PATRICK

21ST CENTURY RELAY BIDDING METHOD

OPTIMAL PRECISION RELAY

Tellwell

Tellwell Talent
www.tellwell.ca

ISBN
978-0-2288-6671-8 (Paperback)

To my darling wife, my life-long partner in every way.

Your constant support and encouragment gave me the motivation to complete this "labor of love" and your help in writing, improving its substance and its language, editing and proof-reading this book were invaluable.

As my Bridge partner, you were also there, at all times, to help me "test" the effectiveness of the Optimal Precision Relay method presented in this book.

TABLE OF CONTENTS

TABLE OF CONTENTS – CONT'D

FOREWORD

Card playing's technique in Bridge has reached, for quite some time now, a very advanced level and a high degree of scientific and statistical rigor. *That is **not** the case when it comes to **bidding**!*

Perhaps because most of the work devoted to bidding, in the last 50 years or so, has been overly focused on trying to find *specific remedies* to the numerous deficiencies found in most bidding systems played around the world – and often doing so by "grafting" onto them a multitude of new conventions, often worse than the illness itself !...

And while the "Italian Clubs" bidding systems, in the '60s, followed by the "Precision Club", from the '70s on, brought some improvements to bidding by dealing with one clear flaw of *traditional* bidding – openings at the level of one with a point-range way too wide – they *did **not** resolve* the imprecision inherent to *traditional* bidding systems; they only addressed one symptom, not the illness.

Indeed, we need to address the root cause of the communication issues between partners inherent to *traditional* systems : *"dialogue"* bidding.
And the solution was pioneered, as early as in the mid-'50s, through highly innovative thinking and major advances made in ***relay*** * bidding – much of it having, unfortunately, remained unknown as they were not translated into English, a rather limiting factor in Bridge.

* ***Relay*** bidding : refers to one partner asking *the other* to describe his hand, in *"monologue"* fashion, through successive, economical *relay* bids, instead of both partners describing *part of their hand* to each other via a *"dialogue"*.

It is this book's purpose to correct this anomaly and, most importantly, to fully integrate the *relay process* into a bidding method that is modern, comprehensive and effective.
Certainly, it is not for everyone; It is intended for advanced players looking for a better, cutting-edge bidding methodology that could take them to "the next level" as world-class players.
Hopefully, the framework it presents can be used as the basis for continuous improvement and further refinement by these same players.

Before getting into it, identifying here and now four key cornerstones of the method will help capture its fundamental characteristics :

1. The method's first specificity is that it is based on the **Optimal** Hand Evaluation – a hand evaluation point count covered in detail in a separate book previously published and that is summarized at the very beginning of this book, as it is a *critical* element of the method.

The **Optimal** point count clearly establishes that **opening** hands **must** be counted in HLD pts – Honor + Length + Distribution pts – not just H or HL pts, to reflect the total *distributional* value of opening hands.

2. And, as staying within the "bidding safety level" requires any opening bid at the one-level to be within a 6 HLD point zone, the method uses a strong 1 ♣ opening to differentiate hands of 12/17 HLD pts from hands of 18 + HLD pts.

3. It is a *relay* method – which replaces the *traditional* "dialogue" between partners by a *monologue* by which one player asks his partner, economically, to describe his hand's distribution, all 13 cards if needed, allowing him to know how well all 26 cards of the side fit together – to bid the *optimal* contract.

4. And the method extends the use of *transfer* * bids to responses to *all* *opening bids of one*, not just 1 NT, enabling an optimal treatment of hands *in misfit* as well as that of hands with a *trump fit* through a great variety of trial rebids of unmatched precision !

     * *transfer* bids : bidding the suit just *below* the one actually identified, a *forcing* bid allowing further bidding by the responder on his partner's *transfer*. Traditionally used only for responses to a No Trump opening.

I welcome any questions or comments you may have which you can send to this e-mail address : patrick.darricades@gmail.com

Plenty to look forward to – so, good reading !

Patrick Darricades

FOREWORD

Accurate hand evaluation is a fundamental first step in Bridge and its effective communication between Bridge partners is the very foundation from which a bidding system can be designed. Its degree *of accuracy* is often decisive in reaching the *optimal* contract.

But the *traditional* M. Work/C. Goren HD point count – universally taught for over 70 years now and still used today – is far from being sufficiently accurate and is simply *not satisfactory*.

The Foreword, below, from the book « *Optimal* Hand Evaluation », by the same author and published in 2019, illustrates this vividly :

In his 1968 *"Bridge Dictionary"*, the author illustrates perfectly our topic with the following example of these two hands of the same side :

♠ K Q x x	♠ A J x x
♥ x	♥ x x x x
♦ x x x	♦ x x
♣ A Q x x x	♣ K x x

which he comments on as follows : « *One can see that a 4 ♠ contract is virtually assured with these two hands, even though they total only 19 honor points and 23 HDS points (**H**onor, **D**istribution, trump **S**upport) – while it is generally considered that **27** HDS points are needed to bid and make a major suit game. In this specific case, it must be acknowledged that the **Goren** *point count, universally used today, does not adequately translate this perfect Fit* ».

* **Goren** point count : Refers to the great American champion Charles Goren who popularized the addition of **distribution** points for short suits (3 2 1 for void, singleton and doubleton) to M. Work's 4 3 2 1 **honor** point count (for Ace, King, Queen, Jack) to reflect the **total** value of a hand.

Over 50 years after this very pertinent observation, we should have found a more accurate hand evaluation method that correctly assesses the combined value of these two hands at **29** total points – Honors, Length, Distribution and Fit points – rather than only 23 HDS points.

Surprisingly, this is not the case, despite several advances made in hand evaluation since 1968, many of which have yet to be taught today or systematically integrated by a majority of champions and experts – essentially *to avoid counting in **half**-points to keep the point count "simple"*.

A significant error of judgment which has unfortunately resulted in delaying for several decades the correct point count and therefore an accurate hand evaluation.

Nevertheless, most experts tend to agree that we can safely rely on the widely acknowledged accuracy of the 4 3 2 1 honor point count to evaluate *evenly-distributed* hands for a No Trump contract.

But then, how do we account for the 6 NT contract which should be bid with the following hands totalling only 27 honor points, when it is generally considered that a minimum of 33 H pts are needed for 6 NT :

♠ A x x		♠ x x	
♥ x x		♥ A x x	
♦ K x x		♦ A Q J x x	
♣ A Q x x x		♣ K x x	

And adding 1 point for the 5 clubs and another for the 5 diamonds only brings the total up to 29 pts – far below the required 33 total pts !

Here again, we should have found by now a more accurate hand evaluation point count that correctly assesses the *combined* value of these two hands at **36** total points – **H**onor, **L**ength and **F**it points.

And then there is the matter of the value of **tens** – generally ignored, particularly for *suit* contracts. As an example of this, take the deal below, from a tournament where not a single pair found the 4 ♠ game :

♠ A J 10 x x		♠ Q x x	
♥ K J x		♥ Q x	
♦ Q x x x		♦ A J 10 x	
♣ x		♣ x x x x	

The bidding was invariably :

1 ♠	2 ♠
Pass	

But an **optimal** point count will show that East's hand is worth **11** HLD Fit pts, not 9. The bidding could then be :

1 ♠	2 ♦
4 ♣ ("Splinter" bid)	4 ♠

The above is clearly a case where each **10** is of *significant* value. Counting the appropriate value of Tens is critically important to reaching the *right* contracts. This is another example of the *traditional* point count giving these two hands a total of only 23 HDS pts when they actually total **29 HLDFit** pts.

Yet, to obtain an **optimal** hand evaluation, we only needed to apply corrections identified long ago, and *some **new ones*** involving just a few more corrections to make to a point count already very familiar to all. That is precisely what this book proposes to do and illustrate.

2

In the process, this **optimal** hand evaluation also addresses how to precisely evaluate *misfitted* hands – a key issue generally ignored and ***not*** *precisely quantified*. The following example is a good illustration of this. In this deal, from the Final of a National selection, 1981, 3 teams out of 4 played 3 NT, down 2, following East's 2 ♣ response to West's 1 ♥ opening :

♠ x x	♠ Q x x
♥ A J 10 x x	♥ Q
♦ K x x x	♦ Q J x x
♣ K x	♣ A Q x x x

But East's hand, far from being worth 13 H / 14 HL pts, should be counted for less than **10** HL *Misfit* pts, which makes a 2 ♣ response inappropriate. A 1 NT response would have enabled the teams to settle in 3 ♦.

Numerous examples can be found in this book illustrating the *disastrous consequences* of the inadequate point count universally used today and the *significant and decisive advantages of a very accurate* **optimal** *point count.*

A number of necessary corrections clearly **must be made** to the M. Work / C. Goren point count – corrections which result in an **optimal** point count allowing a very precise and very accurate hand evaluation.

These corrections were all identified in « **Optimal** Hand Evaluation », a book by the same author, published in 2019 (by Master Point Press). That book provides all the rationale and justifications for the **optimal** point count and over 100 example deals illustrating its validity and effectiveness, compared to other point count methods.

Reading « **Optimal** Hand Evaluation » is a mandatory, *pre-requisite* to getting familiar with the Optimal Precision Relay bidding method.

For reference, you will find, on the next two pages, a **summary** of the **Optimal** point count and all the corrections that need to be made to the M. Work / C. Goren point count to reach *optimal* accuracy.

COMPLETE **SUMMARY** OF THE **OPTIMAL** POINT COUNT

HONOR POINTS

Ace : **4 ½** pts K : **3** pts Q *accompanied* : **2** pts Q *isolated* : **1 ½** pt
J *accompanied* : **1** pt J *isolated* : **½** pt

10 *isolated* or with an Ace : **0** pt 10 with a K : **½** pt
10 with a Q or a J : **1** pt J 10 x : **2** pts

No Ace : **-1** pt (***opening*** *hands only*)
No King : **-1** pt 3 Kings : **+1** pt 4 Kings : **+2** pts
No Queen : **-1** pt 4 Queens : **+1** pt

Singleton honor : **-1** pt Q or J doubleton : **-½** pt
2 honors doubleton : **-1** pt i.e. : Q x : **1** pt J x : **0** pt
(A K, A Q, K Q, Q J)
*Do **not** deduct **1** point for the **J** doubleton with the Ace or the King*
As A J is better than A x and K J better than K x.

3 honors in a **5**-card suit : **+1** pt + the **10** or a 4th **H** : **+2** pts
3 honors in a **6**-card suit : **+2** pts + the **10** or a 4th **H** : **+3** pts

---

LENGTH POINTS

5-card suit (with Q J or K minimum) : **1** pt **6**-card suit : 2 pts
6-card suit *without* Q J or K : **1** pt

7-card suit (or longer) : **2** pts for *each* card from the 7th on

---

DISTRIBUTION POINTS

Void : **4** pts Singleton : **2** pts <u>2</u> doubletons : **1** pt

<u>1</u> doubleton : **0** pt

4 3 3 3 Distribution : **-1** pt A singleton at a **NT** contract : **-1** pt

---

H + **L** + **D** points must be added to assess the full value of **opening**
hands, counted in **HLD** points. **Responding** hands, however, must
only add **H** + **L** points, initially (2 **L** pts *maximum*) and will **add D**
points only *once a Fit has been found.*

4

COMPLETE **SUMMARY** OF THE **OPTIMAL** POINT COUNT

SEMI-FIT POINTS

+ 1 for **K, Q, J 10** or **J doubleton** in partner's **long** suit (**5** + cards)

FIT POINTS

8-card Fit : **+ 1** pt   9-card Fit : **+ 2** pts   **10** + card Fit : **+ 3** pts

+ 1 for honor(s) in suit(s) with a Fit when the honor(s) are < 4 pts

These Fit points count for **all** suits and **all** contracts (suit or NT)

DISTRIBUTION-FIT POINTS **WITH A TRUMP FIT**

*They are the **difference** between the **number** of **trumps** and the number of **cards** in the support hand's **shortest** suit.*

Number of **trumps** :	4	3	2
Distribution-Fit points Void :	4 pts	3 pts	2 pts
Singleton :	3 pts	2 pts	1 pt
Doubleton :	2 pts	1 pt	0 pt

WASTED HONOR POINTS

Honors (*except* Aces) Opposite a **singleton** : **- 2** pts
                                        Opposite a **void** : **- 3** pts

Not a single Honor :   Opposite a **singleton** : **+ 2** pts
                                        Opposite a **void** : **+ 3** pts

An Ace *without* any *other* honor opposite a **singleton** : + 1 point

MISFIT POINTS

Opposite a **long** suit (5 cards or more) in Partner's hand :

- 1 pt for a **doubleton** <u>*without*</u> honor   - 2 pts for a **singleton**
- 3 pts for a **void**   A **singleton** at NT : **- 1** point

2 perfectly *"mirror"* <u>**hands**</u> : **- 2** pts   2 *"mirror"* <u>**suits**</u> : **- 1** pt

---

OPTIMAL POINT COUNT : IMPLICATIONS ON BIDDING

The **Optimal** Point Count has significant implications on some bidding practices and principles, which should be outlined ahead of presenting a new bidding method. These implications are the following :

– The "quantitative" 4 NT jump on a 1 NT or 2 NT opening must be discontinued as its current meaning totally ignores potential Fit points.

– The same applies to an invitational 2 NT response to a 1 NT opening, for the same reasons. Some other meaning must be attributed to it.

– The discovery that Fit points count for **all** suits and **all** contracts, including NT, now rules out "hiding" a 6-card minor single-suit behind a NT opening. Illustrations :

Readers' mail, 2010 – Le Bridgeur.

	♠ A x x	♠ K x x
	♥ A x	♥ x x x
	♦ x x	♦ x x x x
	♣ A K 10 x x x	♣ Q x x

« We bid as follows :	1 ♣	1 ♦
	2 NT	Pass

« And missed the 3 NT game. What did we do wrong ? ».

The wrongdoing isn't the players' fault – it comes from the poor bidding system played which prevents the appropriate point count.
East, with its 3 ½ pts (-1 pt for 4 3 3 3), cannot bid 3 NT without knowing about West's 6 clubs – a fact well concealed by the opener !
Had East known it, he could have added 3 pts for the 9-card ♣ Fit with the Queen. A different auction could have been :

1 ♣	1 ♦
3 ♣ (6 ♣, 17/19 HLD)	3 ♥ ? (♥ guarded ?)
3 NT (yes, ♥ guarded)	Pass

Regional tournament, 2009.

	♠ K Q x	♠ x x x
	♥ A x	♥ x x x
	♦ A J x x x x	♦ K 10 x x
	♣ x x	♣ A x x

An amusing case where all West hands were invariably opened 1 NT. A NT opening which, for some, was 15/17 or 14/16 HL pts, and for others 13/15 or 12/14 H pts.

You guessed it... In all cases, the response was : *Pass* !
Well, isn't it exactly how we have been taught to count points and to bid for the last 40 years or so ?!... Instead, the bidding could be :

2 ♦ (6 + ♦, 15/17 HLD)	3 ♦ (♦ Fit – Invitation to 3 NT if
3 NT	West guards the Majors)

Right upon West's opening, East can count 10 HLFit pts in diamonds (8 H pts -2 pts for 4 3 3 3 and no Queen + 4 pts for the 10-card ♦ Fit with the King). Opposite a minimum of 15 HLD pts, he can invite 3 NT.

– The critical importance of identifying precisely the *length* of suits, for Fit points, as well as *singletons* (or voids) in order to account for *"wasted honor pts"*, **prohibits** jump raises that do not describe a short suit. Illustration :

♠ A Q x x	♠ K x x x x
♥ x	♥ x x x
♦ A K x x x	♦ x x
♣ x x x	♣ K Q x

In *traditional* bidding : 1 ♦   1 ♠
                           3 ♠ (♠ Fit, 17/19 HL)   ?

What is East to do now? He knows nothing about West's ♥ / ♣ residual distribution. If West has a ♣ singleton, he must *pass*. But then, he will miss 4 ♠ if West has a ♥ singleton..

Instead of :   1 ♦   1 ♠
                           3 ♥ (*"mini-splinter"*)   4 ♠

West's *"mini-splinter"* indicates that he has 17/19 HLDF pts with at least an 8-card ♠ Fit + a third point for a singleton with 4 trumps. Knowing about West's ♥ singleton, East can now add 2 pts for *"no wasted honor pts"* in hearts for a minimum of 27 pts on his side = 4 ♠.

– As well, "trial" bids following a trump raise should no longer be *inquiring* about partner's holding in a suit but should, instead, be *short-suit* trial bids in order to assess *"wasted honor pts"*. Example :

♠ A x x	♠ x x x
♥ A K 10 x x	♥ Q x x x
♦ Q J x x	♦ K 10 x
♣ x	♣ K J x

If, in *traditional* bidding, the auction is :

1 ♥	2 ♥
3 ♦ (♦ strength ?)	4 ♥

8

East will conclude in 4 ♥ as he does have the complementing ♦ honor West is looking for, but it won't help – as the key is for West to identify his singleton, enabling East to assess *"wasted honor pts"*. A 3 ♣ short suit "trial bid" would enable East to settle in 3 ♥.

And hereunder is the ***most significant*** implication.

– **All** opening hands must be counted in HLD pts and opening bids at the level of one must precisely be within a **6** HLD point zone to respect the *"bidding safety level"* and because **no more** than **two** point zones of **3** HLD pts each can be described economically, by any system !

This necessarily **dictates** using one opening bid to identify hands just **above that limit**. The implication is clear and unequivocal : a strong 1 ♣ opening bid **must be used** to do that !

Putting the "break" point, say, at 18 HLD pts, would mean that openings of 1 ♦, 1 ♥ and 1 ♠ could be limited to 17 HLD pts with two HLD point zones of : 12/14 and 15/17 HLD pts, while hands opened 1 ♣ would be in the 18/20 and 21/23 + HLD point zones.

So, now, playing a strong 1 ♣ opening is no longer a "systemic choice or personal preference" – it is an absolute "must", for *any* bidding system !

This definitely fixes the most basic problem of *traditional* bidding : a point range too wide for openings of 1 ♣, 1 ♦, 1 ♥ or 1 ♠, a flaw denouced by H. Schenken as far back as… 1963 !

As well, the forcing nature of a strong 1 ♣ opening prevents an inappropriate *Pass* by a *weak* partner while allowing him to know immediately the partnership's *minimum* strength – a significant benefit when opponents intervene.

Furthermore, the most economical 1 ♣ opening gives both partners the *most bidding space* to describe their hands, particularly the *responder's* hand – and that's as it should be as it is the *strong* hand that should have the *weaker hand* described.

As was just illustrated above, the implications of the **optimal** point count on bidding are significant and applying them is sure to lead to much improved bidding and results "at the table".

PREAMBLE

Assessing the 3 main bidding methodologies will help identify :
A) the key principles that guide them and their effectiveness, *or lack of*, and B) systemic flaws that an effective bidding method should avoid.

It will also help assess whether we need to "**rethink**" the *traditional* methodology used to communicate key information between partners.

Broadly, we can distinguish three distinct bidding methodologies :

– The "**founding**" systems, often called (wrongly) *natural* bidding systems, such as the American Standard or Acol or 5-card Major, successfully promoted by many great champions from the early '30s on. They all use a "*dialogue*" methodology to communicate between partners and their evolution over the years (from 4-card Major to 5-card Major openings, from strong 2 ♠ or 2 ♥ openings to weak 2 openings, from strong jump responses to "limit bids", etc.) did not alter the *dialogue* methodology used by these systems.

– The **strong Club** bidding systems, which use *traditional* dialogue bidding but open 1 ♣ hands strong in Honor points (**16 + H pts**), thus limiting *other* openings to 15 H *maximum*. While also dating back to the early '30s (Vanderbilt's strong Club dates back to 1929), they started to attract a strong following only after the unprecedented successes achieved on the world stage by the Italian *Blue Team* in the '60s, and culminated with the advent of the **Precision Club** in the '70s.

– **Relay** bidding systems, pioneered by the French champion P. Ghestem in the early '50s. These systems replaced the traditional *dialogue* between partners by a *monologue* whereby one of the partners asks the other through successive, economical relay bids – to fully describe his hand and then decides, alone, what the final contract will be.

Relay bidding systems have not been widely known as their early conceptors were mostly French experts who did not publish their work in English – a rather serious handicap.

Around these three types of bidding architectures, a multitude of bidding systems have been developed by a variety of experts and champions – but they do not warrant analysis here as they either did not gain wide acceptance or withstand the test of time.
Instead, I will review *three specific openings* generally used by all systems as they warrant a specific analysis, notably 1 NT and weak 2 openings.

Each of the three main bidding architectures mentioned above will now be analysed to determine what lessons can be learned from them.

I. THE « FOUNDING » TRADITIONAL SYSTEMS

Much space will be devoted to analysing these systems as they constitute the very foundation of most current bidding systems.

Their core methodology consists of a *dialogue* by which each player describes to his partner **part** *of his hand*, in strength and in distribution, until a final contract is decided upon by one of the two players.

To do so, two key principles have generally been retained as "gospel" :

1. E. Culbertson's and C. Goren's « *progressive, approach forcing* » bidding process of : A) **opening** as many hands as possible with an economical one-level bid, from 1 ♣ through to 1 ♠, with the result that these hands will have a wide point range – the hand's *strength* thus taking a back seat to identifying a suit, and B) **responding** as economically as possible, preferably one-over-one – the hand's *strength*, here too, taking a back seat to identifying a suit.

The above's major implication is that opening bids at the one-level (except 1 NT) can have a point range that goes from 11 H/12 HL pts to 20 H/21 HL pts. This equates to **4** point zones of **3 H** pts each : 11/13 H, 14/16 H, 17/19 H, 20/21 HL pts. This will undoubtedly **prevent** any possible future **precise** description of the hand's **strength** as there is no "technical" way to describe a hand in **four** different point zones.

The other implication is that very strong hands will then have to be opened at the level of two : 2 ♣ or 2 ♦ or 2 NT.

2. The principle of « *anticipation* » which means that the bid you make should, first and foremost, pave the way to making your next rebid as **easy** as possible – **not as precise** as possible, as *easy* as possible.
This has some implications, as well, and major ones at that :

Should partner's response make your rebid difficult, you may have to rebid a "false" second suit of 3 cards only instead of 4, or bid NT with a singleton in partner's suit, or support his suit with one card *short* of what he would expect, or make a *"conventional"* forcing bid to keep the dialogue going, or "improvise" – and many conventions exist to get you out of trouble : over 300 of them, actually, which you can find in books entirely devoted to them. Already in 1975, *"Bridge Conventions Complete"* outlined 190 of them in a 650 page book…

Let's now illustrate the above by some example hands, taken from international tournaments and excerpts from Bridge magazines.

World Championship, Brazil - 1961.

♠ K Q J x x x   ♠ x x
♥ A Q x   ♥ x x x x
♦ x   ♦ K Q J x x
♣ Q J x   ♣ x x

The bidding was most often :

1 ♠	1 NT
3 ♠ (17/19 HD pts)	Pass

Down one. The opening bid's wide point range forces East to respond, even with a rather minimum hand, and leads West to jump-rebid with such a strong ♠ holding. And strong ♣ bidders would not have fared any better as West does not have 16 H pts to open 1 ♣.

And the opening bid's wide point range can lead the *responder* to over-shoot, as the following deal, from the same championship, shows :

♠ x   ♠ Q J x x
♥ K Q x x x   ♥ x x
♦ A J 10 x   ♦ K Q x x
♣ K x x   ♣ x x x

The bidding was most often :

1 ♥	1 ♠
2 ♦	3 ♦

Down one. The opening bid's wide point range forces East to bid 3 ♦ even with a minimum hand, as West could have as many as 17 HL pts and a 3 NT contract could be odds on.

In the example below, the bidding was most often :   1 ♥   Pass

♠ A K   ♠ x x x
♥ A x x x x x   ♥ x
♦ x   ♦ x x x
♣ A x x x   ♣ K x x x x x

And the 6 ♣ slam was missed. Here again, West's non-forcing 1 ♥ opening bid has too wide a point range and leads to a disastrous result ! And strong ♣ bidders would have fared no better as West has 14 H pts.

World Championships, teams of four - 2008.

♠ A K x x x   ♠ Q x x
♥ K Q x x x   ♥ A x x x
♦ ---   ♦ x x x x
♣ Q x x   ♣ K x

The bidding was most often as follows :

1 ♠	2 ♠
3 ♥	4 ♥

And not a single team found the slam! West counts his hand for 18 HD pts and his 3 ♥ rebid indicates 17 to 19 HLD pts. East describes up to 10 HDS pts in spades and 10 to 12 HDS pts in hearts. This gives West little motivation to bid further as his own 20 pts (+ 2 for the 9-card ♥ Fit) + 12 pts maximum in East = 32 pts maximum.

But West has 20 HLD pts, not 18 HD pts ! (2 pts for the two 5-card suits, 4 pts for the void). And East has 12 HDFit pts in spades, not 10 ! His first mistake was therefore to bid 2 ♠ which limits his hand to 10 HDS pts.

While the wrong point count is the primary reason for the flawed bidding, West's 3 ♥ rebid does not indicate its key ♦ void, at the level of 3 or 4. *Dialogue* bidding is not being precise enough.
And a strong ♣ bidding system would not have fared any better here as West does not have the mandatory 16 H pts to open 1 ♣.

« *Readers' mail* » — Le Bridgeur, 2010.

♠ A x x		♠ K x x	
♥ A x		♥ x x x	
♦ x x		♦ x x x x	
♣ A K J x x x		♣ Q x x	

« *We bid as follows* :	1 ♣	1 ♦
	2 NT	Pass

« *What did we do wrong ?* ».

The wrongdoing isn't the players' fault – It comes from the poor bidding system played! As well as using *an inaccurate point count !*...

West has 21 ½ HLD pts (no Queen but + 2 pts for 3 H in a 6-card suit), not 18 HL pts! and East, with its 3 ½ pts (-1 point for 4 3 3 3), cannot bid 3 NT without knowing that West has 6 clubs – a fact well concealed by the opener! Had East known it, he could have added 3 pts for the 9-card ♣ Fit with the Queen. Now that we know that Fit points **do count** for NT contracts, it becomes out of the question to hide from partner a 6-card minor suit behind a NT bid !

Playing a strong 1 ♣ opening, a different auction could have been :

1 ♣ (16 + H pts)	1 ♦ (weak hand)
3 ♣ (6 ♣, 18/20 HLD pts)	3 ♥ ? (♥ guarded ?)
3 NT (yes, ♥ guarded)	Pass

« *Techniques* » – Le Bridgeur, 2007.

« *West opened the following hand 1 ♠. What should his **rebid** be on a 1 NT response from his partner ? :*

      ♠ K J 10 x x
      ♥ A x
      ♦ K J x
      ♣ A x x

« *2 NT would indicate 18 / 19 H pts while 2 ♠ would promise 6 spades. The only option left is to bid a **false** second suit at an economic level : 2 ♣* ».

« *Or, with the following hand opened 1 ♦, what to rebid on partner's 1 ♠ response ? :*

      ♠ A Q x
      ♥ K Q x
      ♦ A Q J x x x
      ♣ x

« *The hand is one spade short for a 3 ♠ Fit and is too strong for a 3 ♦ rebid. Again, the only option left is to bid a **false** second suit : 2 ♥, this time a forcing reverse bid* ».

So now, when unable to describe your hand, "lying" to your partner becomes O.K. ?!... Actually, the only serious option with both example hands above is to play a strong ♣ bidding system! Opening both hands 1 ♣ will not cause you to "lie" to your partner on your rebid !

« *Bidding contest* » – Le Bridgeur, 2008.

« *With the hand below, what is your **rebid** after the following auction ? :*

		♠ A x x
2 ♣ (strong, forcing)	2 ♠ (♠ Ace)	♥ x x x x x
3 ♠	?	♦ x x x x
		♣ x

« *No rebid is satisfactory : 4 ♠ or 5 ♠ would not identify the ♣ singleton, while a 5 ♣ "splinter" bid would promise a 4-card ♠ Fit. As for a 4 ♣ bid, will it be understood as a natural bid describing clubs, or as a ♣ control ?* ».

The wonders of opening a very strong hand by a very *uneconomical* 2 ♣ : the level of 3 ♠ has been reached *before* East could indicate a ♠ Fit !...

As illustrated by the examples above – a small sample among many – the *"founding"* bidding systems clearly have many flaws. To address some of them, experts and champions have devised multiple *artificial conventions* which could be "grafted" on these systems, such as :

« Bidding contest » – Le Bridgeur.

*« What is your **rebid**, with this responder's hand, after the following auction :*

		♠ J x x x x
1 ♦	1 ♠	♥ Q x x
2 ♥	?	♦ ---
		♣ K Q x x x

*« No rebid seems adequate : we cannot Pass with 8 H pts opposite a forcing reverse bid by partner, nor can we support hearts with only 3 ♥, and the hand is not strong enough for bidding 3 ♣ which is the conventional "4th suit game forcing" bid. As for bidding spades again with such weak spades, no thanks... To resolve this dilemna, many experts use a 2 NT rebid as a conventional **relay** to get the opener to bid again... ».*

But then, if you are to resort to *relays*, wouldn't it be simpler for West, the strong hand, to relay by 1NT over 1♠, to enable East to describe, economically, the balance of his hand : 2 ♣, 2 ♦ or 2 ♥ with a two-suiter, or 2 ♠ with a single-suit hand, or 2 NT to 3 ♠ with a strong hand...

Here is another : *« A convention worth trying ? »* – Le Bridgeur, 2008.

*« This opening hand's **rebid** is problematic after the following auction :*

♠ A J x x x		
♥ A K	1 ♠	1 NT (< 10 H)
♦ x x x	?	
♣ A Q		

*« The hand is much too strong for a 2 ♠ rebid but the spade suit is too weak for 3 ♠. As for 2 ♦ or 3 ♦, no thank you !... Here is **a new convention** which would deal with this type of situation : Use 2 NT as a conventional, forcing rebid, indicating a strong hand over 17 H pts, with either a 6-card single-suit of mediocre quality, or a 5 - 4 or 6 - 4 two-suiter. On this 2 NT, partner's 3 ♣ bid will be a conventional **relay** bid asking the opener to "clarify" his distribution – rebid his 6-card single suit or his second suit ».*

Wow! How creative : first get the opener to "burn" 4 bidding steps to describe nothing more than a strong hand over 17 H pts and then describe, at the level of 3, nothing more than either 6 cards or 9 cards !

Wouldn't it be simpler to play a strong ♣ bidding system to describe a hand of 16 H pts by a 1 ♣ opening followed by a 1 ♠ rebid, followed by either 2 ♠ or his second suit.

Yet, these conventions must still not be enough to resolve these systems' numerous dilemmas, as resorting to "improvisations" followed by *conventional* bids seems to also be part of today's arsenal, as illustrated by the following :

« *Readers' Mail* » – Le Bridgeur, 2008.

« **Not** *playing the "inverted minor-suit raise" convention, what should my response be on partner's* 1 ♣ *opening, with the following hand :*

♠ K x x
♥ Q x x
♦ Q
♣ A Q 10 x x x

Reply by the expert managing the *Readers' mail* : « *The least dangerous response seems to be…* 1 ♦ *and if the opener rebids* 1 ♥, *I would recommend you adopt the following* **convention** *to "correct" the initial response : with a "true" suit in diamonds, show your support of clubs by bidding* 3 ♣, *while if you are* **short** *in diamonds, as here, then bid* 2 ♠, *conventionally showing your* ♣ *Fit but* **without** *a* ♦ *suit* ».

Wow ! Would it not have been simpler to suggest to the writer to adopt *the "inverted minor-suit raise"* convention without delay ?…

SUMMARY SYNTHESIS ON *TRADITIONAL* BIDDING SYSTEMS

A multitude of other examples are continuously provided by Bridge magazines that delight us, monthly, with "bidding contests" which illustrate the state of absurd chaos *traditional* Bridge bidding is in and has been in for many, many years.
Based on a hand evaluation point count which has *never been right,* and on opening hands counted in H or HL points instead of HLD points – total heresy – these systems all have in common :

– Their lack of precision on hands' **strength** – due to point zones far too wide, with its direct consequence : the partnership is placed outside the *bidding safety level* right from the opening bid !

– Their lack of precision on hands' **distribution** – beyond describing 9 cards in a two-suited hand or 6 cards in a single-suit hand, a hand's *residual* distribution is rarely described fully, due to a lack of bidding space inherent to the *dialogue* methodology.

– Their use of **multiple conventions** "grafted" onto these systems to deal with their many deficiencies. Often ambiguous and unecono-mical, these modern day conventions often provide medicine that is worse than the sickness (*splinter* bids at the level of 4, *quantitative* 4 NT, Jacoby 2 NT raise, and many more).

– Continuous **improvisations** – often nonsensical (NT opening with a singleton, bidding a false suit as a rebid, etc.) – requiring from the partner infallible interpretations of… divine inspiration !

– As for systems **not** playing a strong 1 ♣ opening, they offer the additional "privilege" of strong 2 ♣ openings (and for some, game-forcing 2 ♦ openings !…).

The results are well known and observed every day : bad contracts declared, good contrats missed and a great deal of dissatisfaction often leading to partnership disputes and break-ups.

And none of this is news to most experts and champions who have known it for many years. H. Schenken, the great American champion and pioneer, wrote, as far back as 1963 in his introduction to his bidding system « *Better Bidding in 15 minutes / The Schenken Club* » that, in his opinion « *traditional (American) bidding is* **inaccurate** *and* **ineffective** *and has become* **obsolete***… and its biggest problem is the* **wide range** *of the opening of* **one** ».

II. THE STRONG CLUB BIDDING SYSTEMS

It is the very purpose of **strong Club** bidding systems to address the wide range of the opening of one and they all have two key goals :
First, to limit all other openings to *less* than 16 H pts (the only exception being the opening of 2 NT which has generally been retained for balanced hands of 20/22 H pts), thereby addressing the problem of the wide range of the opening of one and, second, to indicate to partner a strong hand at an economical level – much more frequent than the 2 ♣ opening which requires 22 + HL/HD pts.

The strong 1 ♣ opening also has several other benefits :

– Being a *forcing* bid, for at least one round, it avoids an inappropriate *Pass* by a weak partner, while also allowing partner much *more frequently* to know immediately what is the minimum strength of their side – which can be a significant advantage when opponents intervene.

– It preserves maximum bidding space for ulterior communication with the partner, not just for the opener's rebids, but also by giving partner the most bidding space possible for him to describe *his hand* – and that's as it should be as the strong hand should be the team's captain and have the *weaker* hand described.

This, in turn, makes it possible to more precisely describe most opening hands – **all** opening hands, not just the ones opened 1 ♣ – through economical and precise rebids without having to resort to jumps and other "contortions".

– Just as importantly, it allows partner to make precise and aggressive *"limit"* response bids directly at the two and three levels with 8/10 HL pts with the assurance that their side has no less than 24 HL pts.

These are major, significant improvements over *traditional* bidding !

Which explains the constantly growing adoption by more and more players of strong ♣ systems which went from being played by just a few pioneers in the mid-'50s to being played, today, by over half of the teams represented in world championships – a majority of which have been won, since 1957, by teams playing strong ♣ systems.
At this pace, one can foresee the likely – and justified – disappearance of *traditional* systems within the next 30 to 40 years.

Thus, the energy still spent by so many on inventing new conventions to deal with *traditional* systems' many deficiencies appears rather futile, but worse yet is the continued practice to teach and advocate such *traditional* systems : that is maintaining in *"artificial life support"* a patient afflicted by an illness for which there is no possible cure !...

The early '70s saw the advent of the **Precision Club** bidding system which : A) reduced the H points needed to open 1 ♣ from 17 H to 16 H pts – a significant improvement – and B) converted the Italian strong ♣ systems to 5-card Majors and weak 1 NT openings (13/15 H pts).

For some time now, the Precision Club system has become the most widely adopted strong ♣ system played worldwide and will, therefore, be the one we focus on.

Yet, having said all of this, strong ♣ bidding systems – as most have been played since the '60s – have surprisingly retained many of the flaws typically associated with *traditional* systems, such as :

– Counting opening hands in H or HL pts instead of H<u>L</u>D pts, therefore placing the partnership outside the *bidding safety level* right from the opening bid as well as guaranteeing ulterior bids' lack of precise point zoning in HLD pts.

– **Not** succeeding in limiting all other openings to *no more than* two HLD point zones – as a 16 + H 1 ♣ opening limits other openings to 11/15 H pts openings : that's **four** HLD point zones! from an 11 H/12 HL 5 3 3 2 hand to a 15 H 7 3 3 0 hand of 23 HLD pts = 12/14, 15/17, 18/20 and 21/23 ! Totally unplayable !

– Communicating between partners through flawed, uneconomical *dialogue*, thus guaranteeing lack of *distributional* precision.

– Retaining the use of prehistoric relics of the past (*jump* bids and rebids with strong hands, the strong 2 NT opening, etc.) as well as numerous, nonsensical "modern day" conventions (uneconomical "*splinter*" bids at the level of four, the "*quantitative*" 4 NT jump, etc.) and many more.

All of the above "doom" strong club bidding systems as an acceptable alternative to *traditional* bidding systems – even though they are far superior to them.

Several examples, hereafter, will illustrate the above mentioned flaws and deficiencies.

In his 1972 book on the Precision Club system, « *Precision Bidding and Precision Play* », British champion Terence Reese states that « *with less than 8 H pts, and no trump Fit, there is no reason to bid over a 1 ♠ opening (5-card major) limited to 15 H pts, such as with a hand like the one below* » :

♠ x x
♥ Q 10 x x x
♦ K x x
♣ x x x

20

But a 4 ♥ contract should be bid opposite an opener having the follow-ing hand :

- ♠ A x x x x
- ♥ A K x x
- ♦ A x x
- ♣ x

And that's because the opener has, in fact, 18 ½ HLD pts (minus 1 for no Queen), not 15 H pts! And he should have opened a strong, forcing 1 ♣. Counting opening hands based on **H** pts only dooms strong Club systems, just as it does *traditional* systems.

Here is another example which clearly debunks T. Reese's above stated assertion – taken from the 2009 United States championship in which the following hand was invariably opened 1 ♥ :

- ♠ A K 10 x x
- ♥ A Q 10 x x x
- ♦ x
- ♣ x

Well, the hand only has 13 H pts, right? Therefore, no harm could come from hearing partner *pass* should he have **less** than 8 H pts without a ♥ Fit… Perhaps, with a hand such as the one below :

- ♠ Q x x
- ♥ J x
- ♦ x x x x
- ♣ x x x x

Unfortunately, a 4 ♥ or 4 ♠ game will be missed and that is because, far from having 13 H pts, the opening hand has 22 ½ HLD pts !
It should have been opened a strong, forcing 1 ♣.

A different example can be found in Charles Goren's 1975 book on the Precision Club system « *Charles Goren presents the Precision system* » where he shows the following hand opposite a 1 ♥ opening (5-card major) limited to 15 H pts :

- ♠ A x x
- ♥ K x x
- ♦ x x
- ♣ K x x x x

And makes this comment : « *With the ♥ Fit, responder knows : 1) the **trump** suit, 2) that a **slam** is **excluded**, and 3) that a ♥ game can be considered if the opener is at the **maximum** of his point range, 14/15 H pts. He now only needs to make an **invitational** bid for a ♥ game* ».

An astonishing assessment and conclusion when, with an opening hand such as the one below :

♠ x
♥ A Q 10 x x
♦ A x
♣ A 10 x x x

Instead of just considering and inviting a ♥ game − it is 7 ♣ that should be played! Here again, the wrong point count leads straight to the wrong conclusion! And the responder has a hand of 13 ½ HLDF pts (no Queen), not 12, and therefore a simple invitation is not at all appropriate.

But the initial error is due to counting the opening hand in H pts only. Had West properly counted his hand and opened a strong, forcing 1 ♣, East could have described his 5 ♣ 3 ♥ 3 ♠ 2 ♦ hand and 10/12 HL pts and the side would easily find the 7 ♣ contract.

Rosenblum Cup, USA, 2010.

♠ x	♠ x x x x
♥ A J x x x	♥ K x
♦ ---	♦ J x x x
♣ A K x x x x x	♣ J 10 x

The team considered the World's best for a 15 to 20 year period opens West's hand a non-forcing 2 ♣ ! (natural, 5 + ♣, 11/15 H pts).
Rather difficult for East to be motivated to bid over this opening...

Astonishing opening of a non-forcing 2 ♣ − the hand doesn't have the 16 H pts prescribed to open 1 strong ♣ − a hand which has a 5-card Major and a 7 – 5 two-suiter of 8 to 9 winning tricks ! (23 HLD pts).

But then, the pair may not have to worry too much about their bidding system in view of their opponents' bidding, in the other room, which was as follows :

1 ♥	1 ♠
3 ♣ (non forcing < 16 H pts)	Pass

Wow! A good demonstration of how to miss a game contract, or a possible slam!... and further illustration that counting an opening hand in H points *only* will often lead to embarrassing situations !
Again, that is because **one** point zone counted in H pts can equate to **four** HLD point zones. Here, 12 H pts = 23 HLD pts !
It is mandatory to count opening hands in HLD pts and a forcing 1 ♣ opening bid should be used here.

And the Precision Club's 2 ♣ opening fares no better as this opening, also counted in H pts only, covers an 11/15 H point zone, much too wide to respect the *bidding level safety*! Illustration :

In his book on the Precision Club, T. Reese states that, with either of the following two hands, North can *Pass* on partner's 2 ♣ opening (5 + clubs) as he does **not** have 8 H pts while the opener's hand is limited to 15 H pts – a game will not be missed :

Responder A	Responder B
♠ x x	♠ K x x
♥ Q J x x x	♥ x x x
♦ A x x x	♦ A x x x
♣ x x	♣ x x x

Really ? But with the following opening hands there is 4 ♥ to play with opener A, and 3 NT with opener B :

Opener A	Opener B
♠ x	♠ Q x
♥ K 10 x	♥ A x x
♦ K x x	♦ x x
♣ A K x x x x	♣ A K Q x x x

And that's because the 11/15 H 2 ♣ opening covers a point zone way too wide : opener A has, in fact, 18 HLD pts, not 13 H pts! and opener B has 19 HL/20 HLD pts, not 15 H pts !
Strong ♣ systems are just as doomed as *traditional* bidding systems right from their opening bids because these are counted in **H** pts only !

And then, there is the 2 NT opening – the most absurd of all opening bids in its *traditional* meaning : a very strong, balanced hand of 20/22 H pts. But a strong 2 NT opening is *pre-emptive*... to the partner !
It defies the principle that *"the stronger the hand, the lower the bid"* to preserve bidding space when it is most likely to be needed, and prevents the partner from describing a possible singleton to the strong hand !
A 2 NT opening, or jump-rebid, must *never, ever* be used to describe strong, balanced hands – that should be Bridge bidding 101 !

Why would a strong Club system retain such an absurd opening is beyond comprehension! Illustrations :

Le Bridgeur, 2008.

♠ A Q J x	♠ x x x
♥ A x x	♥ x
♦ A K Q x	♦ x x x
♣ x x	♣ A K J x x x

The bidding was :   2 NT   3 ♠ (*transfer* for ♣)
                     3 NT   Pass

« *West, with his weak ♣ doubleton and stoppers in both ♠ and ♥, favored proposing* 3 NT *over transfering to ♣* ». And the 6 ♣ slam was missed.

To reach the right contract would have required knowing about East's singleton : with a ♦ singleton, 3 NT would be the right contract, while with a ♥ singleton, 6 ♣ is the right contract. But the 2 NT opening prevents such a description.

While on a strong 1 ♣ opening, East would have had no difficulty describing his singleton : 2 ♣ (5 + clubs, 7 + HL pts), followed by 3 ♣ (6 clubs) followed by his ♥ singleton. West would then just have to inquire about East's Key Cards in clubs before concluding in 6 ♣.

Another example : « *Readers' mail* » – Le Bridgeur, 2008.

♠ A Q x	♠ x
♥ K Q x	♥ A J x x x
♦ A Q x x	♦ K J x x
♣ A x x	♣ x x x

« *We were not able to come up with a convincing way to reach the ♦ slam after the following start :*

                     2 NT   3 ♦ (transfer for ♥)
                     3 ♥ (transfer to ♥)   ?

As our understanding is that a natural 4 ♦ *bid, at this stage, would guarantee spade* **and** *club controls, right ?* ».

Reply from the expert managing the *Readers' mail* : « *You are correct, but then, you may elect to "depart" from the rule by "ignoring" your lack of club control* ».

Rather than "departing from" and "ignoring" rules, wouldn't better advice be to never again open such hands 2 NT? Opening West's hand 1♣, instead, would allow plenty of bidding space for East to describe his hand's 5 ♥ 4 ♦ and ♠ singleton, allowing West to inquire about East's Key Cards and reach the ♦ slam.

As can be seen from the example hands just shown, strong ♣ bidding systems, as most are still played nowadays, do not offer a satisfactory solution as they retain most of the *traditional* systems' flaws and deficiencies.

SUMMARY SYNTHESIS ON (MOST) STRONG ♣ BIDDING SYSTEMS

– Based on a hand evaluation which has *never been right* and on opening hands counted in H or HL points instead of HLD points – total heresy – these systems all have in common their **lack of precision** on hands' *strength* due to point zones far too large, with its direct consequence : the partnership is placed *outside* the "bidding safety level" right from the opening bid! They have **not** fixed the *traditional* systems' major problem, the excessively wide point range of the opening of one.

– Their **lack of precision** on hands' *distribution*. Beyond describing 9 cards in a two-suited hand or 6 cards in a single-suit hand, a hand's "residual" distribution is rarely described fully, due to a lack of bidding space inherent to the *dialogue* methodology used.

Based on the two observations above, the term *Precision* most often used by these systems : *Precision* Club, Power *Precision*, Super *Precision*, etc. are, in fact, totally misleading...

Because of the above, these systems also use **multiple conventions** "grafted" onto them to deal with their many deficiencies (*Splinter* bids at the 4 level, *quantitative* 4 NT, and many, many more) and most have retained the non-sensical opening of 2 NT for strong, balanced hands !

Conclusion : Clearly, strong Club bidding systems do **not** constitute – at least not in their current configuration – the right path to what we are looking for : an effective, precise and satisfactory bidding method for the 21st Century.

III. RELAY BIDDING SYSTEMS

When it comes to Bridge bidding, the revolution already occurred… over 60 years ago, but it has generally remained a well-kept secret.

That is, in part, due to the fact that the the first **Relay** bidding systems were devised by French experts and champions who did not have their books translated in English.

The very first pioneer was the French champion Pierre Ghestem, who designed the ***Monaco*** *relay* system in the early '50s and played it in tournaments for the first time in 1955 – and won, playing it, the European championship that same year, the world championship the following year and the first Olympiad in 1960 (the only time the Italian Blue Team's 12 consecutive victories as the world's best was broken).

Other French champions soon followed in his footsteps and devised their own Relay systems, notably P. Collet (the *Beta* system, 1964) and B. Romanet (The *Alpha* system, 1967).

All of them were convinced – rightfully so – that knowing the precise *distribution* of a hand was fundamental to reaching the *optimal* contract and that this could **not** be achieved by the *traditional* dialogue between two partners, describing only part of their hand to each other.

Their bidding revolution was to ***replace*** this *dialogue* by a ***monologue***, whereby one partner asks the other, through successive, economical relays (the suit just above his partner's bid), to describe his hand's precise distribution – all 13 cards, if needed.

Armed with that precise knowledge, the *relaying* partner will then be able to conclude in the *optimal* contract, his own hand's distribution being totally unknown to the opponents.

Their revolution was **not** the *relay* bid – which existed since Stayman's 2 ♣ response over a 1 NT opening and which *traditional* systems occasionally use, such as the forcing 1 NT response over a 1 ♥ or 1 ♠ opening – but was, rather, the *monologue* process involving successive, economical relays by one player, asking his partner to describe his hand according to a *specific process*.

From there, they developped a systematic description *process* of a hand's distribution. P. Ghestem, in particular, developed the most natural "Monaco" process : the first suit bid is a 5-card suit, the second suit bid is a 4-card suit and the third suit bid is a 3-card suit, thus describing 12 cards out of 13. If and when needed, another relay bid will ask the responder to describe his 13th card.

Furthermore, whenever one partner's complete hand distribution has been described without exceeding the level of 3 NT, a 4 ♣ bid can now be used by *the relayer* as a **R**oman **K**ey **C**ard **A**sk instead of the very uneconomical 4 NT Blackwood.

Let's now look at a few examples to illustrate the above :

♠ A K x x x	♠ Q J x x
♥ x x	♥ A x
♦ x x	♦ A x
♣ A Q x x	♣ K x x x x

In *traditional* bidding, whether playing a strong ♣ or not, the above hands can be expected to be bid as follows :

1 ♠	2 ♣
3 ♣	3 ♠ (slam interest)
4 ♠ (no ♦ or ♥ control)	4 NT (RKC Blackwood)
5 ♣ (3 Key Cards)	?

What now? If West has the ♣ Queen, 6 NT is lay-down, but if he has, instead, the ♦ Q and/or the ♥ Q, better stop in 5 ♠ … How can East now inquire about which Queen West has without getting over 5 ♠ ?

With a **strong ♣** / *Relay* bidding system, this would be the auction :

1 ♠ (5 + ♠, 13/18 HLD)	1 NT ? (relay)
2 ♣ (4 clubs)	2 ♦ ? (relay)
2 NT (2 ♦ 2 ♥, 16/18 HLD)	4 ♣ ? (RKC Ask, ♠ trump)
4 ♦ (3 Key Cards)	5 ♣ ? (K & Q ♣ Ask)
5 ♥ (♣ Queen)	6 NT

West cannot have another King (for 7 NT) which would give him 17 H/ 19 HLD pts : he would have opened a strong 1 ♣.
West's point zone and 13-card distribution is known at a very low level which allows a 4 ♣ Key Card Ask, instead of 4 NT. This, in turn, allows a ♣ Ask and 6 NT can now be bid in economical certainty.

Note : A *relay* bid being an inquiry will, in all cases, and throughout this book, be followed by a question mark.

Another example : 2007 National selection, teams of four – Le Bridgeur.

♠ A x x x x	♠ K Q x
♥ K J x	♥ A x
♦ A x x x	♦ K Q x x x
♣ x	♣ x x x

Both teams missed the slam and stopped at 4 ♠. One can imagine the bidding to have been as follows :

1 ♠	2 ♦
3 ♦	3 ♠ (slam interest)
4 ♠	Pass

West, judging his hand minimum in H points, prefers not to encourage further bidding. Now, East can hardly bid further at the 5-level and risk going down should the opener also have 3 small clubs…

With a **strong ♣ / Relay** bidding system, this would be the auction :

1 ♠ (5 + ♠, 13/18 HLD)	1 NT ? (relay)
2 ♦ (4 diamonds)	2 ♥ ? (relay)
3 ♥ (3 hearts = ♣ singleton, 16/18 HLD)	

On West's 3 ♥ bid, East can then count : 16 HLD pts minimum in West + its own 17 HLDFit pts + 2 pts for the 9-card ♦ Fit + 2 pts for "no wasted honor pts" in clubs = 37 total pts. Grand slam zone ! All that is needed now is for East to discover West's controls to play 6 ♠ and a 4 ♣ KC Ask will do just that. The bidding would then proceed as follows :

	4 ♣ ? (RKC Ask, ♠ trump)
4 ♠ (2 KCards w/o Q)	4 NT ? (other Kings ?)
5 ♥ (♥ King)	6 ♠

Plain good sense suggests that it is East, the strong hand, that should take control and have West describe his hand, fully, thus discovering his ♣ singleton, the key to reaching the right contract.

Regional tournament, 2009.

♠ K Q x x x	♠ A x x
♥ A x x	♥ x x
♦ Q x x x	♦ K J 10 x
♣ x	♣ x x x x

The bidding was often :

1 ♠	2 ♠
Pass	

West, being minimum, cannot envision a game opposite a maximum of 10 S pts. And strong ♣ bidders would fare no better.

With a **strong ♣ / Relay** bidding system, this would be the auction :

1 ♠ (5 + ♠, 13/18 HLD)	1 NT ? (relay)
2 ♦ (4 diamonds)	2 ♥ ? (relay)
2 ♠ (13/15 HLD)	2 NT ? (relay)
3 ♥ (3 ♥ = ♣ singleton)	4 ♠

Upon West's 2 ♦ bid, East can add 1 point for the 8-card ♦ Fit to his own 10 ½ HDFit pts in spades and can safely continue to *relay*.

Discovering West's ♣ singleton now allows him to add to this total 2 pts for "no wasted honor pts" in clubs = 26 ½ pts minimum = Game.

Had West bid 3 ♣, instead of 3 ♥, indicating 3 clubs and therefore a ♥ singleton, East would have signed off in 3 ♠.

Regional tournament, 2006.

♠ K 10 x x	♠ A Q x x
♥ x	♥ x x x x
♦ x x x	♦ x x
♣ A Q 10 x x	♣ K x x

These two hands were, almost invariably, *passed* out !... But West has 14 HLD pts, **not** 9 H pts, and should open !

With a **strong ♣** / *Relay* bidding system, this would be the auction :

2 ♣ (5 + ♣, 14 / 17 HLD)	2 ♦ ? (relay)
2 ♠ (4 spades)	2 NT ? (relay)
3 ♦ (3 ♦ = ♥ singleton)	4 ♠

On West's 2 ♣ opening, East can count his hand for 12 ½ HDFit pts with his 8-card ♣ Fit (2 Fit points, 1 D point for the ♦ doubleton), more than enough points to *relay*. To which he can then add 1 ♠ Fit point + 2 pts for "no wasted honor pts" in hearts = 29 ½ pts! = 4 ♠.

Had West bid 3 ♥, instead of 3 ♦, indicating 3 hearts and therefore a ♦ singleton, East would have signed off in 3 ♠.

Here are now a couple of examples where knowing the opener's exact distribution, at a very economical level, enables the relayer to avoid bad slam contracts :

Regional tournament, 2004.

♠ A 10 x	♠ K x x
♥ A 10 x x	♥ K Q x x
♦ A K x	♦ J x x
♣ K x x	♣ A Q x

Counting West's hand for 18 H pts and East's hand for 15 H pts, one will not be surprised that the large majority of pairs ended up bidding 6 ♥ or 6 NT. Unfortunately, these two perfectly "mirror" hands can only deliver 11 tricks – but you would have to know about the two "mirror" hands to stop short of slam.

First, West only has 17 ½ pts (-1 for no Queen and -1 for 4 3 3 3) and East only has 14 pts (-1 for 4 3 3 3), not 15. And the 1 point for the ♥ Fit point is offset by minus 2 pts for two perfectly *"mirror"* hands.

With a **strong ♣** / *Relay* bidding system, the auction would be :

1 ♣ (16 + H pts)	1 ♦ ? (relay)
1 NT (16/18 HL)	2 ♣ ? (relay)
2 ♥ (4 hearts)	2 ♠ ? (relay)
2 NT (4 ♥ 3 3 3)	3 NT

East stops in 3 NT as he knows that his side cannot have more than 31 pts with two "mirror" hands.

Here is another example deal with two 4 3 3 3 hands without a Fit where 6 NT must **not** be bid despite the honor point count :

♠ A 10 x	♠ K Q J
♥ K x x x	♥ A Q x
♦ A 10 x	♦ J x x x
♣ K J x	♣ A Q x

In the tournament this deal comes from, the bidding was most often : 1 NT – 6 NT   down 2, and experts' comments generally blamed East players for overvaluing their hand. But, had East players downgraded their hand by one point, how would that have changed the bidding and outcome ?... It is West's hand that is not worth a strong 15/17 1NT opening! It only has 14 pts : - 1 pt for 4 3 3 3 and - 1 pt for no Queen.

With a **strong ♣** / *Relay* bidding system, the auction could be :

1 NT (13/15 HL)	2 ♦ ? (forcing Stayman)
2 ♥ (4 hearts)	2 ♠ ? (relay)
2 NT (4 ♥ 3 3 3)	3 NT

East has 18 ½ pts (-1 for 4 3 3 3) and can deduct 1 point for two "mirror" suits : without an 8-card Fit, he knows that his side cannot have more than 32 ½ pts : not the points for 6 NT.

The next example combines the multiple absurdities of a game-forcing 2 ♦ or 2 NT opening or rebid, with a 4 NT *"quantitative"* bid :

European Championships, 2004.

♠ A x	♠ Q x x
♥ A x x	♥ x
♦ A Q J x	♦ K 10 x x
♣ A K x x	♣ Q J x x x

One team plays 3 NT, the other plays 4 NT after the following auction :

2 ♦ (game forcing)	2 ♥ (7 + H pts, no Ace)
2 NT (22/24 H pts)	4 NT (*quantitative*)
Pass	

Wow! In the above auction, neither the diamond nor the club suits are mentioned and East proposes to play a NT contract with a ♥ singleton! And the following alternative auction was proposed by an expert :

2 NT (21/23 H pts)	3 ♣
3 NT	5 ♣
6 ♣	Pass

Here too, the diamond suit is not mentioned, nor is the ♥ singleton !

With a **strong ♣ / *Relay*** bidding system, the auction would be :

1 ♣	2 ♣ (5 + ♣, 9/12 HL pts)
2 ♦ ? (relay)	3 ♦ (4 ♦)
3 ♥ ? (relay)	3 ♠ (3 ♠ = ♥ singleton)
4 ♣ ? (RKC Ask)	4 ♥ (No Key Card)
4 ♠ ? (trump Q/♣ ?)	5 ♦ (Yes, ♣ Q <u>and</u> ♦ K)
7 ♦	

A little better than 4 NT or 6 ♣, right ?…

Another advantage of only one player describing his hand is that it leaves opponents in the dark about the unknown hand. And when the contract is bid and played by the unknown hand, the lead can occasionally give away one trick, sometimes two.
Following is an interesting, and not so rare, illustration of this :

World Championship, teams of four – Istanbul, 2004.

♠ J x	♠ A x x x
♥ A K Q 9 x x	♥ x
♦ Q x	♦ K J x x x
♣ K Q J	♣ x x x

In one room, West, dealer, opens 1 ♥ and rebids 3 ♥, and the team ends up playing 3 NT – down two, on a club lead and a spade return. In the other room, West's team plays a **strong ♣/Relay** system and the bidding was :

1 ♣	2 ♦ (5 + ♦, 8 + H pts)
2 ♥ ? (relay)	2 ♠ (4 spades)
2 NT ? (relay)	3 ♣ (3 ♣ = ♥ singleton)
3 NT	

Knowing nothing about West's hand, and not imagining he could have 6 hearts, North leads in dummy's known short suit, with a small heart, under J 10 – allowing West to score his ♥ 9 and 6 hearts for 9 tricks !

The point has been made : **Relay** bidding is clearly *THE* solution to reach the right contracts through a precise, economical description of partner's full hand distribution.

But it can only be the solution **if** played *in conjonction* with the **optimal** hand evaluation point count **and** a strong 1 ♣ opening, counted in HLD pts, not H or HL pts. And, of course, without the absurdities of *traditional* systems such as the strong 2 NT opening, the *"quantitative"* 4 NT, *"splinter"* bids at the level of 4, and many, many more…

Not meeting the above criteria (strong 1♣ opening and counting opening hands in HLD pts) is a major reason why *Relay* systems have not prevailed, in the past, despite their clear superiority over other bidding methodologies.
There are other reasons : many – most – *Relay* systems do not use the simple *"Monaco"* hand description process and are too complicated, taxing considerably the memory, and few have been sufficiently developed and published.

And resistance to change is also a factor – just consider that it took more than 45 years just to get out of the "medieval dark ages" of *traditional* systems before the Precision Club system started being more widely adopted among champions, from 1975 on.
One may wonder how many years it will take before **Relay** *bidding becomes widely accepted. Perhaps this book can contribute to its advancement…*

Before drawing some preliminary conclusions from the preceding analysis, we first need to analyse three opening bids common to all three types of bidding systems identified, specifically :

➢ Pre-emptive openings at the level of 3 and 4.
➢ Weak *2* openings of 2 ♠ and 2 ♥.
➢ The **strong** 1 NT opening.

We will analyse these three openings next.

Three opening bids, generally common to most, if not all, bidding systems, warrant a specific analysis – and for reasons that will become quickly apparent, namely : *Pre-emptive* openings at the level of 3 and 4, **Weak 2** openings of 2 ♠ and 2 ♥, and the **strong** 1 NT opening.

PRE-EMPTIVE OPENINGS FROM 3 ♣ UP

In 2000, J-R. Vernes (French statistician, conceptor of *"The Law of Total Tricks"*) revealed, in his book « *Bridge Distributionnel* » (*Distributional Bridge,* not translated into English), the findings of a substantial statistical study he conducted over 5000 deals from 40 world championships played between 1955 and 1998.
His statistical study dealt specifically with *pre-emptive* openings bids, from 2 ♥ up through to 5 ♦. And his findings were enlightening and several were surprising.

➤ **Pre-emptive** openings of 3 ♣ and 3 ♦ at these championships did **not**, in a majority of cases, correspond to the *traditional* pre-emptive parameters – 7 cards and less than 9 H pts.

Instead, because these openings were not considered to be effective as *pre-emptive* bids, they were most often used as *semi-constructive* with a **6**-card suit and **9** or **10** H pts – in other words, a light opening looking for a potential 3 NT contract. And, interestingly, they were found to be the ***most effective*** of all pre-emptive bids, gaining a total of 150 IMPs – an average of 2 IMPs per deal, twice the average IMPs won per deal! Clearly a winning strategy.

➤ While *pre-emptive* openings in Majors, 3 ♥, 3 ♠, 4 ♥ and 4 ♠ were found to be "neutral", meaning that they did **not** generate favorable results compared to a *Pass* with the same hand at another table.

It appears that the cases where the results were **un**favorable belonged to either of two possibilities :

– When the pre-emptive opening *did not prevent* the opponents from finding and making their own contract. *Passing*, in these cases, achieved the same results, or *better* results as it did not reveal the opener's distribution.

– When the pre-emptive opening *led to a costly penalty* – heavier than what opponents would have scored playing their own contract – or to *missing their own game*, or bidding a game *played from the wrong hand*.
And these two cases reveal that this could have been avoided had the contract been *bid and played by the opener's* **partner**, the player with the *stronger* hand.

This is due to : A) Unfavorable *leads*, made *through* the stronger hand, and B) Having the stronger hand exposed as the dummy hand, making it easier for the opponents to defeat the contract. Makes perfect sense. And, come to think of it, it does **not** make much sense to have *the weak* hand bid and play a final contract – *at any level*.

The implication is clear and the solution simple : pre-emptive openings should be made via **transfer** bids! Therefore : 3 ♦ for hearts, 3 ♥ for spades, 3 NT for clubs, 4 ♣ for diamonds, all the way up to 5 ♥ for spades (and if partner's hand is not the *stronger* hand – less than 9 H pts – it means that the opponents have 24 + H pts and will likely bid).

Now, in order to retain the benefit of the light opening of 3 ♦, which has proved to be effective, we need to find a replacement bid for it. Well, it so happens that a 2 NT opening bid – which must *never, ever* be used to describe strong, balanced hands – can be used to describe just that hand : a 6 + card ♦ single-suit of 12/14 HLD pts.

And a 2 NT opening for these hands has the additional advantage of allowing partner to use 3 ♣ as a *relay* bid – should he want the opener's hand further described – an economical relay below the level of 3 ♦ !

WEAK 2 ♠ / 2 ♥ PRE-EMPTIVE OPENINGS

And when it comes to weak 2 ♥/2 ♠ openings, J-R. Vernes' statistical study reveals rather compelling findings : These openings lead to *negative* results, losing 60 IMPs, overall – an average loss of 1 IMP per deal (it takes *a gain* of 1 IMP per deal to win a tournament).

Considering that weak 2 ♥ and 2 ♠ openings have become widely adopted and played worldwide for about 50 years now, this warrants some analysis.

While such negative results could, in part, be explained by the fact that these openings are occasionally misused and/or over-used by players and that effective counter-measures have been devised over the years, there are, in fact, more compelling explanations for their poor results :

– The first one was previously mentioned as it relates to pre-emptive openings of 3 ♥ and up, as well : pre-emptive openings should be made via *transfer* bids – as it simply makes no sense to have the *weak* hand bid and play a final contract, at any level.

– And the second reason is even more compelling : these opening hands being, like all others, counted in H pts only – generally, **7** to **10** H pts – lead right into predictable failure ! Illustration :

Suppose you hold this hand :   ♠ K x
                             ♥ Q J x x x
                             ♦ A x x x
                             ♣ x x

And your partner opened a weak 2 ♠ of 7/10 H pts. Which of these two hands could he have ? :

Hand A	Hand B
♠ Q J 10 x x x	♠ A Q x x x x
♥ K x	♥ K x x
♦ x x x	♦ x
♣ Q x	♣ x x x

If he has hand A, you must **not** bid on as 2 ♠ already goes down one, when the opponents don't even have a play for a game in a Major – but then you will miss a 4 ♥ game opposite hand B.

And that is because hand A only has 10 HLD pts (one point only for the ♣ Q doubleton, one point only for the two doubletons, minus 1 point for an Aceless opening hand). With your 13 ½ HLFit pts in spades in North, the total isn't close to 27 pts – if you knew it, you would *Pass*.

Hand B, on the other hand, has 13 ½ HLD pts + 2 pts for the 8-card ♥ Fit with the King + your own 13 ½ pts = 29 pts. If you could rely on an opening hand of no less than 12 HLD pts, you would safely *relay* and discover South's 6 ♠ 3 ♥ 3 ♣ 1 ♦ distribution and play 4 ♥, such as :

♠ A Q x x x x	♠ K x
♥ K x x	♥ Q J x x
♦ x	♦ A x x x
♣ x x x	♣ x x
2 ♠ (6 ♠, 12/14 HLD)	2 NT ? (relay)
3 ♦ (6 ♠ <u>3 ♥</u> 3 ♣ <u>1 ♦</u>)	4 ♥

Counting an opening hand in H pts only is pure heresy! And when weak 2 ♠ or 2 ♥ openings "boomerang" against their own side, it is often the count in H pts, instead of HLD pts, that is the primary reason for it. The **optimal** point count has taught us that any opening in a 3 H point-zone immediately places the partnership **outside** the bidding level safety !

So now, the question is : do we retain the weak 2 openings for hearts and spades by using a 2 ♦ opening as a *transfer* bid ?
To answer that question, two things need to be considered : first, a 2 ♦ opening is much less effective than opening 2 ♥ or 2 ♠, as it becomes a *forcing* bid for partner which makes it easier for opponents to intervene.

And, second, opposite a weak 2 opening bid, partner will, statistically, have about 10 H pts and the side will therefore have, more often than not, less than 20 H pts, meaning a part-score, not a game.

All in all, not a very compelling case, particularly since these very hands could be opened 1 ♥ or 1 ♠, in the 12/14 HLD point zone (8 or 9 H pts + 2 L pts + 2 D pts = 12 /13 HLD pts).

A much better option exists, as the *optimal* point zone is *the **next** zone up* i. e. 15/17 HLD pts. In that zone, a 6-card single-suit hand will have 12 to 14 H pts and can expect about 9 + H pts in his partner's hand. Adding to these H points Length pts + Distribution pts + potential Fit pts places the partnership in *game* zone, more often than not !

And it is precisely in that very point-zone that the opener's side should try its best to avoid and *pre-empt* opponents' intervention ! And what better to do that than to open 2 ♥ or 2 ♠, describing a 15/17 HLD 6-card single-suit Major suit, bid by the *stronger* hand !

And this, without sacrificing 2 ♦ as a natural opening bid, in the process : 2 ♦ can now be an opening describing the very same 15/17 HLD 6-card ♦ single-suit, and so can an opening bid of 2 ♣. Two opening bids which could be hugely helpful in the search for a potential 3 NT contract! And which do not need to be *transfer* bids.

Here are some illustrations of the benefits of such openings :

Regional tournament, 2009.

♠ K Q x	♠ x x x
♥ A x	♥ x x x
♦ A x x x x x	♦ K 10 x x
♣ x x	♣ A x x

An amusing case where all West hands were invariably opened 1 NT. A NT opening which, for some, was 15/17 or 14/16 HL pts, and for others 13/15 or 12/14 H pts. In all cases, you guessed it.. the response was : Pass! Well, isn't it exactly how we have been taught to count points and to bid in the last 40 years or so ?!... Instead, the bidding could be :

2 ♦ (6 ♦ single-suit, 15/17 HLD)	2 ♥ ? (relay)
2 NT (6 ♦ 3 2 2)	3 ♦ *
3 NT (Majors guarded)	

* 3 ♦ = ♦ Fit, invitation to 3 NT **if** West guards the Majors.

Right upon West's opening, East can count 10 HFit pts in diamonds (8 H pts - 2 pts for 4 3 3 3 and no Queen + 4 pts for the 10-card ♦ Fit with the King). He *relays* to detect a possible singleton in West's hand.

Regional tournament, 2006.

♠ A x x	♠ K Q x x x
♥ x x x	♥ x x
♦ A K x x x x	♦ Q x
♣ x	♣ x x x x

The auction was most often :

1 ♦	1 ♠
2 ♦	Pass

What else can East bid but *pass*? As he doesn't know about the ♦ Fit or the ♠ Fit, nor about the ♣ singleton which is ideal opposite his 4 small clubs – neither does he have enough points to pursue the dialogue beyond 2 ♦ as rebidding his spades could be costly should he find West minimum with a ♠ singleton. As a result, 4 ♠ is missed.

The system's problems are numerous : 1) the 1♦ opening invites an easy, no-risk 1 ♥ intervention from the opponents, 2) the 2 ♦ rebid indicates only 5 diamonds, not 6, and 3) East's 1 ♠ response only describes 4 spades, not 5 – *another major deficiency common to most bidding systems*... Instead, the bidding could be :

2 ♦ (6 + ♦, 15/17 HLD)	2 ♠ (5 ♠, 7/9 HL pts)
3 ♣ (♠ Fit, ♣ singleton)	4 ♠

East's 2 ♠ response indicates 5 spades, not 4, since a 2 ♦ opening, showing a single-suit hand, cannot have 4 spades. Similarly, West cannot have a second suit in clubs and a 3 ♣ bid can then be a "short suit" trial bid, showing a ♣ singleton with the ♠ Fit.
East can then add to his initial count of 9 HLFit pts in diamonds, 2 pts for *no* "wasted honor pts" in clubs + 1 D point for his 2 doubletons = 12 pts + 15 HLD pts minimum in West = 27 total pts minimum = 4 ♠.

From « *Evaluation of Bridge Hands* » – J-R. Vernes & B. Charles, 1995.

♠ A x x	♠ x x x
♥ x x	♥ A x x
♦ x x	♦ A x x x
♣ A K 10 x x x	♣ Q x x

The example deal above puzzled the authors of the book as 3 NT should be bid but the two hands only add up to 21 H pts + 2 L pts for the six clubs, in *traditional* point count.
And nowadays most advocates of a 12/14 HL pts 1 NT opening would be delighted to open West's hand 1 NT to deny their opponents a "cheap" overcall of 1 ♥ or 1 ♠ or 1 NT.

But on such 1NT opening, East would Pass. He only has 8 ½ pts (4 3 3 3 and no King) and does not know about West's 6 clubs and the 9-card ♣ Fit.

The modern day practice of "hiding" a 6-card minor suit behind a NT bid is heresy! Particularly when the alternative is to open at a level even higher than 1 NT while precisely indicating a 6-card suit ! Instead, the bidding could be :

2 ♣ (6 ♣, 14/17 HLD pts)	2 ♦ ? (relay)
2 NT (6 ♣ 3 2 2)	3 ♠ ? (guard ♠ ?)
3 NT (yes, I guard spades)	Pass

On West's 2 ♣ opening, East can immediately add 3 pts to his hand for the 9-card ♣ Fit with the Queen. He *relays* to determine whether West has a singleton and upon West's description of a 6 3 2 2 hand and guarding the spades, he can now play 3 NT.

Clearly, we need to "rethink" the *traditional* approach to opening bids at the level of two as these opening bids can be used in a considerably more effective way.

THE 1 NT OPENING

When it comes to 1 NT openings, here too J-R. Vernes' latest statistical research, unveiled in 2011, which he conducted on more than 1600 openings of 1 NT – both strong and weak – in European Champion-ships, reveals rather compelling findings : Strong 1NT openings of 15/17 H pts lead to negative results, losing 118 IMPs (686 openings) while weak 1 NT openings of 12/14 H pts (961 openings) gained 301 IMPs – a substantial net difference of 419 IMPs.

As proponents of a strong 1 NT opening, whether 15/17 or 14/16 H pts, still outnumber those playing a weak NT, this opening warrants, as well, some analysis.

While the negative results of strong 1 NT openings could, in part, be explained by the fact that these openings have been substantially disfigured over the years – by including some 5 4 2 2 or 6 3 2 2 distributions and/or a 5-card Major – thus losing valuable precision, there are, in fact, more compelling explanations for such results :

– A 1 NT opening, by-passing four lower bids, is *pre-emptive* in nature and a strong NT therefore pre-empts… the partner! As well, it defies the key principle that *"the stronger the hand, the lower the bid"* to preserve bidding space when most needed i.e. with strong hands that could lead to a game or a slam. And 15/17 H pts is precisely the point zone most likely to find 8 + H pts in partner's hand which, combined with **L**ength pts, **D**istribution pts and **F**it pts will, more often than not, add up to the points for a game, whether in NT or in a suit !

Not so for a 12/14 HL NT which will likely find 9 H pts in partner's hand, adding up much more rarely to the points needed for game.

– A strong 1 NT opening defies the *"balanced hand principle"* : An *unbalanced* hand is the one which *should describe* its singleton as the balanced hand is the one best able to judge whether partner's singleton "meshes" well, or poorly, with his hand. In other words, applying the "wasted honor pts" count! Yet, this fundamental principle is totally overlooked by the proponents of a strong 1NT opening !

It follows logically from the two observations made above that, if we divide balanced hands into point zones of : 12/14 HL pts, 15/17 HL pts and 18/20 HL pts, the strongest hand should be opened with the lowest bid, 1 ♣, the next strongest opened with the second lowest, 1 ♦, and the weakest one opened with the highest bid, 1 NT – that is :

1 ♣ : 18/20 HL pts   1 ♦ : 15/17 HL pts   1 NT : 12/14 HL pts

Here are some illustrations of the key observations made above :

Opener A	Opener B
♠ A x x	♠ A x x
♥ K Q x	♥ x x x
♦ A Q J x	♦ A Q J x
♣ x x x	♣ K Q x

Responder

♠ K Q x x x x
♥ J x x
♦ x x x
♣ x

Only the opener can judge what the *optimal* contract is – 4 ♠ with opener A, but only 3 ♠ with opener B – and for that he needs to have his partner describe his 6 spades and his ♣ singleton. But how can the responder do that on his partner's strong 1 NT opening ?

Had the opening bid been 1 ♦, instead, *relay* bidding could be :

1 ♦	1 ♠ (5 + ♠, 7/9 HL pts)
1 NT ? (relay)	2 ♠ (6 ♠, single-suit)
2 NT ? (relay)	3 ♣ (♣ singleton)

With hand A : 4 ♠ (no "wasted honor pts" in clubs)
With hand B : 3 ♠ ("wasted honor pts" in clubs)

The strong hand is in control and can *relay* to have the responder describe *his* hand. Perfect illustration of the *"balanced hand principle"*.

Now, remove the ♦ Q J from both openers' hands, which would now be in the 12/14 HL point zone, and the bidding would then be :

1 NT (12/14 HL)	2 ♥ (*transfer* for spades)
2 ♠	Pass

A 7/9 HLD point zone will not likely produce a game opposite a 12/14 HL 1NT opening – unless the opener "super-accepts" spades – so, the responder does not need to describe his ♣ singleton.

In the next example, responder's hand is very close to the one shown in the above deal, but this time the opening bid was my favorite 2 NT !

National selection, teams – 2009.

♠ A J x	♠ K Q x x x x
♥ A K J x	♥ Q x x
♦ A K x	♦ x x x
♣ x x x	♣ x

40

Almost invariably, the bidding was :

2 NT	3 ♥ (*transfer* for spades)
3 ♠	4 ♠
Pass	

And the slam was missed by all teams. East players did not "see" a slam opposite 20/21 H pts and West's two Jacks and 4 3 3 3 distribution discouraged him from considering a slam.

Had West's opening been 1 strong ♣, *relay* bidding could have been :

1 ♣ (18 + HLD pts)	2 ♠ (6 + ♠, 7/9 HL pts)
2 NT ? (relay)	3 ♣ (♣ singleton)
3 ♦ ? (relay)	3 ♠ (6 ♠ 3 3 1 ♣)

Followed by a 4 ♣ Roman Key Card Ask leading to 6 ♠.

East can jump to 2 ♠ directly to identify 6 spades, not just 5, with only 7/9 HL pts, at no risk opposite an 18 + HLD 1 ♣ opening, and by indicating a 6 3 3 1 distribution, he denies a ♣ void – a key precision as a 7 3 3 0 distribution, instead, would lead to 7 ♠.
(with a void, East's last bid would be 4 ♣, repeating his short suit).

Such a precise description is simply *pre-empted* by a 2 NT opening.

Cap Volmac, 1995.

♠ K Q x x	♠ A x x x
♥ K x x x	♥ Q J 10
♦ A Q x	♦ K x x
♣ K x	♣ x x x

The auction at 5 of the 8 tables was : 1 NT – 3 NT, down 200, as the opponents cashed the ♥ Ace and 5 clubs. An 11 IMPs swing as 4 ♠ could not be beaten.

It would have been best for West to make the final decision as he is the one with the doubleton. But the strong 1 NT opening makes East the captain – and leads to the wrong outcome.

As it happens, a strong 1 NT opening is misguided as West's point count is 18 ½ pts (+ 1 point for 3 Kings), not 17. Playing a strong 1 ♣ and *relays* could have led to the following auction :

1 ♣	1 NT (7/12 HL pts)
2 ♣ ? (relay-stayman)	2 ♠ (4 spades, 10/12 HL)
4 ♠	

And for those concerned about the weak NT opening's vulnerability to *penalty doubles* when finding a partner also with a weak hand, don't be : weak 1NT openings are very rarely doubled for penalty and this is attested by most experts and champions and by statistical studies. Relative to that unsubstantiated concern, here is now a compelling illustration of the *pre-emptive* effectiveness of the weak 1 NT opening, an example deal taken from one of Edgar Kaplan's books :

♠ K Q x x	♠ J 10 x
♥ A x x	♥ x x
♦ A 10 x	♦ J 9 x x
♣ 10 x x	♣ x x x

At one table, West opened 1 ♦, North *doubled* and North/South found their vulnerable 4 ♥ contract. At the other table, Kaplan/Sheinwold, not vulnerable, bid as follows :

1 NT (12/14 H)	2 ♣ (Stayman)
2 ♠ (4 spades)	3 ♠ (!)
Pass	------ All pass -------

Down 100. A rather cheap save against a vulnerable 4 ♥ !...

Here is another example, from the 1969 Bermuda Bowl world championship : South dealer, all vulnerable.

♠ A K x	♠ x x x x x
♥ A x x	♥ J 10 x
♦ x x x	♦ J x
♣ K x x x	♣ Q x x

At the first table, West opened 1 ♣, North overcalled by 1 ♦ and North/South eventually ended in 3 NT. South led a high spade and, from there, 3 NT was sure to make.

At the other table, West opened 1 NT and the bidding was as follows :

1 NT (12/14)	Double	2 ♥ (*transfer* for ♠)
2 ♠	-------- All pass --------	

Down one. Some save against a vulnerable 3 NT !...

Regional tournament, 2012.

♠ x x	♠ A x x
♥ A J x	♥ x x x
♦ A Q x x x	♦ K J
♣ K x x	♣ A Q J 10 x

Not a single team found the slam as East players counted their hand for 16 HL pts and did not "see" a slam on partner's 1 NT opening, which was, for some, 14/16 H, for others 13/15 H or 12/14 H pts. Opposite the few West players who opened 1 NT 15/17 HL pts, a few Easts invited by a *"quantitative"* 4 NT, on which openers *passed.*

But West has 16 HL pts (9 pts for two Aces and 1 point for the 5 diamonds), not 14, and East has 20 HL pts, not 16! You would expect the bidding to have been : 1 NT (15/17 HL)   –   6 NT !

The issue here is not whether to open 1 NT or 1 ♦ but to count points properly and to find the 8-card ♣ Fit (+ 2 pts). But how to discover the ♣ Fit after a 1 NT opening if you do not play a *relay* bidding system? *Relay* bidding which could look like this :

1 NT (15/17 HL pts)	2 ♦ ? (forcing Stayman)
3 ♦ (5 diamonds)	3 ♥ ? (relay)
3 ♠ (♠ doubleton)	4 ♣ ? (RKC Ask, ♦ trump)
4 NT (2 Keys and ♦ Q)	5 ♣ ? (K & Q ♣ Ask)
5 ♠ (♣ King)	6 NT

Note : Trump is diamonds, West's long suit.
East knows West's exact 5 ♦ 3 ♣ 3 ♥ 2 ♠ distribution upon West's 3 ♠ bid. The rest is child's play…

National Division 1, teams of four, 2015.

♠ A x x	♠ x
♥ K x x x	♥ A J 10 x
♦ A K x x	♦ J 10 x x x
♣ K x	♣ x x x

In the semi-finals of ND 1, in 2015, 3 teams out of 4 bid as follows :

1 NT (15/17 H)   Pass

Cumulative point count errors and the wrong opening bid leading to missing the 4 ♥ game.
This example illustrates several features of the **optimal** point count.
First, East must count his HLD points on a NT opening ! **not** his H pts only, and, of course, his tens! Which gives him 8 ½ HLD pts (- 2 for no King and no Queen), not 6 H pts! He should make a 2 ♣ Stayman inquiry. With 1 point for the ♥ Fit + 1 more point for the ♠ singleton with 4 trumps, the side *may* now be able to find the ♥ game… *Maybe.*

But the first point count mistake comes from the opener who has 18 H pts, not 17 ! (9 pts for two Aces + 1 point for 3 Kings minus 1 point for no Queen). A 1 NT opening was therefore **not** the right bid.

43

A strong 1 ♣ opening would enable to bid the game, and from the right hand, West, thus protecting the ♣ King against a club lead :

1 ♣ (18 + HLD)	1 ♦ (< 7 HL pts)
1 NT (18/20 HL)	2 ♣ ? (Stayman)
2 ♥ (4 hearts)	4 ♥

10 ½ HDF pts in East + 18 HL pts in West = 28 ½ pts = 4 ♥
A little better than : 1 NT   Pass   *right ?!...*

Conclusion : A 1 NT opening bid is *pre-emptive* in nature – therefore, to pre-empt the opponents, **not** the partner, this opening should be weak : « *The weaker the hand, the higher the bid* ».

– The "balanced hand principle" dictates that it is the partner of a strong, balanced hand who should describe his hand, when it is *unbalanced*. To do so requires bidding space. *"The stronger the hand, the lower the bid"*.

– Furthermore, to increase the frequency of the strong 1 NT opening and to get around a rebid problem, *traditional* bidding has "disfigured" the 1 NT opening by including in it 5 4 2 2 or 6 3 2 2 distributions. But *Relay* bidding has no such rebid problem and the frequency of a 12/14 HL 1 NT opening is twice that of a 15 /17 H 1 NT opening.

– And including a 5-card Major in a NT opening makes no sense !
Here again, we know that the primary reason for *traditional* bidding to do so is to avoid a rebid problem in "dialogue" bidding.
Playing *Relays*, which look for total *distributional* precision, it becomes inconceivable **not** to start by describing a 5-card Major !
And including **both** 4-card Majors in a NT opening is no better !
Considering that the priority objective of a pair is to look for an 8-card Fit in a Major, to open by bidding **over** *both of them* is pure heresy !

The logic is to make the NT opening – or a 1 NT rebid after a 1 ♦ or 1 ♣ opening – exactly *the opposite* of what it has become nowadays :
12/14 HL pts, **not** 15/17 H pts, denying a 5-card Major, denying **both** 4-card Majors, and denying a 6 3 2 2 distribution or a 5 4 2 2 distribution other than one with 5 4 in the minor suits.

FIRST CONCLUSIONS

From the preceding analysis and assessment of the 3 main bidding methodologies and of 3 specific opening bids, we can already reach some key, preliminary **conclusions** whose implications will need to be incorporated in a new bidding method for the 21st Century.

A NEW BIDDING METHOD :

GUIDING PRINCIPLES AND CORNERSTONES

A very accurate hand evaluation can and should serve as the basis for a sound bidding method and a number of key conclusions can be derived from the **Optimal** hand evaluation and its essential implications : they provide "pathways" and guiding principles for what a modern / effective bidding method should look for, such as :

1. A first consideration is the need to identify : A) the exact **Length** of each suit, to be able to count Fit points which count for **all** suits and **all** contracts, and B) short suits, their nature (singleton or void) and their exact location, to allow the count of "wasted honor points".
Implication : Achieving optimal *distributional* precision is a priority of critical importance. And to do so, there is only one solution : replacing the *traditional* "dialogue" by a "monologue" – an inquiry made by one player using the most economical bids possible (the suit just above the one bid by his partner) as a *relay*. There is simply no better way to give a player the bidding space needed to describe 12 (or more) of his cards, economically (without going over 3 NT).

To do this, an excellent and simple description methodology was previously devised, in the early '50s; It is the *"Monaco"* process i.e. on successive *relays*, the player interrogated describes his hand in the most natural fashion : first a 5-card suit, second a 4-card suit, and third a **3**-card suit – this describes, in three bids, **12** cards out of 13.
And when the third bid is either No Trump or a repeat of one of the first two suits, it denies a third suit of 3 cards.
And for 6-card single-suit hands, the long suit is first repeated and then the short suit is bid with a 6 3 3 1 hand. With a 6 3 2 2 hand, No Trump is bid after repeating the 6-card suit.

2. A second key consideration concerns the precise zoning of a hand's **Strength** and here two key implications come out of the analysis of the **optimal** point count : A) Opening hands must imperatively be counted in HLD points, and B) Point zones **must** be described in zones of 3 HLD points and no wider in order to be sufficiently precise and to remain within the *bidding level safety*.

The challenge now is to reconcile the two requirements of **strength** and **distributional** precision – knowing that the bidding space available to achieve this only allows the description of <u>two</u> point zones, not three or more. Well, the good news is that it is technically possible to describe economically – for 90 % of most frequent distributions – all 13 cards of a hand for two point zones of 3 HLD pts, without going over the level of 3 NT. This can be done as follows :

– 2 point zones for *balanced* hands : 12/14 HL pts : 1 NT opening, 15/17 HL pts : 1 ♦ opening followed by a 1 NT rebid.
– The same 2 point zones for 1 ♥ and 1 ♠ opening bids : 12/14 HLD pts and 15/17 HLD pts. This now means that a 5 4 3 1 hand can be opened with **9 H** pts! Thus, the following hands can be bid to 4 ♥ :

♠ K Q x x	♠ A x x x
♥ A x x x x	♥ K x x x
♦ x x x	♦ x
♣ x	♣ x x x x

With 12 ½ HLD pts, West can open, and the auction could be :

1 ♥ (5 + ♥)	1 ♠
2 ♠ (4 ♠, 13/17 HLDF pts)	3 ♦ (♦ singleton, ♠ or ♥ Fit)
4 ♥	Pass

On East's 1 ♠ response, West's hand has 14 ½ HLDFit pts (+ 1 for the 8-card ♠ Fit + 1 for the ♣ singleton with 4 trumps) and, after East's *short-suit* 3 ♦ trial bid (11/13 Fit pts), West can add 2 pts for "no wasted honor pts" in diamonds : 16 ½ HLDF + 11 HLDF minimum = Game.
A little better than :   Pass   Pass   *wouldn't you say ?...*

– A strong 1 ♣ opening bid can now be used for all hands of **18** HLD pts and over. With two point zones as well : 18/20 and 21/23 HLD pts. 1 ♣ opening followed by a 1 NT rebid : 18 to 20 HL pts.
And all responses to 1 ♣ (except 1 ♦) are in two zones as well : 7/9 HL and 10/12 HL pts. The 1 ♦ response being *relay* (either *less* than 7 HL pts or 13 + HL pts – the next responder's bid will clarify which it is).

On all responses other than 1 ♦, the opener *relays* – done being embarassed by the typical question asked in "bidding contests" : "*After your 1 ♣ opening, what is your rebid over partner's 1 ♠ response ? »*...
As the answer will now invariably be : « 1 NT – *relay*. My partner has started to describe **his** hand : let him continue ! ». The "monologue" process works both ways !

And isn't it, indeed, elementary logic that over a strong 1 ♣ opening, it is the responder who should, in most cases, describe his weaker hand instead of having the opener describe his through... jumps, "splinter" bids at the level of 4 and other absurd conventions and contortions !?...

But then how are 24 + point hands opened ? but 1 ♣ of course! Since *they will **never** have to be described – the **responder** will describe **his** hand.* Well, except when responder has 13 + HL pts and *relays* : Let's see : that's 24 + HLD pts + 13 + HL pts = 37 + pts, and that's *before counting* the responder's distribution pts or Fit pts... that's ***above*** 40 total pts ! Well, I don't know about you, but I haven't had lately that many points so often that a specific opening bid should be dedicated to such hands !

A few examples, now, to illustrate this different methodology :

Bidding contest – Le Bridgeur.

♠ A x	♠ x x x
♥ A x x x x	♥ K J 10 x x
♦ A K Q x x	♦ x x
♣ x	♣ A J x

The three participants in the bidding contest could only reach 6 ♥. Just like the entire field at the tournament this deal comes from where only one pair bid the grand slam – presumably because the pairs did not communicate that they had 10 hearts, not 9, or that West had 5 diamonds by A K Q, or both... Again, dialogue = imprecision.

With a *Relay* system, the bidding could be :

1 ♣ (18 + HLD pts)	1 ♥ (4 ♥ +, 7/12 HL pts)
1 ♠ ? (relay)	2 NT (5 ♥ 3 3 2, 10/12 HL)
3 ♣ ? (relay)	3 ♦ (5 ♥ 3 3 2 ♦)
4 ♣ ? (RKC Ask, ♥ trump)	4 ♠ (2 Keys, w/o ♥ Q)
7 ♥	

West knows everything about East's hand making it easy to bid 7 ♥.

The "monologue" process works both ways : one can see here the value of the *responder* describing precisely his hand to a 1 ♣ opener.

*One has to wonder how such a failure from the entire field, with these two hands, did not lead to serious questioning of **any** and **all** bidding systems ?!...*

« *Lessons in bidding technique* », 2008 – Le Bridgeur.

The question was : « *With the following hand in East, what would you bid, after the following auction ?* » :

West	East	♠ A K x
		♥ Q x
1 ♠	2 ♣	♦ Q J x
2 ♠	?	♣ Q x x x x

Comment from the writer of the article : « *4 ♠. An exceptional trump support associated to... a non-existant source of tricks! Do not make the mistake of "imagining" a partner's hand that will result in a slam. For the one time in ten that it will, you will end up playing very poor slams the other nine times if you encourage partner to bid by bidding 3 ♠.*
Try then to stop a partner who would have, for example, the following hand :

♠ Q 10 9 x x x
♥ A x x
♦ A K x
♣ x

Astonishing assessment ! – No doubt revealing of a rather powerless bidding system... Isn't it, indeed, the very purpose of a good bidding system to be able to determine when there is a slam and when there isn't? and to provide the means to bid the *good* slams – and to *avoid* the *bad* ones. Such as this, for example, for the two hands shown above :

2 ♠ (6 ♠ single-suit, 15/17 HLD)	2 NT ? (relay)
3 ♣ (♣ singleton)	4 ♠

East stops in 4 ♠ as West's ♣ singleton is *in misfit* opposite East's ♣ suit : no slam. While, if the same West had a ♥ singleton instead of clubs, the two hands being, for example, as follows :

♠ Q 10 9 x x x	♠ A K x
♥ x	♥ Q x
♦ A x x	♦ Q J x
♣ A K x	♣ Q x x x x

The bidding could then be as follows :

2 ♠ (6 + ♠, 15/17 HLD)	2 NT ? (relay)
3 ♥ (♥ singleton)	4 ♣ ? (KC Ask, ♠ trump)
4 NT (2 Key Cards w/ ♠ Q)	5 ♣ ? (K & Q ♣ Ask)
5 ♠ (♣ K)	6 ♠

The writer's problem is the system he plays – a system which does nothing to obtain the precise information needed to reach the right contracts. A system H. Schenken appropriately called « *inaccurate, ineffective and obsolete* » over 55 years ago !...

Yet, H. Schenken's own system couldn't have solved the above issue then or now because this has nothing to do with using a strong 1 ♣ opening – it has to do with using a *relay* system, to have *one hand fully described* instead of describing only "part" of each hand...

3. A third key consideration concerns the identification of a 6-card minor suit because it will find a Fit of 8 + cards between partners 75 % of the time and we know that Fit points count for **all** suits and **all** contracts.

The same 6-card minor suits that *traditional* systems do their very best to carefully hide from their partner, particularly behind a NT bid for 6 3 2 2 hands, the surest way to "bury" them... This allows them, then, on one hand, to reserve the 2 ♣ opening bid for those wonderful, very frequent, very strong hands... and, on the other hand, to open 6-card minor suits 1 ♣ or 1 ♦ – an open invitation for opponents to intervene very *economically* with a 1 ♥ or 1 ♠ overcall.

The result of these practices is well-known and observed every day : a multitude of contracts in minor suits and in NT repeatedly missed – at all levels : part-scores, games and slams !

Conclusion : we must "rethink" the *traditional* approach to treating 6-card minor suits – for opening bids as well as for *responding* bids. And it is not very difficult, by opening these hands as follows :

– 3 ♣ and 2 NT (for diamonds) opening bids for 6-card single-suit hands of 12/14 HLD pts (*weak hand, bid high : preemptive*).

– 2 ♣ and 2 ♦ opening bids for 6-card single-suit hands of 15/17 HLD pts (*stronger hand, bid low*).

– Open 1 ♣ these same 6-card single-suit hands of 18 + HLD pts.
On a 1 ♦ response : rebid 2 ♣ or 2 ♦ with 21/23+ HLD
                rebid 3 ♣ or 2 NT (diamonds) with 18/20 HLD pts
(*stronger hand : bid low, weaker hand : bid high*).

On any *other* response : the opener *relays* – by the suit just above the one bid by his partner.

Illustrations for such openings were shown in the previous section.

To the above implications – directly drawn from the **optimal** hand evaluation – we must add the implications to be drawn from the most glaring absurdities of contemporary bidding systems, such as :

– Get rid of *"the horrible threes"*, that is the worse three opening bids ever devised and which **must not** be part of a sound new bidding method, in their current traditional meaning : The strong 2 NT, strong 2 ♣ and strong 1 NT opening bids – the first two made obsolete by a strong 1 ♣ opening.

– Get rid of the *"quantitative"* 4 NT jump, in fact get rid of all *double, triple* and *quadruple* jumps (other than for *pre-emptive* purposes), bidding a "false" second suit as a rebid, *"splinter"* bids at the level of four, and many others which are too many to list...

– Last, but certainly not least, the 4 NT Blackwood Ask is far too high to be of much help! It must be replaced by a much more economical 4 ♣ Roman Key Card Asking bid.

The above **cornerstones** could constitute the foundation of a new bidding method.

Upon that foundation remains to be designed a comprehensive and coherent bidding method which will also have to address numerous situations which *traditional* systems have badly mistreated since... the beginning of time, such as : responder's *misfits* on 1♥ and 1♠ openings, *trial* bids on 1 ♥ and 1 ♠ openings, responses to **all** opening bids, the 1 ♦ opening bid, and many others...

But before doing that, let's clearly define what we *should* expect of a sound, modern bidding method – in other words, what should be its objectives. That is what we will do next.

Had other systems gone through such definition process, they would likely have come up with something far, far different from what they ended up with...

THE OPTIMAL PRECISION RELAY CONSTITUTION

« *We hold these truths to be self-evident that all bidding methods "are **not** created equal", that "traditional **dialogue** bidding is ineffective and obsolete" and destined to be abandoned and that "the future is in **monologue, relay** bidding" based on **optimal hand evaluation** and precise, **pertinent** hand description **effectively** leading to positive results* ».

The author

PREAMBLE

The preceding analysis clearly points to the numerous deficiencies most bidding systems have.

And their negative impact seems confirmed by a relatively recent study conducted by D. Kleinman – on deals bid and played in regional tournaments across the U.S. – which led him to conclude that 55 % of errors and failures can be attributed to *poor bidding*, 30 % to *defensive* play and less than 15 % to *declarer's* play.

The need for a different bidding method has been clearly established, but before outlining such a method, we need, first, to define clear **objectives** and **criteria** – something generally lacking from designing bidding systems.

KEY OBJECTIVES

Three key objectives are fundamental :

– Being *effective*, i.e. performing, meaning : 1) bid your **optimal** contracts 2) **avoid** bidding **bad** contracts, and 3) make it as difficult as possible for **opponents** to find **their** best contract.

– Being *playable*. The first objective is not likely to be achieved if the bidding method is **not** playable by being too imprecise, too complex or does not respect the "bidding safety level".

Ely Culbertson once said that his slam *Asking* bids had been his greatest *technical* innovation but his greatest *psychological* failure as they were so complex as to be unplayable, even by the very best world-class players.

– Being *satisfying* to… *both* partners! And that is not incidental judging
by the number of disputes and break-ups between partners, most of which stem from disagreements over bidding.

Let's now define which **criteria** will be used to do so and what **means** are available to achieve these objectives.

MEANS AND CRITERIA

I. Achieving the first objective – being *effective* – requires three key elements : *Precision, pertinent description* and *competitive initiative*.

– **Precision**, on both hand *distribution* and hand *strength*. And precision goes hand in hand with the **economical** use of bidding space. Such precision and economy can only be achieved through a *"monologue"* using *relays*, **not** through a *"dialogue"* process.

As previously illustrated, achieving **strength** precision requires four elements : 1) counting opening hands in HLD pts, not H or HL pts only, 2) counting *total* points between two hands as HLD + Fit pts, 3) opening 1 ♣ hands of 18 + HLD pts in order to *limit* all other openings to 17 HLD pts maximum, and 4) to precisely "zone" any opening or response to no more than **two** point zones of 3 pts each.

And **distribution** precision calls for two elements : 1) one player descri- bing to the other his hand's complete distribution, and 2) identify a singleton, or void, and its location ("wasted honor points").

Furthemore, ultimate precision calls for two elements : 1) identify, whenever asked to do so, "guards" in specific suits (to play NT contracts), and 2) identify, precisely, **K**ey **C**ards as well as Kings and Queens in *specific suits* in response to a slam inquiry – and to do this, using economical bids will be *mandatory* as a 4 NT Blackwood is much too high to be of much value and **must** be replaced by a 4 ♣ RKC Ask.

– **Pertinent description**, meaning bids which have **useful value** that describe a hand's key features. Interestingly, this is rarely referred to in Bridge books, and yet it is a critically important criteria! Example:

♠ A Q J x x	♠ K x x x
♥ x x	♥ x x
♦ K Q x x	♦ A x x x x
♣ Q x	♣ x x

Traditional bidding will most often be :

1 ♠	2 ♠
3 ♦	4 ♠

West's 3 ♦ bid is invitational, looking for support in the diamond suit and, preferably, a 4-card ♠ Fit. With both, East bids 4 ♠. Down one, with four losers in hearts and clubs.

That is because East's 2 ♠ bid gives West no *useful, pertinent* infor- mation – in addition to wrongly evaluating his hand which has 12 ½ HLDFit pts. And a direct jump-raise to 3 ♠ would not be more useful.

The pertinent information here is three-fold : a good ♦ suit, a 4-card ♠ Fit and *nothing* in the other two suits, no Ace, no King, no singleton. And describing these specific, useful features could be done as follows :

1 ♠	2 ♦
3 ♦	3 ♠

A much more useful auction than using 3 ♠ as a slam invitation – with a strong hand and slam interest, the responder can just *relay*.

On East's very descriptive, useful bids, West can now *Pass* as he knows about the four losers in hearts and clubs.

54

World Championship, pairs – 2006, Italy.

♠ A Q x x x		♠ K	
♥ ---		♥ Q J 10 x x x	
♦ K Q x x x		♦ A J x x	
♣ x x x		♣ x x	

Only 3 pairs out of 72 found the 5 ♦ game, the result of uneconomical *"dialogue"* and disastrous lack of *precision*, the bidding having generally been as follows :

1 ♠	2 ♥
2 ♠	3 ♥
Pass or 3 NT	

The ♦ suit is never mentioned by either player! *Pertinent description?* In 2006, 96 % of the world's best pairs unable to find this 5 ♦ contract… What does that say about **any** and **all** bidding systems being played ?...

The 5 ♦ contract could easily be reached with *relay* bidding such as :

1 ♠	1 NT ? (relay)
2 ♦ (5 ♠ 4 ♦, 12/17 HLD pts)	2 ♥ ? (relay)
3 ♣ (3 ♣ : ♥ singleton, 15/17)	3 ♥ ? (relay)
4 ♦ (5 ♦ = 5 ♠ 5 ♦ 3 ♣ 0 ♥)	5 ♦

All relevant, *pertinent* features of West's hand are described : the second suit of 5 diamonds and the ♥ void – and with 3 "wasted honor pts" in hearts, East knows his side doesn't have the points for a slam.

– *Competitive initiative*. The importance of this criteria has been understood for quite some time now and is reflected in opening bids such as pre-emptive bids at the levels of three and four, the weak 1 NT opening, weak-two Major suit openings, etc.

And a strong 1 ♣ opening of 18 + HLD points now enables extending the *competitive initiative* to 1 ♥ and 1 ♠ openings with hands of 12/14 HLD pts which can now be bid with 9 **H** pts when with a singleton !

And this applies, as well, to **all** openings *at the level of two* as these openings, in the 15/17 HLD point zone, can be made with as little as **9** H pts when the hand has a void (4 L pts for a 7-card suit + 4 D pts for the void).

So now, **All Optimal** Precision Relay opening bids from 1 ♥ up represent a *competitive initiative!* Particularly since Aces are valued 4 ½ pts each, Tens can be worth one whole point when with a Queen or a Jack, etc. The following hands illustrate this vividly :

♠ A J 10 x x	Q 10 x	A x x	A J x
♥ x	x x	K Q J x x x	x
♦ A x x x	K x x	x	x x x
♣ x x x	A J 10 x x	x x x	Q J 10 x x x

1 ♠	1 NT	2 ♥	3 ♣
12 HLD pts	13 HL pt	16 ½ HLD pts	12 ½ HLD pts
(no K, no Q)		(+ 2 for K Q J)	(no K)

Other factors contribute to a bidding method's effectiveness but the three referred to above are absolutely key and **must** be part of a bidding method for the 21st Century.

Some have said that *concealment* should be one criteria to minimize the information communicated to opponents; but that is just not rational as it would also mean concealing to… the partner! and that is certainly **not** going to provide *pertinent description* to the partner.

Having said this, *relay* bidding **is** actually the best possible way to *conceal to opponents* the hand of the *interrogator* while the latter obtains *precise* and *pertinent* information from his partner.

II. Achieving the second objective – being *playable* – also requires three key elements :

– Stay within the "*bidding safety level*". This means that bidding must describe a hand's strength within a point zone that will never place the partnership **outside** the bidding safety level.

This may sound rather elementary, yet any bidding system counting opening hands in H or HL points only does **not** respect this mandatory requirement! In fact, asking two questions is all that is needed to determine whether a system is *playable* or *not* :

– Are *opening* hands counted in HLD pts, rather than H or HL pts ?

– Do *opening* bids at the one-level *limit* the hand's point zone to **6 HLD** pts ? (other than the opening bid used for *strong* hands).

If the answer to either question is **no**, the system is **unplayable** !

– Have **systemic coherence**, logical, rational. This is needed to find the right bid without having to rely solely on memory.

Actually, it is the reverse that is observed in contemporary bidding systems due to the "grafting" of multiple conventions to the system or simply "inconsistencies" such as retaining the strong 2 NT opening while playing a strong 1 ♣ opening, playing a strong NT opening in conjunction with a strong 1 ♣ opening, or playing a 1NT opening which would include a 5-card Major or both 4-card Majors, and many more.

– **No *ambiguous*** or ***improvised*** bids. These have no place in a method seeking *precision* through a *monologue / relay* process.

Such bids are among the most debilitating in contemporary bidding systems as illustrated so often by the *bidding contests* appearing in Bridge magazines. Ely Culbertson once said that *"a bid is only effective **if partner understands** it, easily and quickly"*. How true but often totally overlooked! Hereunder is a telling example of such bids :

Bidding contest – Le Bridgeur, 2010.

« *What would you bid as West, the opener, after the auction below ?* » :

```
♠ A Q x
♥ Q x          1 NT  (15/17 H)       4 NT  (16/17 H)
♦ A K x x      ?
♣ J x x x
```

No less than six different bids were advocated by the experts consulted, with their comments : Pass (*"my NT is rather minimum"*), 5 ♣ (*"we will find a Fit in one of the minor suits"*), 5 ♦ (*"my clubs are too weak, I'd rather try diamonds"*), 5 ♥ (*"I accept the slam invitation and indicate my number of Italian controls : 5 ♦ = 3 controls, 5 ♥ = 5 controls, etc."*), 5 ♠ (*"indicates specifically 4 – 4 in the minors and 3 ♠"*), 5 NT (*"I have the minors and give my partner a choice of slams : NT or a minor"*).

Well now, who wouldn't be motivated to play Bridge after such a demonstration?!.. And not a single comment on the absurdity of the *"quantitative"* 4 NT bid which *"burns"* 14 bidding steps only to elicit... wild interpretations from the opener and six different bids from Pass to... a small slam ! *Surely, there has got to be a better way !?...*

And how would such bidding get the partnership to 7 NT opposite a hand such as this one :

```
♠ K x
♥ A K x
♦ Q x x x x x
♣ A x
```

On the same strong 1 NT opening, *Relay* bidding could be :

1 NT (15/17 HL)	2 ♣ ? (relay / stayman)
2 ♦ (no 4-card Major)	2 ♥ ? (relay)
2 NT (no 5-card minor)	3 ♣ ? (relay)
3 ♠ (3 ♠ 2 ♥ 4 ♦ 4 ♣)	4 ♣ ? (RKC Ask, ♦ is trump)
4 ♦ (3 Key Cards)	4 ♠ ? (K & Q ♠ Ask)
5 ♣ (♠ Queen)	5 ♥ ? (K & Q ♥ Ask)
5 NT (♥ Queen)	7 NT

Economical, precise and pertinent description (had West had 3 ♥ and 2 ♠, instead, there would only be 6 NT). Upon West's 4 ♦ bid, East knows that a 6 ♦ contract is 100 %, upon his 5 ♣ bid that 7 ♦ is 100 %, and upon his 5 NT bid that 7 NT is 100 %. *Highly satisfying !...*

III. Achieving the third objective, being ***satisfying***, also requires three key elements :

– Being ***effective*** and ***playable***, that is achieving the method's first two objectives. This requires achieving **all** the elements previously identified : *Economical precision, pertinent description, competitive initiative, staying within the bidding safety level, systemic coherence,* and *no ambiguous or improvised bids.*

– ***Minimize complexity****.* Complexity is a frequent source of errors and failures, in all systems. To minimize complexity requires minimizing the key factors which contribute to it, and they are :

1) The multiple *conventions* "grafted" to the system; they overtax the memory, particularly since they often apply to very specific situations that can be rather infrequent. They have no place in *relay* bidding.

2) *Lack of precision* contributes to complexity, such as a point zone too wide can lead to delicate decisions, so can a bid which has more than one meaning, etc. This also has no place in *relay* bidding.

3) The principle of *"anticipation"*, the very foundation of *dialogue* bidding – and the biggest contributor to lack of precision or pertinent description. It has no place in a monologue/*relay* bidding method.

4) Multiple choices between several bids possible is a very frequent source of complexity and… of totally non-sensical bids, as well ! Hereunder is an excellent illustration of it :

« *Exercices* » – Le Bridgeur, 2008.

« *After opening the hands below 1 ♦, what do you rebid on a 1 ♠ response?*» :

♠ A Q x x	♠ A Q x x	♠ Q J x x	♠ A Q J x
♥ A J 10 x	♥ A x	♥ K x x x	♥ K x
♦ A x x x	♦ A K 10 x x	♦ A Q x	♦ K J x x x
♣ x	♣ x x	♣ A K	♣ A Q

Answers and comments from the expert writing the article :

3 ♠	3 NT	4 ♠	No good answer…
too *weak* for	too *strong*		*should have*
a *"splinter"*	for 3 ♠		*opened it* 2 NT !

Wow! *The more choices, the merrier...* And what choices! Each of these answers being totally absurd in addition to being very uneconomical : the first hand carefully "hides" the *other* 4-card Major and the club singleton, the second hides the strong 5-card ♦ suit and the lack of club control, the third one hides the *other* 4-card Major and the *"false"* ♦ suit, and as for opening the fourth one 2 NT... no comment !
Precision ? Economy ? Pertinent description ? Effective ? Satisfying ?...

And to think that, had each of these hands been opened a strong 1 ♣, as they should be, the simple answer to the question asked would be, in **all** cases : « 1 NT – *relay. My partner has started to describe **his** hand; let him continue !...* ». Isn't it elementary to have the *weaker* hand describe itself to the *stronger* hand, instead of the absurd bids above ?!...
Such multiple choices have no place in *monologue / relay* bidding.

– Being **versatile, multi-purpose**, meaning having the ability to pro-vide *flexible* solutions to a variety of situations *along general principles* – rather than specific conventions to fix specific problems.

A strong 1 ♣ opener relaying over his *partner's* response – to have *him* describe *his* hand – is a typical example of the method's versatility : the *monologue* process works both ways !
So is minimizing, as much as possible, the use of *"special conventions"* which tax the memory, and avoiding bids that produce *"multiple choices"* which tax one's judgment. Instead, rely on a simple principle : when the responder bids the suit just above the opener's suit, it is a *relay* and the *opener* describes his hand; *On any other response* from the responder, the opener *relays,* by bidding the suit just above his partner's bid, and the responder continues to describe his hand.

Another example is the inappropriate use of *"splinter"* bids at the level of four which do **not** respect the *bidding safety level*. Since their use have become part of every player's tool box, let's look at the following deal which will generate a *"splinter"* jump to 4 ♦ on a 1 ♠ opening :

♠ A K x x x	♠ Q x x x
♥ x	♥ Q J x x
♦ K J x x	♦ x
♣ x x x	♣ A x x

And the 4 ♠ contract will be down one, due to West's "wasted honor pts" in diamonds opposite East's singleton. And *"splinter"* bids have other flaws, as well : they do **not** describe whether the trump Fit has 4 cards, or 5, whether the shortness is a singleton or a void, and say nothing about the distribution of the other two suits.
And 11 bidding steps have been *"burned"* for such imprecision !

Whatever happened to the principle that *"the higher the bid, the more precise it should be"*? *"Splinter"* bids at the level of four are among the most misguided conventions ever devised – in close competition with the strong 2 NT and 2 ♣ opening bids, and the *"quantitative"* 4 NT jump!

While the **Optimal** Precision Relay equivalent would be as follows :

1 ♠   3 ♦ : *"mini-splinter"*

3 ♠ : Final

The 3 ♦ *"mini-splinter"* bid becomes possible because a strong East would **not** describe a strong ♦ suit by a jump (uneconomical *dialogue*), he would either bid 2 ♦ or he would *relay*.

With the hands above, the **Optimal** Precision Relay bidding would be:

1 ♠	1 NT ? (relay)
2 ♦ (4 diamonds)	2 ♥ ? (relay)
2 ♠ (12/14 HLD pts)	2 NT ? (relay)
3 ♣ (3 clubs = ♥ singleton)	3 ♠ - Final

East signs-off in 3 ♠ because of the "wasted honor pts" in hearts.

While, with the following two hands :

♠ A K x x x	♠ Q x x x
♥ x	♥ A x x x
♦ K Q x x	♦ A x x x
♣ x x x	♣ x

The bidding in **Optimal** Precision Relay would be as follows :

1 ♠	3 ♣ (*"mini-splinter"*)
3 ♦ ? (relay)	3 ♥ (4 ♥)
4 ♣ ? (RKC Ask)	4 NT (2 Key Cards & ♠ Q)
6 ♠	

On West's 3 ♦ *relay*, East can now further describe precisely the balance of his hand : with a ♣ void, instead of a singleton, he would rebid 4 ♣, with 5 spades, instead of just 4, he would bid 3 ♠ – so, his 4 ♥ bid doesn't just describe 4 hearts, it describes precisely a 4 4 4 1 hand !

Economical Precision, Pertinent Description, Systemic Coherence, Simplicity, Versatility, Effectiveness, Satisfying ! You be the judge...

The table below summarizes the key **objectives** and **criteria** above :

OBJECTIVES	CRITERIA AND MEANS
Being *Effective*	⇒ *Economical precision*
	⇒ *Pertinent description*
	⇒ *Competitive initiative*
Being *Playable*	⇒ *Respect the "Bidding level safety"*
	⇒ *Systemic coherence*
	⇒ *No ambiguous or improvised bids*
Being *Satisfying*	⇒ *Effective and Playable*
	⇒ *Minimise complexity*
	⇒ *Versatility*

THE OPTIMAL PRECISION RELAY PLEDGE

*"In **Precision** We Trust" and **pledge** to dedicate every effort toward **pertinent** hand description, in a manner that is **economical** and respectful of the "bidding level safety". We intend to achieve this through systemic **versatility** and "**competitive initiative**" aimed at delivering an **effective** and **playable** bidding method. We do this, not because it is easy, but to fulfill the pursuit of **happiness** between partners ».*

The author

CHAPTER 1

FUNDAMENTALS OF THE BIDDING METHOD

I. CORNERSTONE PROCESSES OF THE METHOD

Having defined the method's **objectives** and **criteria** now leads us into identifying which **processes** will be used to achieve our "Mission" :
Design an *effective, playable* and *satisfying* bidding method for the 21st Century through *economic precision, pertinent description, competitive initiative, systemic coherence* and *versatility*, with *no ambiguous* or *improvised* bids and respecting the *bidding safety level*.

Hereafter are the 5 key **cornerstone processes** specific to the *Relay* bidding method presented in this book.

1. DESCRIPTION PROCESS APPLYING TO 1 ♥ and 1 ♠ OPENINGS

The *traditional* process of describing an opening hand's upper point zone by a jump is simply **not** economical or precise enough and does **not** meet the **Optimal P**recision Relay criteria. Illustration :

	1 ♠	1 NT	1 ♠	1 NT
	2 ♦ : 5 ♠ 4 ♦ 11/15 H pts		3 ♦ : 5 ♠ 4 ♦ 16/20 H pts	
Or :	1 ♠	1 NT	1 ♠	1 NT
	2 ♠ : 6 ♠ 11/15 H pts		3 ♠ : 6 ♠ 16/20 H pts	

This process only describes, at the level of three, 9 cards in the first case, and 6 cards in the second. And, for two-suiters, each rebid covers **3** HLD point zones : 13 (5 4 2 2) to 21 (6 4 3 0) HLD pts in the 11/15 H point range, or two HLD point zones : 18 to 23 HLD pts in the 16/20 H point range. Way outside the "bidding level safety". Totally **unplayable**!

And a *Relay* method following the same process would do no better.
A totally different process is needed to always describe, at the level of three, the hand's **residual** cards i.e. at least **12** cards out of 13.

And such a process exists : it is the *"Monaco"* process, which does exactly the reverse : instead of *jumping* with the *stronger* hands, it uses an economical *"braking"* bid for hands in the *lower* point zone.

This *"braking"* bid is used either **ahead** of the opener's rebid when the two suits are touching or **after** the opener's rebid when the two suits are **not** touching. Illustration :

A) The *"brake"* is applied ***ahead*** of opener's rebid :

1 ♥			1 ♠ ? (relay)	
1 NT : *"brake"*	**12/14** HLD pts		2 ♣ ? (relay)	
2 ♦ :	5 ♥ 4 ♦		2 ♠ ? (relay)	
3 ♣ :	3 ♣	5 ♥ 4 ♦ 3 ♣ : **12** cards out of 13		

Therefore, the same 3-suiter, in the **15/17** HLD point zone, will be described *without* the *"brake"* :

1 ♥			1 ♠ ? (relay)	
2 ♦ :	5 ♥ 4 ♦	**15/17** HLD pts	2 ♠ ? (relay)	
3 ♣ :	3 ♣	5 ♥ 4 ♦ 3 ♣ : **12** cards out of 13		

B) The *"brake"* is applied ***after*** the opener's rebid :

1 ♠			1 NT ? (relay)	
2 ♦ :	5 ♠ 4 ♦	**12/17** HLD pts	2 ♥ ? (relay)	
2 ♠ :	*"brake"*	**12/14** HLD pts	2 NT ? (relay)	
3 ♣ :	3 ♣	5 ♠ 4 ♦ 3 ♣ : **12** cards out of 13		

Therefore :

1 ♠			1 NT ? (relay)	
2 ♦ :	5 ♠ 4 ♦	**12/17** HLD pts	2 ♥ ? (relay)	
3 ♣ :	3 ♣	**15/17** HLD pts	5 ♠ 4 ♦ 3 ♣ : 12 cards	

C) While **6 + card single-suits** are described as follows :

1 ♥			1 ♠ ? (relay)	
2 ♥ :	6 + ♥	**12/14** HLD pts	2 ♠ ? (relay)	
2 NT :	6 ♥ 3 2 2 :	**12** cards out of 13		
3 ♣ :	♣ singleton	6 ♥ 3 ♦ 3 ♠ 1 ♣ :	**12** cards out of 13	
3 ♦ :	♦ singleton	6 ♥ 3 ♣ 3 ♠ 1 ♦ :	**12** cards out of 13	
3 ♥ :	♠ singleton	6 ♥ 3 ♣ 3 ♦ 1 ♠ :	**12** cards out of 13	

6 + card single-suits of **15/17** HLD pts are described the same way but after being opened 2 ♥.

The **13th** card will be identified, if asked for, on the next (last) *relay*.

2. TRANSFER RESPONSES TO 1 ♠ and 1 ♥ OPENINGS

Paradoxally, *traditional* bidding experiences its greatest difficulties when responding to the most frequent openings, 1 ♠ and 1 ♥, when :
A) the responder is *weak* and ***misfit*** in the Major suit opened, and
B) the responder is *strong* and ***with*** a Fit in the Major suit opened.

In the first case, a *conventional* 1 NT response is used to alert the opener that the responder does not have enough points for a 2 over 1 response; this bid *says nothing* about his hand's *distribution* and does *not propose* an *alternative suit* to consider.

In the second case, it resorts to *conventions* and *contortions* to describe, as best as possible, the responder's strength, Fit and distribution – having to overcome the initial handicap of starting at the level of two. Thus were born conventions such as : *"3rd suit forcing"*, *"4th suit forcing"*, the Jacoby 2 NT Major suit *"raise"*, double jump *"splinter"* bids at the level of four, etc, etc…

Yet, elementary logic would suggest that it is exactly the **reverse** that should be done : when *weak* and **misfit**, the responder should identify, as quickly as possible, an **alternative** suit which should be considered, while, when *strong* and **with** a Fit, he should either *relay* or describe, economically, specific, *pertinent* features of his hand.

And the good news is that both can be done, *using the **same** first response !*
Here again, the solution was provided, over 60 years ago, by the same relay pioneer, P. Ghestem, as part of the *"Monaco"* process : it consists of using **transfer** bids as a first response. Illustrations :

1. Responder with a *weak*, **misfit** hand :

♠ K Q x x x	♠ x
♥ A x x x	♥ x x
♦ J x	♦ K Q x x x x x
♣ Q x	♣ J 10 x

While *traditional* bidding would be :

1 ♠	1 NT
2 ♥	? *Not the points for a 3 ♦ rebid*

In **Optimal** Precision Relay the bidding will be :

1 ♠	2 ♣ (*Transfer* for diamonds)
2 ♦ (*Transfer*)	Pass

2. Responder **with** a Fit in opener's suit and *invitational* strength :

♠ A K x x x	♠ Q x x x
♥ Q x	♥ x x x
♦ A x x	♦ K Q x x x
♣ x x x	♣ x

In **Optimal** Precision Relay the bidding will be :

1 ♠	2 ♣ (*Transfer* for diamonds)
2 ♦ (*Transfer*)	3 ♣ * (*trial* bid)
4 ♠	

* East's *trial* bid is a *"mini-splinter"* and indicates : 13/15 HLDF pts, a solid ♦ suit, a 4-card ♠ Fit, a ♣ singleton, and *nothing* in the 4th suit, hearts (no Ace, no King, no singleton). West easily concludes in 4 ♠. *Pertinent description* with *economical precision !*

While with 2 clubs and 2 hearts in East's hand, East's rebid would be 3 ♠ which West will pass, knowing of 4 losers in clubs and hearts.

3. 1 ♣ OPENING, RESPONSES AND REBIDS

Next to limiting all other openings to 17 HLD pts, the most important benefit of opening 1 ♣ hands of 18 + HLD pts is to provide maximum bidding space to **both** *partners*, to fully describe one of the two hands. This is **not** what is done by most *traditional* strong ♣ systems which quickly revert to *dialogue* bidding, with its uneconomical imprecision.

The **Optimal P**recision **R**elay method takes a different approach to deal effectively and simply with this issue :

– The 1 ♦ response to 1 ♣ is *relay*, indicating either a *weak* hand of less than 7 HL pts or a *strong* hand of 13 + HL pts, which means that *any other response* is of **7**/**12** HL pts, in **two** point zones of **7**/**9** and **10**/**12** HL pts. Responder's next bid will clarify whether he has **< 7** or **13 +** HL pts.

– On a 1 ♦ response, the opener will describe **his** hand by rebids having the *very* same meaning they had as *opening* bids, also in two point-zones, but with **18 +** HLD pts : 1 ♥/1 ♠ : 5-card Major, 1 NT : balanced distribution, 2 ♣/♦/♥/♠, as well as 2 NT (♦) and 3 ♣ : 6 + card single-suit of **18 +** HLD pts.

– Any response *other* than 1 ♦ indicates that the *responder* is describing **his** hand, in two point zones of **7**/**9** or **10**/**12** HL pts, by bids having the *very* same meaning they had as opening bids, but with **7**/**12** HL pts. Furthermore, these responses are made via **transfer** bids to enable the **strong** hand, the 1 ♣ opener, to bid the intended suit. Thus, a response of 1 ♥ is for **spades**, 1 ♠ is for **No Trump**, 1 NT is for **clubs**, etc. These *transfer* responses have the added benefit of enabling *economical rebids* to describe various hand distributions : *versatility !*

4. 1 ♦ OPENING, « SEMI-STRONG » : 14 / 19 HLD PTS

Most *traditional* bidding systems have made their 1♦ opening a complete nonsense : it has the same *wide point-range* as the 1 ♥/1 ♠ openings, yet does not promise more than 3 diamonds! It includes hands with a 6 + card ♦ single-suit as well as hands having both 4-card Majors. Thus, it maximizes the frequency of an opening which is considerably less precise than 1 ♥/1 ♠ openings and much more vulnerable to interventions !

What should happen, instead, is exactly the *reverse* : **minimize** the frequency of a 1 ♦ opening which is an open invitation for opponents to intervene, economically with 1 ♥ or 1 ♠, and at very little risk !

Here again, the **O**ptimal **P**recision **R**elay method takes a different approach to deal effectively and simply with this issue : it looks to *minimizing* the frequency of the 1 ♦ opening and does so as follows :

– It *excludes* a 6 + card ♦ single-suit from the 1 ♦ opening : these should be opened either 2 ♦ or 3 ♦ (2 NT) as precise *"competitive initiatives"* !

– It also excludes from this opening hands with *both* 4-card Majors (this eliminates the *Precision Club* system's absurd 2 ♦ opening for 4 4 1 4 or 4 4 0 5 hands in a 11/15 H point zone = 13 to 20 HLD pts ! Three HLD point zones at the level of two! Totally **unplayable** !).

– Furthermore, while keeping it a two point zone opening of **6** HLD pts, it **raises** its point-range to **14/19** HLD pts. The purpose of this sole *exception* to opening 1 ♣ hands of 18 + HLD is to allow the description of two-suiter hands with 5 + ♦ in *one point zone only* after a 1 ♣ opening which does not provide the bidding space needed to describe such a two-suiter in **two** point zones.

The result of applying the above mentioned three criteria is that it substantially **reduces** the frequency of the 1♦ opening to **15** % of all openings – precisely what is aimed at ! (vs **25** % of openings in *traditional* bidding).

And such an opening offers other substantial benefits, as well :

– With a point count starting at **14** HLD pts, it allows a responder with a hand of **7/9** HL pts to make a "limit" bid at the level of two *without exceeding* the "bidding level safety" (**14** HLD minimum + **7** HL minimum = **21** HLD pts minimum). A great *competitive initiative* limit bid !

– Furthermore, the 1 ♦ opening being used for a strong NT hand of **15/17** HL pts, lends itself quite naturally to *transfer* responses : 1 ♥ is a *relay*, 1 ♠ is natural and specifically describes a **5**-card spade suit of 7/9 HL pts, and *any other bid* can now be a *transfer* bid, i.e. 1 NT for clubs, 2 ♣ for diamonds, 2 ♦ for hearts, 2 ♥ for spades.

– Last, but not least, excluding a 6 + card ♦ single-suit from the 1 ♦ opening now allows giving a different meaning to a 2 ♦ rebid, such as describing, *conventionally*, a 5 ♦ 4 ♥ in the lower point zone of **14/16** HLD pts – an issue which has "dogged" *traditional* systems for... ever !

5. 4 ♣ AND 4 ♦ SLAM ASKING BIDS

While the Roman Key Card Blackwood was a major improvement over the previous Ace Response Blackwood, it still does **not** resolve the fact that the 4 NT RKC Blackwood is way *too high* a bid to make it of much value. Total precision requires, in most cases, to also inquire about Kings and Queens in *specific suits*, and to be able to do so economically requires that the RKC Ask be made at the *much lower level* of 4 ♣ or 4 ♦.

Doing so is precisely what the **Optimal** P**recision** R**elay** method attempts to achieve, as often as possible, through having the hand interrogated describe 12, or all 13, of its cards *below* the level of 4 ♣.

Furthermore, the RKC Blackwood cannot be used when one, or more, suit is **not** controlled (two direct losers) and the process currently used, of identifying, first, controls in specific suits *before* getting to the 4 NT Ask is simply not satisfactory.

To address that issue, the **Optimal** P**recision** R**elay** method uses 4 ♦ as a **Control A**sk bid to inquire about controls in specific suits *not controlled*.

The five characteristics just reviewed constitute key cornerstones of the **Optimal** P**recision** R**elay** method and the following table, on the next page, summarizes the key features of the method.

OPTIMAL PRECISION RELAY : CORNERSTONE PROCESSES

CRITERIA	CORNERSTONE PROCESSES
Economical Precision	• **Relay** / *"monologue"* • *"Monaco"* process (**5 4 3**, *brake* **vs** *jump*) • **12** , or all 13 cards, at the level of three • **18** + HLD 1 ♣ opening = Others : **12**/**17** HLD • 4 ♣ as Roman **K**ey **C**ard **A**sk rather than 4 NT
Pertinent Description	• *"Monaco"* description process of **12** + cards • **Multiple** *"trial"* bids on **most** suit openings • *Transfer* bids on openings of one from 1♣ up • **Responder** describes **his** hand on 1 ♣ opening
Competitive Initiative	• **All** opening bids **from 1 ♥ up** • *Transfer responses* to 1 ♣ and 1 ♦ openings at the level of **two** with hands of **7**/**9** HL pts
Bidding level safety	• **Opening** hands counted in HLD pts, **not H** pts • All bids always within a **3** or **6** HLD point-zone • **No** double / triple **jump**, *quantitative* 4 NT
Systemic Coherence	• **Two** point zones for openings **and** responses • *"Mirror"* **rebids** & **responses** on 1 ♣ opening • **No** conventions *"grafted"*, no *improvised* bids • Bid *strong* hands **low**, *weak* hands **high**
Effective & Playable	• **Optimal precision** ⇒ performance • Always within the *"Bidding level safety"* • Complexity is **minimized**
Versatility	• *Transfer* Bids • Multiple *"trial"* bids on 1 ♥ / ♠ openings • *"Mirror"* **rebids** & **responses** on 1 ♣ opening

II. FUNDAMENTAL PRINCIPLES AND STRUCTURE OF OPENINGS

After a brief summary of the key principles which govern the **Optimal** Precision Relay bidding method, we will overview the **structure** of all opening bids.

The following chapters will then cover each opening bid with the **responses**, **rebids** and **further developments** specific to each opening. At the end of each chapter, a table will summarize the key elements specific to each opening.

I. FUNDAMENTALS OF THE BIDDING METHOD

POINT COUNT

– **Opening** hands are counted in HLD points, **not** H or HL pts.

– **Responding** hands are counted in **HL** pts, with a maximum of **2 L** pts, initially, on any opening *other than* 1 NT. Responders to a 1 NT opening, or NT rebid, count their HLD points. The principle being that *one* of the two hands of a partnership **must** count its distribution points.

– Once a Fit of 8 cards or more has been found, then **total** points are counted in **HLDFit** pts.

KEY PRINCIPLES OF THE OPTIMAL PRECISION RELAY METHOD

– The **OPTIMAL PRECISION RELAY** method is a *relay* bidding method, using a *monologue* methodology by which one player asks his partner, through successive, economical *relay* bids, to describe his hand's distribution, all **13** cards if needed, allowing him to know all **26** cards of the side to bid the *optimal* contract.

On *successive relays*, it uses the "Monaco" **5 4 3** description process, that is bidding, first, a 5-card suit, a 4-card suit next, and a **3**-card suit next. *Without* a 3-card suit, the third bid will be 2 NT or rebidding one of the first 2 suits, thus *lengthening* it by one card while *denying* a 3-card suit.

– All hands opened 1 ♦, 1 ♥ or 1 ♠ are described, initially, within a **6** HLD point zone and, later, within a **3** HLD point zone.

– It opens 1 ♣ all hands of **18 +** HLD pts. Cornerstone of the method, it **limits** any *other* opening to **17** HLD pts and therefore to **two** point zones : 12/14 and 15/17 HLD pts.

It is also intended to give *maximum* bidding space for the responder to describe *his* hand, also in two point zones : **7/9** and **10/12** HL pts.

71

– Hands opened 1 ♣ are then described – on a 1 ♦ *relay* – in exactly the *same way* as if they had been opened otherwise, i.e. 1 ♥/♠ : 5-card Major, 1 NT : balanced distribution, 2 ♣/♦/♥/♠ : 6 + card single-suit, etc. And the same description process applies to *responses* to a 1 ♣ opening other than a 1 ♦ *relay*, except that *transfer* bids are used for these responses i.e. 1 ♥ for spades, 1 ♠ for No Trump, etc.

– The *"semi-strong"* 1 ♦ opening is another cornerstone of the method. It describes hands in a **14/19** HLD point zone – *sole exception* to the 1 ♣ opening with 18 + HLD pts – that are *specifically* either a balanced distri- bution of 15/17 HL pts (equivalent to the *traditional* strong 1 NT open- ing) or two-suiter hands with 5 + ♦ : 5 + ♦ 4 ♥ or 4 ♠, or ♦/♣.
It also describes two point-zones : 14/16 and 17/19 HLD pts, and it specifically excludes a 6 + card ♦ single-suit hand as well as **both** 4-card Majors.
As a *"semi-strong"* opening, it is intended to give *maximum* bidding space for the *responder* to describe his hand.

– The method also uses extensively ***transfer*** bids, in *response* to **all** openings of one, not just 1 NT, as part of the method's approach to precisely describe responders' hands through bids that will enable economical rebids after the initial transfer bid.
Transfer bids are also used for *pre-emptive* openings of 3 ♦ and up.

In addition to often enabling *"right-siding"* contracts, these *transfer* bids provide *economic precision, pertinent description, competitive initiative* and *versatility.*

– Last but not least, the method uses two *unique slam inquiry* bids : 4 ♣ and 4 ♦ – both **K**ey **C**ard **A**sks, but used in different circumstances.
Their *economic* level allows the *specific* description of Kings and Queens in suits *other than the trump suit*, whenever possible.

The table on the next page summarizes the method's key *characteristics.*

OPTIMAL PRECISION RELAY : KEY CHARACTERISTICS

FEATURES	CORNERSTONE CHARACTERISTICS
Point Count **Point Zones**	• **Opening** hands counted in HLD points. • **Two** point zones, of **3** HLD (or HL) pts each.
Relay **Process**	• « *Monaco* » process (*5 4 3*, *brake* vs *jump*) • *Transfer* bids on *all* openings of one.
1 ♣ **Opening**	• **18** + HLD = *other* openings : **12/17** HLD pts. • **Eliminates** *strong* 2 NT, 2 ♣, 1 NT openings • "*Mirror*" **rebids** & **responses** on 1 ♣ opening • Responder describes **his** hand on 1 ♣ opening
1 ♦ **Opening**	• **14/19** HLD pts. **14/16** and **17/19** HLD pts. • **Not** 6 + ♦ single-suit, **not** *both* 4-card Majors • Balanced **15/17** HL *or* 5 + ♦ 4 ♥ or ♠ or 4/5 ♣
Competitive **Initiative**	• 1 ♥/♠ openings : 5-card Major, **12/17** HLD pts. • 1 NT opening : **12/14** HL pts. • 2 ♣/♦/♥/♠ openings : 6 + single-suit, **15/17** • *Pre-emptive* openings, 3 ♦ up, via *transfer* bids
Others	• **Multiple** "*trial*" bids on 1 ♥ / ♠ openings • RKC Ask at 4 ♣ rather than 4 NT

III. STRUCTURE OF OPENING BIDS

---

1 NT Opening   12/14 HL pts   4 3 3 3   4 4 3 2   5 3 3 2   5 4 ♦/♣ 2 2

Denies : a 5-card Major   **both** 4-card Majors   a 6-card suit

---

Pre-emptive in nature, the 1 NT opening must be a *weak* NT in order to pre-empt the opponents, *not the partner* – regardless of vulnerability.

– It must **not** include a 5-card Major which, unlike *traditional* systems, does **not** present a rebid problem after an opening of 1 ♠ or 1 ♥.

– It must **not** include **both** 4-card Majors! When you consider that finding an 8-card Fit in a Major is a partnership's top priority, **not** to bid *either* Major and, worse yet, to bid ***over*both** of them is pure heresy !

– It must **not** include hands that have a 6-card suit! Hiding a 6-card suit behind a NT bid defies elementary logic as well as any claim of "precise hand description". Minor 6-card suits can easily be described by openings of 2 ♣ and 2 ♦, in the 15/17 HLD point-zone, 3 ♣ and 3 ♦ (2 NT), in the 12/14 HLD point-zone.

– It must also **not** include 5 4 2 2 hands which could not be described later on. The only exception allowed by the **Optimal** Precision Relay method is to include a *minor* 5 4 2 2 two-suiter which the method precisely describes on a 2 ♣ *relay-Stayman* by the responder.

Thus, in **Optimal** Precision Relay, the 1 NT opening gives a very precise picture of the hand, on *strength* as well as on *distribution* – and the same applies to No Trump rebids after a 1 ♦ or 1 ♣ opening.

Example hands opened 1 NT in **Optimal** Precision Relay :

♠ Q 10 x	K x x	Q J x	K x	A J x
♥ x x	A x	A J 10 x	A x	K J x
♦ K Q x x	K J 10 x x	K 10 x x	K J x x	K Q 10 x
♣ A x x x	x x x	x x	Q 10 x x x	x x x
12 H	12 ½ HL	13 H	14 H	14 ½ H
(10 w/Q)	(no Q)	(10 w/K)	(15 HD)	(4 3 3 3)

Note that hands 1, 2 and 3 would **not** be opened in *traditional* **H** point count (counted as 11 H pts).

Opening bid **frequency** : the 1 NT opening represents **15** % of all openings in **Optimal** Precision Relay (vs 7 % for a 15/17 H 1NT opening in *traditional* bidding).

75

---

1 ♠/♥ Openings : **12/17** HLD pts   All hands with a **5** + card Major
                                       Hands with **both** 4-card Majors

---

Hands opened 1 ♠ or 1 ♥ must have a minimum of **9** H points.

Key guiding principle : ***Absolute priority given to Majors*** !
This means that we open 1 ♠ or 1 ♥ hands that have a *longer* minor suit,
i.e. 4 ♠ 4 ♥ 0 ♦ 5 ♣ or 5 ♠ 1 ♥ 6 ♦ 1 ♣.
With two Majors of unequal length, the *longest* Major is bid first; when
of equal length, 5 or 6 cards each, the *highest ranking* Major is bid first.

Two observations / comments :

– Opening 1 ♠ or 1 ♥ hands of 12/14 HLD pts means that hands with
a 5-card Major and a singleton, as well as **all** hands with a 6-card Major
can now be opened with only **9** H pts. The ultimate *"competitive initiative"* bid! These "light" openings, along with the weak NT, enable the
method to open **60** % of the time, instead of 50 % in *traditional* bidding!

– **Not** opening 1 ♠ or 1 ♥ hands which have **both** 4-card Majors defies
logic as well as probabilities : a 4-card suit will find a 4 - 4, or 4 - 5/6 Fit
33 % of the time. With **both** 4-card Majors, the chances of finding a Fit
in one of the two Major suits are **over 55** *%*! *By-passing that opportunity*
is pure nonsense! The reason given for doing so is that it will mislead
the partner who will be expecting a 5-card Major – but hands with both
4-card Majors only represent about 5 % of hands opened 1 ♥ or 1 ♠ !

Actually, the only valid justification is that, in *traditional* bidding, the
opener will **never** be able to alert his partner, later, that his Major only
had 4 cards, **not** 5. Well, **not so** with the **Optimal** Precision Relay
method which addresses this issue by alerting the partner, quickly, that
the Major opened was of **4** cards only. It does so by using a *specific rebid*,
as simple and natural as can be : the *immediate* rebid of the *other* Major!
(*Hands* **5 – 4** *in Majors are described differently, as we will see later*).

  Example hands opened 1 ♠ or 1 ♥ in **Optimal** Precision Relay :

♠ A Q J x x	x	A Q x x x	K Q x x	x x
♥ x x x	A Q 10 x x	K x	A x x x	A K 10 x x
♦ K 10 x	x x x	K 10 x x	x	K Q x x x
♣ x x	A x x x	x x	A x x x	x
13 HL	**14** HLD	**15** HLD	**16** HD	**17** HLD

  Opening bid **frequency** : the 1 ♠ and 1 ♥ openings represent, *together*,
30 % of all openings in **Optimal** Precision Relay (**17** % for 1 ♠, which is
in the lower, more frequent point-zone, when 4 – 4 in the Majors).

---

1 ♦ opening : **14/19** HLD pts   Hands with 5 + ♦ 4 ♠ or 4 ♥ or 4/5 ♣
  or   **15/17** HL pts   **Balanced** distribution

Denies a 6 + card ♦ single-suit, **both** 4-card Majors, a 5-card Major

---

Hands opened 1 ♦ must have a minimum of **9 H** points.

The 1 ♦ opening in **Optimal** Precision Relay has four objectives :

1. Open 1 ♦, instead of 1 NT, the strong **balanced** hands of 15/17 HL pts in order to give both players *maximum bidding space* to describe their hand, particularly the **responder** (*"the balanced hand principle"*).

2. Describe very precisely **two-suiter** hands with diamonds, including the ♦ / ♣ two-suiters − too often neglected in *traditional* bidding.

3. Relieve the 1 ♣ opening from having to describe strong two-suiters with 5 + diamonds in *two* point-zones, as there is only bidding space to describe **one** point zone after a 1 ♣ opening and 2 ♦ rebid.

4. Minimize the frequency of 1 ♦ openings as they facilitate a 1 ♥ or 1♠ intervention with little to no risk to opponents.

The last two objectives lead to raising the 1 ♦ opening's point-zone to **14/19** HLD pts. This point-zone, along with the exclusion of both 4-card Majors and of 6 + ♦ single-suiters (much more effectively described by openings of 2♦ and 2 NT) from the 1 ♦ opening, make this opening very precise and even more so upon the *first rebid*.

  Note that, while the 1 ♦ opening includes *balanced* hands of 15/17 HL pts, the diamond suit will be of **4** cards *or more* in about 85 % of cases. It will be of **3** cards in only 13 % of cases (4 3 3♦ 3, 4 2 3♦ 4, 5 ♣ 3♦ 3 2) and of **2** cards in only 3 % of cases (4 ♠ 3 ♥ 2 ♦ 4 ♣, 4 ♥ 3 ♠ 2 ♦ 4 ♣, 3 3 2 ♦ 5 ♣).

  Example hands opened 1 ♦ in **Optimal** Precision Relay :

♠ x x x	Q 10 x x	Q J x	x x	K 10 x x
♥ K Q x x	---	K 10 x x	A x	x
♦ A J 10 x x	K J x x	A Q x	K Q 10 x x	A Q x x
♣ x	A x x x x	K J x	A x x x	A Q x x
14 ½ HLD	**16 HLD**	**16 H**	**17 HLD**	18 ½ HD
	(void : 4 pts)	(4 3 3)	(2 doubletons)	

  Opening bid **frequency** : the 1 ♦ opening represents **15** % of all openings in **Optimal** Precision Relay (vs **25** % in *traditional* bidding).

1 ♣ Opening : **18 +** HLD pts **Any** and **all** distributions. **Forcing** bid

Limits every *other* opening to *17* HLD pts (*except for the* 1 ♦ *opening*)

Hands opened 1 ♣ must have a minimum of **10 H** points.

The key characteristic of the 1 ♣ opening is that further *rebids*, on a 1 ♦ response, as well as *responses* to 1♣, other than 1♦, are perfect "*mirrors*" to opening bids :
– On a 1 ♦ response (initially considered a *relay*), the opener describes his hand in exactly the same way as he would if he had **not** opened 1 ♣ i.e. : 1 ♥/♠ : 5-card Major in two point zones, 18/20 and 21/23 + HLD pts, 1 NT : balanced hand (in two point-zones), 2 ♥ / 2 ♠ : 6 + card single-suit in one point zone, 18/20 HLD pts, 2 ♣ /2 ♦ : 6 + card single-suit or two-suiter, in one point-zone.

– Any response *other* than a 1 ♦ *relay* describes the *responder's* hand in the same way as if he had opened, but does so via *transfer* bids : 1 ♥ for spades, 1 ♠ for No Trump, in two point zones, 7/9 and 10/12 HL pts, 1 NT for clubs, in one point zone, 9/12 HL pts, 2 ♣ for diamonds, in one point-zone, etc. *Systemic coherence, economical, pertinent description !*

Example hands opened 1 ♣ in **Optimal** Precision Relay :

♠ A x	Q J x	K Q 10 x	K Q x x	A K 10 x
♥ K Q x x	A K x x x x	x	A Q J x	K Q x
♦ A x x x	x	K Q J x x	A K x x	A Q x
♣ K J x	A x x	A x x	x	A x x
18 H	**19 HLD**	**20 1/2 HLD**	**22 HLD**	**23 H**

Opening bid **frequency** : the 1 ♣ opening represents **25 %** of all openings – about the same as in *traditional* bidding but the **Optimal** Precision Relay 1 ♣ opening guarantees **18 +** HLD pts !

2 ♣ Opening : **14/17** HLD pts. **6 +** ♣ single-suit
or : **two-suiter** with **5 +** ♣ and **4 ♥** or **4 ♠**

Denies **4 +** ♦   denies a **5 +** card Major   denies **both** 4-card Majors

Hands opened 2 ♣ must have a minimum of **9 H** points.

Note that the opening is limited to a **4 HLD** point-zone, the maximum point-range *allowed* at the two-level to stay *within the bidding level safety.*

The **Optimal** Precision Relay 2 ♣ opening is considerably more precise than the *Precision Club* 2 ♣ opening as it **excludes** diamonds as a second- ary 4-card suit – thus eliminating an awful 3 ♦ rebid which would only describe 9 cards at the three-level and would land above the 3 ♣ level !

Most importantly, the *Precision Club* 2 ♣ opening is simply **unplayable** as, counted in H pts, its 11/15 H point-range equates to a 13/21 HLD point-range (6 4 3 0), or **3** HLD point zones – *way outside the bidding level safety*. At the two-level, a point zone must **not** exceed **4** HLD pts.
A simple example, below, will illustrate this point very clearly :

♠ A Q x x	♠ K x x x
♥ x	♥ x x x
♦ x x	♦ x x x
♣ A K x x x x	♣ Q x x

In *Precision Club*, the West hand is opened 2 ♣ (13 H pts), which East will *pass* (less than 8 H pts). In **Optimal** Precision Relay the bidding will be :

1 ♣ (18 + HLD pts)	1 ♦ (less than 7 HL pts)
2 ♣ (5 + ♣, forcing)	2 ♦ ? (relay)
2 ♠ (4 ♠, 18/20 HLD)	2 NT ? (relay)
3 ♣ (6 clubs)	4 ♠

West's 3 ♣ bid guarantees a singleton in one of the red suits. East can add to his 7 ½ HF pts (2 Fit pts in clubs + 2 Fit pts in spades with the King) 2 pts for "no wasted honor pts" in hearts or diamonds.
Opposite 18 + HLD = 27 ½ pts = 4 ♠.

Example hands opened 2 ♣ in **Optimal** Precision Relay .

♠ K Q 10 x	K x x	x	K x	K 10 x x
♥ x x	x	Q J x x	x x	x
♦ x x	Q J x	K 10 x	K J x	x x
♣ A J 10 x x	A J x x x x	A Q x x x	A Q x x x x	A Q J x x x
14 ½ HLD	15 ½ HLD	16 HLD	16 ½ HLD	17 HLD

Opening bid **frequency** : the 2 ♣ opening represents **5 %** of all openings in **Optimal Precision Relay**.

---

2 ♦ / 2 ♥ / 2 ♠ Openings : **15/17** HLD pts   6 + ♦ / ♥ / ♠ single-suit

---

Hands opened 2 ♦ / 2 ♥ / 2 ♠ must have a minimum of **9 H** points.

The case against weak, *pre-emptive* 2 ♥ / 2 ♠ openings and in favor of **15/17** HLD pts 2 ♥ / 2 ♠ openings was previously made.

And this applies just as well to a 2 ♦ opening for two reasons : A) This opening will be of substantial help in the search for a NT contract (identifying at once a 6-card suit and potential Fit – *or misfit* – points), and B) As a *competitive initiative* opening, instead of an absurd 1♦ opening, an open invitation for the opponents to intervene, risk-free.

Example hands opened 2 ♦ / 2 ♥ / 2 ♠ in **Optimal** Precision Relay :

♠ A x x	K 10 x	K Q 10 x x x	A J x
♥ Q J 10 x x x	x x	x x	x x
♦ x	K Q x x x x	A K x	K Q 10 x x x x
♣ K x x	A x	x x	x
15 ½ HLD	16 HLD	16 ½ HLD	17 ½ HLD

Opening bid **frequency** : the 2 ♦ / 2 ♥ / 2 ♠ openings represent, *together*, 5 % of all openings in **Optimal** Precision Relay.

---

2 NT (♦) / 3 ♣ Openings : **12/14** HLD pts. 6 + ♦ / ♣ single-suit

---

Hands opened 2 NT (♦) / 3 ♣ must have a minimum of **9** H points.

We have shown, earlier, statistics which validate the effectiveness of opening 3 ♣ /3 ♦ *semi-constructive* hands of 6 cards and 9 to 10 H pts – facilitating the search for a possible NT contract.

And, in **Optimal** Precision Relay, these openings can be used to great advantage as they can be further described, economically, on *relays* such as : on a 3 ♦ *relay* to a 3 ♣ opening : 3 ♥ : ♥ singleton, 3 ♠ : ♠ singleton, 3 NT : **no** singleton (6 3 2 2 or 7 2 2 2), 4 ♣ : ♦ singleton.

And the 2 NT opening for 6 + diamonds enables a description at an *even more economical* level, as the *relay*, 3 ♣, is made *below* the level of 3 ♦. Descriptive rebids can then be : 3 ♦ : **no** singleton, 3 ♥ : ♥ singleton, 3 ♠ : ♠ singleton, 3 NT : ♣ singleton.

Example hands opened 2 NT (♦) / 3 ♣ in **Optimal** Precision Relay :

♠ x x	x x x	x	x
♥ x x	x	x x x	K x x
♦ K Q x x x x	K 10 x	K Q x x x	x x
♣ K Q x	A J 10 x x x	A x x	A J 10 x x x x
12 HLD	13 HLD	13 ½ HLD	14 ½ HLD
(no Ace)	(no Queen)		(no Queen)

Opening bid **frequency** : the 2 NT (♦) / 3 ♣ openings represent, *together*, **3** % of all openings in **Optimal** Precision Relay.

80

---

3 ♦ (♥) / 3 ♥ (♠) Openings : Pre-emptive *Transfer* bids   7 + ♥ / ♠

Less than **9 H** pts   **6** or **7** tricks *(vulnerability)*   Denies **2** Aces

---

The case for opening weak, *pre-emptive* hands via **transfer** bids is so elementary that it hardly has to be made (like pre-empt 101…).

For this purpose, the **Optimal** Precision Relay method uses *pre-emptive* bids of 3 ♦ for hearts, and 3 ♥ for spades, and on, up the line.

Other than using *transfer* opening bids, the criteria used by the **Optimal** Precision Relay method for pre-emptive bids are the same as in *traditional* bidding.

Example hands opened 3 ♦ (♥) / 3 ♥ (♠) in **Optimal** Precision Relay :

♠ x x	Q J 10 x x x x	x
♥ K Q J x x x x	---	K Q J x x x x x
♦ x x x	A x x	x x
♣ x	x x x	x x
3 ♦ (♥)	3 ♥ (♠)	3 ♦ (♥)
< than 9 H **6 Tricks**	< than 9 H **6 Tricks**	< than 9 H **7 Tricks**

---

3 ♠ Opening : Pre-emptive *Transfer* bid for *either* **NT** or a **minor** suit

5 + ♣ **5** + ♦ **2 1**   **10 / 12 H** pts   **7** or **8 tricks** *(vulnerability)*

Denies **2** Aces **and** denies **3** cards in a Major

Pre-emptive openings via *transfer* bids also enable the use of the 3 ♠ opening in a unique way for 5 - 5 minor two-suiters which would benefit greatly from a *competitive initiative* opening rather than being opened 1 ♦.

This allows the responder to *transfer* to 3 NT to play this contract from *the stronger* hand while only having to guard *two* suits – the Majors. But then, to allow playing 3 NT for which distribution pts do **not** count, this opening must guarantee a given number of **H** pts. For that reason, the 3 ♠ opening promises specifically **10/12 H** pts.

Furthermore, to ensure that a Fit in a Major is **not** missed – with partner having a 5-card Major – the minor two-suiter opening hand **must not** have **three** cards in either Major.

81

If the responder does **not** guard both Majors or does **not** have the points to play 3 NT, he *transfers* into his best minor suit, 4 ♣ or 4 ♦.

Note : The risk of not finding an 8-card Fit in one of the minor suits is limited, knowing that the probabilities of finding an 8, 9 or 10-card Fit opposite a 5-card suit are over 54 %, finding such a Fit in one of *two* 5-card suits is substantially higher, 75 %.

Example hands opened 3 ♠ in **Optimal** Precision Relay :

♠ x	♠ x x	♠ x
♥ x x	♥ ---	♥ x
♦ K Q 10 x x	♦ K Q x x x x	♦ K J 10 x x
♣ K J 10 x x	♣ K Q J x x	♣ A K 10 x x x
10 H (no Ace)	**11** H (no Ace)	**12** H (no Q)
7 tricks	**7 ½ tricks**	**8 1/2 tricks**

Openings of : 3 NT (♣) / 4 ♣ (♦) / 4 ♦ (♥) / 4 ♥ (♠) / 4 ♠ (♣), etc.

Pre-emptive *Transfer* bids   8 + ♣ / ♦ / ♥ / ♠ single-suits

Less than **9 H** pts   **7** or **8** tricks (*vulnerability*)   Denies **2** Aces

---

Other than using *transfer* opening bids, the criteria used by the **Optimal** Precision Relay method for the above *pre-emptive* bids are the same as in *traditional* bidding.

Example hands opened 3 NT and up in **Optimal** Precision Relay :

♠ x	♠ Q J 10 x x x x x	♠ x
♥ x x	♥ x	♥ x x
♦ x x	♦ A x x	♦ K Q J x x x x x x
♣ K Q J x x x x x	♣ x	♣ x
3 NT (♣)	**4 ♥ (♠)**	**5 ♣ (♦)**
7 H pts 7 tricks	7 ½ H pts 7 tricks	7 H pts 8 tricks

Opening bid **frequency** : *Pre-emptive* openings from 3 ♦ up represent, *together*, **2** % of all openings in **Optimal** Precision Relay.

This concludes the overview of opening bids in Optimal Precision Relay.

Note : *Modifications can easily be made to some of the above openings by players who favor more "traditional" openings such as playing "natural" pre-emptive openings (rather than transfer bids) or "weak two" Major suit openings (just switch their point zone from 15/17 to 12/14 HLD pts). But playing a strong NT is not an option as the 1 ♦ opening must be 14/19 pts.*

Two observations are warranted here : 1) The **only** time you face a "choice" of openings, between 1 ♦ and 1 NT, is with a 5 - 4 - 2 - 2 hand (5 - 4 minors) of 14 HL pts, and 2) you never have to wonder about your rebid *in advance* : on a relay by partner, you will never have a rebid problem and when partner does not relay, he is the one describing his hand, not you. The *traditional* "anticipation" principle does not apply !

Before covering responses and further *developments* after each opening, two elements warrant mention and comment : A) the relative *frequency* of each opening, and B) specific key *reference points* found throughout the method.

RELATIVE FREQUENCY OF OPENING BIDS

Opening	Pass	1 ♠ 1 ♥	1 ♣	1 ♦	1 NT
Frequency	40 %	30 %	25 %	15 %	15 %

Opening	2 ♣	2 ♠ 2 ♥ 2 ♦	2 NT (♦) 3 ♣	3 ♦ & up	3 ♠ (NT, ♣ / ♦)
Frequency	5 %	5 %	3 %	2 %	1 %

The above table undelines several key features of the method :

– The HLD point count and the "light" openings of 1 ♥, 1 ♠ and 1 NT enable the **Optimal** Precision Relay method to open the bidding **60 %** of the time, while *traditional* bidding generally opens the bidding about 50 % of the time. A significant *competitive initiative* benefit !

And *"competitive initiative"* openings of 1 ♥, 1 ♠, 1 NT, 2 NT and up represent **50 %** of **all** openings! Furthermore, the two-level openings of 2 ♣, 2 ♦, 2 ♥ and 2 ♠, are effectively *pre-emptive* in nature as well as being descriptive of both *suit-length **and** hand strength,* making most interventions rather inoperative.

– The 1 ♣ opening has a frequency of **25 %**, as it does in *traditional* bidding, but while the latter means nothing, other than opening points, the **Optimal** Precision Relay 1 ♣ opening promises **18 +** HLD pts !

83

– Last, but certainly not least, the 1♦ opening, an open invitation for low-risk interventions of 1 ♥ and 1 ♠, has been limited to a frequency of **15** % – unlike a disastrous **25** % in *traditional* bidding !

KEY REFERENCE POINT ZONES IN OPTIMAL PRECISION RELAY

The study of bidding *developments* following opening bids will identify recurring "reference point zones" that are specific to the method; it will be helpful to identify them now :

FOR OPENINGS :	12/14 HL/HLD	15/17 HL/HLD	18/20 HL/HLD

– The **12/14** HLD point zone is the *lower* point zone of several openings : 1 ♥, 1 ♠, 2 NT (♦) and 3 ♣, and 1 NT in HL points.

– The **15/17** HLD point zone is the *higher* point zone of the 1 ♥ and 1 ♠ openings as well as the point zone of the 2 ♣, 2 ♦, 2 ♥ and 2 ♠ openings. It is also the point zone, in HL pts, for *balanced* hands opened 1 ♦.

– The **18/20** HLD point zone is the *lower* point zone of the 1 ♣ opening. Over **75** % of 1 ♣ openings are in this lower point zone.

FOR RESPONSES :	7/9 HL	10/12 HL	13/15 HLDF / 13 + HL

– The **7/9** HL point zone is the *lower* point zone for responses to **All** openings (except for openings limited to 14 HLD pts : 1 NT, 2 NT, 3 ♣).

– The **10/12** HL point zone is the *higher* point zone for responses to the 1 ♣ opening. It is also the "*limit*" bid zone for responses on 1 ♥ and 1 ♠ openings and the "*invitational*" zone on 1 NT openings.

– The **13/15** HLDF point zone is the "*trial*" bid / *mini-splinter* zone for responses on 1 ♥ and 1 ♠ openings.

– **13 +** HL pts are the points that justify *multiple relays* on any opening.

POINT ZONES "AVERAGES"

In closing, a practical "tip" : the simplest and most practical way to add up the *combined* points of two hands is to count the *average* of a given point zone i.e. count 8 pts for a 7/9 HL point zone, 11 pts for a 10/12 HL point zone, 14 pts for a 13/15 HL point zone.

So, if your own hand's count is 14 HLDFit pts and your partner has described a 12/14 HLD point zone, count the total as : 14 + 13 = 27.

This "*averaging*" will often be used in this book and will give you plenty of opportunities to see how practical it is.

SUMMARY OF OPENING BIDS IN OPTIMAL PRECISION RELAY

OPENINGS	HAND DESCRIPTION	POINTS
1 ♣	ANY AND ALL DISTRIBUTIONS	18 + HLD
1 ♦	TWO-SUITER ♦ / ♣, 5 ♦ 4 ♥, 5 ♦ 4 ♠ BALANCED hands 4333 4432 5332 Denies 5-card Major, **both 4**-card Majors and **denies 6** + card ♦ single-suit	14 /19 HLD 15 /17 HL
1 ♥ / 1 ♠	5–card Major Any distribution Both 4-card Majors (15/17 HLD : 1 ♥)	12 /17 HLD
1 NT	BALANCED hands 4333 4432 5332 Denies 5-card Major, **both 4**-card Majors and **denies 6** + card suit	12 /14 HL
2 ♣	TWO-SUITER 5 + ♣ 4 ♥, 5 + ♣ 4 ♠ 6 + card ♣ single-suit Denies both 4-card Majors, 5-card Major	<u>14</u> /17 HLD
2 ♦ / 2 ♥ / 2 ♠	6 + card ♦ / ♥ / ♠ single-suit	15 /17 HLD
2 NT (♦) / 3 ♣	6 + card ♦ (2 NT) / ♣ single-suit	12 /14 HLD
3 ♦ and up	*Transfer* Bid (3 ♦ : ♥, 3 ♥ : ♠) *Pre-emptive* 7 + card single-suit	< than 9 H 6 / 7 Tricks
3 ♠	*Transfer* Bid for NT or ♣ or ♦ *Pre-emptive* 5 + ♣ 5 + ♦ two-suiter ***without*** 3 cards in a Major	<u>10/12 H</u> 7 / 8 Tricks

We are now ready to study each opening and the *full developments* that follow them. We will start with 2 ♥ and 2 ♠ openings as they are the easiest and will familiarize us with the whole description process. But, first, let's look at some key probabilities about hand distributions and point zones that you may find helpful.

MOST FREQUENT HAND DISTRIBUTIONS

DISTRIBUTIONS	PROBABILITIES	LD pts
4 4 3 2	21.5 %	0
5 3 3 2	15.5 %	1
5 4 3 1	13 %	3
5 4 2 2	10.5 %	2
4 3 3 3	10.5 %	- 1
6 3 3 1 & 6 3 2 2	9 %	4, 3
6 4 2 1 & 6 4 3 0	6 %	4, 6
Hands w/ 5 + cards	65 %	

HONOR POINTS IN ONE HAND

POINTS	FREQUENCY	POINT ZONES	FREQUENCY
8	9 %		
9	9.5 %	7 to 9	26.5 %
10	9.5 %		
11	9 %	10 to 12	26.5 %
12	8 %		
13	7 %	12 to 14	21 %
14	5.5 %	13 to 15	17 %
15	4.5 %	15 to 17	10 %
16 +	< 10 %	16 +	< 10 %

LIKELY POINT ZONES OPPOSITE OPENING HANDS

POINTS	POINT ZONE	POINT ZONE	POINT ZONE	POINT ZONE
10 to 12	< 7 21 %	7 to 9 28 %	10 to 12 27 %	13 + 24 %
12 to 14	< 7 26 %	7 to 9 30 %	10 to 12 26 %	13 + 18 %
13 to 15	< 7 28 %	7 to 9 31 %	10 to 12 25 %	13 + 15 %
15 to 17	< 7 35 %	7 to 9 32 %	10 to 12 22 %	13 + 11 %
16 +	< 7 47 %	7 to 9 30 %	10 to 12 15 %	13 + 6 %

PROBABILITIES OF FITS AND MISFITS

NUMBER OF CARDS	MISFIT	8-CARD FIT	9-CARD FIT	10-CARD FIT
3	75 %	13 %	4 %	1 %
4	65 %	22 %	9 %	2 %
5	45 %	30 %	18 %	5 %
6	25 %	33 %	28 %	12 %
7	7 %	25 %	35 %	23 %
8	0 %	11 %	35 %	35 %

The above table shows that finding an **8**-card Fit is much more frequent (**30** %) starting from a **5**-card suit than starting from a **4**-card suit (**22** %), just like finding a **9**-card Fit is much more frequent (**18** %) starting from a **5**-card suit than starting from a **4**-card suit (**9** %).

Overall, the probabilities of finding an **8** + card fit starting from a **5**-card suit are **55** %, while they are only **35** % starting from a **4**-card suit.

As well, a **6**-card suit will find a Fit of **8** or **more** cards **75** % of the time, while a **7**-card suit will find a Fit of **9** or **10** cards almost **60** % of the time.

CHAPTER 2

OPENING BIDS, RESPONSES AND DEVELOPMENTS

---

2 ♥ / 2 ♠ OPENINGS – RESPONSES AND DEVELOPMENTS

PREAMBLE

Covering these two openings first will facilitate getting familiar with :
A) The complete description of 6 + card ♥ and ♠ single-suit hands on
successive relays – so we won't have to do it again with the same hands
opened 1 ♥, 1 ♠ or 1 ♣, and B) responses *other* than *relays*, particularly
"trial" bids.

As will be done for all openings, we will cover, first, the complete
description of opener's hand on successive *relays*, before studying
responses *other* than *relays*.

We will then cover the *same description* and *responses* after a 1 ♣ opening
with the same hands of 18 + HLD pts and will close each section with a
summary table of all *responses* and *rebids*, and with example deals
illustrating them

KEY PRINCIPLES

– **Responding** hands are counted in HL pts, with a maximum of **2 L**
pts, initially. Once a Fit of 8 + cards has been found, then **total** points
are counted in HLDFit pts.

– Whenever possible and pertinent, the method will endeavour to
identify a singleton, in either hand, in order to assess "wasted honor
pts". This means that, in addition to describing 12 out of 13 cards – and
therefore singletons – on successive *relays*, the method will use "trial"
bids and *"mini-splinter"* bids to identify singletons.

– Contrary to what proponents of strong Club systems advocate, a
responder **must** bid with hands of **7** HL pts (not 8 H pts) on any opening
which goes up to 17 HLD pts, and therefore on a 2 ♥ opening.

And **7** HL pts will be sufficient to make a first relay, while **10 +** HLDF
pts will be needed for a *second* relay.

The responder will elect to *relay* when : A) No *specific descriptive* response corresponds to his hand, or B) He needs *more information* on opener's hand to find the *"optimal"* contract. Illustrations :

Opener	Responder A	Responder B
♠ x x x	♠ Q J x	♠ x x
♥ A K x x x x	♥ Q x x	♥ Q x
♦ x	♦ K J x	♦ x x x x
♣ K Q x	♣ J x x x	♣ A J 10 x x

Opposite a 2 ♥ opening, there are no *specific* responses descriptive of the responder's hand. Therefore, responder will *relay*, by 2 ♠ over 2 ♥, on which the opener will bid his singleton, 3 ♦.

Responder A's 11 HFit pts (4 3 3 3) now become 9 pts (- 2 pts for *"wasted honor pts"* in diamonds) : 16 pts (average of 15/17 pts) + 9 = 25, **not** the points for game. He will conclude in 3 ♥. As can be seen, it would have been a mistake for the responder to conclude directly in 4 ♥.

While, responder B's 9 ½ HLFit pts (no King) now become 11 ½ pts (+ 2 pts for no *"wasted honor pts"* in diamonds) : 16 pts + 11 ½ = 27 ½, the points for game. He will conclude in 4 ♥.

---

2 ♥ Opening   **6 + ♥** single-suit   **15/17** HLD pts   **9 +** H pts
RESPONSES AND DEVELOPMENTS

We will start with the detailed description of the opener's hand on successive *relays*, before covering responses *other* than relays.

I. DESCRIPTION OF OPENER'S HAND ON SUCCESSIVE RELAYS

1. **Semi-regular** hands (**no** singleton) : 6 3 2 2 and 7 2 2 2

   Process : On a first *relay*, 2 ♠ : Opener's first rebid will be 2 NT

   Then, on a *second relay*, 3 ♣ : The 3-card suit with 6 3 2 2

   Rebid ♥ with 7 2 2 2

Therefore, such hands will be described as follows :

2 ♥		2 ♠ ?
2 NT	**no** singleton	3 ♣ ?
3 ♦	6 ♥ <u>3 ♦</u> 2 2	
3 ♥	7 ♥ 2 2 2	No 3-card suit, therefore rebid ♥ = 7 ♥
3 ♠	6 ♥ <u>3 ♠</u> 2 2	
3 NT	6 ♥ <u>3 ♣</u> 2 2	3 NT = the 3-card suit is in the *relay* suit.

As can be seen, a 2 ♠ *relay* allows a 2 NT rebid which immediately describes a semi-regular hand *without* a singleton. A potential 3 – 5 ♠ Fit can and will be found on opener's next bid.

Note that if responder does **not** need to identify opener's 3-card suit and favors a 3 NT contract, he can skip further relaying after 2 NT and *inquire about guards* in ♦ or ♠ : 3 ♦ or 3 ♠. Or he can *pass* or bid 3 NT.

2. **Unbalanced** hands (**with** a singleton) : 6 3 3 1, 7 3 2 1, 7 3 3 0

   Process : On a first *relay*, 2 ♠ : Opener's rebid will be in his *short suit*.
   Then, on a *second relay*, 3 ♦ or 3 ♠ : With 6 3 3 1 : 3 NT, nothing else.
   With 7 <u>3</u> 2 1 : the 3-card suit.   With 7 3 3 <u>0</u> : Rebid the short suit.

Therefore, such hands will be described as follows :

6 ♥ 3 3 1<u>♣</u>		6 ♥ 3 3 1<u>♦</u>		6 ♥ 3 3 1<u>♠</u>	
2 ♥	2 ♠ ?	2 ♥	2 ♠ ?	2 ♥	2 ♠ ?
<u>3 ♣</u>	3 ♦ ?	<u>3 ♦</u>	3 ♠ ? *	3 ♥ * *	3 ♠ ?
3 NT – Final		3 NT – Final		3 NT – Final	

* the *relay* is <u>3 ♠</u> here, not 3 ♥.

* * 3 ♥ is used to describe the ♠ *singleton*, more *economical* than 3 ♠.

All most *frequent* distributions – 6 3 2 2 and 6 3 3 1 – are fully described *below* the level of 4 ♣, allowing the latter bid to be used as a RKC Ask.

7-card suits will be described as follows :

7 ♥ and *short* in ♣		7 ♥ and *short* in ♦		7 ♥ and *short* in ♠	
2 ♥	2 ♠ ?	2 ♥	2 ♠ ?	2 ♥	2 ♠ ?
3 ♣	3 ♦ ?	3 ♦	3 ♠ ?**	3 ♥	3 ♠ ?
3 ♥ * 7 ♥ 2 ♠ 3 ♦ 1 ♣		4 ♣ 7 ♥ 2 ♠ 3 ♣ 1 ♦		4 ♣ 7 ♥ 3 ♣ 2 ♦ 1 ♠	
3 ♠ 7 ♥ 3 ♠ 2 ♦ 1 ♣		4 ♥ * 7 ♥ 3 ♠ 2 ♣ 1 ♦		4 ♦ 7 ♥ 2 ♣ 3 ♦ 1 ♠	
4 ♣ 7 ♥ 3 ♠ 3 ♦ 0 ♣		4 ♦ 7 ♥ 3 ♠ 3 ♣ 0 ♦		3 ♠ * 7 ♥ 3 ♣ 3 ♦ 0 ♠	

3 ♥ * : More *economical* than 4 ♦.

3 ♠ ** : The *relay* is 3 ♠ here, not 3 ♥.

4 ♥ * : More *economical* than 4 ♠ / avoids exceeding the 4 ♥ level.

3 ♠ * : Bid *directly* over the 2 ♠ *relay* to *avoid having to conclude in 4 ♠*.

Note that a 7 3 3 0 distribution will be rather rare in the 15/17 HLD point zone as the 2 ♥ opening requires a minimum of **9** H pts which would add up to 17 HLD pts with the 8 LD pts given to a 7 3 3 0 distribution. But its description is shown here as it will mostly apply after a 1 ♣ opening / 2 ♥ rebid.

And the same applies to 8 + card suits (0,4 % frequency) whose 9 LD pts, added to a *minimum* of 9 H pts, add up to a *minimum* of 18 HLD pts. These hands should be opened 1 ♣ and, in most cases, it is the *responder* who will describe *his* hand on this opening, and the opener will very rarely have to describe an 8 + card suit.

Following is a **summary** table of the **full description** of opener's hand on *successive relays*.

SUMMARY OF HAND DESCRIPTION ON SUCCESSIVE RELAYS

DISTRIBUTION	ON 2 ♠ ?	2nd Relay	DESCRIPTION	FINAL BID
6 ♥ 3 2 2	2 NT	3 ♣ ?	The 3-card suit	3 ♦ / 3 ♠ / 3 NT
7 ♥ 2 2 2			Rebid ♥	3 ♥
w/ singleton	Singleton		Nothing else to describe	
6 ♥ 3 3 1 ♣	3 ♣	3 ♦ ?		3 NT
6 ♥ 3 3 1 ♦	3 ♦	3 ♠ ?	Final - 3 NT	3 NT
6 ♥ 3 3 1 ♠	3 ♥ (♠)	3 ♠ ?		3 NT
7 ♥ 3 2 1 ♣	3 ♣	3 ♦ ?	The 3-card suit	3 ♠ / 3 ♥ (♦)
7 ♥ 3 2 1 ♦	3 ♦	3 ♠ ?		4 ♣ / 4 ♥ (♠)
7 ♥ 3 2 1 ♠	3 ♥ (♠)	3 ♠ ?		4 ♣ / 4 ♦
w/ a void	The void			
7 ♥ 3 3 0 ♣	3 ♣	3 ♦ ?	Rebid the void suit	4 ♣
7 ♥ 3 3 0 ♦	3 ♦	3 ♠ ?		4 ♦
7 ♥ 3 3 0 ♠	3 ♠		3 ♠ was Final	

II. RESPONSES OTHER THAN SUCCESSIVE RELAYS

DETERMINING PARAMETERS

Three key parameters determine which responses to select :

1. The hand's **strength**, therefore its number of points.

This first parameter comes down to something rather simple : hands with *fewer* than **7** pts (whether HL or HLDFit pts) will almost never produce a game (16 + 6 = 22) while hands of **13** + pts will almost always produce a game (16 + 13 = 29). Which means that, in the first case, with or without a Fit, the response will always be *pass*.

In the second case, the responder will *relay*, or conclude directly in game. Therefore, we will only have to develop responses for hands in the 7/12 point-zone, in two point-zones : **7/9** and **10/12** pts.

Note the *approximate* frequency of points in responder's hand : fewer than **7** pts : 20 %, **7/9** pts : 30 %, **10/12** pts : 27 %, **13** + pts : 20 %.

93

2. The second parameter is the **presence** or **absence** of a ♥ **Fit**.

As a reminder, a 6-card suit will find an 8 + card Fit for the side 75 % of the time; A 7 + card suit will find an 8 + card Fit 93 % of the time. Therefore, the priority should be to develop *"trial"* bid responses which identify a singleton, in either hand, when the side has a ♥ Fit.

– With a Fit of two cards, meaning an 8-card Fit for the side, a singleton in responder's hand is not likely (less than 5 % probability of 10 cards in the other two suits, ♠ excluded) and the responder will either *pass* with **7/9** Fit pts or, with **10/12** Fit pts, he will *relay* to detect a potential singleton (*"wasted honor pts"*) in the opener's hand.

– With a Fit of **3 +** cards (43 % probability), meaning an 9 + card Fit, and a singleton, the responder's priority should be to identify his singleton, and ♥ Fit.
And this can very easily be done by bidding his singleton directly on 2 ♥ : 3 ♣, ♣ singleton and 3 + hearts, 3 ♦ : ♦ singleton and 3 + hearts, 3 ♥ : ♠ singleton and 3 + hearts. And this, even with 8 or 9 pts as 16 + 8/9 + 2 pts for *"no wasted honor pts"* opposite the singleton = 26 + pts.

Compare this to *traditional* bidding's practice to use the 3 ♣ and 3 ♦ bids to suggest an *alternative* suit of at least 6 cards, preferably 7, when the responder is misfit in ♥ – a low frequency bid and very risky as it elevates the contract bid to 9 tricks. A rather useless, misguided bid.
Illustration :

♠ A x	♠ K x x x
♥ A J 10 x x x	♥ Q x x
♦ A x x	♦ x
♣ x x	♣ J x x x x

The bidding will be :

| 2 ♥ | 3 ♦ : ♦ singleton, 3-card ♥ Fit |
| 4 ♥ | 10 HLDFit pts |

With a ♥ Fit but **no** singleton, the responder will *relay* to detect a potential singleton in opener's hand and assess *"wasted honor pts"*.

– With a ♥ *misfit*, meaning a ♥ singleton (or void), the responder should look for a possible 8-card Fit in the *other* Major, if he has 5 + ♠. Having, or not, 5 + cards in the other Major is the third parameter.

3. The third parameter is the ***presence,*** or *not,* of **5 + ♠**, the other Major.

This becomes a consideration when the responder has a ♥ *misfit* or even a semi-Fit with a ♥ doubleton without any honor, as a spade contract may be better than one in hearts.

To identify a 5 + ♠ suit in responder's hand, the method uses the *conventional* response of 2 **NT** – a very pertinent use of this bid, rather than using it to propose a NT contract : with a balanced hand of 11 HL pts, the responder can *relay* to detect a singleton in opener's hand.

On a 2 NT response, the opener *without* a ♠ Fit – fewer than 3 cards in spades – goes back to hearts by bidding 3 ♥.

With a ♠ Fit, the opener bids his singleton, 3 ♣ or 3 ♦, exactly as he would have on a *relay*. *Without* a singleton, he will support spades, by 3 ♠, or 4 ♠ – thus describing precisely a 6 ♥ 3 ♠ 2 2 hand. Illustration :

♠ Q x x	♠ K J 10 x x
♥ A K x x x x	♥ x x
♦ x	♦ x x x
♣ K 10 x	♣ Q J x

The bidding will be :

2 ♥	2 NT : 5 + ♠
3 ♦ : ♦ singleton, ♠ Fit	4 ♠

With *"no wasted honor pts"* in diamonds, East can bid 4 ♠ – better than 4 ♥ as diamonds can be ruffed from the hand *short* in trumps, West. As can be seen, 4 ♠ will likely succeed (ruffing a heart before discarding a diamond on hearts), while 4 ♥ will fail.
Had West's singleton been in clubs, East would conclude in 3 ♠.
Had West rebid 3 ♠ (6 ♥ 3 ♠ 2 2), East would *pass*.

As can be seen, the **Optimal** Precision Relay method provides a simple solution to an issue which has "dogged" *traditional* bidding for ever, that is how to find a 3 - 5 Fit in the *other* Major when the responder holds 5 cards in that Major, not just 4, but can only bid that suit once. It answers the question about how does a *relay* system find a 3 - 5 Fit when the *relay* is in the 5-card suit.

In summary, the **Optimal** Precision Relay responses to 2 ♥, whether *relays* or other, are simple, natural and consistent with the method's objectives and methodology : *economical precision, pertinent description, versatility, minimal complexity – effective, playable and satisfying.*

UNUSUAL *CONVENTIONAL* BIDS TO "FLAG"

OPENING	UNUSUAL *CONVENTIONAL* RESPONSE	POINTS
2 ♥	2 NT : 5 + ♠	7/12 HL

The summary of **responses**, below, illustrates their simplicity :

SUMMARY OF RESPONSES TO A 2 ♥ OPENING

POINTS	MISFIT	8-card ♥ FIT (two ♥)	9 + card ♥ FIT (3 + ♥)
< than 7	Pass	Pass	Pass
7 / 9	Pass	Pass	5 + ♠ 3 ♥ 3 2 : 2 NT or *singleton* : 3 ♣ / ♦ / ♥ or *Relay*
10 / 12	2 NT (5 ♠) or *Relay*	5 + ♠ 2 ♥ 3 3 : 2 NT or *Relay*	5 + ♠ 3 ♥ 3 2 : 2 NT or *singleton* : 3 ♣ / ♦ / ♥ or *Relay*

A few hands now to practice our **responses** to a 2 ♥ opening :

♠ A x x	♠ K Q x x x	♠ K x x x	♠ A x x
♥ x	♥ Q x	♥ Q x x	♥ Q x x
♦ J x x x x	♦ x x x	♦ x	♦ K J x x
♣ K Q x x	♣ x x x	♣ J x x x x	♣ Q x x
8 H (- 2 in ♥)	9 HLF	10 HDF	13 ½ HF
♥ *misfit*, **not** 5 ♠	♥ Fit, 5 ♠	♥ Fit, ♦ singleton	No short suit
Pass	2 NT : 5 ♠	3 ♦	3 NT

♠ Q x x	♠ x	♠ x x x	♠ Q 10 x x x
♥ A x x	♥ K x x x	♥ K J x	♥ Q x x
♦ Q J x x x	♦ x x x x	♦ A x x x	♦ x x
♣ x x	♣ Q J x x	♣ Q x x	♣ A 10 x
12 HLDF (no K)	13 HDF	11 HDF (4333)	11 ½ HDF (no K)
2 ♠ : *relay*	2 ♠ : *relay*	2 ♠ : *relay*	2 ♠ : *relay*
		(or 4 ♥)	♠ *too weak for* 2 NT

Note the versatility of these various responses which would **not** be possible on a *traditional* weak 2 ♥ opening, much too weak for such responses. These responses contribute greatly to making the **Optimal Precision Relay 2 ♥** opening considerably more effective and vastly superior to the *traditional* weak 2 ♥ opening.

---

6 + ♥ single-suit **18 + HLD** pts Open 1 ♣
REBIDS, RESPONSES AND DEVELOPMENTS

OPENER'S REBID ON 1 ♦ RESPONSE

In **Optimal** Precision Relay, the opener will describe **his** hand on a 1 ♦ response to a 1 ♣ opening. He will do so with rebids that will be the same as if he had **not** opened 1 ♣, but with *reversed* point zones.

With 6 + ♥ and **18/20** HLD pts, his *minimum* zone, he will rebid 2 ♥. With 21/23 + HLD pts, he will rebid 1 ♥, followed by 2 ♥ on a 2nd *relay*. The point zones are reversed to keep the *most economical* rebid for the *stronger* hand to give bidding space to *the responder* to describe his hand. Further bidding developments will be *the same* as after a 2 ♥ opening.

RESPONSES TO 1 ♣ OTHER THAN 1 ♦

The same applies to direct responses to a 1 ♣ opening, except that the 6 + card heart suit will be described via a *transfer* bid to have the hearts bid by the *strong* hand, the 1 ♣ opener. Its point zone is also *reversed* : he will bid 2 ♦, for hearts, with **7/9** HL pts. With 6 + ♥ and **10/12** HL pts, the response will be 1 ♥, then rebid 2 ♥.

On responder's 2 ♦ response, the opener will *transfer* to 2 ♥ which will be a *relay* (18 + HLD + 7 HL = 25 total pts *minimum*) on which the responder will *describe his* hand the same way as previously described.

Note : If the opener is *minimum* and *misfit* in hearts (18 pts - 2 pts for the *misfit* + 7 = 23 pts), but with 5 + spades, instead of transferring to 2 ♥, he can bid 2 ♠ over 2 ♦, looking for a Fit in spades.

Let's conclude this chapter with a few deals taken from tournaments :

Final of National selection, teams – 2008.

♠ x x	♠ J x x x x x
♥ A J x x x x	♥ K x x
♦ K Q x	♦ x
♣ K x	♣ Q x x

At all four tables the contract bid and played was 4 ♥ – down one.

To stop short of 4 ♥, East's ♦ singleton, opposite *"wasted honor pts"*, needs to be identified, as it would be in the following auction :

2 ♥ (6 + ♥, 15/17 HLD)   3 ♦ (♦ singleton, ♥ fit)
3 ♥ - Final (*"wasted honor pts"* in diamonds)

Cap Gemini – 1999.

♠ A K	♠ J x x x
♥ A Q x x x x	♥ K J
♦ Q J x	♦ A x
♣ Q x	♣ A K J x x

Only two pairs out of 8 found the 7 NT contract. Three pairs bid to 7 ♥ or 7 ♣, two pairs played 6 NT, and the Italian world champions stopped in 4 ♥! How could 7 NT be missed with these two hands' overabundance of points ?! And the ♠ King or ♦ Q J are not needed for 7 NT !

So, let's remove the ♠ King and ♦ Q J from the opener's hand and see how these hands would be bid in **Optimal** Precision **R**elay :

2 ♥ (6 + ♥, 15/17 HLD)	2 ♠ ? (relay)
2 NT (6 ♥ 3 2 2)	3 ♣ ? (relay)
3 ♦ (6 ♥ 3 ♦ 2 2)	3 ♠ ? (♠ guarded ?)
3 NT (yes, ♠ guarded)	4 ♣ ? (RKC Ask, ♥ is trump)
4 NT (2 Keys w/ ♥ Q)	5 ♣ ? (K & Q ♣ Ask)
5 ♥ (♣ Queen)	7 NT

East wants to know where West's 3-card suit is, as if it is clubs and without the ♣ Queen, a slam could be compromised. Then he needs to ensure that spades are controlled to be able to use the 4 ♣ RKC Ask. *Economic precision, pertinent description, effective and... very satisfying !*

And with the hands as they were in the tournament (with the ♠ King and ♦ Q J), West would have 20 HLD pts, would open 1 ♣, rebid 2 ♥ on responder's 1 ♦ *relay*, and the rest of the auction would be the same as above.

Bidding contest – Le bridgeur, 2008.

♠ Q J x	♠ 10 x
♥ Q J 10 x x x	♥ x x x
♦ A x	♦ K Q x
♣ K x	♣ A Q J x x

A 9-card Fit and the points for game led all contestants straight to 4 ♥ – down one, with four direct losers. 3 NT was the right contract.
In **Optimal** Precision **R**elay the bidding would be :

2 ♥ (6 + ♥, 15/17 HLD)	2 ♠ ? (relay)
2 NT (6 ♥ 3 2 2)	3 ♠ ? (♠ guarded ?)
3 NT (yes, ♠ guarded)	Pass

Without supporting honor cards in hearts and a 5 3 3 2 distribution favoring a NT contract, East should give preference to NT and *pass*.
In this case, the hearts suit does not contribute a single trick to 3 NT !

National division, mixed teams – 2012.

♠ A x x	♠ K Q x x x
♥ A K x x x x x	♥ x x
♦ x x	♦ A x
♣ x	♣ A K x x

Only 6 pairs out of 20 found the right contract of 6 ♥. 7 pairs played 6 ♠, down one, 4 pairs played 6 NT, doomed on a ♦ lead, and 3 others bid to 7 ♥ or 7 NT.

In **Optimal P**recision **R**elay the bidding will be :

2 ♥ (6 + ♥, 15/17 HLD)	2 ♠ ? (relay)
3 ♣ (♣ singleton)	3 ♦ ? (relay)
3 ♠ (<u>7 ♥ 3 ♠ 2 ♦ 1 ♣</u>)	4 ♣ ? (RKC Ask, ♥ is trump)
4 ♦ (3 Key Cards)	6 ♥

The key to finding the right contract of 6 ♥ is to know West's exact distribution, as if West's hand is 6 ♥ 3 3 1 ♣ instead of 7 ♥ 3 ♠ 2 ♦ 1 ♣, there is no slam !

Note that East does not need to inquire about a potential ♥ Queen as he cannot have it : it would give West 22 HLD pts (2 pts for 3 H in hearts) and he would not have opened 2 ♥.

Economical precision, pertinent description, systemic coherence, no ambiguous or improvised bid, minimal complexity – effective and satisfying !

Next, we will look at suggested bids by the opener's partner following an intervention by the opponents over a 2 ♥ opening.

BIDDING AFTER INTERVENTIONS OVER A 2 ♥ OPENING

The table below summarizes suggested bids by the opener's *partner* following an intervention by the opposite team over a 2 ♥ opening.

The suggested bids are guided by two key **principles / objectives** :

1. Retain, whenever possibe, *"trial"* bids with a 3-card ♥ support and a singleton, as they represent a pertinent description of a key feature.

2. *Double* for **penalty** when the opener's partner has **10 +** H pts as the opener's side has the large majority of honor points and risky interventions must be penalised and used to advantage by the opener's side.

INTERVENTIONS over a 2 ♥ opening	SUGGESTED BIDS BY OPENER'S PARTNER **Key principles** : Retain *"**trial**"* bids **Double** : for **penalty**
Double (*Take-out*)	2 ♠ : *Relay* Same as **w/o** the take-out double 2 NT : 5 + ♠. 3 ♣, 3 ♦, 3 ♥ (♠) : *"trial"* bids ***Redouble*** : 11/12 HL pts Invitation for 3 NT
2 ♠ (5 + ♠)	**Double** : *Penalty* double (with **4 +** spades) 2 NT : *Relay* 3 ♣, 3 ♦, 3 ♥ (♠ singleton) : *"trial"* bids
2 NT (5 - 5 in minors)	3 ♣, 3 ♦, 3 ♥ (♠ singleton) : *"trial"* bids **Double** : Replaces the **2 NT** response : **5 + ♠**
3 ♣ (6 + ♣)	**Double** : *Penalty* double 3 ♦, 3 ♥ (♠ singleton), 4 ♣ : *"trial"* bids
3 ♦ (6 + ♦)	**Double** : *Penalty* double 3 ♠, 4 ♣, 4 ♦ : *"trial"* bids 3 ♥ : ♥ fit, *no single.*
3 ♥ (*Cue-bid*)	**Double** : Replaces **2 NT** bid : 5 + ♠, ♥ *semi-Fit* 3 ♠, 4 ♣, 4 ♦ : *"trial"* bids
3 ♠ (♠ *pre-empt*)	**Double** : *Penalty* double 4 ♣, 4 ♦ : *"trial"* bids

---

2 ♠ Opening   6 + ♠ single-suit   **15/17 HLD** pts   9 + H pts
RESPONSES AND DEVELOPMENTS

I. DESCRIPTION OF OPENER'S HAND ON SUCCESSIVE RELAYS

1. **Semi-regular** hands (**no** singleton) : 6 3 2 2 and 7 2 2 2

Process : On the first *relay*, 2 NT : The opener does not have here the option to rebid 2 NT to describe a semi-regular hand. So, the process will be *reversed* : the opener will bid his **3**-card suit first, when 6 3 2 2, followed by 3 NT. When 7 2 2 2, the opener's *rebid* will be 3 ♠. Therefore, such hands will be described as follows :

6 ♠ <u>3</u> ♣ 2 2			6 ♠ <u>3</u> ♦ 2 2			6 ♠ <u>3</u> ♥ 2 2	
2 ♠	2 NT ?		2 ♠	2 NT ?		2 ♠	2 NT ?
<u>3</u> ♣	3 ♦ ?		<u>3</u> ♦	3 ♥ ?		3 NT * directly	
3 NT			3 NT				

** 6 ♠ <u>3</u> ♥ 2 2 is described by a direct 3 NT rebid to reserve a 3 ♥ rebid for a singleton in a 6 ♠ 3 3 1 ♥ hand.

2. **Unbalanced** hands (**with** a singleton) : 6 3 3 1, 7 3 2 1, 7 3 3 0

Process : On the first *relay* of 2 NT : Opener will rebid his *short* suit. Then, on a *second relay*, with 6 3 3 1 he will return to spades : 3 ♠. With 7 3 ? 1 : the 3-card suit, with 7 3 3 0 : Rebid the short suit. Therefore, such hands will be described as follows :

6 ♠ 3 3 1 ♣			6 ♠ 3 3 1 ♦			6 ♠ 3 3 1 ♥	
2 ♠	2 NT ?		2 ♠	2 NT ?		2 ♠	2 NT ?
<u>3</u> ♣	3 ♦ ?		<u>3</u> ♦	3 ♥ ?		3 ♥ - Final	
<u>3</u> ♠			<u>3</u> ♠				

As was the case for semi-regular distributions, all 6 3 3 1 distributions are fully described below the level of 4 ♣, which can be a RKC Ask.

7-card suits will be described as follows :

7 ♠ and *short* in ♣			7 ♠ and *short* in ♦			7 ♠ and *short* in ♥	
2 ♠	2 NT ?		2 ♠	2 NT ?		2 ♠	2 NT ?
<u>3</u> ♣	3 ♦ ?		<u>3</u> ♦	3 ♥ ?		*see below :*	
<u>3</u> ♥	7 ♠ <u>3</u> ♥ 2 ♦ 1 ♣		4 ♣	7 ♠ <u>3</u> ♣ 2 ♥ 1 ♦		4 ♣ *	7 ♠ <u>3</u> ♣ 2 ♦ <u>1</u> ♥
<u>4</u> ♦	7 ♠ <u>3</u> ♦ 2 ♥ 1 ♣		4 ♥	7 ♠ <u>3</u> ♥ 2 ♣ <u>1</u> ♦		4 ♦ *	7 ♠ <u>3</u> ♦ 2 ♣ <u>1</u> ♥
<u>4</u> ♣	7 ♠ 3 ♥ 3 ♦ <u>0</u> ♣		4 ♦	7 ♠ 3 ♥ 3 ♣ <u>0</u> ♦		4 ♥ *	7 ♠ 3 ♦ 3 ♣ <u>0</u> ♥

* The 3 ♥ rebid on the 2 NT *relay* being *final* for the 6 ♠ 3 3 1♥ distribution, hands with 7 ♠ are *conventionally* described directly at the level of four, *the short suit* being hearts.

Following is a summary table of the **full description** of opener's hand.

SUMMARY OF HAND DESCRIPTION ON SUCCESSIVE RELAYS

DISTRIBUTION	ON 2 NT ?	2nd Relay	DESCRIPTION	FINAL BID
	The 3-card Suit		Bid NT	
6 ♠ 2 2 3 ♣	3 ♣	3 ♦ ?		3 NT
6 ♠ 2 2 3 ♦	3 ♦	3 ♥ ?		3 NT
6 ♠ 2 2 3 ♥	3 NT			
7 ♠ 2 2 2	3 ♠			
W/ singleton	Singleton		Return to 3 ♠	
6 ♠ 3 3 1 ♣	3 ♣	3 ♦ ?		3 ♠
6 ♠ 3 3 1 ♦	3 ♦	3 ♥ ?		3 ♠
6 ♠ 3 3 1 ♥	3 ♥		3 ♥ is final	
W/singleton	Singleton		The 3-card Suit	
7 ♠ 3 2 1 ♣	3 ♣	3 ♦ ?		3 ♥ / 4 ♦
7 ♠ 3 2 1 ♦	3 ♦	3 ♥ ?		4 ♣ / 4 ♥
7 ♠ 3 2 1 ♥	4 ♣ / 4 ♦			4 ♣ / 4 ♦
W/ a void	The void		Rebid the void suit	
7 ♠ 3 3 0 ♣	3 ♣	3 ♦ ?		4 ♣
7 ♠ 3 3 0 ♦	3 ♦	3 ♥ ?		4 ♦
7 ♠ 3 3 0 ♥	4 ♥		4 ♥ is final	4 ♥

II. RESPONSES OTHER THAN SUCCESSIVE RELAYS

DETERMINING PARAMETERS

The same three key parameters as on a 2 ♥ opening apply here :

1. The hand's **strength**, therefore its number of points.

Hands below 7 pts (whether HL or HLDFit pts) will not produce a game and should be *passed*. Hands of 13 + pts will *almost always produce a game* and the responder will *relay*, or conclude directly in game.

Therefore, responses *other than relays* will be for 7/12 point hands, in *two* point zones : **7/9** and **10/12** pts.

2. The second parameter is the **presence** or **absence** of a ♠ **Fit**.

Priority is given to *"trial"* bid responses which identify a singleton, in either hand, when the opener's partner has a 3-card ♠ Fit.

– With a two-card Fit, meaning an 8-card Fit for the side, a singleton in responder's hand is not likely and the responder will either *pass* with 7/9 Fit pts or, with 10/12 Fit pts, he will *relay*, to detect a potential singleton (*"wasted honor pts"*) in the opener's hand.

– With a **3 +** card Fit, meaning a 9 + card Fit, and a singleton, the responder's priority should be to identify his singleton, and ♠ Fit. To do so, he will bid his singleton directly on 2 ♠ : 3 ♣, ♣ singleton and 3 + ♠, 3 ♦ : ♦ singleton and 3 + ♠.

With a ♥ singleton, however, the response will be 3 ♠, instead of 3 ♥, to reserve the direct 3 ♥ response for hands with **5 +** hearts.

With a ♠ Fit but **no** singleton, the responder will *relay* to detect a potential singleton in opener's hand and assess *"wasted honor pts"*.

Illustration :

♠ A J x x x x x	♠ x x x
♥ Q x x	♥ K J x
♦ K x	♦ A J x x
♣ x	♣ x x x

The bidding will be :

2 ♠ (6 + ♠, 15/17 HLD)	2 NT ? (relay)
3 ♣ (♣ singleton or 3 ♣)	3 ♦ ? (relay)
3 ♥ (7 ♠ <u>1 ♣</u> <u>3 ♥</u> 2 ♦)	4 ♠

With *"no wasted honor pts"* in clubs, East can bid 4 ♠ as he can count : 16 HLD + 7 ½ H (no Queen and 4 3 3 3) + 3 Fit pts for 10 spades + 2 pts for *"no wasted honor pts"* in clubs = 28 ½ pts.

– With a ♠ **misfit**, meaning a ♠ singleton (or void), the responder should look for a possible 8-card Fit in the other Major, if he has 5 + ♥. Having, *or not*, 5 + cards in the other Major is the third parameter.

3. The third parameter is the ***presence,*** or *not*, of 5 + ♥, the other Major.

This should also be considered when the responder has a *semi-Fit* with a ♠ doubleton without any honor, as a heart contract may be better than one in spades. With 5 + hearts, the responder will bid 3 ♥.

On a 3 ♥ response, the opener **without** a ♥ Fit – less than 3 cards in hearts – goes back to spades by bidding 3 ♠. With a ♥ Fit, the opener will chose the best contract between hearts, spades, and NT.

With a ♠ *misfit* and **without** 5 + ♥, an opener with 10/12 pts should *relay* to find an alternative suit or to play 3 NT if opener is 6 ♠ 3 2 2.

A summary of **responses** to a 2 ♠ opening can be found below :

SUMMARY OF RESPONSES TO A 2 ♠ OPENING

POINTS	MISFIT	8-card ♠ FIT (2 ♠)	9 + card ♠ FIT (3 + ♠)
< than 7	Pass	Pass	Pass
7/9	Pass	Pass	*w/singleton* : 3 ♣/ ♦/ ♠ or 3 ♥ (5 + ♥) or *pass*
10 / 12	3 ♥ (5 + ♥) or *Relay*	3 ♥ (5 + ♥) or *Relay*	*w/singleton* : 3 ♣/ ♦/ ♠ or 3 ♥ (5 ♥) or *Relay*

A few hands now to practice our **responses** to a 2 ♠ opening :

♠ x	♠ Q x	♠ Q x x	♠ A x x
♥ A x x	♥ K Q x x x	♥ K x x x	♥ K x x
♦ J x x x x	♦ x x x	♦ x	♦ K x x x x
♣ K Q x x	♣ x x x	♣ J 10 x x x	♣ x x
8 H	9 HLF	11 ½ HDF	13 ½ HLDF
♠ *misfit*, not 5 ♥	2-card ♠ Fit	♠ Fit	♠ Fit
Pass	3 ♥ (5 ♥)	3 ♦	2 NT
		(♦ singleton)	*relay*

6 + ♠ single-suit   18 + HLD pts   Open 1 ♣

REBIDS, RESPONSES AND DEVELOPMENTS

OPENER'S REBID ON 1 ♦ RESPONSE

In **Optimal** Precision Relay the opener will describe his hand on a 1 ♦ response to a 1 ♣ opening. He will do so with rebids that will be *exactly the same* as if he had *not* opened 1 ♣, but with **reversed** point zones. With 6 + ♠ and **18/20** HLD pts, his *minimum* zone, he will rebid 2 ♠. With 21/23 + HLD pts, he will rebid 1 ♠, followed by 2 ♠ on a 2nd *relay*. The point zones are reversed for the same reasons previously given. Further bidding developments will be the same as after a 2 ♠ opening.

RESPONSES TO 1 ♣ OTHER THAN 1 ♦

The same applies to direct responses to a 1 ♣ opening, *except* that the 6 + card spade suit will be described via a **transfer** bid, also with its point zone *reversed* : he will bid 2 ♥, for spades, with **7/9** HL pts. With 6 + ♠ and **10/12** HL pts, the response will be 1 ♥, *transfer* for spades, then rebid 2 ♠.

On responder's 2 ♥ *transfer* response, the opener will *transfer* to 2 ♠ which will be a *relay* (18 + HLD + 7 HL = 25 total pts *minimum*) on which the responder will *describe his* hand in the same way previously described, *except* that he can now bid 2 **NT** with semi-balanced hands.

Note : On responder's 2 ♥ response, a minimum opener, *misfit* in ♠, may want to look for a Fit *in another suit* by bidding a **5** + card minor suit, 3 ♣ or 3 ♦, or 2 NT with 5 hearts.

Let's conclude this chapter with some deals taken from tournaments :

Olympiads – 2004.

♠ K Q 10 x x x	♠ A x
♥ x x x	♥ A x
♦ A Q x	♦ K x x x x
♣ x	♣ x x x x

The bidding was most often :

1 ♠	2 ♦
2 ♠	2 NT
3 ♠	4 ♠

And the slam was missed. Dialogue = imprecision. Instead of :

2 ♠ (6 + ♠, 15/17 HLD)	2 NT ? (relay)
3 ♣ (♣ singleton or 3 ♣)	3 ♦ ? (relay)
3 ♠ (♣ singleton)	4 ♣ ? (RKC Ask, ♠ is trump)
4 NT (2 Keys w/ ♠ Q)	5 ♦ ? (K & Q ♦ Ask)
5 ♠ (♦ Queen)	6 ♠

Once West's distribution is known to be 6 ♠ 3 3 1 ♣, East can count 16 HLD pts + his own 12 HL pts + 2 pts for the spade and diamond Fits + 2 pts for *"no wasted honor pts"* in clubs = 32 HLDF pts = slam zone. *Economical precision + pertinent description = Effective and satisfying !*

Deal from the book « *How good is your Bridge hand* » − 2000.

♠ A K x x x x	♠ Q x x x
♥ x x x	♥ A x
♦ x	♦ A x
♣ A 10 x	♣ K Q J x x

The authors report the following auction :

1 ♠	3 ♣
4 ♣	4 ♠
Pass	

And ask : « *Which partner is the most to blame for stopping in game ?* ».

Perhaps the blame should be laid on the bidding system instead; Dialogue = Imprecision! The **Optimal** Precision Relay bidding will be :

2 ♠ (6 + ♠, 15/17 HLD)	2 NT ? (relay)
3 ♦ (♦ singleton or 3 ♦)	3 ♥ ? (relay)
3 ♠ (♦ singleton)	4 ♣ ? (RKC Ask, ♠ is trump)
4 ♦ (3 Key Cards)	7 NT

East, with its 23 ½ HLDF pts, knows their side is in grand slam zone right upon West's opening! From there, reaching 7 NT is child's play !

Final of National Division, teams of four − 2008.

♠ A Q x x x x	♠ K x
♥ A x x	♥ K x x
♦ J 10 x	♦ A Q x x x
♣ x	♣ Q 10 x

At both tables, the bidding was :

1 ♠	2 ♦
2 ♠	3 NT

Another typical example where the bidding did not indicate that the long suit had 6 cards, not just 5, and neglected to identify the club singleton.

The **Optimal** Precision **Relay** bidding will be :

2 ♠ (6 + ♠, 15/17 HLD)	2 NT ? (relay)
3 ♣ (♣ *singleton* or 3 ♣)	3 ♦ ? (relay)
3 ♠ (♣ singleton)	4 ♠

East's knowledge of West's ♣ singleton opposite three clubs to the Queen prohibits playing 3 NT. Knowing about West's 6 spades, not just 5, he concludes in 4 ♠.

Regional tournament – 2000.

♠ K 10 x x x x	♠ A x x x
♥ x x	♥ A x x
♦ A Q	♦ K J 10 x
♣ A x x	♣ K x

The contract most often reached was 6 ♠. In **Optimal** Precision **Relay** the bidding would be :

2 ♠ (6 + ♠, 15/17 HLD)	2 NT ? (relay)
3 ♣ (♣ *singleton* or 3 ♣)	3 ♦ ? (relay)
3 NT (6 ♠ 3 ♣ 2 2)	4 ♣ ? (RKC Ask, ♠ is trump)
4 ♦ (3 Key Cards)	5 ♦ ? (K & Q ♦ Ask)
5 ♠ (♦ Q)	7 NT

The ♦ Jack must be known to bid 7 NT. East can count 13 tricks.

European Championship – 2012.

♠ K Q 10 x x x	♠ A x x x
♥ x x x	♥ A x x
♦ A x	♦ K x x
♣ K Q	♣ A J x x

Only 23 pairs out of 50 were able to get to 7 ♠. Instead of :

2 ♠ (6 + ♠, 15/17 HLD)	2 NT ? (relay)
3 NT (6 ♠ 3 ♥ 2 2)	4 ♣ ? (RKC Ask, ♠ is trump)
4 NT (2 Keys and ♠ Q)	5 ♣ ? (K & Q ♣ Ask)
5 NT (♣ K and Q)	7 NT

Here again the ♣ J must be known to bid 7 NT. East can count 13 tricks.

BIDDING AFTER INTERVENTIONS OVER A 2 ♠ OPENING

The table below summarizes *suggested* bids by the opener's partner following an intervention by the opposite team over a 2 ♠ opening.

The suggested bids are guided by the same two key **principles** or **objectives** which applied after a 2 ♥ opening :

1. **Retain**, whenever possibe, *"trial"* bids with a 3-card ♠ support and a singleton, as they are very precise and descriptive.

2. **Double** for **penalty** when the opener's partner has **10 + H** pts as the opener's side has the large majority of honor pts and risky interventions must be penalised and used to advantage by the opener's side.

INTERVENTIONS over a 2 ♠ opening	SUGGESTED BIDS BY OPENER'S PARTNER Key principles : Retain « *trial* » bids Double : For **penalty**
Double (*Take-out*)	2 NT : Relay *Same as **w/o** the take-out double* 3 ♣, 3 ♦ : *"trial"* bids 3 ♥ : 5 + ♥ 3 ♠ : pre-emptive **Redouble** : 11 / 12 HL pts Invitation for 3 NT
2 NT (5 - 5 in minors ?)	3 ♣, 3 ♦ : *"trial"* bids 3 ♥ : 5 + ♥ 3 ♠ : pre-emptive **Double** : Invitational to 3 NT w/ ♥ *guarded*
3 ♣ (6 + ♣)	**Double** : for penalty 3 ♦, 4 ♣ : *"trial"* bids 3 ♥ : 5 + ♥ 3 ♠ : pre-emptive
3 ♦ (6 + ♦)	**Double** : for penalty 3 ♥ : 5 + ♥ 3 ♠ : pre-emptive 4 ♣, 4 ♦ : *"trial"* bids
3 ♥ (6 + ♥)	**Double** : for penalty 3 ♠ : pre-emptive 4 ♣, 4 ♦ : *"trial"* bids
3 ♠ (Cue-bid)	**Double** : 5 + ♥ / semi-Fit ♠ *Replaces the 3 ♥ bid* 4 ♣, 4 ♦ : *"trial"* bids

---

2 ♦ Opening   **6 + ♦** single-suit   **15/17 HLD** pts   9 + H pts

RESPONSES AND DEVELOPMENTS

As was done with the 2 ♥ and 2 ♠ openings, we will cover, first, the complete description *of* opener's hand on successive *relays*, before studying responses *other* than *relays*. We will then cover the same *description* and *responses* after a 1 ♣ opening with the same hands of 18 + HLD.

I. DESCRIPTION OF OPENER'S HAND ON SUCCESSIVE RELAYS

1. **Semi-regular** hands (**no** singleton) : 6 3 2 2 and 7 2 2 2

> *Process* : On a first *relay*, 2 ♥ : Opener's first rebid will be 2 NT
> Then, on a *second relay*, 3 ♣ : The 3-card suit with 6 3 2 2
> with 7 2 2 2 : Rebid diamonds

Therefore, such hands will be described as follows :

2 ♦		2 ♥ ?
2 NT	**no** singleton	3 ♣ ?
3 ♦	7 ♦ 2 2 2	No 3-card suit, therefore rebid diamonds = 7 ♦
3 ♥	6 ♦ <u>3 ♥</u> 2 2	
3 ♠	6 ♦ <u>3 ♠</u> 2 2	
3 NT	6 ♦ <u>3 ♣</u> 2 2	3 NT means that the 3-card suit is in the *relay*.

The 2 NT rebid immediately describes a semi-regular hand without a singleton. A potential 5 – 3 ♥ Fit can be found on opener's next bid.

If responder does **not** need to identify opener's 3-card suit and favors a 3 NT contract, he can skip further relaying after 2 NT and inquire *about guards* in hearts or spades : 3 ♥ or 3 ♠. Or he can bid 3 NT directly.

2. **Unbalanced** hands (**with** a singleton) : 6 3 3 1, 7 3 2 1, 7 3 3 0

> *Process* : On a first *relay*, 2 ♥ : Opener's rebid will be in his *short suit*.
> Then, on a second *relay* : With 6 3 3 1 : 3 NT, nothing else to describe.
> With 7 3 2 1 : the 3-card suit.   With 7 3 3 0 : Rebid the short suit.

Therefore, such hands will be described as follows :

6 ♦ 3 3 1 ♠		6 ♦ 3 3 1 ♣		6 ♦ 3 3 1 ♥	
2 ♦	2 ♥ ?	2 ♦	2 ♥ ?	2 ♦	2 ♥ ?
<u>2 ♠</u>	2 NT ?	<u>3 ♣</u>	3 ♥ * ?	<u>3 ♦</u> **	3 ♥ ?
3 NT – Final		3 NT – Final		3 NT – Final	

* 3 ♥ is used as the *relay*, here, as 3 ♦ would be final, to play.
** 3 ♦ is used to describe the ♥ singleton, more *economical* than 3 ♥.

109

As was the case after 2 ♥ and 2 ♠ openings, all most frequent distributions – 6 3 2 2 and 6 3 3 1 – are fully described below the level of 4 ♣.

7-card suits will be described as follows :

7 ♦ and *short in* ♠		7 ♦ and *short in* ♣		7 ♦ and *short in* ♥	
2 ♦	2 ♥ ?	2 ♦	2 ♥ ?	2 ♦	2 ♥ ?
<u>2 ♠</u>	2 NT ?	<u>3 ♣</u>	3 ♥ ?	<u>3 ♦</u>	3 ♥ ?
<u>3 ♣</u> 7 ♦ <u>3 ♣</u> 2 ♥ 1 ♠		<u>3 ♠</u> 7 ♦ <u>3 ♠</u> 2 ♥ 1 ♣		<u>3 ♠</u> 7 ♦ <u>3 ♠</u> 2 ♣ 1 ♥	
<u>3 ♥</u> 7 ♦ <u>3 ♥</u> 2 ♣ 1 ♠		<u>4 ♦</u> * 7 ♦ <u>3 ♥</u> 2 ♠ 1 ♣		<u>4 ♣</u> 7 ♦ <u>3 ♣</u> 2 ♠ 1 ♥	
<u>3 ♠</u> 7 ♦ 3 ♣ 3 ♥ <u>0 ♠</u>		<u>4 ♣</u> 7 ♦ 3 ♠ 3 ♦ <u>0 ♣</u>		<u>4 ♦</u> *7 ♦ 3 ♠ 3 ♣ <u>0 ♥</u>	

4 ♦ * : More economical than 4 ♥.

Reminder : A 7 3 3 0 distribution will rarely occur in the 15/17 HLD point zone – 9 H pts *minimum* required + 8 LD pts given to a 7 3 3 0 distribution = 17 HLD. Its description is shown here as it would be after a 1 ♣ opening.

Below is a summary table of the **full description** of opener's hand

DISTRIBUTION	ON 2 ♥ ?	2nd **Relay**	DESCRIPTION	FINAL BID
6 ♦ 3 2 2 7 ♦ 2 2 2	2 NT	3 ♣ ?	The 3-card suit Rebid ♦	3 ♥ /3 ♠ /3 NT 3 ♦
Singleton	Singleton		Nothing else to describe	
6 ♦ 3 3 1 ♠ 6 ♦ 3 3 1 ♣ 6 ♦ 3 3 1 ♥	2 ♠ 3 ♣ <u>3 ♦</u>	2 NT ? <u>3 ♥</u> ? 3 ♥ ?	Final - 3 NT	3 NT 3 NT 3 NT
7 ♦ 3 2 1 ♠ 7 ♦ 3 2 1 ♣ 7 ♦ 3 2 1 ♥	2 ♠ 3 ♣ 3 ♦	2 NT ? <u>3 ♥</u> ? 3 ♥ ?	The 3-card Suit	3 ♣ / 3 ♥ 3 ♠ / 4 ♥ 3 ♠ / 4 ♣
Void 7 ♦ 3 3 <u>0 ♠</u> 7 ♦ 3 3 <u>0 ♣</u> 7 ♦ 3 3 <u>0 ♥</u>	2 ♠ 3 ♣ 3 ♦	2 NT ? <u>3 ♥</u> ? 3 ♥ ?	Rebid the void suit	3 ♠ 4 ♣ <u>4 ♦</u>

II. RESPONSES OTHER THAN SUCCESSIVE RELAYS

DETERMINING PARAMETERS

Three key parameters determine *which* responses to select. Two of them are the same as those applying to 2 ♥ and 2 ♠ openings : the hand's *strength* and the presence, or absence, of a Fit in a Major suit.

The third one, however, a Fit in the suit opened and «*"trial"* bids, does **not** apply on a 2 ♦ opening as the priority then becomes to look for a potential 3 NT contract rather than a potential 5 ♦ contract.

1. The hand's **strength**, therefore its number of points.

As was the case on 2 ♥ and 2 ♠ openings, with less than 7 pts, the responder *passes*, while with 13 + pts, he *relays*. Here too, we only have to develop responses in *two* point zones : 7/9 and 10/12 pts.

2. The second parameter is to identify a potential Fit in a Major suit.

2.1 5 + card ♠ suit.

With 10/12 pts – game zone – the responder will relay to discover the opener's hand distribution.
With 7/9 pts, the responder will identify his 5 + card ♠ suit by bidding 2 ♠ over 2 ♦. Over this 2 ♠ response, the opener has three options :
   – With a ♠ *misfit* (singleton, therefore with 6 ♦ 3 3 1 ♠ or 7 ♦ 3 2 1 ♠), he will revert back to his long suit, 3 ♦.
   – With a *semi-fit* of 2 ♠, therefore with a 6 ♦ 3 2 ♠ 2 or 7 ♦ 2 2 2 hand, the opener will bid 2 NT.
   – With a ♠ Fit of 3 cards, he will identify his singleton, if he has one : 3 ♣ or 3 ♥. Without a singleton, therefore with a 6 ♦ 3 ♠ 2 2 hand, he will raise spades to 3 ♠, or 4 ♠.

The following deal illustrates the effectiveness of this response :

♠ A x x	♠ K Q x x x
♥ x x x	♥ x x
♦ A K x x x x	♦ Q x
♣ x	♣ x x x x

Typical *traditional* bidding would be :

	1 ♠ (4 + ♠)
1 ♦	
2 ♦ (5 + ♦, 11/15 H pts)	?

What now? The responder does **not** know about the ♦ Fit, nor the ♠ Fit, nor West's ♣ singleton and he does not have enough points to bid further as he could find a ♠ singleton in opener's hand. The ♠ game will be missed.

111

While in **Optimal** Precision Relay, the bidding will be :

2 ♦	2 ♠ (5 + ♠, 7/9 HL pts)
3 ♣ (♠ Fit, ♣ singleton)	4 ♠

The responder has all the pertinent elements – in two bids – and can count a minimum of 27 HLDF pts on their side with Fit pts in diamonds and spades and 2 pts for *"no wasted honor pts"* in clubs.

2.2 **5 +** card ♥ suit.

With 5 + ♥, rather than using 2 NT as a *conventional* response to identify his 5 + card Major, a *relay* from the responder will readily uncover whether or not there is a ♥ Fit : 2 ♠ : ♠ singleton, 6 ♦ <u>3 ♥</u> 3 1 ♠, 3 ♣ : ♣ singleton, 6 ♦ <u>3 ♥</u> 3 1 ♣, 3 ♦, ♥ singleton, 2 NT, Fit or semi-fit in ♥.

This has the additional advantage of *preserving* the direct 2 NT response for the search for a 3 NT game – the next key parameter.

2.3 With **both** 5-card Majors or **no** 5-card Major.

– In the (rare) case of having both 5-card Majors, the responder will *relay* to discover the opener's hand distribution and a Major suit Fit.

– **Without** a 5-card Major and 7/9 pts, the responder will *pass*.

3. The third parameter is to facilitate the search for a NT game.

To do so, the method uses three response bids : 2 NT, 3 ♣ and 3 ♦. These responses can be used with 10/12 pts, as with 7/9 pts, without a ♦ Fit, there will be no NT game (16 HLD pts – 1 point for two doubletons = 15 HL pts + 9 HL pts = 24 pts) and responder will *pass*.

– The 2 NT response is used for balanced hands of 10/12 HLF pts, without a 5-card Major but with **both** Major suits **guarded**. It is *invitational* to play 3 NT from the right hand i.e. the hand *guarding the Majors*.

On this response, the opener can either *pass*, or raise to 3 NT, or revert to 3 ♦, or bid 3 ♣ if he has a ♣ singleton (a singleton in a Major suit would be a negative because of *"wasted honor pts"*). Illustration :

♠ x x x	♠ A x
♥ A 10 x	♥ K J x
♦ A K x x x x	♦ x x x x
♣ x	♣ x x x x

Traditional bidding would likely bid these two hands as follows :

1 ♦	1 NT
2 ♦	3 ♦
Pass	

The key feature of these two hands, the ♣ singleton opposite *"no wasted honor pts"*, is not identified. While in **Optimal Precision Relay**, the bidding will be :

2 ♦	2 NT
3 ♣ (♣ singleton)	5 ♦

East can count : 16 HLD + 12 ½ HDF + 2 pts for *"no wasted honor pts"* in clubs = 30 ½ pts = 5 ♦.

– The 3 ♣ response is used for semi-balanced hands of 10/12 HLF pts with a good 5 + ♣ suit, and of course **without** a 5-card Major.

Identifying a 5 + ♣ suit facilitates finding potential Fit pts in clubs, while inviting a 3 NT contract. It enables the opener to either revert back to 3 ♦ or to inquire about guards in either hearts or spades.

Example hands for a 3 ♣ response :

♠ x x	♠ K x x	♠ A x x
♥ Q 10 x	♥ x x x	♥ x x
♦ x x x	♦ Q x	♦ x x x
♣ K Q x x x	♣ A x x x x	♣ K J 10 x x
11 ½ HLDF pts	11 ½ HLF pts	12 ½ HLDF pts

– The 3 ♦ response is used for balanced hands of 10/12 HLF pts **without** a 5-card Major or with a good 5 + ♣ suit and a 3 + card ♦ Fit and only one of the two Majors guarded (with *both* Majors guarded, the direct response is 2 NT). It is *invitational* to a 3 NT contract bid by the opener.

It is **not** intended to be a *pre-emptive* bid in diamonds which is much more effective when bid at the level of 4 ♦ with a 4-card ♦ Fit.

Example hands for a 3 ♦ response :

♠ x x	♠ Q x x x	♠ K x x
♥ Q J x x	♥ x x x	♥ x x
♦ x x x	♦ Q J x	♦ K x x
♣ K Q x x	♣ A x x	♣ Q 10 x x x
10 HF pts	10 HF pts	11 ½ HF pts
11 HDF pts	(4 3 3 3, no K)	12 ½ HDF pts

In closing, inquiring for *"guards"* in specific suits is always an option after the responses of 2 ♠, 3 ♣, 3 ♦ just as it is after a *relay*. Illustration :

♠ x x	♠ A x x
♥ A x x	♥ x x
♦ A K x x x x	♦ Q x x
♣ x x	♣ A x x x x

In **Optimal** Precision **Relay**, the bidding will be :

2 ♦	2 ♥ ?
2 NT (6 ♦ 3 2 2)	3 ♥ ? (♥ guarded ?)
3 NT (yes, ♥ guarded)	Pass

East is too strong for a direct 3 ♣ response (14 ½ HLDF pts) so he *relays*.

A summary of **responses** on a 2 ♦ opening can be found below.

POINTS	MISFIT	5 + ♠ *(with 2 + ♦)*	Balanced distribution **Without** a 5-card Major
< than 7	Pass	Pass	Pass
7 / 9	2 ♠ w/ 5 ♠	2 ♠	Pass
10 / 12	*Relay*	*Relay*	***both** Majors **guarded** : 2 NT* with 5 good ♣ : 3 ♣ ***without** 5 good ♣ : 3 ♦* or *Relay*

A few hands now to practice our responses to a 2 ♦ opening :

♠ K x x x	x x x	K Q x x x	x
♥ Q x x	K J x x	x x x	Q J x x x
♦ x	x x	Q x	x x x
♣ Q J x x x	Q J 10 x	x x x	Q J 10 x
6 ½ HLMisfit ♦	8 HF	9 HLF	11 HLDF (no K)
Pass	Pass	2 ♠ : 5 ♠	2 ♥ ? *Relay*

♠ K x	x	K Q x x x	A x x
♥ x x x	Q x x x	A x x	Q x x
♦ J x x	K x x x	A x	A x x x
♣ A x x x x	x x x x	x x x	x x x
11 HLF/12 HLDF	11 ½ HDF	16 HLF	11 ½ HF
Balanced, 5 ♣	*weak* in H pts	2 ♥ ? *Relay*	2 NT
3 ♣	4 ♦ *pre-emptive*		**Both** Majors Guarded

---

6 + ♦ single-suit   18 + HLD pts   Open 1 ♣

REBIDS, RESPONSES AND DEVELOPMENTS

OPENER'S REBID ON A 1 ♦ RESPONSE

In **Optimal** Precision Relay the opener will describe *his* hand on a 1 ♦ response to a 1 ♣ opening. He will do so with rebids that will be *exactly the same* as if he had opened 2 ♦.

With 6 + diamonds, he will rebid 2 ♦ with **21/23** + HLD pts. With 18/20 HLD pts, he will bid 2 NT (*strong hand, bid low; weaker hand, bid high*).

However, bidding *developments* beyond this rebid will be different from the ones after a 2 ♦ opening as *modifications* will be needed to accomodate the two-suiters opened 1 ♦, a bid which is *no longer available* after a 1♣ opening. These modifications will be covered in the chapter dealing specifically with the 1 ♣ opening.

RESPONSES TO 1 ♣ OTHER THAN 1 ♦

The same applies to **direct responses** to a 1 ♣ opening : any response *other* than 1 ♦ will be exactly the same as if the responder had opened, *except* that a 6 + card diamond suit of **10/12** HL pts will be bid via a *transfer* bid : 2 ♣. With 7/9 HL pts, he will bid 2 NT .

On responder's 2 ♣ response, the opener's transfer to 2 ♦ will be *relay* and the responder will describe *his* hand. However, here too, bidding *developments* beyond the 2 ♣ response will need *modifications* to describe the *two-suiters* opened 1 ♦, a bid no longer available.

These modifications will be covered now.

1. 6 + ♦ SINGLE-SUIT HAND : 10/12 HLD PTS

On opener's *transfer* to 2 ♦, the responder's rebid will be :

- 2 NT with semi-balanced hands (6 ♦ 3 2 2), followed by the tripleton (3 ♦ with 7 ♦ 2 2 2).
- With *unbalanced* hands, the singleton directly at the level of **three**, i.e. 3 ♥, 3 ♠, 3 NT with a ♣ singleton.
- 3 ♦ with 7 ♦ 3 3 0 hands, followed by the void (3 ♠, 4 ♣, 3 NT w/ ♥)

2. TWO-SUITERS WITH 5 + ♦ AND A SECOND SUIT : 9/12 HL PTS.

In addition to allowing the diamonds to be bid by the *strong* hand, the 1 ♣ opener, the *transfer* response of 2 ♣ for diamonds adds the great benefit of enabling the economical rebid of 2 ♥ with hearts as the second suit of a 5 ♦ 4 ♥ hand.

On opener's *transfer* to 2 ♦, the responder will rebid his second suit :
2 ♥, 2 ♠ or 3 ♣, which only leave room to describe **one** point-zone,
9/12 HL pts. Hands of 7/8 HL pts will be assimilated to *weak* hands
of less than 7 HL pts and will be answered 1 ♦.
Following the responder's bid of his second suit, his next bid will be
either NT with a 5 4 2 2 hand or a repeat of diamonds with a 6 ♦ 4
two-suiter or its 3-card suit with a 5 4 3 hand.

Let's conclude this chapter with some deals taken from tournaments :

International tournament – 2004.

♠ x	♠ x x x
♥ x x	♥ A K x x
♦ K Q x x x x x	♦ A x
♣ A Q x	♣ K x x x

The bidding was most often :

1 ♦	1 ♥
2 ♦	2 ♠ (3rd suit forcing)
3 ♦	3 NT or 5 ♦

And the slam was missed. Dialogue = imprecision. Instead of :

2 ♦ (6 + ♦, 15/17 HLD)	2 ♥ ? (relay)
2 ♠ (♠ singleton)	2 NT ? (relay)
3 ♣ (3 ♣, 7 ♦ 2 ♥ 1 ♠)	4 ♣ ? (RKC Ask, ♦ is trump)
4 NT (2 Keys w/ ♦ Q)	5 ♣ ? (K & Q ♣ Ask)
5 ♥ (♣ Queen)	6 ♦

East knows their side is in slam zone right upon West's 2 ♠ rebid !
(+ 2 pts for *"no wasted honor points"* in spades). And his next rebid, 3 ♣,
shows 7 diamonds, not just 6. The rest is kids' play...
Economical precision, pertinent description, competitive initiative !

Cap Gemini – 2000.

♠ x x	♠ A K x x x x x
♥ A x	♥ K x
♦ A K x x x x	♦ Q x
♣ x x	♣ A x

Only 3 pairs out of 8 found the 7 ♦ contract. The other **5** pairs played
either 6 ♠, 7 ♠ or 6 ♦.

In **Optimal** **P**recision **R**elay, the bidding would be :

116

2 ♦	2 ♥ ? (relay)
2 NT (semi-regular)	3 ♣ ? (relay)
3 ♦ (7 ♦ 2 2 2)	4 ♣ ? (RKC Ask, trump is ♦)
4 ♦ (3 Key Cards)	7 ♦

The key is to find out about West's 7 ♦, not just 6. And there is no need to inquire about a potential ♠ Queen (for 7 NT) which West cannot have as it would give him 18 pts : he would have opened 1 ♣.

San Remo European Open, semi-finals – 2009.

♠ K x	♠ A 10 x x
♥ K Q x	♥ A J x x x
♦ A Q 10 x x x	♦ x x
♣ x x	♣ Q x

At one table, the bidding was : 1 NT   3 NT
Down one, on a ♣ lead. A vivid illustration of *what **not** to do* : opening 1 strong NT, *including* in this opening a 6-card suit, and an *absurd* jump response to 3 NT with 5 hearts ! *From European semi-finalists, in 2009 ?!...*

Instead of :   2 ♦   2 ♥ ? (relay)
                          2 NT (semi-regular)   3 ♣ ? (relay)
                          3 ♥ (6 ♦ 3 ♥ 2 2)   4 ♥

« *Readers' mail* » – Le Bridgeur, 2011.

♠ A x x	♠ K x x x x
♥ x	♥ J 10 x x x x
♦ A J 10 x x x	♦ Q x
♣ A x x	♣ ---

« *Our bidding was :*   1 ♦   1 ♥
                                  2 ♦   Pass

« *We missed the* ♠ *Fit and the game. How should we have bid ?* »
The response given to the reader was : « *I am a proponent of the conventional response of* 2 ♥, *describing* 5 ♠ 4 ♥ *and less than 10 H pts.*
*But I will admit that it would be rather annoying to hear the opener **pass** on* 2 ♥, *with 3 hearts but a* ♠ *misfit, thus missing a 4* ♥ *game* ».

But it is trying to describe a 6 5 2 0 distribution through a totally *artificial convention* that is absurd and a vivid example of "a remedy worse than the illness"! In **Optimal** **P**recision **R**elay the bidding would be :

2 ♦	2 ♥ ? (relay)
3 ♦ (♥ singleton)	3 ♥ ? (relay)
3 NT (6 ♦ 3 3 1 ♥)	4 ♠

BIDDING AFTER INTERVENTIONS OVER A 2 ♦ OPENING

The table below summarizes *suggested* bids by the opener's *partner* following an intervention by the opposite team over a 2 ♦ opening.

The suggested bids are guided by two key **principles** or **objectives** :

1. Over a 2 ♥ or 2 ♠ overcall, **double** is **not** for *penalty* : it is a *relay*. Over any *other* overcall, 3 ♣ and up, **double** is for **penalty** and applies when the opener's partner has 10 + H pts.

2. **Retain**, whenever possible, the 2 NT, 3 ♣ and 3 ♦ responses which are very useful in the search for a NT contract.

INTERVENTIONS over a 2 ♦ opening	SUGGESTED BIDS BY OPENER'S PARTNER Key principles : Retain "*trial*" bids for NT Double : *Relay* over 2 ♥ / ♠ / 2 NT
Double (*Take-out*)	2 ♥ : *Relay* Same as *w/o* the take-out double 2 ♠, 2 NT, 3 ♣, 3 ♦ : keep their meaning 4 ♦ : pre-emptive **Redouble** : 11 / 12 HL pts Invitation for 3 NT
2 ♥ (5 + ♥)	**Double** : *Relay* Replaces the 2 ♥ bid 2 ♠, 2 NT, 3 ♣, 3 ♦ : keep their meaning 4 ♦ : pre-emptive
2 ♠ (5 + ♠)	**Double** : *Relay* 2 NT, 3 ♣, 3 ♦ : keep their meaning 4 ♦ : pre-emptive
2 NT (5 ♠ 5 ♥ ?)	**Double** : *Relay* 3 ♣, 3 ♦ : keep their meaning 4 ♦ : pre-emptive 3 NT, 5 ♦ : to play
3 ♣ (6 + ♣)	**Double : Penalty** double 3 ♦ : keeps its meaning 3 NT, 5 ♦ : to play 4 ♦ : pre-emptive
3 ♦ (*Cue-bid, strong* 5 ♠ 5 ♥ ?)	**Double** : Invites opener to bid 3 NT 4 ♦ : pre-emptive 3 NT, 5 ♦ : to play

2 ♣ Opening – **RESPONSES AND DEVELOPMENTS**

14/17 HLD / **9 +** H pts   **6 +** ♣ single-suit **or** **5 +** ♣ 4 ♥ or 4 ♠

The 2 ♣ opening is different from the 2 ♠, 2 ♥ and 2 ♦ openings in that it is also used for two-suiter hands with 5 + ♣ and **one** 4-card **Major**, as well as 6 + ♣ single-suit hands. It will therefore be our first opportunity to get familiar with the description of **5 4 2 2, 5 4 3 1, 6 4 2 1** and **6 4 3 0** distributions (7 - 4 two-suiters rarely exist in a 2 ♣ opening as such hands have 8 LD pts which, added to the 9 H pts minimum required for this opening, would add up to 17 HLD pts *minimum*).

As a reminder, these 5 + ♣ two-suiters **cannot** have **4 diamonds** as a second suit, **nor** can they have **both** 4-card Majors.

As was done with the 2 ♠, 2 ♥ and 2 ♦ openings, we will cover, first, the complete description *of* opener's hand on successive *relays*, before studying responses *other* than *relays*. We will then cover the same description and responses after a 1 ♣ opening with the same hands of 18 + HLD pts and will close each section with a summary table of full description bids and responses other than *relays*.

I. DESCRIPTION OF OPENER'S HAND ON SUCCESSIVE RELAYS

All hands opened 2 ♣ are described in **one** point-zone only, of 4 pts instead of 3 : 14/17 HLD pts.
The opener's **first rebid** will immediately identify the opener's hand **structure** – single-suit **or** two-suiter – on responder's *relay*, as follows :

2 ♣	2 ♦ ?	
2 ♥	: 5 + ♣ 4 ♥	denies 4 ♠
2 ♠	: 5 + ♣ 4 ♠	denies 4 ♥
2 NT	: 6 ♣ single-suit with**out** a singleton	
3 ♣	: 6 ♣ single-suit **with** a singleton	

1. **Semi-regular** hands (**no singleton**) : 6 3 2 2 and 7 2 2 2

   Process : On a first *relay*, 2 ♦ : Opener's first rebid will be 2 NT
   Then, on a *second relay*, <u>3 ♦</u> ? : The 3-card suit with 6 3 2 2
                                         Rebid ♣ with 7 2 2 2

Therefore, such hands will be described as follows :

2 ♣	2 ♦ ?
2 NT **no** singleton	<u>3 ♦</u> ? instead of 3 ♣ which would be final.

3 ♥	6 ♣ 3 ♥ 2 2	
3 ♠	6 ♣ 3 ♠ 2 2	
3 NT	6 ♣ 3 ♦ 2 2	3 NT = the 3-card suit is in the *relay* suit.
4 ♣	7 ♣ 2 2 2	No 3-card suit, therefore rebidding ♣ = 7 ♣.

If responder does **not** need to identify opener's 3-card suit and favors a 3 NT contract, he can skip further relaying after 2 NT and *inquire about guards* in hearts or spades : 3 ♥ or 3 ♠. Or he can bid 3 NT directly.

2. **Unbalanced** single-suit hands (**with** a singleton) : 6 3 3 1, 7 3 2 1

Unbalanced single-suit hands with 7 ♣ will be described *directly* **beyond** a 3 ♣ rebid – thus, rebids of 3 ♦, 3 ♥ and 3 ♠ immediately describe a 7-card suit. Therefore, a 3 ♣ rebid denies 7 ♣ and guarantees a **6** ♣ single-suit.

Process : On a first *relay*, 2 ♦ : Opener's **rebid** will be :
– With 6 ♣ 3 3 1 : 3 ♣, then the singleton on a second *relay* (3 ♦).
– With 7 ♣ : the singleton, directly at the level of 3 : 3 ♦ / 3 ♥ / 3 ♠.
 Then, with 7 3 2 1 : the 3-card suit. With 7 3 3 0 : rebid the short suit

Therefore, such hands will be described as follows :

6 ♣ 3 3 1 hands :	2 ♣	2 ♦ ?
	3 ♣	3 ♦ ?
	3 ♥	6 ♣ 3 3 1 ♥
	3 ♠	6 ♣ 3 3 1 ♠
	3 NT	6 ♣ 3 3 1 ♦ singleton in the *relay* suit.

A 3 ♣ rebid therefore *denies* 7 ♣ as well as a void.

7 ♣ suits will be described as follows :

7 ♣ and *short* in ♦		7 ♣ and *short* in ♥		7 ♣ and *short* in ♠	
2 ♣	2 ♦ ?	2 ♣	2 ♦ ?	2 ♣	2 ♦ ?
3 ♦	3 ♥ ?	3 ♥	3 ♠ ?		
3 ♠	7 ♣ 3 ♠ 2 ♥ 1 ♦	3 NT	7 ♣ 3 ♠ 2 ♦ 1 ♥	3 ♠	7 ♣ 3 ♥ 3 ♦ 0 ♠
3 NT	7 ♣ 3 ♥ 2 ♠ 1 ♦	4 ♦	7 ♣ 3 ♦ 2 ♠ 1 ♥	3 NT	7 ♣ 3 ♦ 2 ♥ 1 ♠
4 ♦	7 ♣ 3 ♥ 3 ♠ 0 ♦	4 ♥	7 ♣ 3 ♦ 3 ♠ 0 ♥	4 ♥	7 ♣ 3 ♥ 2 ♦ 1 ♠

With a 7 3 3 0 distribution, the short suit is **rebid**. A spade void is described by the direct rebid of 3 ♠, while any *other* direct rebid above 3 ♠ describes a 7 3 2 1 distribution.

Note that **all** *most frequent* distributions – 6 3 2 2 and 6 3 3 1 – as well as 5 of 9 hands with 7 ♣, are fully described below the level of 4 ♣, allowing the 4 ♣ bid to be used as a RKC Ask.

3. **Two-suiter hands** : 5 ♣ 4 Major, 6 ♣ 4 Major

Process : On a first *relay*, 2 ♦, the 4-card Major, then on the next relay:
– With 5 ♣ 4 2 2 : NT - Final
– With 5 ♣ 4 <u>3</u> 1 or 6 ♣ 4 <u>3</u> 0 : the 3-card suit (cannot be 5 4 4 0 as it
  cannot have both 4-card Majors, nor can it have 4 diamonds).
– With 6 ♣ 4 2 1 (no 3-card suit) : rebid clubs, 3 ♣, then the doubleton.

Therefore, such hands will be described as follows :

5 + ♣ 4 ♥	:	2 ♣	2 ♦ ?
		2 ♥	2 ♠ ?
5 ♣ 4 ♥ 2 ♠ 2 ♦	:	2 NT	
5 ♣ 4 ♥ <u>3</u> ♦ 1 ♠	:	3 ♦	3 ♥ ?
		3 NT	
6 ♣ 4 ♥ <u>3</u> ♦ 0 ♠	:	3 ♦	3 ♥ ?
		3 ♠	4th suit = void = <u>6</u> ♣
5 ♣ 4 ♥ <u>3</u> ♠ 1 ♦	:	3 ♠	Final = 5 4 3 1
6 ♣ 4 ♥ <u>3</u> ♠ 0 ♦	:	3 ♥	*Impossible* ♥ rebid = <u>6</u> 4 3 ♠ 0 ♦
6 ♣ 4 ♥ <u>2</u> ♠ 1 ♦	:	3 ♣	3 ♦ ?
		3 ♠	
6 ♣ 4 ♥ <u>2</u> ♦ 1 ♠	:	3 ♣	3 ♦ ?
		3 NT	*two* cards in the *relay* suit

---

5 + ♣ 4 ♠	:	2 ♣	2 ♦ ?
		2 ♠	2 NT ?

5 ♣ 4 ♠ 2 ♥ 2 ♦ : Here there are 2 options :
– with a sure "stopper" in **both** hearts and diamonds : 3 NT
– with**out** a "stopper" in **both** hearts and diamonds : 3 ♠, an *impossible*
bid allowing the side to stop in 3 ♠ with 4 direct "losers" in ♥ and ♦.
Illustration : with these two hands :

♠ K Q x x	♠ A J x x
♥ x	♥ x x x x
♦ x x x	♦ x x
♣ A Q x x x	♣ K x x

The **Optimal** Precision Relay bidding will be :

2 ♣	2 ♦ ?
2 ♠	2 NT ?
3 ♦ (3 diamonds)	4 ♠

While, with these two hands :

♠ K Q x x	♠ A J x x
♥ x x	♥ x x x x
♦ x x	♦ x x
♣ A Q x x x	♣ K x x

The **Optimal** **P**recision **R**elay bidding will be :

2 ♣	2 ♦ ?
2 ♠	2 NT ?
3 ♠ (5 4 2 2 w/**o** stoppers)	Pass

East passes on West's 3 ♠ as he knows of 4 direct "losers" in ♥ and ♦.

While, with these two hands :

♠ Q x x x	♠ A J x x
♥ A x	♥ x x x x
♦ K x	♦ x x
♣ A Q x x x	♣ K x x

The **Optimal** **P**recision **R**elay bidding will be :

2 ♣	2 ♦ ?
2 ♠	2 NT ?
3 NT (5 4 2 2 w/ stoppers)	4 ♠

Knowing that his side does **not** have 4 direct "losers" in the red suits, East can now bid 4 ♠.

5 ♣ 4 ♠ <u>3 ♦</u> 1 ♥ :	3 ♦	3 ♥ ?
	3 NT	

6 ♣ 4 ♠ <u>3 ♦</u> 0 ♥ :	3 ♦	3 ♥ ?
	<u>3 ♠</u>	*Impossible* ♠ rebid = <u>6</u> 4 3 ♦ <u>0 ♥</u>

5 ♣ 4 ♠ 3 ♥ 1 ♦ :	3 ♥	Final = 5 4 3 1

6 ♣ 4 ♠ 3 ♥ 0 ♦ :	<u>3 ♠</u>	*Impossible* ♠ rebid = <u>6</u> 4 3 ♥ <u>0 ♦</u>

6 ♣ 4 ♠ <u>2 ♥</u> 1 ♦ :	3 ♣	3 ♦ ?
	3 ♥	

6 ♣ 4 ♠ <u>2 ♦</u> 1 ♥ :	3 ♣	3 ♦ ?
	3 NT	two cards in the *relay* suit

All two-suiters are fully described below the level of 4 ♣.

You will find, on the next page, a summary table of the **full description** of opener's hand on *successive relays*.

Below is a summary table of the **full description** of opener's hand on *successive relays*.

SUMMARY OF HAND DESCRIPTION ON SUCCESSIVE RELAYS

DISTRIBUTION	On 2 ♦ ?	2nd Relay	DESCRIPTION	FINAL BID
Semi-regular				
6 ♣ 3 2 2	2 NT	3 ♦ ?	3-card suit	3 ♥ /3 ♠ /3 NT
7 ♣ 2 2 2			Rebid ♣	4 ♣
Singleton	Rebid ♣		The 3-card suit	
6 ♣ 3 3 1 ♥	3 ♣	3 ♦ ?		3 ♥
6 ♣ 3 3 1 ♠	3 ♣	3 ♦ ?		3 ♠
6 ♣ 3 3 1 ♦	3 ♣	3 ♦ ?		3 NT
7 ♣ single-suit				
7 ♣ 3 2 1 ♦	3 ♦	3 ♥ ?	The 3-card suit	3 ♣ / 3 ♥
7 ♣ 3 2 1 ♥	3 ♥	3 ♠ ?		3 ♠ / 4 ♥
7 ♣ 3 2 1 ♠	3 ♠ /3 NT			4 ♣
7 ♣ 3 3 0 ♦	3 ♦	3 ♥ ?	Rebid void	4 ♦
7 ♣ 3 3 0 ♥	3 ♥	3 ♠ ?		4 ♥
7 ♣ 3 3 0 ♠	3 ♠		3 ♠ is final	
Two-suiters				
5 ♣ 4 ♥ or 4 ♠	2 ♥ / 2 ♠	2 NT ?	NT	3 NT
5 ♣ 4 M 3 ♦ 1	2 ♥ / 2 ♠	2 ♠ /NT	The 3-card suit	3 ♦
5 ♣ 4 3 ♥ / ♠ 1	2 ♥ / 2 ♠	2 NT ?		3 ♥ / ♠
6 ♣ 4 3 ♦ 0	2 ♥ / 2 ♠	2 NT ?	The 3-card Suit	3 ♥ / ♠
6 ♣ 4 3 ♥ / ♠ 0	2 ♥ / 2 ♠	2 NT ?		3 ♥ / ♠
6 ♣ 4 2 ♦ 1	2 ♥ / 2 ♠	2 NT ?	Rebid ♣ : 3 ♣ then the 2-card suit	3 ♥ / ♠ / NT
6 ♣ 4 2 ♥ / ♠ 1	2 ♥ / 2 ♠	2 NT ?		3 ♥ / ♠ / NT

II. RESPONSES OTHER THAN SUCCESSIVE RELAYS

DETERMINING PARAMETERS

The same three key parameters applying to responses over a 2 ♦ opening apply to the responses over a 2 ♣ opening : the hand's *strength*, the search for a Fit in a Major suit, and without such Fit, the search for a potential 3 NT contract rather than a potential 5 ♣ contract.

1. The hand's *strength*, therefore its number of points.

As was the case on the 2 ♦ opening, with less than 7 pts, the responder *passes*, while with 13 + pts, he *relays*. Therefore, here too, specific responses only apply to 7/12 point hands : 7/9 and 10/12 pts.

2. The second parameter is to identify a potential **Fit** in a Major suit.

2.1 With a 4-card Major, *or both*, the responder will *relay*, 2 ♦, with any hand of 7 + HL pts – the easiest and surest way to find out whether the side has an 8-card Fit in a Major suit.

2.2 With a 5-card Major.

With 10/12 pts – game zone – the responder will *relay* to discover the opener's hand distribution.
With 7/9 pts, the responder **bids** his 5-card Major directly, 2 ♥ or 2 ♠, over the 2 ♣ opening. Over this response, the opener has three options :

– With a **misfit** in responder's Major bid (singleton), he will revert back to his long suit, 3 ♣.

– With a **semi-fit** of 2 cards in the Major, the opener will bid 2 NT or can *pass* as the response of 2 ♥ or 2 ♠ is **not** forcing.

– With a **Fit** of 3 or 4 cards, he will identify his singleton, if he has one, at the level of three : <u>3</u> ♦ or <u>3</u> ♥ (not 3 ♠ which would go over a 3 ♥ raise). **Without** a singleton, he will raise the Major to 3 or 4. Example :

♠ K Q x x	♠ A x x x x
♥ x x x	♥ x x
♦ x	♦ x x x x
♣ A Q x x x	♣ K x

In **Optimal** Precision Relay, these two hands will be bid as follows :

2 ♣	2 ♠ (5 ♠, 7/9 HL)
3 ♦ (♠ Fit, ♦ singleton)	4 ♠

With + 2 pts for *"no wasted honor pts"* in diamonds, East can count on 16 HLDF pts from partner + his own 11 ½ pts (no Queen but 1 point for two doubletons + 1 pt for the King in opener's 5-card suit) = 27 ½ pts.

2.3 With **5 – 4** in the Majors.

With 5 ♥ and 4 ♠, the responder will bid 2 ♥ over which the opener will bid 2 ♠ if he has 4 spades. Thus, there is no possibility to miss an 8-card Fit in a Major.

However, with 5 ♠ and 4 ♥, bidding 2 ♠ would not enable the side to find an 8-card ♥ Fit and the opener would have to revert back to 3 ♣ without having 6 clubs . Therefore, we need to find a way to identify a 5 ♠ 4 ♥ two-suiter – preferably immediately and directly.

To do this, the method uses a *conventional* direct response of 2 NT, rather than using this bid as invitational to 3 NT. This bid, being *forcing*, can be bid in both point zones, 7/9 and 10/12 HL pts.

This addresses a very problematic situation in *traditional* bidding with a weak hand. Example :

♠ x	♠ A x x x x
♥ A J 10 x	♥ K x x x
♦ x x x	♦ x
♣ A J 10 x x	♣ x x x

In **Optimal P**recision **R**elay, these two hands will be bid as follows :

2 ♣	2 NT (5 ♠ 4 ♥)
3 ♥ (♥ Fit)	4 ♥

With 12 ½ HLDF pts (3 pts for the singleton with 4 trumps, 1 additional point for the ♥ K and 1 pt for the 8-card ♣ Fit), East can count on his side having the points for game. A game not likely to be found in *traditional* bidding...

With 5 ♥ and 5 ♠ (rare), the responder will *relay* to look for a Fit in one of the Majors as he would have no way to describe such a two-suiter as well as its singleton.

3. The third parameter is to facilitate the search for a NT game.

With**out** a 4-card or 5-card Major, the priority is obviously to look for a possible 3 NT game. To do so, the responder has the choice between *relaying* and using the *invitational* 3 ♣ response. A 3 ♣ response will mean : a ♣ Fit, by 3 or 4 cards, 11/12 HlFit pts, and **both** Major suits *guarded*. Example hands corresponding to the 3 ♣ *invitational* bid :

Hand A :	♠ A x x	♥ Q J x	♦ J 10 x x	♣ Q x x
Hand B :	♠ K x x	♥ A x	♦ x x x x	♣ Q x x x

Here is an illustration of the 3 ♣ response :

♠ x x x	♠ A x
♥ A x x	♥ K Q x
♦ x	♦ x x x x
♣ A K 10 x x x	♣ x x x x

In **Optimal** Precision Relay, these two hands will be bid as follows :

2 ♣	3 ♣ (invitation for 3 NT)
3 ♦ (♦ singleton)	5 ♣

West's ♦ singleton rules out 3 NT but the 2 additional pts for *"no wasted honor pts"* in diamonds now gives the side the points for 5 ♣.

While the hands below would be right for a *pre-emptive* 4 ♣ raise :

♠ x x	♠ x x x
♥ x x x	♥ x
♦ Q J x x	♦ J 10 x x
♣ K x x x	♣ K Q x x x

This concludes the study of responses to the 2 ♣ opening. A summary of the **responses** can be found below.

SUMMARY OF RESPONSES TO A 2 ♣ OPENING

POINTS	w/o 4 or 5-card Major	*With* 4-card Major	*With* 5-card Major
< than 7	Pass	Pass	Pass
7 / 9	Pass	*Relay* (2 ♦)	2 ♥ / 2 ♠ w/ 5 ♠ 4 ♥ : 2 NT
10 / 12	3 ♣ (for 3 NT) or *Relay* (2 ♦)	*Relay*	w/ 5 ♠ 4 ♥ : 2 NT or *Relay*

UNUSUAL CONVENTIONAL BIDS TO "FLAG"

OPENING	UNUSUAL CONVENTIONAL RESPONSE	POINTS
2 ♣	2 NT : 5 ♠ 4 ♥	7 / 12 HL

126

A few hands now to practice our **responses** to a 2 ♣ opening :

♠ K x x	♠ K x x x	♠ K Q x x x
♥ J 10 x	♥ Q x x x	♥ Q x
♦ A x x x x	♦ x x	♦ x x x
♣ x x	♣ K x x	♣ x x x
8 ½ HL (no Q)	10 ½ HDF	9 HLDF
Pass	2 ♦ relay	2 ♠ (5 ♠)

♠ A x x x x	♠ K x x	♠ x x x
♥ Q x x x	♥ Q J x	♥ x
♦ A x	♦ x x x	♦ K x x x
♣ x x	♣ Q J 10 x	♣ Q x x x x
9 ½ HL (no K)	11 HF	10 ½ HDF
2 NT : 5 ♠ 4 ♥	3 ♣ (for 3 NT)	4 ♣
		pre-emptive

---

6 + ♣ single-suit **or 5 + ♣ 4 ♥** or **4 ♠**   **18 + HLD** pts   Open 1 ♣

REBIDS, RESPONSES AND DEVELOPMENTS

OPENER'S REBID ON A 1 ♦ RESPONSE

On a 1 ♦ response to a 1 ♣ opening, the opener will now have **two** point-zones to describe, not just one. His first rebid of 2 ♣ will describe either a two-suiter hand of 18/20 HLD pts **or** a 6 + ♣ single-suiter of 21/23 + HLD pts (with 6 + ♣ single-suiters of 18/20 HLD pts, he will rebid 3 ♣). The hand's further description will be the same as after a 2 ♣ opening. How to describe two-suiter hands in the 21/23 + HLD point-zone will be covered in the chapter dealing with the 1 ♣ opening.

RESPONSES TO 1 ♣ OTHER THAN 1 ♦

The same applies to **direct responses** to a 1 ♣ opening, *except* that the clubs will be described via a *transfer* bid : a response of 1 **NT** will describe either a 5 + ♣ two-suiter hand of **7/9** HL pts or a 6 + ♣ single suiter of **10/12** HL pts (with a 6 + ♣ single suiter of 7/9 HL pts, the response will be 3 ♣). On a 1 NT response, the opener's transfer to 2 ♣ will be a *relay* on which the responder will describe his hand.

The description of two-suiter hands of 10/12 HL pts will be covered in the chapter dealing specifically with the 1 ♣ opening.

Here too, the *transfer* response of 1 NT for clubs adds the great benefit of enabling the economical rebid of 2 ♦ with diamonds as the second suit of a 5 ♣ 4 ♦ hand. On opener's *transfer* to 2 ♣, the responder's rebid will be:

1. 6 + ♣ SINGLE-SUIT HAND : 10/12 HLD PTS

– 2 NT with semi-balanced hands (6 ♣ 3 2 2), followed by the tripleton (followed by 3 ♣ with 7 ♣ 2 2 2).
– With *unbalanced* hands, the singleton directly at the level of **three**, i.e. 3 ♦, 3 ♥, 3 ♠.
– 3 ♣ with 7 ♣ 3 3 0 hands, followed by the void (3 ♥, 3 ♠, 3 NT w/ ♦)

2. TWO-SUITERS WITH 5 + ♣ AND A SECOND SUIT : 9/12 HL PTS.

On opener's *transfer* to 2 ♣, the responder will rebid his second suit : 2 ♦, 2 ♥, 2 ♠, which only leave room to describe **one** point-zone, 9/12 HL pts. Hands of 7/8 HL pts will be answered 1 ♦ (as if < than 7 HL). Following the responder's bid of his second suit, his next bid will be either NT with a 5 4 2 2 hand or a repeat of clubs with a 6 ♣ 4 two-suiter hand or its 3-card suit with a 5 4 3 hand.

Let's conclude this chapter with some deals taken from tournaments :

« *Technique* » – Le Bridgeur, 2009.

♠ x x	♠ A x x
♥ Q x x x	♥ A K x x x
♦ x	♦ A x x
♣ A K Q x x x	♣ x x

The grand slam was very rarely bid because East did **not** know about West's 6 ♣ to A K Q. In **Optimal** Precision Relay the bidding would be :

2 ♣ (5 + ♣, 14/17 HLD)	2 ♦ ?
2 ♥ (4 hearts)	2 ♠ ?
3 ♣ (6 clubs)	3 ♦ ?
3 ♠ (2 spades)	4 ♣ ? (RKC Ask, trump is ♣)
4 NT (2 Keys w/ ♣ Q)	5 ♥ ? (K & Q ♥ Ask)
5 NT (♥ Queen)	7 ♥

East knows everything about West's hand and can count 13 tricks with ruffing a club, if needed, to develop the suit, and ruffing a diamond.

Regional tournament, 2010.

♠ x x	♠ x x x x
♥ A Q x x	♥ J 10 x x x
♦ x x	♦ A x
♣ A Q 10 x x	♣ K x

In the tournament this deal was played, the bidding was, most often :

1 ♣	1 ♥
2 ♥	Pass

In **Optimal** Precision Relay the bidding would be :

2 ♣	2 ♥ (5 + ♥, 7/9 HL)
3 ♥ (no singleton)	4 ♥

East can add 1 point for his King in partner's 5-card suit + 1 point for J 10 of hearts + 1 D point for his two doubletons = 11 ½ HDF pts opposite 16 HLDF pts minimum (14 + 1 ♥ Fit point + 1 D point for a doubleton in a hand with 4 trumps) = 27 ½ pts = 4 ♥.

Readers' mail – Le Bridgeur, 2010.

♠ A 10 x	♠ K x x
♥ A x	♥ x x x
♦ x x	♦ 10 x x x
♣ A K J x x x	♣ Q x x

« *Our bidding was :*   1 ♣   1 ♦
                        2 NT   Pass

« *We missed the* 3 NT *game. Where did we go wrong ?* »

The wrong doing isn't the players' but rather the bidding system played! And then, the correct point count has yet to be learned !...

West has 21 HLD / 20 HL pts, not 18 HL pts, but a 2 NT opening would still not enable East to bid to 3 NT without knowing West's 6 clubs which would allow him to add 3 Fit pts to his own 3 ½ pts (4 3 3 3).

In **Optimal** Precision **Relay** the bidding would be :

> 1 ♣ (18 + HLD)   1 ♦ (< 7 or 13 + HL pts)
> 2 ♣ (5 + ♣, forcing)   3 ♣ (♣ Fit, 4/6 HLDF)
> 3 NT

In this case, the 3 ♣ bid does **not** promise that both Majors are guarded as the responder has fewer than **7** HL pts.

National Division I, open, semi-finals − 2011.

> ♠ x   ♠ A J 10 x
> ♥ x x x   ♥ x
> ♦ K x x   ♦ Q J 10 x x
> ♣ A K J x x x   ♣ x x x

At one table, the auction was :

West	North	East	South
1 ♣	1 ♠	1 NT	2 ♠
3 NT	Pass	Pass	Pass

Down three for a loss of 14 IMPs! The above bidding is a very good example of *what **not** to do* : First, opening 1 ♣ a 17 HLD point hand is an open invitation for opponents to intervene in a Major suit.
Second, West's conclusion in 3 NT is flabbergasting! as he has a singleton and has no idea what East holds in hearts. Instead of the following :

> 2 ♣ (5 + ♣, 14/17 HLD)   2 ♦ ? (relay)
> 3 ♣ (6 ♣ 3 3 1)   3 ♥ ? (♥ guarded ?)
> 4 ♣ (no, ♥ *not guarded*) 5 ♣

First, the 2 ♣ opening would have prevented the ♠ overcall. Second, East learns about the lack of guards in hearts and, third, he can count 30 + HLDF pts on his side (16 + 14 ½) for a game in clubs.

Interclub finals – 2011.

♠	A J 10 x x x	♠ x x
♥	A x	♥ Q x x x
♦	A K x x x	♦ x x
♣	---	♣ A Q 10 x x

The pair titled "World's best pair for 2011" – Fantoni/Nunes – play 5 ♦, with 7 trumps, instead of 4 ♠, because West describes a <u>5 ♠</u> 5 ♦ two-suiter, and the 8-card ♠ Fit is not found.

Instead of :   1 ♣   2 ♣ (5 + ♣, 7/12 HL)
                 2 ♦ ?   2 ♥ (5 ♣ 4 ♥, 7/9 HL)
                 2 ♠ ?   2 NT (5 ♣ 4 ♥ 2 2)
                 4 ♠

It is simply absurd to have a hand worth 24 ½ HLD pts try to describe itself – particularly when 6 5 2 0 – instead of describing the weaker hand!

131

BIDDING AFTER INTERVENTIONS OVER A 2 ♣ OPENING

The table below summarizes *suggested* bids by the opener's partner following an intervention by the opposite team over a 2 ♣ opening.

The suggested bids are guided by two key **principles** or **objectives** :

1. Over a 2 ♦, 2 ♥, 2 ♠, 2 NT or 3 ♣ overcall, **double is not** for penalty : it is a *relay*. Over any *other* overcall, 3 ♦ and up, **double** is for **penalty** and applies when the opener's partner has 10 + H pts.

2. Retain, when possible, the 2 NT and 3 ♣ responses which are very useful in the search for a contract in NT or in a Major suit.

INTERVENTIONS over a 2 ♣ opening	SUGGESTED BIDS BY OPENER'S PARTNER **Key principles : Retain** 2 NT / 3 ♣ responses **Double :** *Relay* over 2 ♦ / ♥ / ♠ / 2 NT
Double *(Take-out)*	2 ♦ : *Relay* Same as w / o the take-out double 2 ♥, 2 ♠, 2 NT, 3 ♣, 4 ♣ : keep their meaning
2 ♦ (5 + ♦)	**Double :** *Relay* 2 ♥, 2 ♠, 2 NT, 3 ♣, 4 ♣ : keep their meaning 3 ♦ *"cue-bid"* : ♦ singleton 4 + card ♣ Fit 3 ♥, 3 ♠ : pre-emptive 7 + card suit, **no** ♣ Fit
2 ♥ (5 + ♥)	**Double :** *Relay* (Replaces the 2 ♦ bid) 2 ♠, 3 ♣, 4 ♣ : keep their meaning 2 NT : Same as 3 ♣ but with **two** stoppers in ♥ 3 ♥ *"cue-bid"* : ♥ singleton 4 + card ♣ Fit
2 ♠ (5 + ♠)	**Double :** *Relay* "Sputnik" type **with 4 +** ♥ 3 ♣, 4 ♣ : keep their meaning 2 NT : Same as 3 ♣ but with **two** stoppers in ♠ 3 ♠ *"cue-bid"* : ♠ singleton 4 + card ♣ Fit
2 NT (?)	**Double : Relay** "Sputnik" type **with** ♥ / ♠ 3 ♣, 4 ♣ : keep their meaning
3 ♣ (Cue-bid 5 ♠ 5 ♥ ?)	**Double :** Invites 3 NT **without** Majors guard 3 ♦ : Invites 3 NT **with both** Majors guarded 4 ♣ : Remains pre-emptive raise

CHAPTER 3

OPENING BIDS, RESPONSES AND DEVELOPMENTS

DEVELOPMENT PROCESSES COMMON TO 1 ♥ / 1 ♠ OPENINGS

PREAMBLE

Covering these two key openings now gets us into the very "heart" of the method in terms of **responses** and following developments. These are extremely important as responses to 1 ♥ and 1 ♠ openings have been particularly poorly handled by *traditional* bidding systems.

I am not just referring here to the *dialogue* methodology, and the imprecision associated with it, compared to the *relay* methodology; I am referring to **all** responses to 1 ♥ and 1 ♠ openings and the fundamental premise they are based on in *traditional* bidding, which is :
« *The responder to a 1 ♥ or 1 ♠ opening must have* **10 + H** *pts to bid a* **new** *suit at the level of* **two**; *with* **fewer** *than 10 H pts, he must bid 1 NT, regardless of his hand's distribution − or raise to 2 ♥ or 2 ♠ with a Fit* ».

So, with a *misfitted* hand, such as the one below, the bidding will be :

♠ K Q x x x		♠ x x
♥ A x x x		♥ x x x
♦ x x		♦ K Q J x x x
♣ A x		♣ x x
1 ♠		1 NT
2 ♥		Pass or 2 ♠

Down one, or two. 2 ♦ would have been a better contract…

Or, worse yet, the deal below, where a majority of pairs played in 4 ♠ while many stopped in 2 ♠, instead of playing 6 ♣ :

♠ A K x x x x		♠ Q x
♥ A x x		♥ x x
♦ x		♦ A x x
♣ A x x		♣ K x x x x x
1 ♠		1 NT
2 ♠		Pass

I. USE OF TRANSFER BIDS AS RESPONSES TO 1 ♥ / 1 ♠ OPENINGS

The **Optimal** Precision **Relay** method takes a totally different approach to handling theses cases : it immediately identifies the responder's *long suit* with **weak** hands, and to differentiate weak hands from stronger hands, the responder retains control of the bidding by using *transfer* bids i.e. a response of 2 ♣ on a 1 ♥ or 1 ♠ opening is a *transfer* bid for diamonds, and so on up the line. Thus the bidding on the first deal shown on the previous page would be :

1 ♠ (12/17 HLD pts)	2 ♣ (*transfer* for diamonds)
2 ♦ (*transfer* to ♦)	Pass

While on the second deal shown on that page, the bidding would be :

1 ♣ (18 + HLD pts)	1 NT (transfer ♣, 7/12 HL pts)
2 ♣ ? (transfer / relay)	2 NT (6 ♣ 3 2 2, 10/12 HL)
3 ♣ ? (relay)	3 ♦ (6 ♣ 3 ♦ 2 2)
4 ♣ ? (RKC Ask)	4 ♠ (2 KC w/o the ♣ Q)
4 NT * ? (K & Q ♠ Ask)	5 ♦ (♠ Queen)
6 ♣	

* We will see later how 4 NT is here a K & Q Ask in spades.

Many other embarassing situations occur in *traditional* bidding, paradoxally when the responder has a 4-card Fit in opener's suit. Such as :

♠ A Q x x x	♠ K x x x
♥ A x x x	♥ K Q x x x
♦ D x	♦ x x
♣ x x	♣ Q x

The bidding would likely be :

1 ♠	2 ♥
3 ♥	3 ♠
4 ♠	

Traditional bidding is quite likely to bid these hands to game – but there are four direct losers in diamonds and clubs. While using *transfer* bids provides a very precise solution for such hands :

1 ♠	2 ♦ (*transfer* for hearts)
2 ♥ (*transfer* to ♥)	3 ♠ *
Pass	

 ** East's successive bids specifically mean : **strong** *first* suit (Ace or K Q), 4 + card Fit in opener's suit, 13/15 HLDF pts, and **nothing** in the **other two** suits (no Ace or King or singleton). The opener *passes*, knowing of four direct losers in diamonds and clubs.

The next example features *traditional* bidding's favorite modern convention, the *"splinter"* bid :

	♠ x x x	♠ x x x
	♥ A Q x x x	♥ K J x x
	♦ K Q x	♦ x
	♣ A x	♣ K Q x x x
	1 ♥	4 ♦ (*"splinter"* bid)
	4 ♥	

or, for others :	1 ♥	2 ♣
	2 ♥	4 ♦ (*"splinter"* bid)
	4 ♥	

Down one. Here again, the **Optimal P**recision **R**elay method's use of *transfer* bids provides a very precise solution for such hands :

1 ♥	1 NT (*transfer* for clubs)
2 ♣ (*transfer* to ♣)	3 ♦ * (*"mini-splinter"*)
3 ♥ - Final	Pass

* East's successive bids specifically mean : **strong** *first* suit (Ace or K Q), 4 + card Fit in opener's suit, 13/15 HLDF pts, and **nothing** in the **fourth suit** (no Ace or King or singleton or doubleton).

The opener concludes in 3 ♥, knowing of three sure direct losers in spades and one very likely in diamonds.

As the above examples show, beyond the use of successive *relays* to have one hand fully described economically, the second key characteristic of the **Optimal P**recision **R**elay method is its extensive use of *transfer* bid responses to the 1 ♥ and 1 ♠ openings.

On 1 ♥ and 1 ♠ openings, **all** responses at the level of 2 are **transfer** bids – that is bidding the suit *just below* the one being described, i.e. on a 1 ♥ opening, 1 NT is a *transfer* bid for clubs, 2 ♣ for diamonds, 2 ♦ for hearts, and 2 ♥ for spades.

Transfer bid responses are used in two specific cases :

A. With **weak** hands – less than **10** HL pts – **misfit** in the Major suit opened, with a **long** suit (or two) as a preferred alternative suit to play. The deal shown on page 129 is one example of it.

Here is another, with a two-suiter. The **second** suit bid **must** have 5 + cards :

	♠ A x x x x	♠ x
	♥ x x	♥ K J 10 x x
	♦ K x	♦ Q J x x x
	♣ K Q x x	♣ x x

1 ♠	2 ♣ (*Transfer* for diamonds)
2 ♦ (*Transfer* to ♦)	2 ♥ (5 + ♥, 4 + ♦, ♠ *misfit*)
Pass	

On a 1 ♠ opening, East has 8 HL **misfit** pts. Bidding both suits, showing a ♠ *misfit*, gives the opener a choice between hearts and diamonds.

B. Hands with a **4**-card **Fit** in the Major suit opened – those very hands which *traditional* bidding tries to describe through artificial conventions, *"splinter"* bids at the level of 4, and other "contorsions" !

In sharp contrast to that, the **Optimal** Precision Relay method uses *transfer* bid responses as *"trial"* bids to precisely and economically describe *specific* hands' features. These *transfer* bids at the level of **two** are combined with direct bids at the level of **three**, which are natural bids, **not** *transfer* bids. All of them have in common a 13/15 HLDF point zone and a 4-card Fit in the Major opened. The options are :

– Hands <u>with a singleton</u> *with* controls (Ace or K) in *both* other suits : **jump** directly to the level of **three** in the singleton suit.
– Hands <u>with a singleton</u> *without* controls (Ace or K) in *either* other suit : *transfer-Fit* first, at the level of **two**, followed by the singleton suit at the level of **three**.
– Hands <u>with a singleton</u>, a *strong side-suit* and *no* controls (Ace or K) in the *fourth* suit : the **strong** side-suit via a *transfer* bid at the level of **two**, followed by the singleton suit at the level of **three**.

Example hands of above responses – on a 1 ♥ opening :

♠ A x x x	♠ Q x x x	♠ x x x
♥ J x x x	♥ K x x x	♥ Q x x x
♦ K J x x	♦ Q J x x	♦ A J 10 x x
♣ x	♣ x	♣ x
14 HDF pts (no Q)	13 ½ HDF pts	14 HLDF pts (no K)
3 ♣ (singleton)	2 ♦ (♥) then 3 ♣	2 ♣ (♦) then 3 ♣
♦ & ♠ controlled	♦ & ♠ **not** controlled	**nothing** in spades

On the responder's most economical bid of 3 ♣, the opener can make one more *relay* to obtain further precisions on the responder's hand :

3 ♦ ?	3 ♥	: <u>5</u> ♥
	3 ♠	: 4 ♠
	3 NT	: nothing else to describe
	4 ♣	: Void in ♣

– On a 1 ♥ or 1 ♠ opening, the direct *transfer* bid of <u>2 ♠</u> is used, *conventionally*, to signal a **void** (vs a singleton), **and** a **5**-card trump support.

On partner's transfer to 2 NT, responder will identify his void : 3 ♣, 3 ♦ or 3 ♥ (♠ void). This bid corresponds to the *direct bid* of the singleton at the level of 3, that is **with** controls in both other suits, and with specifically : a **5**-card trump Fit in the suit opened, a void, and **16/18** HLDF pts, the points which correspond to the additional **2 D** pts (void vs singleton) and 1 Fit point (10 cards vs 9). *Precision, pertinent description !*

Compare this to the *traditional* "splinter" bid which, at the level of four, does **not** differentiate between a singleton or a void, 4 or 5 trumps, 15/17 or 16/18 pts, and says nothing about controls in *the other two suits* !...

Example hands for a 2 ♠ *transfer* response – on a 1 ♥ opening :

	♠ A x x x	♠ K x x x	♠ ---
	♥ J x x x x	♥ A x x x x	♥ Q x x x x
	♦ K J x x	♦ ---	♦ A x x x
	♣ ---	♣ K 10 x x	♣ K x x x
	16 HDF pts (no Q)	18 HLDF pts (no Q)	17 HDF pts
	2 ♠ then 3 ♣	2 ♠ then 3 ♦	2 ♠ then 3 ♥ (♠)

– Hands <u>without</u> a singleton with *one **strong** suit* (Ace or K Q) and **no** *control* in the *other two suits* : *transfer* bid the *strong* suit, followed by a raise, at the level of three, of the Major suit opened.
Example hands – on a 1 ♥ opening :

	♠ x x x	♠ Q x
	♥ Q J x x	♥ K J x x
	♦ K Q x x	♦ x x
	♣ x x	♣ K Q x x x
	13 HDF pts	15 HLDF pts
	2 ♣ (♦) then 3 ♥	1 NT (♣) then 3 ♥

The second bid of 3 ♥, invitational and very descriptive, is much more useful than its *traditional* counterpart's indicating *slam interest*. Such bids, with no specific meaning, have no place in a *relay* bidding method. *Relaying* is used, instead, in search of additional, useful information !

II. NATURAL BID FOLLOWING A FIRST RELAY

A first *relay* bid can be followed by a **natural** bid (non-relay) whenever the responder, instead of relaying, choses to : A) pass, or B) conclude directly in a part-score or game contract, or C) make an *invitational* bid, generally in the **10/12** point zone.
For this, the sole condition, for the responder, is to have **4** cards, or more, in the *other* Major suit. Thus, further development bids could be :

1 ♥   1 ♠ ? (relay)
1 NT : 12/14 HLD   2 ♣ : *relay*
                                     2 ♦ : 5 ♦, <u>4 ♠</u>, ♥ *misfit* or *semi-fit*   7/9 HL
                                     2 ♥ : ♥ *preference* <u>4 ♠</u> *no game* 7/9 HL
                                     2 ♠ : <u>5 ♠</u>, ♥ *semi-fit* 10/12 HL pts
                                     2 NT : Balanced, <u>4 ♠</u> ♥ *semi-fit* 10/12 HL
                                     3 ♣/3 ♦ : ♣/♦ singleton 3-card ♥ Fit <u>4 ♠</u>
                                                     10/12 HLDF pts
                                     Pass is ***not*** an option as opener could have 4 ♠

1 ♥   1 ♠ ? (relay)
2 ♣ : 5 ♥ 4 ♣, *denies* 4 ♠   Pass : ♥ *misfit* ♣ *preference* <u>4 ♠</u> 7/9 HL
       12/17 HLD   2 ♦ : *relay*
                                     2 ♥ : ♥ *preference* <u>4 ♠</u>   7/9 HL pts
                                     2 ♠ : <u>5 ♠</u>, ♥ *semi-fit*   10/12 HL pts
                                     2 NT : Balanced <u>4 ♠</u> ♥ *semi-fit* 10/12 HL
                                     3 ♣ : ♣ support <u>4 ♠</u> no ♥ Fit 10/12 HL
                                     3 ♦ : ♦ singleton 3-card ♥ Fit   <u>4 ♠</u>
                                                     10/12 HLDF pts

1 ♥   1 ♠ ? (relay)
2 ♦ : 5 ♥ 4 ♦, *denies* 4 ♠   2 ♥ : ♥ *preference* <u>4 ♠</u>   7/9 HL pts
       15/17 HLD   2 ♠ : *relay*
                                     2 NT : Balanced <u>4 ♠</u> ♥ *semi-fit* 7/9 HL
                                     3 ♣ : ♣ singleton 3-card ♥ Fit <u>4 ♠</u>
                                                     10/12 HLDF pts
                                     3 ♦ : ♦ support <u>4 ♠</u> no ♥ Fit 10/12 HL

Note that the 3 ♣ and 3 ♦ bids above describe **4 +** cards in the *other minor*
suit, as they guarantee **4 +** ♠, 3 ♥ and a ♣ or ♦ singleton.

1 ♥   1 ♠ ? (relay)
2 ♥ : 6 + ♥ 12/14 HLD   2 ♠ : *relay*
                                     2 NT : <u>5 ♠</u> *conventional* ♥ *misfit* 10/12 HL
                                     3 ♣/♦ : ♣/♦ singleton, ♥ Fit 10/12 HDF
                                     3 ♥ : ♠ singleton, ♥ Fit 10/12 HLDF

After a 2 ♠ rebid by opener, which specifically describes 4 ♥ and 4 ♠ :

1 ♥   1 ♠ ? (*relay*)
2 ♠ : 4 ♥ 4 ♠ **15/17** HLD   2 NT : **natural** / final – to play.
                                     3 ♣ : *relay*
                                     3 ♦ : ♦ *singleton* 4-card ♠ Fit 10/12 HDF

Most often, a first *relay*, followed by a *natural* bid, will be used for invitational hands of 10/12 HLDFit pts with a **3**-card Fit in the Major opened.

138

III. FUNDAMENTAL PRINCIPLES OF HAND DESCRIPTION ON RELAYS

Before covering the specific description process on responder's relays, let's first cover the **key principles** which govern such descriptions.

A. **Successive *relays*** : A *second* relay is **never** made in the **first** suit bid by the partner. Therefore :

1 ♥	1 ♠ ?
2 ♦ : 5 ♥ 4 ♦ 2nd relay is :	**2 ♠ ?** **not** 2 ♥

While *further* relays, the third one and on – which require a hand of 10 + pts – will be done in the suit just over the last suit bid by partner :

1 ♥		1 ♠ ?
2 ♦ : 5 ♥ 4 ♦		2 ♠ ?
3 ♣ : 5 ♥ 4 ♦ 3 ♣	3rd relay is :	3 ♦ ?
3 NT : 5 ♥ 4 ♦ 3 ♣ 1 ♠	Final	
3 ♥ : <u>6 ♥</u> 4 ♦ 3 ♣ 0 ♠	Final	
<u>3 ♠</u> : 5 ♥ <u>5 ♦</u> 3 ♣ <u>0 ♠</u>	Final	4th suit = void
4 ♣ : 5 ♥ 4 ♦ 4 ♣ 0 ♠	Final	

B. **Distributional** description : The **5 4 3** process : that is, the first suit bid has 5 cards, the second has 4 cards and the third has **3** cards. The third bid identifying a 3-card suit is key here as it describes **12** cards.

And the **corollary** of this process is just as fundamental : a third bid which does **not** describe a third suit **denies** a 3-card third suit i.e. a rebid of the **first** suit describes a <u>6</u> 4 2 1 hand while a rebid of the **second** suit describes a **5 <u>5</u> 2 1** hand.

– Thus, a third bid of **2 NT** promises **2** cards in the *last relay* bid and **denies** a singleton in that suit. Thus 2 NT will be bid **before** rebidding the first or second suit whenever this applies, while **not** bidding 2 NT first means that the hand has a singleton in the *last relay* bid. Examples :

1 ♥	1 ♠ ?	
2 ♦ : 5 ♥ 4 ♦	2 ♠ ? (relay)	
2 NT : 2 spades	3 ♣ ? (relay)	
3 ♦ : 5 ♥ <u>5 ♦</u> 2 ♠	thus ♣ singleton	
3 ♥ : <u>6 ♥</u> 4 ♦ 2 ♠	thus ♣ singleton	
3 NT : 5 ♥ 4 ♦ 2 2		

While with a singleton in the *last relay* bid, the bidding will be :

1 ♥	1 ♠ ? (relay)
2 ♦ : 5 ♥ 4 ♦	2 ♠ ? (relay)
3 ♦ : 5 ♥ <u>5 ♦</u>	denies 2 ♠, therefore : ♠ singleton, 2 ♣
3 ♥ : <u>6 ♥</u> 4 ♦	denies 2 ♠, therefore : ♠ singleton, 2 ♣

The **key principle** governing this description process is that a bid at the level of three **must always** describe the residual **4** cards left, after having described the first **9** cards of a two-suiter.

C. **Strength** description : The *"braking"* process :

A *relay* method would **not** fare better than *traditional* bidding if it used the same "jump" rebids to describe strong hands, such as :

1 ♥	1 ♠ ?
2 ♦ : 5 ♥ 4 ♦	11/15 H = **3** HLD zones : 13/15, 16/18, 19/20
3 ♦ : 5 ♥ 4 ♦	16/20 H = **2** HLD zones : 18/20, 21/23

Awful bidding which, at the level of **two**, describes point zones way too wide – and well outside the *"bidding safety level"* – and at the level of **three** describes no more than **9** cards.

A different process is clearly needed to differentiate : A) two HLD point zones, and **two only**, and B) **more** than just 9 cards.

And such a process exists – the *Monaco* process – and consists of **reversing** the *traditional* process : *"brake"* with *weaker* hands instead of *jumping* with *stronger* hands. And this process is rather simple and logical : the *"brake"* is bid **before** bidding the second 4-card suit when the two suits are **touching**, while the *"brake"* is bid **after** bidding the second 4-card suit when the two suits are **not** *touching*. Illustration :

1 ♥	1 ♠ ?
1 NT : "brake" **12/14** HLD	2 ♣ ? (relay)
2 ♦ : 5 ♥ 4 ♦	2 ♠ ? (relay)
3 ♣ : 3 ♣ **12** cards are described	

While in the **15/17** HLD point zone, the same hand will be bid :

1 ♥	1 ♠ ?
2 ♦ : 5 ♥ 4 ♦ **15/17** HLD	2 ♠ ? (relay)
3 ♣ : 3 ♣ **12** cards are described	

When the two suits are **not** touching, the "brake" is used **after** bidding the second suit, such as :

1 ♥	1 ♠ ?
2 ♣ : 5 ♥ 4 ♣	2 ♦ ? (relay)
2 ♥ : "brake" **12/14** HLD	2 ♠ ? (relay)
3 ♦ : 3 ♦ **12** cards are described	

While in the **15/17** HLD point zone, the same hand will be bid :

1 ♥	1 ♠ ?
2 ♣ : 5 ♥ 4 ♣	2 ♦ ? (relay)
3 ♦ : 3 ♦ **15/17** HLD **12** cards are described	

140

Note : The method's *"braking"* process, and its limitation to only *two* HLD point zones, enable *"light"* opening bids as a 5 4 3 1 hand can now be opened with **9 H** pts! Let's again illustrate this by reproducing here the two hands previously shown on page 43, which were :

♠ K Q x x	♠ A x x x
♥ A x x x x	♥ K x x x
♦ x x x	♦ x
♣ x	♣ x x x x

With 12 ½ **HLD** pts, West can open, and the auction could be :

1 ♥ (5 + ♥)	1 ♠
2 ♠ (4 ♠, 13/17 HLDF pts)	3 ♦ (♦ singleton, ♠ or ♥ Fit)
4 ♥	Pass

On East's 1 ♠ response, West's hand has 14 ½ HLDFit pts (+ 1 for the 8-card ♠ Fit + 1 for the ♣ singleton with 4 trumps) and, after East's *short-suit* 3 ♦ trial bid (11/13 Fit pts), West can add 2 pts for "no wasted honor pts" in diamonds : 16 ½ HLDF + 11 HLDF minimum = Game.
A little better than : Pass   Pass   *wouldn't you say ?...*

Note that this, in turn, eliminates the need for the *Drury* convention – intended to verify whether a 3rd or 4th hand opening *is below norm* or not. The **Optimal** Precision Relay's 1 ♥ and 1 ♠ "light" openings in any and all positions eliminate the need for even *lighter* openings.

In closing, one **critical observation** needs to be made : it has been said, by many, that a Relay method is excellent for finding games and slams but not so much when it comes to bidding part-score contracts – and that is generally true of most relay bidding methods which favor the description of hand shape over that of precise point zones to avoid space consuming jumps.
But that is certainly **not** true true of the **O**ptimal **P**recision **R**elay bidding method which gives **both** shape and point zone **equal** value – which is accomplished through replacing jumps by the economical "braking" process. The very knowledge of a hand's precise strength within a very narrow 3 HLD point zone known upon a player's rebid at the level of two makes the **O**ptimal **P**recision **R**elay unique and just as effective for bidding part-score contracts as it is for bidding games and slams.

This concludes the overview of the key principles which govern the 1 ♥ and 1 ♠ openings, responses and developments.
We can now cover, first, the 1 ♥ opening and further developments, and then the 1 ♠ opening and further developments.

1 ♥ Opening – RESPONSES AND DEVELOPMENTS

5 + ♥ any distribution	12/17 H**LD** pts	**9 +** H pts
4 ♥ 4 ♠	15/17 H**LD** pts	**9 +** H pts

Example hands opened 1 ♥ in **Optimal** Precision Relay :

♠ Q J x	K Q x	x x x	A x x x
♥ A J x x x	A x x x x x	K Q x x x	K Q 10 x
♦ x x	x	A Q J x	x
♣ K x x	J x x	x	A x x x
5 ♥ 3 3 2	6 ♥ 3 3 1	5 ♥ 4 3 1	4 ♥ 4 ♠
12 ½ HL pts	14 HLD pts	15 ½ HLD pts	17 HLD pts

As done for all previous openings, we will cover, first, the complete description of opener's hand on successive *relays*, before studying responses *other* than *relays*.

We will then cover the same description and responses after a 1 ♣ opening with the same hands of 18 + HLD pts and will close each section with example deals from tournaments and a summary table of full description bids as well as responses other than *relays*.

KEY PRINCIPLES – REMINDER

– **Responding** hands are counted in **HL** pts, with a *maximum* of **2 L** pts, initially. When a Fit of 8 cards, or more, has been found, then **total** points are counted in **HLDF**it pts.

7 HL pts are needed to respond, not 5 or 6, because the opener's hand is limited to **17** HLD pts. And 7 HL pts are sufficient to make a first *relay*, while **10 +** HL or HLDF pts will generally be needed for a *second* relay.

– Whenever possible, and pertinent, the method will endeavour to identify a singleton, in *either* hand, in order to assess *"wasted honor pts"*. This means that, in addition to describing **12** out of 13 cards, and therefore singletons, on successive *relays*, the method will use *"trial"* bids and *"mini-splinter"* bids to identify singletons.

– The responder will elect to *relay* when : A) No *specific descriptive* response corresponds to his hand, or B) He needs *more information* about opener's hand to find the "optimal" contract.

DESCRIPTION OF OPENER'S HAND ON SUCCESSIVE RELAYS

1. 6 + CARD SINGLE-SUIT HANDS : 12/14 HLD PTS.

In the 15/17 HLD point zone, these hands are opened 2 ♥.

Process : On a first *relay*, 1 ♠ : Opener **rebids** his long suit : 2 ♥
On a *second relay*, 2 ♠, the hand description is exactly the same as previously shown for the 2 ♥ opening − so, we will not repeat it here.
There is no need to memorize the descriptions below : just follow the key principles stated and use rational logic, when not sure.

2. BALANCED 5-CARD SINGLE-SUIT HANDS : 12/17 HL PTS.

Process : On a first *relay*, 1 ♠ : Opener bids NT : 2 NT directly with **15/17** HL pts, or, with **12/14** HL pts, 1 NT, *"brake"*, then 2 ♥.
On a *second relay*, he will then bid his doubleton : 3 ♦, 3 ♠, or 3 NT.

Therefore, such hands will be described as follows :

1 ♥		1 ♠ ?	1 ♥		1 ♠ ?
1 NT	12/14 HL pts	2 ♣ ?	2 NT	15/17 HL pts	3 ♣ ?
2 ♥	5 ♥ 3 3 2	2 ♠ ?		5 ♥ 3 3 2	
2 NT	5 ♥ 3 3 2 ♠	doubleton in the *relay* suit.			
			3 NT	doubleton in the *relay* suit.	
3 ♣	5 ♥ 3 3 2 ♣		3 ♦	5 ♥ 3 3 2 ♦	
3 ♦	5 ♥ 3 3 2 ♦		3 ♠	5 ♥ 3 3 2 ♠	

3. 4 ♥ 4 ♠ HANDS : 15/17 HLD PTS.

With **12/14** HLD pts, these hands are opened 1 ♠ and rebid 2 ♥.

Process : On a first *relay*, 1 ♠ : Opener **rebids** the other Major : 2 ♠.
That is the way the **Optimal** Precision Relay method ***immediately alerts*** the relayer that his hearts do **not** have **5** cards and that his hand is *specifically* **4 - 4** in the Majors.

On a *second relay*, of 3 ♣ (**not** 2 NT which is natural, to play), the opener bids 3 NT when 3 2 in the minor suits (*only case* where the residual 5 cards are not specifically described, whether 3 ♦ 2 ♣ or 3 ♣ 2 ♦), or his **third** suit : 3 ♦, if with 4 or 5 diamonds, or, *conventionally*, by 3 ♥ or 3 ♠, with 4 or 5 clubs. Therefore, such hands will be described as follows :

		1 ♥			1 ♠ ?	
		2 ♠	4 ♥ 4 ♠	15/17 HLD pts	3 ♣ ? (**not** 2 NT)	
With ♣ :	3 NT	4 ♥ 4 ♠ 3 ♣ 2 ♦ or 3 ♦ 2 ♣				
	3 ♥	4 ♥ 4 ♠ 4 ♣ 1 ♦	An *impossible* rebid = 4 4 4 ♣ 1 ♦			
	3 ♠	4 ♥ 4 ♠ 5 ♣ 0 ♦	An *impossible* rebid = 4 4 5 ♣ 0 ♦			

<u>With ♦</u> : 3 NT 4 ♥ 4 ♠ 3 ♦ 2 ♣ or 3 ♣ 2 ♦
              3 ♦   4 ♥ 4 ♠ <u>4 + ♦</u>   3 ♥ ?
              <u>3 ♠</u>   4 ♥ 4 ♠ <u>4</u> ♦ <u>1 ♣</u>   An *impossible* rebid = 4 4 4 ♦ 1 ♣
              <u>3 NT</u> 4 ♥ 4 ♠ <u>5</u> ♦ <u>0 ♣</u>   An *impossible* rebid = 4 4 5 ♦ 0 ♣

4. ALL OTHER HANDS / 5 + ♥ TWO-SUITERS : 12/17 HLD PTS.

Process : On a first *relay*, 1 ♠ : Opener bids his second suit ***directly*** when 15/17 HLD, and when 12/14 HLD, ***after*** *"braking"* with two suits touching, ***before*** *"braking"* with two suits **not** touching. Then, a 3-card suit, if any, will be bid next. The bidding will therefore be as follows :

4.1 With **clubs** as the *second* suit : 5 ♥ 4 ♣, 5 ♥ 5 ♣, 6 ♥ 4 ♣

The suits are **not** touching, therefore the *"braking"* will occur ***after*** bidding the second suit with **12/14** HLD pts. For hands **15/17** HLD pts, the description will be exactly the same but **without** the *"brake"*.

          1 ♥   1 ♠ ?
          2 ♣ : 5 ♥ 4 ♣   2 ♦ ?

First, with **diamonds** as the *third* suit :

	------ **12/14** HLD ------			------ **15/17** HLD ------	
5 ♥ 4 ♣ 2 2	2 ♥ *"brake"*	2 ♠ ?			2 ♦ ?
	2 NT : 2 ♠	3 ♣ ?	2 NT : 2 ♦	3 ♣ ?	
	3 NT		3 NT		
5 ♥ 4 ♣ 3 ♦ 1 ♠	2 ♥ *"brake"*	2 ♠ ?			2 ♦ ?
	3 ♦ : 3 ♦	3 ♥ ?	3 ♦ : 3 ♦	3 ♥ ?	
	3 NT Final		3 NT Final		
5 ♥ <u>5</u> ♣ 3 ♦ 0 ♠	2 ♥ *"brake"*	2 ♠ ?			2 ♦ ?
	3 ♦ : 3 ♦	3 ♥ ?	3 ♦ : 3 ♦	3 ♥ ?	
	4 ♣ : 5 ♣		4 ♣ : 5 ♣		
<u>6</u> ♥ 4 ♣ 3 ♦ 0 ♠	2 ♥ *"brake"*	2 ♠ ?			2 ♦ ?
	3 ♦ : 3 ♦	3 ♥ ?	3 ♦ : 3 ♦	3 ♥ ?	
	<u>3 ♠</u> 4th suit = *void* <u>6 ♥</u>		<u>3 ♠</u> 4th suit = *void* <u>6 ♥</u>		
<u>6</u> ♥ 4 ♣ 2 ♦ 1 ♠	2 ♥ *"brake"*	2 ♠ ?			2 ♦ ?
	3 ♥ Final		3 ♥ Final		
	with <u>2 ♠</u> 1 ♦ *bid* 2 NT *first*		*with* <u>2 ♠</u> 1 ♦ *bid* 2 ♠ *first*		
5 ♥ <u>5</u> ♣ 2 ♦ 1 ♠	2 ♥ *"brake"*	2 ♠ ?			2 ♦ ?
	3 ♣ : <u>5 ♣</u>	3 ♦ ?	3 ♣ : <u>5 ♣</u>	3 ♦ ?	
	3 NT Final <u>2</u> ♦ 1 ♠		3 NT Final <u>2</u> ♦ 1 ♠		
	with <u>2 ♠</u> 1 ♦ *bid* 3 ♠		*with* <u>2 ♠</u> 1 ♦ *bid* 3 ♠		

Now for the same hands, but with **spades** as the *third* suit :

	1 ♥	1 ♠ ?
	2 ♣ : 5 ♥ 4 ♣	2 ♦ ?

	------ **12/14** HLD ------	----- **15/17** HLD -----
5 ♥ 4 ♣ 3 ♠ 1 ♦	2 ♥ "brake" 2 ♠ ?	2 ♦ ?
	3 ♠ : 3 ♠ Final	3 ♠ : 3 ♠ Final
5 ♥ 4 ♣ <u>4</u> ♠ 0 ♦	*Not applicable* : opener will rebid spades **first**	
5 ♥ <u>5</u> ♣ 3 ♠ 0 ♦	2 ♥ "brake" 2 ♠ ?	2 ♠ : 2 ♠ 2 NT ?
	2 NT : 2 ♠ 3 ♣ ?	3 ♣ : 5 ♣ 3 ♦ ?
	3 ♠ : 3 ♠ <u>5 ♣</u>	3 ♠ : 3 ♠ <u>5 ♣</u>
<u>6</u> ♥ 4 ♣ 3 ♠ 0 ♦	2 ♥ "brake" 2 ♠ ?	2 ♦ ?
	2 NT : 2 ♠ 3 ♣ ?	2 ♠ : 2 ♠ 2 NT ?
	<u>3 ♦</u> : 4th suit = *void* <u>6 ♥</u>	<u>3 ♦</u> : 4th suit = *void* <u>6 ♥</u>
<u>6</u> ♥ 4 ♣ 2 ♠ 1 ♦	2 ♥ "brake » 2 ♠ ?	2 ♦ ?
	2 NT : 2 ♠ 3 ♣ ?	2 ♠ : 2 ♠ 2 NT ?
	3 ♥ <u>6 ♥</u> 2 ♠ 1 ♦ Final	3 ♥ <u>6 ♥</u> 2 ♠ 1 ♦ Final
5 ♥ <u>5</u> ♣ 2 ♠ 1 ♦	2 ♥ "brake" 2 ♠ ?	2 ♦ ?
	3 ♣ : 5 ♣ 3 ♦ ?	3 ♣ : 5 ♣ 3 ♦ ?
	3 ♠ Final	3 ♠ Final

4.2 With **diamonds** as the *second* suit : 5 ♥ 4 ♦, 5 ♥ 5 ♦, 6 ♥ 4 ♦

The suits are **touching**, therefore the *"brake"* will occur **before** bidding the second suit with **12/14** HLD pts. For hands **15/17** HLD pts, the description will be exactly the same but **without** the *"brake"*.

	------- **12/14** HLD -------	------ **15/17** HLD ------
	1 ♥ 1 ♠ ?	1 ♥ 1 ♠ ?
	1 NT : "brake" 2 ♣ ?	
	2 ♦ : 5 ♥ 4 ♦ <u>2 ♠</u> ?	2 ♦ : 5 ♥ 4 ♦ <u>2 ♠</u> ?
5 ♥ 4 ♦ 2 2	2 NT : 2 ♠ 3 ♣ ?	2 NT : 2 ♠ 3 ♣ ?
	3 NT	3 NT

First, with **clubs** as the *third* suit :

5 ♥ 4 ♦ 3 ♣ 1 ♠	3 ♣ : 3 ♣ 3 ♦ ?	3 ♣ : 3 ♣ 3 ♦ ?
	3 NT Final	3 NT Final
5 ♥ 4 ♦ <u>4</u> ♣ 0 ♠	3 ♣ : 3 ♣ 3 ♦ ?	3 ♣ : 3 ♣ 3 ♦ ?
	4 ♣	4 ♣

146

	------- 12/14 HLD -------		------ 15/17 HLD ------	
5♥ <u>5♦</u> 3♣ 0♠	3♣ : 3♣	3♦?	3♣ : 3♣	3♦?
	<u>3♠</u> : 4th *suit* = *void* = 5–5		<u>3♠</u>	
5♥ <u>5♦</u> 2♣ 1♠	3♦ : 5♦ 2♣ *with* <u>2♠</u> 1♣ *bid* 2 NT *first*			
<u>6♥</u> 4♦ 3♣ 0♠	3♣ : 3♣	3♦?	3♣ : 3♣	3♦?
	3♥ : 3♥		3♥ : 3♥	
<u>6♥</u> 4♦ 2♣ 1♠	3♥ Final		3♥ Final	
	with <u>2♠</u> 1♣ *bid* 2 NT *first*			

Now with **spades** as the *third* suit :

5♥ 4♦ 3♠ 1♣	3♠ : 3♠ Final		3♠ : 3♠ Final	
5♥ 4♦ <u>4♠</u> 0♣	*Not applicable here* : opener will rebid spades **first**			
5♥ <u>5♦</u> 3♠ 0♣	2 NT : 2♠	3♣?	2 NT : 2♠	3♣?
	3♦ : 5♦	3♥?	3♦ : 5♦	3♥?
	3♠ : 3♠ Final		3♠ : 3♠ Final	
<u>6♥</u> 4♦ 3♠ 0♣	2 NT : 2♠	3♣?	2 NT : 2♠	3♣?
	<u>3♠</u> : 3♠ 6♥		<u>3♠</u> : 3♠ 6♥	
<u>6♥</u> 4♦ 2♠ 1♣	2 NT : 2♠	3♣?	2 NT : 2♠	3♣?
	3♥ : 6♥		3♥ : 6♥	
5♥ <u>5♦</u> 2♠ 1♣	2 NT : 2♠	3♣?	2 NT : 2♠	3♣?
	3♦ : 5♦		3♦ : 5♦	

4.3 With **spades** as the *second* suit : 5♥ 4♠, 6♥ 4♠

The suits are **touching**, therefore, with **12/14** HLD pts, the *"brake"* will occur **before** bidding the second suit.
However, and this is a *unique exception*, for hands **15/17** HLD pts, the description *cannot be* to bid the second suit directly as this rebid is *reserved* for 4 ♥ 4 ♠ hands. Instead, the method uses *direct jumps*, at the level of **three**, into the *third* suit of 3 cards. This *conventionally* indicates that the *second* suit is the *other Major* : spades.

In this case, the responder may want to stop in 3 ♥ or 3 ♠ should the opener's *singleton* find *"wasted honor pts"* opposite the singleton.
Therefore, A) on a jump to 3 ♦, a *second relay* will **not** be possible, and B) the opener's rebid cannot be *beyond* 3 ♥, to allow the side to stop at 3 ♥.

As a result, some modifications to the normal description process needs to be made to describe hands in the 15/17 HLD point zone, shown next.

First, with **clubs** as the *third* suit :

	------- **12/14** HLD -------	------- **15/17** HLD -------
	1 ♥ 1 ♠ ?	1 ♥ 1 ♠ ?
	1 NT : *"brake"* 2 ♣ ?	
	2 ♠ : 5 ♥ 4 ♠ 2 NT ?	
5 ♥ 4 ♠ 2 2	3 NT	3 ♣ : <u>2 +</u> ♣ 3 ♦ ?
		3 NT Final 5 ♥ 4 ♠ 2 2
5 ♥ 4 ♠ 3 ♣ 1 ♦	3 ♣ : 3 ♣ 3 ♦ ?	3 ♣ : <u>2 +</u> ♣ 3 ♦ ?
	3 NT - Final	3 ♥ - 5 ♥ 4 ♠ <u>3 ♣</u> 1
5 ♥ 4 ♠ <u>4 ♣</u> 0 ♦	3 ♣ : 3 ♣ 3 ♦ ?	3 ♣ : <u>2 +</u> ♣ 3 ♦ ?
	4 ♣	4 ♣
5 ♥ <u>5 ♠</u> 3 ♣ 0 ♦ or 2 ♣ 1 ♦ *Not applicable* : with 5 ♠, it is opened 1 ♠		
6 ♥ 4 ♠ <u>2 ♣</u> 1 ♦	3 ♣ : <u>2 ♣</u> 3 ♦ ?	3 ♣ : <u>2 +</u> ♣ 3 ♦ ?
	3 ♥ : 6 ♥ <u>2 ♣</u>	<u>3 ♠</u> *: 6 ♥ <u>2 ♣</u>
		*3 ♠ : *impossible suit* : <u>6 ♥</u> 4 ♠ <u>3 ♣</u> 1 ♦
<u>6 ♥</u> 4 ♠ <u>3 ♣</u> 0 ♦	3 ♣ : <u>2 ♣</u> 3 ♦ ?	3 ♣ : <u>2 +</u> ♣ 3 ♦ ?
	4 ♦ : 4th suit = void = 3 ♣	4 ♦ : 4th suit = void

Now with **diamonds** as the *third* suit :

5 ♥ 4 ♠ 2 2	*Start with Clubs and then* 3 NT – *see above.*	
5 ♥ 4 ♠ 3 ♦ 1 ♣	3 ♦ - Final	3 ♦ - Final
5 ♥ <u>5 ♠</u> 3 ♦ 0 ♣ or 2 ♦ 1 ♣ *Not applicable* : with 5 ♠, it is opened 1 ♠		
<u>6 ♥</u> 4 ♠ <u>2 ♦</u> 1 ♣	3 ♥ - Final 6 ♥ <u>2 ♦</u>	3 ♥ - Final 6 ♥ <u>2 ♦</u>
<u>6 ♥</u> 4 ♠ 3 ♦ 0 ♣	<u>3 ♠</u> : 6 hearts - Final	<u>3 ♠</u> : 6 hearts - Final
5 ♥ 4 ♠ <u>4 ♦</u> 0 ♣	<u>3 NT</u> - Final	<u>3 NT</u> - Final
	Or 4 ♦ if 3 NT is found to be too *unnatural.*	

Note that the complete description of all 13 cards in all hands described above exceed the level of 3 NT only twice, in each point zone – thus allowing the use of 4 ♣ as a RKC Ask, rather than 4 NT, in most cases.

This concludes the detailed description of most hands opened 1 ♥. A **summary** of these descriptions appears on the following page.

SUMMARY OF HAND DESCRIPTION ON SUCCESSIVE RELAYS

DISTRIBUTION	ON 1 ♠ ?	2nd Relay	DESCRIPTION	FINAL BID
6 ♥ 3 2 2 6 ♥ 3 3 1	2 ♥	2 ♠ ?	*See 2 ♥* Opening	*See 2 ♥* Opening
7 ♥ 3 2 1	*Opened 2 ♥*	N/A	N/A	N/A
5 ♥ 3 3 2	1 NT/2 NT	3 ♣ ?	doubleton	3 ♦ / ♠ / NT
4 ♥ 4 ♠	2 ♠	3 ♣ ?	*conventional*	3 ♦ / ♥ / ♠ /NT
Two-suiters	The 2nd suit			
5 ♥ 4 ♣ / ♦	2 ♣ / 2 ♦	2 ♠ ?	2 NT *or*	3 NT *or*
5 ♥ 5 ♣ / ♦	2 ♣ / 2 ♦	2 ♠ ?		
6 ♥ 4 ♣ / ♦	2 ♣ / 2 ♦	2 ♠ ?	The 3rd suit	3 ♣ / ♦ / ♠
	12/14 HLD			
5 ♥ 4 ♠ 2 2	1NT / 2 ♠	2 NT ?	3 NT	3 NT
5 ♥ 4 ♠ 3 1	1NT / 2 ♠	2 NT ?	The 3rd suit	3 NT
6 ♥ 4 ♠	1NT / 2 ♠	2 NT ?		3 ♥
	15/17 HLD			
5 ♥ 4 ♠ 2 2	3 ♣		3 NT	3 NT
5 ♥ 4 ♠ 3 1	3 ♣/3 ♦	3 ♦ ?		3 NT
6 ♥ 4 ♠	3 ♣/3 ♥			3 ♥

RESPONSES OTHER THAN SUCCESSIVE RELAYS

DETERMINING PARAMETERS

The same three key parameters applying to responses over a 2 ♣ opening apply to the responses over a 1 ♥ opening : the hand's **strength**, the search for a **Fit in a Major** suit, and without such Fit, the search for a potential 3 NT contract.

1. The hand's **strength**, therefore its number of points.

As was the case for all openings previously covered, with fewer than 7 HL pts, the responder *passes*, while with **13 +** HL pts, he *relays*, unless his hand corresponds specifically to one of the *trial* bids previously covered. Therefore, here too, specific responses only apply to **7/12** point hands, in two point-zones : **7/9** and **10/12** pts.

149

2. The second parameter is to identify a potential **Fit** in a Major suit.

2.1 With a **4**-card Major, or both, the responder will *relay*, 1 ♠, with any hand of **7** + HL pts – to discover a potential **8**-card Fit in a Major.

2.2 With **5** + cards in the *other* Major, spades.

With **10/12** pts – game zone – the responder *relays* to discover the opener's hand distribution, followed by a natural bid, *propositional* or *concluding*.

With **7/9** pts and ♥ *misfit* (singleton or doubleton without honor) the responder **bids** his **5**-card Major directly : 2 ♥ *transfer* bid for spades. Over this response, the opener has three options :
– With a *misfit* or a *semi-fit* of **2** cards in spades, he will be disciplined and will *transfer* to 2 ♠, as asked.
– With a **Fit** of **3** or **4** cards, he will identify his singleton, if he has one : 3 ♣ or 3 ♦. **Without** a singleton, and 15/17 HLF pts, he will bid 2 NT or raise the Major to 3 ♠. Example :

♠ A x x x	♠ K Q x x x
♥ A K x x x	♥ x x
♦ x	♦ A x x x
♣ x x x	♣ x x

In **Optimal Precision Relay**, these two hands will be bid as follows :

1 ♥	2 ♥ (*Transfer* : 5 ♠, 7/9 HL)
3 ♦ * ("*mini-splinter*")	4 ♠

* **3 ♦** : " *mini-splinter*" i.e ♠ Fit, ♦ singleton, 15/17 HLDF pts.

With 1 additional point for 4 diamonds to the Ace opposite a singleton, East can count on 16 HLDF pts from partner + his own 11 ½ pts (+ 1 point for two doubletons) = 27 ½ pts = 4 ♠.

2.3 With a **3**-card Fit in the Major opened, hearts.

With **7/9** Fit pts and a good 4 + card minor suit – Ace or K Q – the responder will identify his minor-suit strength via a *transfer* bid (1 NT for clubs, 2 ♣ for diamonds) before indicating *both* his **3**-card ♥ support and his *minimum* hand by bidding 2 ♥.

Without a strong minor suit he will either *relay*, with 4 cards in the *other* Major, and then support hearts at the level of 2 ♥ = 10/12 HLDF pts, or, with 7/9 HLDF pts, he will raise ♥ directly, 2 ♦ (*transfer* bid for Hearts).

2.4 With a **4**-card Fit in the Major opened, hearts, and **13/15** HLDF pts, the responder will make a "*trial*" bid whenever his hand corresponds exactly to a specific "*trial*" bid. As a reminder, they are as follows :

– Hands <u>with**out** a singleton</u> with *one* **strong** suit (Ace or K Q) and **no** control in the *other two suits* : *transfer* bid the *strong* suit (1 NT for clubs, or 2 ♣ for diamonds, or 2 ♥ for spades), followed by a raise at the level of three : 3 ♥.

– Hands <u>with a singleton</u> **without** controls (Ace or King) in **either** other suit : **transfer-Fit** first, at the level of two : 2 ♦, followed by the singleton suit at the level of three.

– Hands <u>with a singleton</u> and a **strong side-suit** and **no** controls (Ace or King) in the **fourth** suit : *transfer* bid the **strong side-suit** at the level of two, followed by the singleton suit at the level of three.

– Hands <u>with a singleton</u> **with** controls (Ace or King) in **both** other suits : **jump** directly to the level of three in the singleton suit.

– Hands <u>with a **void**</u> **with** controls (Ace or King) in **both** other suits, a 5-card *trump support* in hearts and **16/18** HDF pts : direct *transfer* to **2 ♠**, *conventional*. On partner's *transfer* to 2 NT, responder will identify his void : 3 ♣ or 3 ♦ or 3 ♥ (for spades).

3. The third parameter is to facilitate the search for a NT game.

With**out** a 4-card or 5-card Major, the priority is obviously to look for a possible 3 NT Game. To do so, the responder will *relay* to discover the opener's hand *distribution* and *strength*.

This concludes the study of responses to the 1 ♥ opening. A summary of the **responses** can be found below.

SUMMARY OF RESPONSES TO A 1 ♥ OPENING

POINTS	w/o 4 or 5-card Major	*With* 4-card Major	*With* 5-card Major
< than 7	Pass	Pass	Pass
7 / 9	*Transfer* to minor suit	*Relay*	2 ♥ : *transfer* / ♠ or : *Relay*
10 / 12	*Relay*	*Relay*	*Relay*

UNUSUAL CONVENTIONAL BIDS TO "FLAG" (*INFREQUENT*)

OPENING	UNUSUAL CONVENTIONAL RESPONSE	POINTS
1 ♥	2 ♠ : <u>5</u> ♥, a **void**, *other* **2** suits controlled	<u>16/18</u> HDF

A few hands now to practice our **responses** to a 1 ♥ opening :

♠ A Q J x x x	♠ K x	♠ A x x x
♥ x	♥ x x x	♥ Q J x
♦ x x x	♦ K J 10 x	♦ K x x
♣ x x x	♣ x x x x	♣ x x x
9 ½ HL *misfit*	9 HDF (no Q)	11 ½ HF (4 3 3 3)
2 ♥ (♠) then *pass*	2 ♣ (♦) then 2 ♥	1 ♠ relay

♠ x x x	♠ x x x	♠ A x x
♥ Q x x x	♥ K J x x	♥ Q x x x x
♦ x	♦ A Q x x	♦ K x x x
♣ K Q x x x	♣ Q x	♣ ---
13 ½ HLDF	15 ½ HDF	17 HDF
1 NT (♣)/3 ♦	2 ♣ (♦)/3 ♥	2 ♠ (5 ♥, void)
nothing in ♠	*nothing in* ♠ & ♣	then 3 ♣, the void

---

5 + ♥ two-suiter   or   4 ♥ - 4 ♠   **18 +** HLD pts   Open 1 ♣

REBIDS, RESPONSES AND DEVELOPMENTS

OPENER'S REBID ON 1 ♦ RESPONSE

On a 1 ♦ response to a 1 ♣ opening, the opener's first rebid will be 1 ♥ with **18 +** HLD pts, as if he had opened 1 ♥, and further bidding developments beyond this rebid will be the very same as after a 1 ♥ opening.

RESPONSE OF 1 ♥ ON A 1 ♣ OPENING

The same applies to a direct response of 1 ♥ to a 1 ♣ opening, which will be made with **7/12** HL pts, *except* that the 1 ♥ response will also be a *transfer* for spades. The ambiguity between hearts and spades will be removed on the next rebid and this will be covered in the next chapter dealing with the 1 ♠ opening.

On responder's 1 ♥ bid, the opener's *transfer* to spades will be a *relay* on which the responder will further describe his hand as will be covered in the next chapter.

Let's conclude this chapter with some deals taken from tournaments :

Olympiads, 1980. Final, teams of four (France / USA).

♠ x x	♠ A J 10 x x
♥ A Q x x x	♥ K
♦ K x x	♦ J x x
♣ A Q x	♣ x x x x

At both tables, the bidding was identical, as follows :

1 ♥	1 ♠
2 ♣	3 ♠ (!!)

3 NT down two at both tables.

East, encouraged by the ♣ Fit (!) and by his King in partner's long suit, "rushes" to 3 ♠ ! And many pairs would likely bid the same way today...

But East's hand is only worth 7 pts ! (2 pts only for the ♥ King, minus 1 point for no Queen, minus 2 pts for the singleton in partner's long suit). In **Optimal** **P**recision Relay the bidding would be :

1 ♥	2 ♥ (*Transfer* for ♠)
2 ♠ (*Transfer* to ♠)	Pass

Cavendish tournament, London – 2011.

♠ A x x x	♠ K Q x
♥ A Q x x	♥ K J x x
♦ A	♦ Q J x
♣ J x x x	♣ A x x

The pair that finished second bid these hands as follows :

1 ♣	1 ♥
3 ♥	4 ♣ (control)
4 ♦ (control)	4 NT ? (RKC Blwood)
5 ♣ (3 clés)	6 ♥

Comment from the expert presenting the deal : « *simple, direct and fast. But the "wasted honor pts" in diamonds make it a bad slam ... ».*

But shouldn't a good bidding system detect *"wasted honor pts"* ? and **not** identifying one's singleton is hardly the way to do that... Instead of :

1 ♥	1 ♠ ?
2 ♠ (4 ♥ 4 ♠, 15/17 HLD)	3 ♣ ?
3 ♥ (4 ♥ 4 ♠ 4 ♣ 1 ♦)	4 ♥

The *"wasted honor pts"* in diamonds rule out a slam.
Just as simple, direct and fast – but more precise and... *more effective !*

FunBridge – Le Bridgeur, 2011.

♠ A x x	♠ J 10 x
♥ K Q J	♥ A x x x x
♦ K Q 10 x x x	♦ A x x
♣ Λ	♣ x x

The column's commentator analyses his own bidding and concludes that *"I was unable to find that East had **5** hearts to get to 7 ♥ instead of 6 ♦"*.

No reflexion on his part that he might be playing a flawed bidding system… Yet, it shouldn't be too complicated to bid up to 7 NT if you trade *dialogue* bidding for *monologue* bidding. Such as :

1 ♣	1 ♥ (5 + ♥, 7/12 HL)
1 ♠ ?	2 NT (5 ♥ 3 3 2, 10/12 HL)
3 ♣ ?	3 NT (♣ doubleton = 3 ♦)
4 ♣ ? (RKC Ask)	4 ♠ (2 Keys w/o ♥ Q)
7 NT	

No chance that East's 5 hearts will not be discovered !

Bidding contest – Le Bridgeur.

♠ A x	♠ x x x
♥ A x x x x	♥ K J 10 x x
♦ A K Q x x	♦ x x
♣ x	♣ A J x

The three participants in the bidding contest could only reach 6 ♥.
Just like the entire field at the tournament this deal comes from where only one pair bid the grand slam – presumably because the pairs did not communicate that they had 10 hearts, not just 9, or that West had 5 diamonds to A K Q, or both… Again, dialogue = imprecision.
*One has to wonder how such a failure from the entire field, with these two hands, did not lead to serious questioning of **all** existing bidding systems ?!...*

In **O**ptimal **P**recision **R**elay the bidding will be :

1 ♣ (18 + HLD pts)	1 ♥ (5 + ♥, 7/12 HL pts)
1 ♠ ? (relay)	2 NT (5 ♥ 3 3 2, 10/12 HL pts)
3 ♣ ? (relay)	3 ♦ (5 ♥ 3 3 2 ♦)
4 ♣ ? (RKC Ask, ♥ trump)	4 ♠ (2 Keys, w/o the ♥ Q)
7 ♥	

West knows everything about East's hand, making it easy to bid 7 ♥.
The *monologue* works both ways : one can see here the value of the *responder* describing precisely his hand to a 1 ♣ opener.

National Division 1, teams of four, 2014.

♠ K Q J x	♠ A x x
♥ A x x x	♥ K J 10 x
♦ K Q x	♦ J 10 x
♣ J 10	♣ x x x

The winning team bid :   1 NT   3 NT   Down two.

That's what "hiding" both 4-card Majors behind a NT opening can lead to !... In **Optimal P**recision **R**elay the bidding will be :

1 ♥ (5 + ♥, 12/17 HLD)	1 ♠ ?
2 ♠ (4 ♥ 4 ♠, 15/17 HLD)	3 ♣ ?
3 NT (4 ♥ 4 ♠ 3 2)	4 ♥

Beyond finding the ♥ Fit, the weak ♣ and ♦ suits favor the 4 ♥ contract over 3 NT.

National selection (France), Open, 2014.

♠ A x	♠ Q x
♥ K Q x	♥ A x x x x x
♦ A K J x	♦ Q x x x
♣ A J x x	♣ x

Only one pair out of four found the optimal contract of 7 ♦ − the 8-card ♦ Fit having, generally, not been identified.

In **Optimal P**recision **R**elay the bidding will be :

1 ♣ (18 + HLD)	1 ♥ (5 + ♥, 7/12 HL)
1 ♠ ?	1 NT (7/9 HL)
2 ♣ ?	2 ♦ (5 ♥ 4 ♦)
2 ♠ ?	2 NT (2 + spades)
3 ♣ ?	3 ♥ (6 ♥ 4 ♦ 2 ♠ 1 ♣)
4 ♣ ? (RKC Ask, trump ♥)	4 ♥ (1 Key Card)
5 ♦ ? (K & Q ♦ Ask)	5 ♠ (♦ Queen)
7 ♦	

West knows all he needs to know about East's hand. Bidding 7 ♦ is as Easy as can be !

BIDDING AFTER INTERVENTIONS OVER A 1 ♥ OPENING

The table below summarizes *suggested* bids by the opener's partner following an intervention by the opposite team over a 1 ♥ opening.

The suggested bids are guided by two key **principles** or **objectives** :

1. Over most interventions below 2 ♠, **double** is **not** for *penalty* : it is a *relay*. Over any *other* overcall, 3 ♥ and up, **double** is for penalty and applies when the opener's partner has **10 +** H pts.

2. **Retain**, when possible, the *Transfer* bids and *trial* bid responses which are very useful.

INTERVENTIONS over a 1 ♥ opening	SUGGESTED BIDS BY OPENER'S PARTNER **Key principles** : **Retain** 2 NT / 3 ♣ responses **Double** : *Relay* over 2 ♦ / ♥ / ♠ / 2 NT
Double (Take-out)	2 ♦ : *Relay* Same as **w/o** the take-out double 2 ♥, 2 ♠, 2 NT, 3 ♣, 4 ♣ : keep their meaning
1 ♠ (5 + ♠)	**Double** : *Relay* 2 ♥, 2 ♠, 2 NT, 3 ♣, 4 ♣ : keep their meaning 3 ♦ "cue-bid" : ♦ singleton 4 + card ♣ Fit 3 ♥, 3 ♠ : pre-emptive 7 + card suit, **no** ♣ Fit
1 NT	**Double** : *Relay* Replaces the 2 ♦ bid 2 ♠, 3 ♣, 4 ♣ : keep their meaning 2 NT : Same as 3 ♣ *but with **two** stoppers in hearts* 3 ♥ "cue-bid" : ♥ singleton 4 + card ♣ Fit
2 ♣ / 2 ♦ (5 + ♣ / ♦)	**Double** : *Relay* "***Sputnik***" type **with** 4 + hearts 3 ♣, 4 ♣ : keep their meaning 2 NT : Same as 3 ♣ *but with two stoppers in spades* 3 ♠ "cue-bid" : ♠ singleton 4 + card ♣ Fit
2 ♥ (Cue-bid)	**Double** : *Relay* "***Sputnik***" type with ♥ / ♠ 3 ♣, 4 ♣ : keep their meaning

1 ♠ Opening – **RESPONSES AND DEVELOPMENTS**

5 + ♠ any distribution	12/17 **HLD** pts	9 + H pts
4 ♠ 4 ♥	12/14 **HLD** pts	9 + H pts

DESCRIPTION OF OPENER'S HAND ON SUCCESSIVE RELAYS

1. 6 + ♠ SINGLE-SUIT HANDS : 12/14 HLD PTS.

These hands are opened 2 ♠ in the **15/17** HLD point zone.

Process : On a first *relay*, 1 NT : Opener **rebids** his long suit : 2 ♠.
On a *second relay*, 2 NT, the hand description is *exactly the same* as previously shown for the 2 ♠ opening – so, we will not repeat it here.
Here too, there is no need to memorize the descriptions below : just follow the key principles stated and use rational logic, when not sure.

2. BALANCED 5 ♠ SINGLE-SUIT HANDS : 12/17 HL PTS.

Process : On a first *relay*, 1 NT : with **15/17** HL pts, opener bids 2 NT *directly*; with **12/14** HL pts, he *"brakes"* first by bidding 2 ♣, then bids 2 NT on a 2 ♦ *relay*.
On the next *relay*, 3 ♣, he will then bid his *doubleton* : 3 ♦, 3 ♥, or 3 NT.

Therefore, such hands will be described as follows :

1 ♠		1 NT ?	1 ♠			1 NT ?
2 ♣	12/14 HL pts	2 ♦ ?	2 NT	15/17 HL pts		3 ♣ ?
2 NT	5 ♠ 3 3 2	3 ♣ ?		5 ♠ 3 3 2		
3 ♦	5 ♠ 3 3 2 ♦		3 ♦	*same as on the left*		
3 ♥	5 ♠ 3 3 2 ♥		3 ♥	*same as on the left*		
3 NT	5 ♠ 3 3 2 ♣	*The* doubleton in the *relay* suit.				

3. 4 ♠ 4 ♥ HANDS : 12/14 HLD PTS.

With **15/17** HLD pts, these hands are opened 1 ♥ and rebid 2 ♠.

Process : On a first *relay*, 1 NT, Opener **rebids** the other Major : 2 ♥. That is the way the **Optimal** Precision Relay method *immediately **alerts*** the relayer that the opener's spades are not by **5** cards and that his hand is *specifically* **4 - 4** in the Majors.

Like after a 1 ♥ opening, on a *second relay* of 3 ♣ (**not** 2 NT), the opener bids 3 NT with 3 2 in the minor suits (*only case where the distribution of the minor suits is not described*) or 3 ♥ or 3 ♠, conventionally, when 4 4 4 1 or 4 4 5 ♣ 0, or 3 ♦ with 4 + diamonds, followed, *conventionally*, by 3 ♠ or 3 NT whith hands distributed 4 4 4 ♦ 1 or 4 4 5 ♦ 0.

157

Therefore, such hands will be described as follows :

1 ♠				1 NT ?	
2 ♥	4 ♠ 4 ♥	**12/14** HLD pts		3 ♣ ?	

With ♣ : 3 NT   4 ♠ 4 ♥ 3 ♣ 2 ♦ or 3 ♦ 2 ♣

        3 ♥   4 ♠ 4 ♥ 1 ♦ <u>4 ♣</u>   ♥ *impossible* rebid = 4 4 1 4

        3 ♠   4 ♠ 4 ♥ 0 ♦ <u>5 ♣</u>   ♠ *impossible* rebid = 4 4 0 5

With ♦ : 3 ♦   4 ♠ 4 ♥ 4 + ♦   3 ♥ ?

        3 ♠   4 ♠ 4 ♥ <u>4 ♦</u> 1 ♣ ♠ *impossible* rebid = 4 4 4 1

        <u>3 NT</u> 4 ♠ 4 ♥ <u>5 ♦</u> 0 ♣   *impossible* rebid = 4 4 5 0

4. ALL OTHER HANDS / 5 + ♠ TWO-SUITERS : 12/17 HLD PTS.

Process : On a first *relay*, 1 NT : Opener ***bids*** his ***second*** suit ***directly***, when **15/17** HLD, and *"brakes"* first, 2 ♣, when **12/14** HLD. A 3-card *third* suit will be bid next. The bidding will therefore be as follows :

4.1 With **clubs** as the *second* suit : 5 ♠ 4 ♣, 5 ♠ 5 ♣, 6 ♠ 4 ♣

1 ♠	1 NT ?
2 ♣ : 5 ♠ 4 ♣	2 ♦ ?

First, with **diamonds** as the *third* suit :

	------- **12/14** HLD -------		------- **15/17** HLD -------	
5 ♠ 4 ♣ 2 2	2 ♠ *"brake"* 2 NT ?		2 NT : 2 ♦ 3 ♣ ?	
	3 NT : 2 ♥ 2 ♦		3 NT : 2 ♥ 2 ♦	
5 ♠ 4 ♣ 3 ♦ 1 ♥	2 ♠ *"brake"* 2 NT ?			2 ♦ ?
	3 ♦ : 3 ♦ 3 ♥ ?		3 ♦ : 3 ♦ 3 ♥ ?	
	3 NT - Final		3 NT - Final	
5 ♠ 5 ♣ 2 ♦ 1 ♥	2 ♠ *"brake"* 2 NT ?			2 ♦ ?
	3 ♦ : 2 + ♦ 3 ♥ ?		3 ♦ : 2 + ♦ 3 ♥ ?	
	4 ♣ : 5 ♣ <u>2 ♦</u> 1 ♥		4 ♣ : 5 ♣ <u>2 ♦</u> 1 ♥	
5 ♠ 5 ♣ 3 ♦ 0 ♥	2 ♠ *"brake"* 2 NT ?			2 ♦ ?
	3 ♦ : 2 + ♦ 3 ♥ ?		3 ♦ : 2 + ♦ 3 ♥ ?	
	4 ♦ : 3 ♦ 5 ♣		4 ♦ : 3 ♦ 5 ♣	
5 ♠ 4 ♣ <u>4 ♦</u> 0 ♥	*Not applicable* – with 4 ♦, opener rebibs 2 ♦ *first*			
6 ♠ 4 ♣ 2 ♦ 1 ♥	2 ♠ *"brake"* 2 NT ?			2 ♦ ?
	3 ♦ : 2 + ♦ 3 ♥ ?		3 ♦ : 2 + ♦ 3 ♥ ?	
	3 ♠ : 6 ♠ 2 ♦ 1 ♥		3 ♠ : 6 ♠ 2 ♦ 1 ♥	
6 ♠ 4 ♣ 3 ♦ 0 ♥	2 ♠ *"brake"* 2 NT ?			2 ♦ ?
	3 ♦ : 3 ♦ 3 ♥ ?		3 ♦ : 3 ♦ 3 ♥ ?	
	<u>4 ♠</u> 6 ♠ <u>3 ♦</u> 0 ♥		<u>4 ♠</u> 6 ♠ <u>3 ♦</u> 0 ♥	

Now for the same hands, but with **hearts** as the *third* suit :

```
1 ♠                1 NT ?
2 ♣ : 5 ♠ 4 ♣      2 ♦ ?
```

------- **12/14** HLD -------   ------ **15/17** HLD ------

5 ♠ 4 ♣ 3 ♥ 1 ♦	2 ♠ *"brake"* 2 NT ?	2 ♦ ?
	3 ♥ : 3 ♥ 3 ♠ ?	3 ♥ : 3 ♥ 3 ♠ ?
	3 NT Final	3 NT Final

5 ♠ 4 ♣ <u>4 ♥</u> 0 ♦   *Not applicable* – with 4 ♥ the opener *rebids Hearts*

5 ♠ <u>5 ♣</u> 2 ♥ 1 ♦	2 ♠ *"brake"* 2 NT ?	2 ♦ ?
	3 ♣ : 5 ♣ 3 ♦ ?	3 ♣ : 5 ♣ 3 ♦ ?
	3 ♥ - Final	3 ♥ - Final

5 ♠ <u>5 ♣</u> 3 ♥ 0 ♦	2 ♠ *"brake"* 2 NT ?	2 ♦ ?
	3 ♥ : 3 ♥ 3 ♠ ?	3 ♥ : 3 ♥ 3 ♠ ?
	4 ♣ : 5 ♣	4 ♣ : 5 ♣

6 ♠ 4 ♣ 2 ♥ 1 ♦   2 ♠ *"brake* 2 NT ?
<u>3 ♠</u> 6 ♠ <u>2 ♥</u> 1 ♦   <u>3 ♠</u> 6 ♠ <u>2 ♥</u> 1 ♦
with 2 ♦ 1 ♥ bid ♦ first

6 ♠ 4 ♣ 3 ♥ 0 ♦	2 ♠ *"brake"* 2 NT ?	2 ♦ ?
	3 ♥ : 3 ♥ 3 ♠ ?	3 ♥ : 3 ♥ 3 ♠ ?
	<u>4 ♦</u> : 4th suit = void <u>6 ♠</u>	<u>4 ♦</u> : 4th suit = void

4.2 With **diamonds** as the *second* suit : 5 ♠ 4 ♦, 5 ♠ 5 ♦, 6 ♠ 4 ♦

The suits are **not** *touching*, therefore the *"brake"* will occur **after** bidding the second suit with **12/14** HLD pts. For hands **15/17** HLD pts, the description will be exactly the same but **without** the *"brake"*.

```
1 ♠                1 NT ?
2 ♦                2 ♥ ?
```

------- **12/14** HLD -------   ------- **15/17** HLD -------

	2 ♠ : *"brake"* 2 NT ?	2 NT : 2 ♥ 3 ♣ ?
5 ♠ 4 ♦ 2 2	3 NT	3 NT

First, with **clubs** as the *third* suit :

5 ♠ 4 ♦ 3 ♣ 1 ♥	3 ♣ : 3 ♣ 3 ♦ ?	3 ♣ : 3 ♣ 3 ♦ ?
	3 NT - Final	3 NT - Final

5 ♠ 4 ♦ <u>4 ♣</u> 0 ♥	3 ♣ : 3 ♣ 3 ♦ ?	3 ♣ : 3 ♣ 3 ♦ ?
	4 ♣	4 ♣

	------- **12/14** HLD -------	------- **15/17** HLD -------
5 ♠ <u>5</u> ♦ 2 ♣ 1 ♥	3 ♦ : 5 ♦ <u>2</u> ♣	3 ♦ : 5 ♦ <u>2</u> ♣
	with <u>2</u> ♥ 1 ♣ bid 2 NT first	
5 ♠ <u>5</u> ♦ 3 ♣ 0 ♥	3 ♣ : 3 ♣ 3 ♦ ?	3 ♣ : 3 ♣ 3 ♦ ?
	4 ♦	4 ♦
6 ♠ 4 ♦ 2 ♣ 1 ♥	3 ♠ - Final	3 ♠ - Final
	with <u>2</u> ♥ 1 ♣ *bid* 2 NT *first, then* 3 ♠	
<u>6 ♠</u> 4 ♦ 3 ♣ 0 ♥	3 ♣ : 3 ♣ 3 ♦ ?	3 ♣ : 3 ♣ 3 ♦ ?
	<u>3 ♥</u> : 4th suit = void = <u>6 ♠</u>	*same as on the left*

Now with **hearts** as the *third* suit :

	1 ♠ 1 NT ?	1 ♠ 1 NT ?
	2 ♦ : 5 ♠ 4 ♦ 2 ♥ ?	2 ♦ : 5 ♠ 4 ♦ 2 ♥ ?
	2 ♠ *"brake"* 2 NT ?	
5 ♠ 4 ♦ 3 ♥ 1 ♣	3 ♥ : 3 ♥ - Final	3 ♥ : 3 ♥ - Final
5 ♠ 4 ♦ 4 ♥ 0 ♣	*Not applicable* – with 4 ♥ the opener bids ♥ *first*	
5 ♠ <u>5</u> ♦ 2 ♥ 1 ♣	3 ♦ : 5 ♦ 3 ♥ ?	2 NT : 2 ♥ 3 ♣ ?
	3 NT	3 ♦ : 5 ♦ 3 ♥ ?
		3 NT
5 ♠ <u>5</u> ♦ 3 ♥ 0 ♣	3 ♦ : 5 ♦ 3 ♥ ?	2 NT : 2 ♥ 3 ♣ ?
	4 ♣ = void = 5 5 3 0	3 ♦ : 5 ♦ 3 ♥ ?
		4 ♣ = void = 5 5 3
6 ♠ 4 ♦ 2 ♥ 1 ♣	3 ♠ : 6 ♠ 2 ♥ 3 ♣ ?	2 NT : 2 ♥ 3 ♣ ?
		3 ♠ : 6 ♠
6 ♠ 4 ♦ 3 ♥ 0 ♣	<u>4 ♣</u> = void = <u>6 ♠</u>	2 NT : 2 ♥ 3 ♣ ?
		3 ♥ : Final

4.3 With **hearts** as the *second* suit : 5 ♠ 4 ♥, 5 ♠ 5 ♥, 6 ♠ 4 ♥

The suits are **touching**, therefore the *"brake"* will occur **before** bidding the second suit with **12/14** HLD pts. However, for hands of **15/17** HLD pts, the description **cannot** be to bid the second suit directly as this rebid is *reserved* for 4 ♠ 4 ♥ hands.

As was done for the 1 ♥ opening, the method uses **direct jump**-rebids, at the level of **three**, into the *third* suit. This *conventionally* indicates that the *second* suit is the **other Major**: hearts. As was done with the 1 ♥ opening, modifications need to be made, as after a 3 ♦ rebid, there is no room for a second relay. These hands will be described as follows :

First, with **clubs** as the *third* suit :

	------- **12/14** HLD -------		------- **15/17** HLD -------	
	1 ♠	1 NT ?	1 ♠	1 NT ?
	2 ♣ : *"brake"*	2 ♦ ?		
	2 ♥ : 5 ♠ 4 ♥	2 NT ?		
5 ♠ 4 ♥ 2 2	3 ♣ : 2 + ♣	3 ♦ ?	3 ♣ : 2 + ♣	3 ♦ ?
	3 NT : 5 ♠ 4 ♥ 2 2		3 NT : 5 ♠ 4 ♥ 2 2	
5 ♠ 4 ♥ 3 ♣ 1 ♦	3 ♣ : 2 + ♣	3 ♦ ?	3 ♣ : 2 + ♣	3 ♦ ?
	3 ♥ : 3 + ♥	3 ♠ ?	3 ♥ : 3 + ♥	3 ♠ ?
	3 NT		3 NT	
5 ♠ <u>5</u> ♥ 2 ♣ 1 ♦	3 ♣ : 2 + ♣	3 ♦ ?	3 ♣ : 2 + ♣	3 ♦ ?
	3 ♥ : 3 + ♥	3 ♠ ?	3 ♥ : 3 + ♥	3 ♠ ?
	4 ♥ : <u>5 ♥</u>		4 ♥ : <u>5 ♥</u>	
6 ♠ 4 ♥ <u>2 ♣</u> 1 ♦	3 ♣ : 2 + ♣	3 ♦ ?	3 ♣ : 2 + ♣	3 ♦ ?
	3 ♠ : 6 ♠ 2 ♣ 1 ♦		3 ♠ : 6 ♠ 2 ♣ 1 ♦	

All other hands, three suiters with a **void**, are described, in the **15/17** point zone through a **jump** *following* an initial "**brake**" :

5 ♠ 4 ♥ <u>4 ♣</u> 0 ♦	3 ♣ : 2 + ♣	3 ♦ ?	<u>2 ♣</u>	2 ♦ ?
	4 ♣ : 4 ♣ 0 ♦		4 ♣ : 4 ♣ 0 ♦	
5 ♠ <u>5</u> ♥ 3 ♣ 0 ♦	3 ♣ : 2 + ♣	3 ♦ ?	<u>2 ♣</u>	2 ♦ ?
	3 ♥ : 3 + ♥	3 ♠ ?	3 ♥ Final 5 ♠ <u>5</u> ♥ 0 ♦	
	4 ♣ : 3 ♣ <u>5 ♥</u>			
<u>6 ♠</u> 4 ♥ <u>3 ♣</u> 0 ♦	3 ♣ : 2 + ♣	3 ♦ ?	<u>2 ♣</u>	2 ♦ ?
	<u>4 ♦</u> : <u>6 ♠ 4 ♥ 0 ♦</u>		3 ♠ : <u>6 ♠</u> 4 ♥ 0 ♦	

Now with **diamonds** as the *third* suit :

5 ♠ 4 ♥ 3 ♦ 1 ♣	3 ♦ : 3 + ♦	3 ♥ ?	3 ♦ : 3 + ♦	3 ♥ ?
	3 NT		3 NT	
5 ♠ 5 ♥ <u>2 ♦</u> 1 ♣	3 ♥ : 5 ♥ <u>2 ♦</u> Final		3 ♥ : 5 ♥ <u>2 ♦</u> Final	
	w/ 2 ♣ 1 ♦ bid 3 ♣ first			
6 ♠ 4 ♥ <u>2 ♦</u> 1 ♣	3 ♠ : 6 ♠ <u>2 ♦</u> 1 ♣		3 ♠ : 6 ♠ <u>2 ♦</u> 1 ♣	

All other hands, three suiters with a **void**, are described, in the **15/17** point zone through a **jump** *following* an initial "**brake**" :

5 ♠ 4 ♥ <u>4 ♦</u> 0 ♣	4 ♦ : 4 ♦ Final	2 ♣ : *"brake"*	2 ♦ ?
		4 ♦ : 4 ♦ <u>0 ♣</u>	

161

5 ♠ 5 ♥ <u>3</u> ♦ 0 ♣   3 ♦ : 3 + ♦   3 ♥ ?   2 ♣ : "*brake*"   2 ♦ ?
                 4 ♥ : 5 ♥   3 ♦ : 3 ♦   3 ♥ ?
                                                     3 NT

<u>6</u> ♠ 4 ♥ 3 ♦ 0 ♣   3 ♦ : 3 + ♦   3 ♥ ?   2 ♣ : "*brake*"   2 ♦ ?
                 3 ♠ : 6 ♠   3 ♦ : 3 ♦   3 ♥ ?
                                                     3 ♠ : 6 ♠

The summary table, below, recaps all above descriptions.

SUMMARY OF HAND DESCRIPTION ON SUCCESSIVE RELAYS

DISTRIBUTION	On 1NT ?	2nd Relay	DESCRIPTION	FINAL BID
6 ♠ 3 2 2 6 ♠ 3 3 1	2 ♠	2NT ?	See 2 ♠ Opening	See 2 ♠ Opening
7 ♠ 3 2 1	*Opened 2 ♠*	N/A	N/A	N/A
5 ♠ 3 3 2	2 NT / 3 NT	3 ♣ ?	doubleton	3 ♦ / ♥ / ♠
4 ♠ 4 ♥	2 ♥	<u>3 ♣</u> ?	***conventional***	3 ♦ / ♥ / ♠
Two-suiters	The 2nd suit			
5 ♠ 4 ♣ or 4 ♦				
5 ♠ 4 min 2 2	2 ♣ / 2 ♦	2 ♦ / ♥ ?	2 NT	3 NT
5 ♠ 4 min 3 1	"	"	The 3-card	3 NT
5 ♠ 5 min	"	"	suit	Rebid the minor
6 ♠ 4 min	"	"		Rebid ♠
	12/14 HLD			
5 ♠ 4 ♥ 2 2	2 ♣ / 2 ♥	2 NT ?	3 ♣	3 NT
5 ♠ 4 ♥ 3 1	"	"	The 3-card	3 NT
5 ♠ 5 ♥	"	"	Suit	
6 ♠ 4 ♥	"	"	The 3rd suit	
	15/17 HLD			
5 ♠ 4 ♥ 2 2	3 NT		3 ♣	3 NT
5 ♠ 4 ♥ 3 1	3 ♣ / 3 ♦	3 ♦ ?	3 ♥	3 NT
5 ♠ 5 ♥	3 ♥	3 ♠ ?		
6 ♠ 4 ♥	3 ♣ / 3 ♠	3 ♦ ?	3 ♠ Final	3 ♠

RESPONSES OTHER THAN SUCCESSIVE RELAYS

DETERMINING PARAMETERS

The *same three* key parameters applying to responses over a 2 ♣ opening apply to the responses over a 1 ♠ opening : the hand's **strength**, the search for a **Fit in a Major** suit, and without such Fit, the search for a potential 3 NT contract.

1. The hand's **strength**, therefore its number of points.

As was the case for all openings previously covered, with fewer than **7** HL pts, the responder *passes*, while with **13 +** HL pts, he *relays*, unless his hand *corresponds specifically* to one of the *"trial"* bids previously covered. Therefore, here too, specific responses only apply to **7/12** point hands : **7/9** and **10/12** pts.

2. The second parameter is to identify a potential **Fit** in a Major suit.

2.1 With a **4**-card Major, *or both*, the responder will *relay*, 1 NT, with any hand of **7 +** HL pts – to discover a potential 8-card Fit in a Major.

2.2 With **5 +** cards in the *other* Major, hearts.

With **10/12** pts – game zone – the responder will *relay* to discover the opener's hand distribution, followed by a *natural* bid, *propositional* or *concluding*.

With **7/9** pts and spade *misfit* (singleton or *doubleton without honor*) the responder **bids** his **5**-card Major *directly*, 2 ♦ *transfer* bid for hearts.
Over this response, the opener has three options :

– With a ***misfit*** or a ***semi-fit*** of 2 cards in hearts, he will be disciplined and will *transfer* to 2 ♥, as asked.

– With a ***Fit*** of **3** or **4** cards, he will identify his singleton, if he has one : 3 ♣ or 3 ♦. **Without** a singleton, and **15/17** HLF pts, he will bid 2 NT or raise the Major to 3 ♥.

2.3 With a **3**-card Fit in the Major opened, spades.

With **7/9** Fit pts and a good **4 +** card *minor* suit – Ace or K Q – the responder will identify his minor-suit *strength* via a *transfer* bid (1 NT for clubs, 2 ♣ for diamonds) before indicating *both* his 3-card ♠ support and his *minimum* hand by bidding 2 ♠.

Without a strong minor suit he will either *relay*, with 4 cards in the other Major, and then support spades at the level of 2 ♠ = 10/12 HLDF pts, or, with 7/9 HLDF pts, he will raise ♠ directly, 2 ♥ (*transfer* bid).

2.4 With a **4**-card Fit in the Major opened, spades, and **13/15** HLDF pts, the responder will make a *"trial"* bid whenever his hand corresponds exactly to a specific *"trial"* bid. As a reminder, they are :

– Hands with**out** a singleton with *one **strong** suit* (Ace or K Q) and **no** *control* in the *other two suits* : *transfer* bid the *strong* suit (2♣ for diamonds, 2 ♦ for hearts, etc.), followed by a raise at the level of 3 : 3 ♠.
– Hands with a singleton **without** *controls* (Ace or King) in **either** other suit : **transfer-Fit** first, at the level of 2 : 2 ♥ (for spades), followed by the singleton suit at the level of three.
– Hands with a singleton and a **strong side-suit** and **no** *controls* (Ace or King) in the **fourth** suit : *transfer* bid for the **strong side-suit** at the level of two, followed by the *singleton* suit at the level of three.
– Hands with a singleton **with** *controls* (Ace or King) in **both** other suits : **jump** *directly* to the level of 3 in the singleton suit.
– Hands with a **void** **with** *controls* (Ace or King) in **both** other suits, a 5-card *trump support* in spades and **16/18** HDF pts : direct *transfer-bid* to 2 ♠, *conventional*. On partner's *transfer* to 2 NT, responder will identify his void : 3 ♣ or 3 ♦ or 3 ♥.

3. The third parameter is to facilitate the search for a NT game.

With**out** a 4-card or 5-card Major, the priority is to look for a possible 3 NT Game. To do so, the responder will *relay*.

SUMMARY OF RESPONSES TO A 1 ♠ OPENING

POINTS	w/o **4** or 5-card Major	*W/*4-card Major	*With* 5-card Major
< than 7	Pass	Pass	Pass
7/9	**Transfer** to minor suit or raise	*Relay*	2 ♥ : *transfer /* ♠ or : *Relay*
10/12	*Relay*	*Relay*	*Relay*

UNUSUAL CONVENTIONAL BIDS TO "FLAG" (*INFREQUENT*)

OPENING	UNUSUAL CONVENTIONAL RESPONSE	POINTS
1 ♠	2 ♠ : 5 ♠, a **void**, *both other* suits controlled	16/18 HDF

---

5 + ♠ two-suiter or 4 ♠ - 4 ♥   18 + **HLD** pts   Open 1 ♣

REBIDS, RESPONSES AND DEVELOPMENTS

OPENER'S 1 ♠ REBID ON A 1 ♦ RESPONSE

On a 1 ♦ response to a 1 ♣ opening, the opener's first rebid will be 1 ♠ with **18 +** HLD pts, as if he had opened 1 ♠ and further bidding *developments* beyond this rebid will be the very same as after a 1 ♠ opening.

RESPONSE OF 1 ♠ (1 ♥) ON A 1 ♣ OPENING

The *same* applies to a direct response of 1 ♠ to a 1 ♣ opening, which will be made with **7/12** HL pts, *except* that it will be done through a **transfer** bid : 1 ♥ for spades.

On responder's 1 ♥ bid, the opener's *transfer* to 1 ♠ will be a *relay* on which the responder will describe *his* hand, in two point zones : 7/9 and **10/12** HL pts. However, the 1 ♥ *transfer* bid being either for hearts or spades, the next rebids will need to remove the ambiguity. How to do this will now be described.

1. 6 + ♠ OR ♥ SINGLE-SUIT HANDS : 10/12 HLD PTS.

On opener's transfer to 1 ♠, the responder's rebid will be 2 ♥ with 6 hearts, 2 ♠ with 6 spades. The ambiguity is immediately removed. The responder's next bids will be as previously outlined.

2. BALANCED 5 ♠ OR ♥ SINGLE-SUIT HANDS : 7/12 HL PTS.

On opener's *transfer* to 1 ♠, the responder's rebid will be **1** NT followed by 2 ♥ with 5 hearts, 2 ♠ with 5 spades.
Therefore, these hands will be described as follows :

1 ♣	1 ♥ (*transfer* for spades)
1 ♠ (*transfer*)	1 NT 5 ♥ or ♠ 3 3 2
2 ♣ (relay)	2 ♥ : 5 ♥ 3 3 2 then 2 NT with 7/9 HL pts
	above 2 NT with 10/12 HL pts
	2 ♠ : 5 ♠ 3 3 2 then 3 ♣ with 7/9 HL pts
	above 3 ♣ with 10/12 HL pts

followed by the doubleton.

3. TWO-SUITERS WITH ♦ OR ♣ AS A SECOND SUIT : 7/12 HL PTS.

After the 1 ♥ *transfer* for spades, the responder will bid his **minor** suit : 2 ♣ with clubs, 2 ♦ with diamonds, followed by his 5 + card Major. Therefore, these hands will be described as follows :

1 ♣	1 ♥ (*transfer* for spades)
1 ♠ (*transfer*)	2 ♣ : 4 + clubs
2 ♦ (relay)	2 ♥ : 5 ♥ 4 ♣ then 2 NT with 7/9 HL pts above 2 NT with 10/12 HL pts
	2 ♠ : 5 ♠ 4 ♣ then 3 ♣ with 7/9 HL pts above 3 ♣ with 10/12 HL pts

1 ♣	1 ♥ (*transfer* for spades)
1 ♠ (*transfer*)	2 ♦ : 4 + diamonds
2 ♥ (relay)	2 ♠ : 5 ♠ 4 ♦ 7/9 HL pts above 2 ♠ with 10/12 HL pts

With 5 ♥ and 4 ♦, *touching* suits that do not allow a *relay* bid between them, the *conventional* **direct** response of 2 ♠ on a 1 ♣ opening will be used to describe this two-suiter, in one point-zone only, 9/12 HL pts. The rest of the hand's distribution will be described on a 2 NT *relay*.

Note: *Players unconfortable with **transfer** responses to a 1 ♣ opening can easily forego this approach and respond, instead, with "**natural**" bids, i.e. 1 ♥ for hearts, 1 ♠ for spades, 1 NT for balanced hands, etc. each in 2 point zones of 7/9 and 10/12 HL pts.*

4. TWO-SUITERS WITH BOTH MAJORS, 7/12 HL PTS.

The importance of these two-suiters, including 4 ♠ 4 ♥, requires that they be immediately identified upon the responder's first rebid.

To do so, the responder's **first** bid on a 1 ♣ opening will be to bid 1 ♠, *transfer* for **NT**, followed by a 2 ♣ rebid, *conventionally* describing the two Majors, either 4 ♠ 4 ♥ or 5 + ♠ 4 ♥ or 5 + ♥ 4 ♠.

On the opener's 2 ♦ *relay*, the responder will then bid 2 ♥ with 5 + hearts, 2 ♠ with 5 + spades, or 2 **NT** with 4 ♠ 4 ♥, 7/9 HL pts, and above 2 NT with 10/12 HL pts.

These hands will therefore be described as follows :

1 ♣	1 ♠ (*transfer* for NT)
1 NT (*transfer*)	2 ♣ : Major two-suiter
2 ♦ (relay)	2 ♥ : 5 + ♥ 4 ♠ then 2 NT with 7/9 HL pts above 2 NT with 10/12 HL pts
	2 ♠ : 5 + ♠ 4 ♥ then 3 ♣ with 7/9 HL pts above 3 ♣ with 10/12 HL pts
	2 NT : 4 ♠ 4 ♥, 7/9 HL pts then the hand's balance
	3 ♣ : 4 ♠ 4 ♥ 3 ♣, 10/12 HL pts.
	3 ♦ : 4 ♠ 4 ♥ 3 ♦, 10/12 HL pts.
	3 ♥ : 4 ♠ 4 ♥ 4 ♦ 1 ♣, 10/12 HL pts.
	3 ♠ : 4 ♠ 4 ♥ 5 ♦ 0 ♣, 10/12 HL pts.

Let's conclude this chapter with deals taken from tournaments :

« *The Precision Bidding System* », C.C. Wei. 1971.

♠ A Q x x	♠ K x x x x
♥ K Q x x	♥ x x
♦ x	♦ x x x
♣ K x x x	♣ Q J x

In his 1971 book presenting the Precision Club bidding system, the author used the above deal to illustrate the system's 2 ♦ opening – *three-suiter short* in diamonds, **11/15** H pts. He bids these two hands and comments on the auction as follows :

2 ♦	3 ♠ !
4 ♠	

« *Knowing, right from the opening bid, that his partner is short in diamonds – no "wasted honor pts" – and assured of a ♠ Fit, East can make a game invitation by jumping to 3 ♠, on which the opener, near maximum with 14 H pts, can bid to game. How many pairs would find this game with only 20 H pts ?* ».
To which he adds, with great honesty : « *It is true that 3 ♠ might fail should West have one King only, instead of two* ».

But it is precisely the 11/15 H point zone, *way too wide* to respect the *"bidding safety level"*, which makes this opening *unplayable* and the jump to 3 ♠ totally unreasonable !
In **Optimal** **P**recision **R**elay, the bidding will be :

1 ♥ (5 + ♥, 12/17 HLD)	1 ♠ ? (relay)
2 ♠ (4 ♥ 4 ♠, **15/17** HLD)	3 ♣ ? (relay)
3 ♥ (4 ♥ 4 ♠ 4 ♣ 1 ♦)	4 ♠

16 HLD pts + 7 HL pts + 3 Fit pts in ♠ + 2 pts for *"no wasted honor pts"* in diamonds = 28 HLDF pts = 4 ♠. While, with only one King *instead of two*, the opening would be 1 ♠, **not** 1 ♥, and the bidding would be :

1 ♠	1 NT ? (relay)
2 ♥ (4 ♠ 4 ♥, **12/14** HLD)	2 ♠ - Final

This time, East stops in 2 ♠ as, even if West has a ♦ singleton, the total number of points will be 3 pts less than in the first case, that is 25 HLDF pts, instead of 28 = **no** game.

« *Readers' mail* », 2008.

♠ A K x x x x	♠ Q x x x
♥ x	♥ K x x
♦ A x x x	♦ K x x x
♣ x x	♣ A x

« Our bidding was :   1 ♠   3 NT (♠ Fit, 13/15 HLD)
                                    4 ♦

« On 3 NT, West bid his diamond control and we ended up in 6 ♠, down two. Where did we go wrong ? ».
Reply from the expert handling the Readers' mail : *« One must be a dreaming optimist to encourage a slam with West's hand!* **Pass** *would have been more reasonable... ».*

But then a slam would be missed with East having the ♦ Queen, instead of the ♠ Queen, and this hand :

                              ♠ J x x x
                              ♥ A x x
                              ♦ K Q x x
                              ♣ K x

Once again, it is the player's judgment that is being questioned rather than *the bidding system!* Yet, it seems clear that it is the 3 NT bid – and the 10 bidding steps it is "burning" in the process – that is questionable !

In **Optimal** Precision Relay, the bidding would be :

    1 ♠ (5 + ♠, 12/17 HLD)   1 NT ? (relay)
    2 ♦ (5 ♠ 4 ♦)   2 ♥ ? (relay)
    3 ♣ (2 + ♣, 15/17 HLD)   3 ♦ ?
    3 ♠ (6 ♠ 4 ♦ 2 ♣ 1 ♥)   4 ♣ ? (RKC Ask, ♠ trump)
    4 ♦ (3 Key Cards)   6 ♦ or 6 ♠

With the East hand submitted by the Reader, on West's 4 ♦ bid, East will know that the ♦ Queen is missing as, if West had it, it would give him 18 HLD pts and he would have opened 1 ♣, not 1 ♠. He will conclude in 4 ♠. While with the second hand, East will bid on to 6 ♦ or 6 ♠ !

Bridge World, 2010.

    ♠ A K x x x   ♠ Q J x
    ♥ A x x   ♥ K x x
    ♦ x x   ♦ K x x x
    ♣ K x x   ♣ A x x

The bidding was :   1 ♠   2 ♦
                    2 ♠   4 ♠

Down one on a ♦ lead through the ♦ King. 3 NT would have been safe. The expert presenting the deal asks the following question : *"When is it preferable to play 3 NT rather than 4 ♥ or 4 ♠ with an 8-card Fit"* ?

168

The answer is : more often than not, when you have a 5 3 3 2 hand opposite a 4 3 3 3 hand i.e. when the trump support hand offers *no ruffing value* while the 5-card suit will contribute the same number of tricks for a 9-trick contract that it would for a 10-trick contract.

Thus, the importance of knowing the precise distribution of a hand.

In **Optimal** Precision Relay, the bidding would be :

1 ♠   1 NT ?

2 NT (5 ♠ 3 3 2, 16 HL)   3 NT

The right contract – bid, furthemore, from the *more appropriate* hand, with the ♦ King protected against a ♦ lead !

One final example, taken from a Bridge book :

♠ A K x x x	♠ x
♥ K x x x	♥ Q J 10 x x x
♦ x	♦ x x x
♣ A x x	♣ x x x

In the tournament this deal comes from, the bidding was most often :

1 ♠   Pass

And the 4 ♥ game was missed.

In **Optimal** Precision Relay, the bidding would be :

1 ♠   2 ♦ (*transfer* for hearts)

3 ♦ (*mini-splinter*)   4 ♥

After his 2 ♦ *transfer* bid, East intended to *pass* on West's transfer to hearts. But West's *mini-splinter* indicates a 4 card ♥ fit and a ♦ *singleton* and asks East to bid 4 ♥ with no "wasted honor pts" in diamonds and 7 + HLDF pts. *Pertinent description, precise, simple and effective !*

Now, we are ready to discover and study the unique 4 ♣ Key Card Ask specific to the **Optimal** Precision Relay bidding method.

OPTIMAL **4** ♣ **6** KEY CARD ASK

Unique and **specific** to the **Optimal Precision Relay** method
RESPONSES AND DEVELOPMENTS

PREAMBULE

The first criterion signaling that a slam can be contemplated is when a partnership knows it has the **points** for it as well as two "fitting" hands. This requires an accurate point count as well as a bidding method that identifies, as precisely as possible, the hands' distribution.
Two criteria that are best met by the **Optimal** point count combined with the **Optimal** Precision Relay bidding method.

Next is the need to identify the Key Cards held to reach the optimal contract. And, as these Key Cards most often include Kings **and** Queens, to obtain that information dictates that a Key Card Ask be as economical as possible – certainly at a much lower level than 4 NT.
That is precisely what the **Optimal** Precision Relay method attempts to achieve, most often, through a Key Card Ask at the level of 4 ♣, when all suits are "controlled", and at the level of 4 ♦, when all suits are **not** controlled or when the relayer's hand has a void.

Furthermore, the method's 4 ♣ Key Card Ask provides **responses** to the 4 ♣ Ask considerably more precise than those provided by the Roman Key Card 4 NT Blackwood. As we will see, those responses are unique and specific to the **Optimal** Precision Relay method as they are only possible with point zones of **precisely** 3 HLD pts.
Before studying these specific responses and further developments, let's identify what makes the **Optimal** Precision Relay's 4 ♣ Key Card Ask far superior to the RKC 4 NT Blackwood :

1. The method's 4 ♣ Ask occurs only after the distribution of the hand interrogated has been *precisely described* to his partner. This eliminates the need to identify a void through a *conventional* jump.

2. In RKC Blackwood, the first two responses, 5 ♣ and 5 ♦, do **not** describe the trump Queen. A further asking bid is needed to find out whether responder has it, or not. At such a high level, this makes the 4 NT Blackwood rather useless! The **Optimal** Precision Relay method avoids this handicap by combining, in its first two responses to a 4 ♣ Ask, **1** Key Card with **3** Key Cards (instead of 4).

The method makes that possible because it precisely **zones** the point-range of any hand to **3** points (whether H, HL, HLD or HLDF), enabling it to avoid, in most cases, a potential confusion between 1 Key and 3 Keys. Still, we will see that the method has devised 3 different ways to clear up a potential confusion.

Thus, a 4 ♦ response describes 1 or 3 Key Cards **without** the trump Queen while a 4 ♥ response describes 1 or 3 Key Cards **with** the trump Queen. A *significant improvement* over the 4 NT RKC Blackwood Ask !

3. "Control *cue-bids*", preliminary to a Blackwood Ask when needed, are **not** used in **Optimal** Precision **R**elay. Instead, when all four suits are not "controlled" or when the inquirer has a void, the method uses a unique 4 ♦ Ask – as this economical asking bid becomes available in a *monologue* process where one player asks and his partner answers.

4. Because of its economical level, a 4 ♣ Asking bid allows **more** than four direct responses, notably 5 ♣, 5 ♦ and 5 ♥ – without exceeding the level of five in a Major suit.

5. Last, but not least, the **Optimal** Precision **R**elay 4 ♣ Ask does not need to resort to the wild "contortions" devised for the RKC Blackwood, such as : the "*induced*" Blackwood, the "*exclusion*" Blackwood, and others such as the "*controlwood*"…

THE OPTIMAL 4 ♣ 6 KEY CARD ASK

This **4 ♣ 6 Key C**ard **A**sk will be identified as the Optimal 4 ♣ 6 Key Card Ask, abbreviated as : OKC 4 ♣ Ask.
The **6 Key C**ards refers to the fact that the trump Queen is identified as a Key Card : the **4** Aces, the trump **K**ing **and** the trump Queen.

PRINCIPLES AND APPLICATIONS

– "Assumed" trump suit. The method, using a *monologue* process, does not identify a trump Fit through raises, other than through "*trial*" bids or "*mini-splinter*" bids. Upon an Optimal 4 ♣ KC Ask, the "*assumed*" trump suit will be defined as the responder's *longest* suit described.
When the responder has described two suits of equal length, the *assumed* trump suit will be the *highest ranking* of the two suits.
Note that the "*assumed*" trump suit may **not** be the trump suit ultimately selected by the inquirer.

After a "*trial*" bid or a "*mini-splinter*" bid, the *assumed* trump will be the actual trump identified.

– Whenever the relayer has *prematurely* stopped relaying, a 4 ♣ bid is natural, **not** an Optimal KC 4 ♣ Ask.

– Just as is the case for a 4 NT Blackwood, *all four suits* should be "controlled" (no suit with *two* direct losers) to use an OKC 4 ♣ Ask.
Nor should the *inquirer* have a void. In these two cases, the method uses a **4 ♦** inquiry, which will be studied later in a specific chapter.

An exception to the above rule can occasionally be made (rare) when a **minor** suit is **not** controlled – whenever a Control Ask can subsequently be made in that specific suit.

RESPONSES TO THE 4 ♣ ASK AND FURTHER DEVELOPMENTS

There are **7** direct responses to the OKC 4 ♣ Ask, from 4 ♦ to 5 ♥.
We will study, first, the first 4 direct responses – the most frequent –
4 ♦, 4 ♥, 4 ♠ and 4 NT, before studying the next 3 : 5 ♣, 5 ♦ and 5 ♥.

I. THE FIRST 4 DIRECT RESPONSES AND FURTHER INQUIRIES

– The first 4 direct responses inform on **all 6 Key Cards**, including the trump Queen, as follows :

    4 ♦   : **1** or **3** or **5** Key Cards **without** the trump Queen.
    4 ♥   : **1** or **3** or **5** Key Cards **with** the trump Queen.
    4 ♠   : **0** or **2** or **4** Key Cards **without** the trump Queen.
    4 NT : **0** or **2** or **4** Key Cards **with** the trump Queen.

– Upon either response, the next bid from the inquirer will either be a conclusion **or a further** asking bid in a *specific* suit inquiring about the King and Queen in that suit. We will call it : the K & Q suit Ask.
Such subsequent specific inquiry will, of course, never inquire about the trump suit, whose holding has previously been revealed in the first direct response.

– There are **4** responses to such suit-specific inquiries, as follows :

    First step   : **No** King or Queen in that suit
    Second step : **Queen** in that suit
    Third step   : **King** in that suit
    Fourth step : King **and** Queen in that suit

Illustration : The "assumed" trump suit is Hearts.
      4 ♣ ? (OKC Ask)   4 ♦ (1 Key Card *without* the trump Q)
      4 ♠ ? (K & Q ♠ Ask)   5 ♣ (♠ Q)

– To save bidding space, after the first response to a 4 ♣ OKC Ask, the method uses the 4 NT bid to inquire about the King and Queen in the *highest ranking suit* – other than the *assumed* trump suit, of course.

Illustrations :

1) 4 ♣ ? with ♥ as **trump** :   <u>4 ♦</u> : 1 or 3 Key Cards w/o the ♥ **Q**

    4 ♥ Conclusion – as trump is hearts

    4 ♠ ? : **K** & **Q** Ask in ♠   4 NT : Neither **K** nor **Q** of spades
                                       5 ♣ : ♠ Queen
                                       5 ♦ : ♠ King
                                       5 ♥ : ♠ King **and** Queen

    4 NT ? : **K** & **Q** Ask in ♦   5 ♣ : Neither **K** nor **Q** of diamonds
                                       5 ♦ : ♦ Queen
                                       5 ♥ : ♦ King
                                       5 ♠ : ♦ King **and** Queen

2) 4 ♣ ? with ♠ as **trump** :   4 ♦ : 1 or 3 Key Cards w/o the ♠ **Q**

    4 ♥ ? : **K** & **Q** Ask in ♥   4 ♠ : Neither **K** nor **Q** of hearts
                                       4 NT : ♥ Queen
                                       5 ♣ : ♥ King
                                       5 ♦ : ♥ King **and** Queen

    4 ♠ Conclusion – as trump is spades

    4 NT ? : **K** & **Q** Ask in ♦   5 ♣ : Neither **K** nor **Q** of diamonds
                                       5 ♦ : ♦ Queen
                                       5 ♥ : ♦ King
                                       5 ♠ : ♦ King **and** Queen

---

1) 4 ♣ ? with ♥ as **trump** :   <u>4 ♥</u> : 1 or 3 Key Cards **with** the ♥ **Q**

    Pass Conclusion – as trump is hearts

    4 ♠ ? : **K** & **Q** Ask in ♠ 4 NT : Neither **K** nor **Q** of spades
                                       5 ♣ : ♠ Queen
                                     5 ♦ : ♠ King
                                     5 ♥ : ♠ King **and** Queen

    4 NT ? : **K** & **Q** Ask in ♦   5 ♣ : Neither **K** nor **Q** of diamonds
                                       5 ♦ : ♦ Queen
                                     5 ♥ : ♦ King
                                     5 ♠ : ♦ King **and** Queen

2) 4 ♣ ? with ♠ as **trump** :   4 ♥ : **1** or **3** Key Cards **with** the ♠ **Q**

    4 ♠ Conclusion − as trump is spades

    4 NT ? : **K** & **Q** Ask in ♥ 5 ♣ : Neither **K** nor **Q** of hearts
                                   5 ♦ : ♥ Queen
                                   5 ♥ : ♥ King
                                   5 ♠ : ♥ King **and** Queen

    5 ♣ ? : **K** & **Q** Ask in ♣ 5 ♦ : Neither **K** nor **Q** of clubs
                                   5 ♥ : ♣ Queen
                                   5 ♠ : ♣ King
                                   5 NT : ♣ King **and** Queen

---

1) 4 ♣ ? with ♥ as **trump** :   4 ♠ : **0** or **2** Key Cards **w/o** the ♥ **Q**

    4 NT ? : **K** & **Q** Ask in ♠ 5 ♣ : Neither **K** nor **Q** of spades
                                   5 ♦ : ♠ Queen
                                   5 ♥ : ♠ King
                                   5 ♠ : ♠ King **and** Queen

    5 ♣ ? : **K** & **Q** Ask in ♣ 5 ♦ : Neither **K** nor **Q** of clubs
                                   5 ♥ : ♣ Queen
                                   5 ♠ : ♣ King
                                   5 NT : ♣ King **and** Queen

2) 4 ♣ ? with ♠ as **trump** :   4 ♠ : **0** or **2** Key Cards **w/o** the ♠ **Q**

    Pass Conclusion − as trump is spades

    4 NT ? : **K** & **Q** Ask in ♥ 5 ♣ : Neither **K** nor **Q** of hearts
                                   5 ♦ : ♥ Queen
                                   5 ♥ : ♥ King
                                   5 ♠ : ♥ King **and** Queen

---

Let's now look at some example hands to illustrate the **Optimal** KC 4 ♣ Ask in action.

Bidding contest, 1978 − Le Bridgeur.

        ♠ A Q J x   ♠ K x x x
        ♥ A K x   ♥ x x
        ♦ A x   ♦ x x
        ♣ K Q x x   ♣ A x x x x

In the tournament the above deal comes from, very few pairs found the ♠ grand slam and neither did the contest's participants.

Most could only reach 6 ♣ or 6 ♠ – thanks to the handicap caused by a 2 ♣ opening… Instead of:

1 ♣ (18 + HLD)	1 NT (5 + ♣, 7/12 HL)
2 ♣ ?	2 ♠ (4 ♠, 7/9 HL)
2 NT ?	3 NT (5 ♣ 4 ♠ 2 2)
4 ♣ ? (trump is ♣)	4 ♦ (1 Key w/o the ♣ Q)
4 ♠ ? (K & Q ♠ Ask)	5 ♦ (♠ King)
7 ♠	

All suits are controlled : the 4 ♣ Ask can be used.
West knows everything about East's hand and can count 13 tricks : 5 clubs, 4 spades, 3 hearts with one ruff, and the ♦ Ace.

National selection, 2013.

♠	K	♠	A x
♥	A x x x	♥	x
♦	Q x x	♦	A J x x x
♣	A K x x x	♣	Q J x x x

Half the field did not find the 6 ♣ slam, concluding in 3 NT or 5 ♣.

This example includes an intervention, which has no impact on the **Optimal P**recision **R**elay bidding which would be as follows :

1 ♣ (18 + HLD)	1 ♥	double (relay)
2 ♣ (5 + ♣)		2 ♦ ?
2 ♥ (5 ♣ 4 ♥, 18/20 HLD)		2 ♠ ?
3 ♦ (♦ tripleton)		3 ♥ ?
3 NT (5 ♣ 4 ♥ 3 ♦ 1 ♠)		4 ♣ ? (trump is ♣)
4 ♦ (3 Keys w/o the ♣ Q)		4 NT ? (K & Q ♦ Ask)
5 ♦ (♦ Queen)		6 ♣

West, with 18 + HLD pts and a ♠ singleton, guarantees that he controls clubs : a 4 ♣ Ask can be used. And no confusion is possible between 1 or 3 Key Cards for the same reasons. 4 NT is a ♦ Ask as 4 ♥ or 4 ♠ would have asked about ♥ or ♠.
East knows all about West's hand and that a response to his 4 NT Ask that exceeds the level of 5 ♣ (♦ Q or K) will allow to play 6 ♣.
And had West indicated ♦ K Q (5 ♠), it is 7 ♣ that would be bid !

National division, mixed pairs, 2012.

♠	J	♠	A x x x
♥	K Q 10 x	♥	A J x
♦	K x x	♦	A x
♣	A J 10 x x	♣	K x x x

A large majority of pairs bid as follows :

1 ♣	1 ♠
1 NT (!)	3 NT

And the 6 ♣ slam was missed. *World-class bidding, in 2012* ? Bidding that fails to identify West's 5 clubs or 4 hearts or ♠ singleton !

But West's hand has 18 ½ HLD pts, not 13 H / 15 HD pts! And these hands would be bid as follows in **Optimal** Precision Relay bidding :

1 ♣ (18 + HLD)	1 ♦ ?
2 ♣ (5 + ♣)	2 ♦ ?
2 ♥ (5 ♣ 4 ♥, 18/20 HLD)	2 ♠ ?
3 ♦ (♦ tripleton)	3 ♥ ?
3 NT (5 ♣ 4 ♥ 3 ♦ 1 ♠)	4 ♣ ? (trump is ♣)
4 ♦ (1 Key w/o the ♣ Q)	4 ♥ ? (K & Q ♥ Ask)
5 ♦ (♥ K Q)	6 ♣

East knows that a response to his 4 ♥ Ask which would exceed the level of 5 ♣ will enable his side to play 6 ♣ as, with 18 + HLD pts, West necessarily has either ♦ K Q or ♣ J 10, and 2 spades can be ruffed.

"Le Dentu's column", 1981 – Le Bridgeur.

The question asked was : « *What is your response, in East, with the following 5 – 5 two-suiter, on partner's 1 ♠ opening* ? » :

♠ A K x x x x	♠ x
♥ A J x	♥ Q 10 x x x
♦ Q	♦ A K x x x
♣ A x x	♣ x x

In one room, East bid 1 NT and West jumped directly to 4 ♠, down one, doubled. In the other room, East bid 2 ♦ and the side ended up in 6 NT! Ah, these wonderful *dialogue* exchanges in *traditional* bidding ! The right contract is 6 ♥. In **Optimal** Precision Relay bidding :

1 ♣ (18 + HLD)	2 ♠ (5 + ♥ 4 ♦, 9/12 HL)
2 NT ?	3 ♦ (5 ♥ 5 ♦)
3 ♥ ?	3 NT (5 ♥ 5 ♦ 2 ♣ 1 ♠)
4 ♣ ? (trump is ♥)	4 ♥ (1 Key with the ♥ Q)
4 NT ? (K & Q ♦ Ask)	5 ♥ (♦ King)
6 ♥	

West knows his side to be in slam zone right upon East's 2 ♠ bid (22 HLD pts + 1 Fit point opposite 9 + HL pts minimum = 32 pts) .
West's 4 NT Ask is for diamonds, the highest ranking suit – spades being a singleton and hearts are trump. Finding 6 ♥ becomes easy.

« *Bidding contest* », 1978 – Le Bridgeur.

♠ A Q x x x x	♠ K J
♥ x x	♥ A x
♦ A Q x	♦ K J x x
♣ A x	♣ K x x x x

In the tournament this deal comes from, not a single pair found the 7 ♠ contract, much less 7 NT! And the contest's participants did no better. The **Optimal** Precision Relay bidding would be as follows :

1 ♣ (18 + HLD)	1 ♦ ?
2 ♠ (6 + ♠, 18/20 HLD)	2 NT ?
3 ♦ (♦ tripleton *or* singleton)	3 ♥ ?
3 NT (6 ♠ 3 ♦ 2 2)	4 ♣ ? (trump is ♠)
4 ♥ (3 Keys **with** the ♠ Q)	5 ♦ ? (K & Q ♦ Ask)
5 ♠ (♦ Queen)	7 NT !

As straightforward and economical as can be! And the key is, of course, to be able to assess the significant value of the two Jacks in East's hand.

Final of National division, teams of four, 2010 – Le Bridgeur.

♠ A x x x x x	♠ x
♥ A K x	♥ Q J x x x
♦ K Q x	♦ A J 10 x x
♣ x	♣ x x

At one table, the bidding was as follows :

1 ♠	1 NT
2 NT (forcing)	3 ♦ (*Transfer* for hearts)
3 ♥ (♥ Fit)	4 ♥

The diamonds were not mentioned, neither were the ♠ and / or ♣ singletons – and the slam was missed. At the other table, the bidding was :

1 ♠	1 NT
3 ♦	4 ♦
4 ♠	Pass

This time, it is the hearts that are not mentioned, nor were the singletons. The slam was missed here too, but worse yet the trump played has only 7 cards when the side has two 8-card Fits! Wow! Instead of :

1 ♣ (18 + HLD)	2 ♠ (5 + ♥ 4 ♦, 9/12 HL)
2 NT ?	3 ♦ (5 ♦)
3 ♥ ?	3 NT (5 ♥ 5 ♦ 2 ♣ 1 ♠)
4 ♣ ? (trump is ♥)	4 ♥ (1 Key w / the ♥ Q)
6 ♥	

Regional tournament, pairs, 2009.

<table>
<tr><td>♠ A K Q x x</td><td>♠ J 10 x</td></tr>
<tr><td>♥ A x x x</td><td>♥ K Q 10 x x</td></tr>
<tr><td>♦ x x</td><td>♦ A</td></tr>
<tr><td>♣ K x</td><td>♣ A x x x</td></tr>
</table>

Only 21 pairs out of 84 (25 %), were able to bid these hands to a grand slam, of which only 6 found the *optimal* contract of 7 NT.
In **Optimal** Precision **Relay**, the bidding would be :

1 ♣ (18 + HLD)	1 ♦ ?
1 ♠ (5 + ♠)	1 NT ?
2 ♣	2 ♦ ?
2 ♥ (5 ♠ 4 ♥, 18/20 HLD)	2 NT ?
3 NT (5 4 2 2)	4 ♣ ? (trump is ♠)
4 ♥ (3 Keys w/the ♠ Q)	5 ♣ ? (K & Q ♣ Ask)
5 ♠ (♣ King)	7 NT

In view of East's honors, West, with 18 + HLD pts, necessarily controls spades. So, a 4 ♣ Ask can be used. And no confusion is possible about West's number of Key Cards. East knows everything about West's hand and can count 13 tricks for 7 NT.
Had West indicated nothing in clubs, East would have inquired about West's holding in diamonds (5 NT ?) – knowing that 7 ♠ was guaranteed. Note that these two hands add up to 38 HLF pts, not 32 HL pts…

It is hard to imagine staying with *traditional, dialogue* bidding after such a fiasco with these two hands loaded with top honors !

« *Enchérodrome* », 2011   Le Bridgeur.

<table>
<tr><td>♠ A R x x</td><td>♠ D V x x x x</td></tr>
<tr><td>♥ A R x</td><td>♥ x</td></tr>
<tr><td>♦ A V x x</td><td>♦ x x</td></tr>
<tr><td>♣ R x</td><td>♣ A x x x</td></tr>
</table>

This time, we are blessed : bidding these hands is a pair playing a strong Club *and* relays. Should be a delight ! Their bidding was :

1 ♣	1 ♦ ? (relay)
2 NT (balanced, 22 + H pts)	3 ♣ ? (relay)
3 ♦ (4 3 3 3 or 4 ♦ and 4 ♠)	3 ♥ ? (relay)
3 ♠ (4 ♦ and 4 ♠)	4 ♦ ? (relay)
4 ♠ (3 Aces & all controls)	4 NT ? (relay)
5 ♥ (♠ & ♥ K's w/o the ♦ K)	6 ♠

Oops ! East, unaware of West's ♣ doubleton, settled for 6 ♠…

Surreal! Why design such a complex system that won't enable your side to uncover the distribution of the ♥/♣ residual – and, worse yet, one which has the **weak** hand of 7 H pts **relay** to have the hand of 22 H pts described ?!... Obviously, just playing a strong club and relays does not do the trick *unless the bidding system makes sense* !...

In **Optimal** Precision Relay, the bidding would be :

1 ♣	1 ♥ (*transfer* for ♠, 7/12 HL)
1 ♠ ?	2 ♣ (4 ♣)
2 ♦ ?	2 ♠ (5 ♠ 4 ♣, 7/9 HL)
2 NT ?	3 ♦ (2 + ♦)
3 ♥ ?	3 ♠ (6 ♠ 4 ♣ 2 ♦ 1 ♥)
4 ♣ ? (trump is ♠)	4 ♥ (1 Key w/the ♠ Q)
7 ♠	

East knows that he will be able to ruff two clubs for 13 tricks.

Let's now look at developments following responses of 4 ♠ and 4 NT :

International tournament, 2011.

♠ A Q x x	♠ K J x x
♥ A x x x	♥ x
♦ J 10 x x x	♦ A K x x x
♣ ---	♣ Q 10 x

In the tournament this deal comes from, only one pair found the 7 ♦ grand slam. Comment from the deal's reporter : « *Once the ♠ fit has been found, how to also find the ♦ 10-card fit and play 7 ♦ instead of 6 ♠ ? Only one pair could – and the spades were divided 4 - 1* ».

While the **Optimal** Precision Relay bidding would be as follows :

1 ♥	1 ♠ ?
2 ♠ (4 ♥ 4 ♠, 15/17 HLD)	2 NT ?
3 ♠ (5 ♦ 0 ♣)	4 ♣ ? (trump is ♦)
4 ♠ (2 Keys w/o the ♦ Q)	4 NT ? (K & Q ♠ Ask)
5 ♦ (♠ Q)	7 ♦

All suits are controlled : a 4 ♣ Ask can be used. And no confusion is possible on West's number of Key Cards because of his 15 + HLD pts.

Istanbul Olympiads, 2004.

♠ A J 10 x x x	♠ K x x x
♥ x	♥ x x x x
♦ K x	♦ A Q x x
♣ A x x x	♣ x

Here is an example of a 4 ♣ Ask following a "trial" bid in **Optimal** **Precision Relay** :

1 ♠ (5 + ♠, 12/17 HLD)	2 ♣ (*Transfer* for diamonds)
2 ♥ ? (Strong - forcing)	3 ♣ (♣ singleton, "trial" bid)
3 ♦ ? (relay)	3 ♥ (4 ♥ = 4 4 4 1, 13/15 pts)
4 ♣ ? (trump is ♠)	4 ♠ (2 Keys w/o the ♠ Q)
5 ♦ ? (K & Q ♦ Ask)	5 ♠ (♦ Queen)
6 ♠	

The precision of East's "trial" bid – ♦ Ace or K Q, nothing in hearts, 13/15 HLDF pts – enables West to add 1 point for his 6th spade + 2 pts for *"no wasted honor pts"* in hearts = 20 pts + 13 minimum = slam zone and the 4 ♣ Ask applies just as it would after successive relays with spades as trump, as established by the "trial" bid.
West, aware of East's 4 spades, knows he does not need the ♠ Q.
East cannot have 0 Key Cards, having previously described the ♦ Ace.

National selection, teams of four, 2007 – Le Bridgeur.

♠ A J x x x	♠ K Q x
♥ K x x	♥ A x
♦ A x x x	♦ K Q x x x
♣ x	♣ x x x

Both teams stopped in 4 ♠, missing the slam.

In **Optimal** **P**recision **R**elay, the bidding would be :

1 ♠ (5 + ♠, 12/17 HLD)	1 NT ?
2 ♦ (5 ♠ 4 ♦)	2 ♥ ?
3 ♥ (3 ♥, 16 HLD)	3 ♠ ?
3 NT (5 4 3 1 ♣)	4 ♣ ? (trump is ♠)
4 ♠ (2 Keys w/o the ♠ Q)	4 NT ? (K & Q ♥ Ask)
5 ♥ (♥ King)	6 ♠

East knows his side is in slam zone right upon West's 2 ♦ rebid !
No confusion is possible about West's number of Key Cards with 15 + HLD pts and his ♣ singleton.

*One wonders how **any** bidding system can miss bidding this slam, in 2007?!*

Regional tournament, 2009.

♠ A J x x x x	♠ K x x x
♥ A Q x	♥ K x
♦ x	♦ A x x x x
♣ Q x x	♣ A x

In **Optimal** Precision **R**elay, the bidding would be :

2 ♠ (6 + ♠, 16 HLD)	2 NT ?
3 ♦ (♦ tripleton or singleton)	3 ♥ ?
3 ♠ (6 ♠ 3 3 1 ♦)	4 ♣ ? (trump is ♠)
4 ♠ (2 Keys **w/o** the ♠ Q)	4 NT ? (K & Q ♥ Ask)
5 ♦ (♥ Queen)	7 ♠

No confusion is possible about West's Key Cards : without the ♠ Queen he cannot have **0** Keys with **15/17** HLD pts and a ♦ singleton.

East knows everything about West's hand : with 10 spades to A K he does not need the ♠ Queen. He can bank on 6 ♠ upon West's 4 ♠ bid and looks for a potential grand slam by asking for his hearts holding. Once the ♥ Queen known, East can bid 7 ♠ : sluff his losing club on the ♥ Queen followed by the ruffing of two clubs.

« *Bidding contest* », 2008.

♠ x x	♠ A x x x x
♥ A Q x x x x	♥ K x x
♦ K x x	♦ A x
♣ A x	♣ K Q x

In **Optimal** Precision **R**elay, the bidding will be :

2 ♥ (6 + ♥, 15/17 HLD)	2 ♠ ?
2 NT (6 ♥ 3 2 2)	3 ♣ ?
3 ♦ (6 ♥ 3 ♦ 2 2)	4 ♣ ? (trump is ♥)
4 NT (2 Keys **w/**the ♥ Q)	5 ♦ ? (K & Q ♦ Ask)
5 NT (♦ King)	7 ♥

East knows all about West's hand and can count 6 tricks in hearts, one in spades, 5 in minor suits plus one diamond ruff.

No confusion is possible about West's number of Keys : without the King and Queen in diamonds, West cannot have **0** Keys with 15 HLD pts (1 point would have to be deducted for no Ace).

« *Bidding contest* » - Le Bridgeur, 2011.

♠ A Q x x x	♠ K J x
♥ x	♥ A x x
♦ x x x	♦ A x x
♣ A Q x x	♣ K J x x

Here, one must avoid picking the wrong trump suit : there is **no** slam in spades, with a 5 – 3 Fit, while there is 7 ♣, with a 4 – 4 Fit.

In **Optimal** Precision **R**elay, the bidding will be :

1 ♠ (5 + ♠, 12/17 HLD)	1 NT ?
2 ♣	2 ♦ ?
3 ♦ (5 ♠ 4 ♣ 3 ♦, 16 HLD)	3 ♥ ?
3 NT (5 ♠ 4 ♣ 3 ♦ 1 ♥)	4 ♣ ? (trump is ♠)
4 NT (2 Keys, w/the ♠ Q)	5 ♣ ? (K & Q ♣ Ask)
5 ♥ (♣ Queen)	7 ♣

No confusion is possible about West's number of Key Cards : he cannot have 0 Keys with 15/17 HLD pts and a ♥ singleton (Q 10 in clubs, K Q J in diamonds and Q 10 in spades would only add up to 12 pts after deducting 1 point for no Ace).

East knows everything about West's hand and can count 4 tricks in clubs, 5 in spades, the two red Aces and ruffing two hearts.

« *Enchérodrome* », 2013 – Le Bridgeur.

♠ A K x	♠ Q x x x
♥ K J 10 x x	♥ A x x x
♦ A	♦ K Q x x x
♣ K Q x x	♣ ---

The above deal in this *"bidding challenge"* comes from the Division 1 National Championship, teams of four. The ♥ *grand* slam must **not** be bid **without** the ♥ Q. Only 4 teams out of 10 bid the right contract of 6 ♥. 4 pairs played 7 ♥, one played 6 NT (down one), and another 5 ♥.

In **Optimal** Precision **R**elay, the bidding will be :

1 ♣ (18 + HLD)	1 ♠ (*transfer* for NT, 7/12 HL)
1 NT ?	2 ♣ (Major two-suiter)
2 ♦ ?	3 ♠ (4 ♥ 4 ♠ 5 ♦, 10/12 HL)
4 ♣ ? (trump is ♦)	4 NT (2 Keys w/the ♦ Q)
5 ♥ ? (K & Q ♥ Ask)	5 ♠ (no ♥ K or Q)
6 ♥	

No confusion is possible about East's number of Key Cards : with 10/12 HL pts and a ♣ void, he cannot have 0 Keys : ♦ Q J 10, the ♥ Q and ♠ Q J would only give East 8 ½ HL pts (- 1 point for no King).

On East's 4 NT bid, West needs the ♥ Queen for 7 ♥, thus the 5 ♥ Ask. Without the ♥ Queen, he settles for 6 ♥ (the ♠ Queen is not needed : ruff one diamond and two spades in dummy reversal play).

Occasionally, inquiring about Jacks may be possible. Here is an example.

<pre>
    ♠ A x x   ♠ K Q J x
    ♥ K Q J x   ♥ A x x
    ♦ A x x   ♦ K Q J x
    ♣ x x x   ♣ A x
</pre>

The bidding will be :

<pre>
    1 NT (12/14 HL)   2 ♣ ? (relay- Stayman)
    2 ♥   (4 ♥)   2 ♠ ? (forcing – relay)
    2 NT (4 ♥ 3 3 3)   4 ♣ ? (RKC Ask, ♥ is trump)
    4 ♥   (3 Keys & ♥ Q)   5 ♦ ? (any Jack ?)
    5 ♥   (♥ Jack)   7 NT
</pre>

The K & Q ♦ Ask would be 4 NT. Thus, the 5 ♦ bid is an Ask for Jacks as it cannot be a "final" contract to play *after **a positive*** response.
With **no** Jack, West would bid 5 NT – and East would conclude in 6 NT.

Also, in the few cases when the responder's hand description is totally known at the level of 2 NT, then 3 ♣ can replace 4 ♣ as the Optimal KC Ask, with the same responses but at the level of 3, i.e. 3 ♦ = 1 or 3 Key Cards w/o the trump Q, 3 ♥ = 1 or 3 Key Cards with the trump Q, etc.
Example :

<pre>
    1 NT   2 ♣ ?
    2 ♥ (4 hearts)   2 ♠ ?
    2 NT (4 ♥ 3 3 3)   3 ♣ ? OKC Ask
                           3 ♥ is invitational
                           3 ♦ / ♠ are guard inquiries
</pre>

II. VERIFICATION OF KEY CARDS

As previously mentioned, the **Optimal** Precision Relay method devised *three* different ways to *clear up* any potential confusion about the number of Key Cards held by the responder to an Optimal KC 4 ♣ Ask. They are outlined below.

A) SPECIFIC ASK IN A SINGLETON.

An **asking** bid in the responder's **singleton** is **not** a K & Q Ask in that suit; instead, it is used to clear up any confusion about his Key Cards. There are three responses to this inquiry :

Step 1 : The *lesser* number of Keys = **1** Key, **not** 3, or 0 Key, **not** 2.

Step 2 : The *greater* number of Keys, one of which is a **King**. i.e.
3 Key Cards (vs 1), including the trump King, or 2 Key Cards (vs 0) including the trump **King**.

Step 3 : The *greater* number of Key Cards (2 vs 0 or 3 vs 1), **all** Aces.

184

Thus, the **Optimal P**recision **R**elay method has a way to differentiate a holding of Key Cards **with** the trump King from one **without** the trump King. Something not done in *traditional* RKC Blackwood !

B) ASKS IN "REVEALING" SUITS.

An alternative – the most frequent – is simply to ask in suits whose responses will "reveal" the number of Key Cards by "inference".
It will often be the preferred alternative, or the only alternative.

C) REPEATED ASK IN A SUIT PREVIOUSLY ASKED.

Asking *a second time* in a suit which had previously been asked about its K & Q holding is another way to ask about clarifying a confusion about the number of Key Cards. It will be used when the responder cannot use the other two. The responses to it are the same as above.

Let's look at some example hands illustrating these 3 options :

Deal from a Bridge book (« *Enriched RKC Blackwood* »).

♠ A x x x x x	♠ K Q x
♥ x	♥ A x x
♦ A J x x	♦ x
♣ A x	♣ K Q J x x x

In **Optimal P**recision **R**elay, these hands will be bid as follows :

1 ♠ (5 + ♠, 12/17 HLD pts)	1 NT ?
2 ♦ (4 ♦)	2 ♥ ?
3 ♣ (2 + ♣, 16 HLD pts)	3 ♦ ?
3 ♠ (6 ♠ 4 ♦ 2 ♣ 1 ♥)	4 ♣ ? (trump is ♠)
4 ♦ (3 Keys w/o the ♠ Q)	<u>4 ♥</u> ? *(verification Ask.)*
<u>5 ♣</u> (3 Aces)	7 NT

West could have 1 Key only, instead of 3, with A J 10 in spades and K Q in diamonds. Thus, East *must verify* which it is, and he does so by an Ask in West's singleton suit.

National tournament, 1981.

♠ A K Q x x x	♠ J x
♥ A Q	♥ K J 10 x x
♦ x x	♦ A x x
♣ x x x	♣ A x x

Very few of the 74 pairs reached 7 NT – the absolute "top".

In **Optimal P**recision **R**elay, these hands will be bid as follows :

1 ♣ (18 + HLD pts)	1 ♦
2 ♠ (6 + ♠, 18/20 HLD)	2 NT ?
3 ♣ (3 ♣ or ♣ singleton)	3 ♦ ?
3 NT (6 ♠ 3 ♣ 2 2)	4 ♣ ? (trump is ♠)
4 ♥ (3 Keys w/the ♠ Q)	5 ♣ ? (K & Q ♣ Ask)
5 ♦ (no ♣ K or Q)	5 ♥ ? (K & Q ♥ Ask)
5 NT (♥ Queen)	7 NT

The ♣ Ask is intended to "clarify" a possible confusion about West's number of Key Cards. With one Key Card, instead of 3, he will necessarily have ♣ honors.

Once assured of West's 3 Key Cards, East can check on West's ♥ holding and count 13 tricks : 6 in spades, 5 in hearts + the 2 minor-suit Aces.

Note that the two hands add up to 36 HLF pts (+2 for 3 honors in a 6-card suit + 2 Fit pts in spades for the doubleton J), not 31 HL pts !

« *Bidding contest* » – Le Bridgeur.

♠ A x	♠ x x x
♥ A 10 x x x	♥ K J x x x
♦ A K Q x x	♦ x x
♣ x	♣ A x x

In the tournament the above deal comes from, only one pair bid 7 ♥. And this failure was confirmed by the three contest participants who all ended up in 6 ♥.

In **Optimal** Precision Relay, these hands will be bid as follows :

1 ♣ (18 + HLD)	1 ♥ (*transfer* for ♠, 7/12 HL)
1 ♠ ? (*transfer*)	1 NT (5 ♥ or 5 ♠ 3 3 2)
2 ♣ ?	2 ♥ (5 ♥ 3 3 2)
2 ♠ ?	2 NT (7/9 HL pts)
3 ♣ ?	3 ♦ (♦ doubleton)
4 ♣ ? (trump is ♥)	4 ♠ (2 Keys w/o the ♥ Q)
5 ♣ ? (K & Q ♣ Ask)	5 ♦ (no ♣ K or Q)
5 ♠ ? (K & Q ♠ Ask)	5 NT (no ♠ K or Q)
7 ♥	

East, with 7/9 HL pts, could have **0** Key Cards, rather than 2. East not having a singleton, West asks in clubs and then spades to clarify East's number of Key Cards. Without a King or Queen in either suit, East has to have **2** Key Cards for 7 + HL pts. West knows everything about East's hand and knows he can play 7 ♥ ruffing one diamond and one club.

Regional tournament, 2011.

♠ x	♠ A K x x x x
♥ A x x x	♥ x
♦ A K x	♦ x x
♣ A K x x x	♣ Q x x x

Not a single pair found the 7 ♣ contract for which one needs to know East's 6 spades to A K, enabling the discard of one heart.

In **Optimal** Precision Relay, these hands will be bid as follows :

1 ♣ (18 + HLD)	1 ♥ (transfer for ♠, 7/12 HL)
1 ♠ (transfer to ♠)	2 ♣ (4 + clubs)
2 ♦ ?	2 NT (5 ♠ 4 ♣ 2 ♦, 10/12 HL)
3 ♣ ?	3 ♠ (6 ♠)
4 ♣ ? (trump is ♠)	4 ♠ (2 Keys w/o the ♠ Q)
5 ♣ ? (K & Q ♣ Ask)	5 ♥ (♣ Queen)
<u>5 NT</u> ? (KC verification)	6 ♦ (2 Key Cards, A & K)
7 ♣	

East could have **0** Key Cards, instead of two. Thus, West's verification Ask in East's ♥ singleton to "clarify" the confusion. Any response bid exceeding the 6 ♣ level will guarantee a 7 ♣ contract.

III. DIRECT RESPONSES TO A 4 ♣ ASK BEYOND 4 NT

Unlike the Blackwood Ask, the economical level of the 4 ♣ Ask allows direct responses **beyond** the level of 4 NT – without exceeding the level of 5 ♥, the lower-ranking Major. Thus, the **Optimal** Precision Relay method uses the 3 direct responses of 5 ♣, 5 ♦ and 5 ♥ to bring further precision to the direct 4 NT response to the 4 ♣ Ask. Let's see how.

We have previously seen the significant benefits ot the inquirer's 4 NT Ask, after a direct response of 4 ♦, 4 ♥ or 4 ♠, to inquire about the K & Q holding in responder's *highest-ranking* suit. However, a 4 NT direct response no longer gives the inquirer this option, which means that he would have to ask about the K & Q holding in a Major suit at the very high level of 5 ♥ or 5 ♠ – generally too high a level.

To overcome this problem, the method uses the 3 direct responses of 5 ♣, 5 ♦ and 5 ♥ to describe the same Key Cards as the 4 NT would, i.e. **2** Key cards **with** the trump **Q, plus** the K and/or Q holding in the **highest-ranking** suit :

– 5 ♣ with the **Q**ueen in that suit
    5 ♦ with the **K**ing in that suit
    5 ♥ with **K** and **Q** in that suit.

And the corollary of this is significant : it is that a direct response of 4 NT now **denies** a Queen, King or K Q in the highest-ranking suit.

This also means that the very economical direct response of 5 ♣ **denies** the K or K Q in the highest-ranking suit – a very valuable precision !

As well, It also means that the level of 5 ♣ will *only be exceeded* when the responder has the K or K Q of the highest-ranking suit.

Two implications that both the inquirer and the responder will need to keep in mind !

These direct responses of 5 ♣, 5 ♦ and 5 ♥ will *often enable* the inquirer to determine *the balance of honors* in responder's hand thanks to the precise 3-point zone identified by the responder.

Illustration : with the following hand, a direct 5 ♣ response from a responder having described a 12/14 HLD pts opening hand or a 10/12 HL pts responding hand, will enable the inquirer to know immediately that *all key honors* of the responder's hand have been described – in just *one bid* :

♠ K Q x x
♥ Q x x
♦ A x x x x
♣ x

Trump is spades. A 5 ♣ response to an OKC 4 ♣ Ask, indicating 2 Key Cards **and** the trump Queen **plus** the ♥ Queen, will tell the inquirer all there is to know about the responder's hand honors.

Actually, in the above example, the inquirer would also know that the responder **cannot** have a Jack in diamonds or hearts or spades as it would put him 1 point over the point zone he described.

The following are example hands of 5 ♣, 5 ♦ and 5 ♥ direct responses :

♠	K Q x x	K Q x x x	K x	x
♥	Q x x	x	A Q x x	K Q x x
♦	x x	Q x x	J 10 x x	K Q 10 x x
♣	A x x x	A x x x	A x x	A x x
Trump :	♠	♠	♥	♦
Response :	5 ♣	5 ♣	5 ♦	5 ♥
	w/ ♥ Q	w/ ♦ Q	w/ ♠ K	w/ ♥ K Q

Note that a 4 NT response would be problematic with the above hands, as it would require from the inquirer a K & Q Ask at the levels of 5 ♥, 5 ♦, 5 ♠ and 5 ♥ for, respectively, each of the hands above. Instead, the direct responses of 5 ♣, 5 ♣, 5 ♦ and 5 ♥ will **tell all** about responder's hand honors !

Here are some examples of these direct responses of 5 ♣, 5 ♦ and 5 ♥.

Rubber game.

♠ A K x x x	♠ Q x x
♥ x	♥ K Q x x x
♦ A K Q x	♦ x x x
♣ K x x	♣ A x

In **Optimal** Precision Relay, these hands will be bid as follows :

1 ♣	1 ♥ (*transfer* for ♠, 7/12 HL)
1 ♠ (*transfer* to ♠)	1 NT (5 ♥ or ♠ 3 3 2)
2 ♣ ?	2 ♥ (5 ♥ 3 3 2)
2 ♠ ?	3 ♣ (♣ doubleton, 10/12 HL)
4 ♣ ? (trump is ♥)	5 ♣ (2 Keys w/ ♥ Q + ♠ Q)
6 ♠	

One can see that a 4 NT response would **deny** the ♠ Q and would enable West to stop in 5 ♠ despite the 37 HLDF pts held by these two hands.

Regional tournament, 2011.

♠ x	♠ A x x
♥ A K x x	♥ Q x x x x
♦ K J 10 x	♦ A Q x
♣ A x x x	♣ x x

Not a single pair found the ♥ grand slam.
In **Optimal** Precision Relay, these hands will be bid as follows :

1 ♣ (18 + HLD)	1 ♥ (*transfer* for ♠, 7/12 HL)
1 ♠ (*transfer* to ♠)	1 NT (5 Major 3 3 2)
2 ♣ ?	2 ♥ (5 ♥)
2 ♠ ?	3 ♣ (♣ doubleton, 10/12 HL)
4 ♣ ? (trump is ♥)	4 NT (2 Keys w/ ♥ Q, no ♠ H)
5 ♦ ? (K & Q ♦ Ask)	5 ♠ (♦ Queen)
5 NT ? (K & Q ♣ Ask)	6 ♣ (no ♣ K nor Q)
7 ♥	

West's 5 NT bid is to check whether East has **0** Key Cards, rather than 2. Without ♣ honors, East's response guarantees **2** Key Cards, thus 7 ♥.

National division 1 selection, teams of four, 2014 – Le Bridgeur.

♠ x	♠ A x x x
♥ K Q x x x x	♥ A 10 x
♦ Q 10 x	♦ A K x x
♣ A x x	♣ K x

Many pairs stopped in 6 ♥. Instead of :

2 ♥ (6 + ♥, 15/17 HLD)	2 ♠ ?
3 ♥ (6 ♥ 3 3 1♠)	4 ♣ ? (trump is ♥)
5 ♣ (2 Keys w/ ♥ Q + ♦ Q)	7 ♥

Here, the 5 ♣ direct response describes the ♦ Queen since spades is a singleton and hearts are trump. 7 ♥ with only two inquiring bids !
Hard to conceive missing this grand slam, with these hands, loaded with top honors, in 2014 ?...

Exercices, 2014 – Le Bridgeur.

♠ x	♠ A 10 x x x
♥ A K x	♥ x
♦ x x x	♦ K Q x
♣ K Q x x x x	♣ A J x x

In **Optimal** Precision **Relay**, these hands will be bid as follows :

2 ♣ (5 + ♣, 14/17 HLD)	2 ♦ ?
3 ♣ (6 ♣ 3 3 1)	3 ♦ ?
3 ♠ (6 ♣ 3 3 1 ♠)	4 ♣ ? (trump is ♣)
5 ♦ (2 Keys w/ ♣ Q + ♥ K)	6 ♣

West cannot have **0** Key Cards with 15/17 HLD pts and a spade single-ton. Note that if West had responded 4 NT, without the precision of the ♥ King, East would not have been able to inquire about West's hearts without exceeding the level of 5 ♣. And had West bid 5 ♣, describing the ♥ Queen, not the King, East would *pass* to play 5 ♣.

One last example, from a National selection, in 2014, where only 3 pairs reached 6 NT and only one reached 7 ♦. The hands were :

♠ K Q x	♠ A x x x
♥ A K Q x	♥ J x
♦ x x x	♦ A K Q 10 x
♣ x x x	♣ A x

In **Optimal** Precision **Relay**, these hands will be bid as follows :

1 NT (12/14 HL)	2 ♣ ?
2 ♥ (4 ♥)	2 ♠ ?
2 NT (4 ♥ 3 3 3)	4 ♣ ? (trump is ♥)
5 ♥ (2 Keys w/ ♥ Q + ♠ K Q)	7 NT

West cannot have **0** key Cards with a minimum of 12 H pts, thus 7 NT.

Summary of responses to the Optimal 4 ♣ 6 KC Ask
FIRST FOUR DIRECT RESPONSES

DIRECT RESPONSE	MEANING	NEXT BIDS	FINAL
4 ♦	**1, 3** or **5** Keys <u>**w/o**</u> the trump **Q**	4 ♥ ? : K & Q ♥ Ask Final if **trump** is ♥ 4 ♠ ? : K & Q ♠ Ask Final if **trump** is ♠ 4 NT ?: K & Q Ask in **higher** ranking suit.	4 NT, 5 ♣, 5 ♦? for ♠ ♣, ♦. 5 ♣, 5 ♦ ? for ♣, ♦ Conclusion
4 ♥	**1, 3** or **5** Keys <u>**w**</u>/the trump **Q**	4 ♠ ? : K & Q ♠ Ask Final if **trump** is ♠ 4 NT ? : K & Q Ask for **higher** ranking suit (♦ or ♥) 5 ♣ /5 ♦ : for ♣ /♦	5 ♣ / 5 ♦ for ♣, ♦ 5 ♦ / 5 ♥ for ♦, ♥ Conclusion
4 ♠	**0, 2** or **4** Keys <u>**w/o**</u> the trump **Q**	4 NT ? : K & Q Ask for **higher** ranking suit (♦ or ♥) 5 ♣ /5 ♦ : for ♣ /♦	Conclusion
4 NT	**0, 2** or **4** Keys <u>**w/**</u> the trump **Q** ***Denies*** K or Q in ***higher*** *ranking* suit	5 ♣ /5 ♦ : for ♣ /♦ Other : conclusion	Conclusion

Summary of responses to the Optimal 4 ♣ 6 KC Ask
LAST THREE DIRECT RESPONSES

DIRECT RESPONSE	MEANING	NEXT BIDS	FINAL
5 ♣	**0, 2** or **4** Keys <u>w/</u> the trump **Q** **And** the **Q** in the *highest* ranking suit.	5 ♦ / 5 ♥ : for ♦, ♥ Other : conclusion *	Conclusion
5 ♦	**0, 2** or **4** Keys <u>w/</u> the trump **Q** **And** the **K** in the *highest* ranking suit.	5 ♥ : for ♥ Other : conclusion *	Conclusion
5 ♥	**0, 2** or **4** Keys <u>w/</u> the trump **Q** **And** **K Q** in the *highest* ranking suit.	Conclusion *	Conclusion

* An Asking bid in responder's singleton, or a *repeat* Ask in a suit previously inquired about, is a *verification* bid to *clarify* the responder's number of Key Cards. 3 step responses : 1st step = *minimum* number of Key Cards, 2nd step = *maximum* number of Key Cards *with* the *trump* K, 3rd step : *maximum* number of Key Cards, all Aces.

N.B. When the 4 ♣ Ask, and its established responses, is not available because *opponents' intervention* disturbed declarer's bidding, then the Asking bid will be 4 NT. For reasons of "bidding level safety", the direct responses to the 4 NT Ask will then be *limited to four:* 5 ♣, for **1, 3** or **5** Key Cards *without* the trump Queen, 5 ♦, for **1, 3** or **5** Key Cards *with* the trump Queen, 5 ♥, for **0, 2** or **4** Key Cards *without* the trump Queen, and 5 ♠, for **0, 2** or **4** Key Cards *with* the trump Q.

THE OPTIMAL PRECISION RELAY BILL OF RIGHTS

« We believe that **all opening** bids, as well as their **responses**, hold **unalienable** rights to be **precisely defined** in **both** distribution and point-range, that **pertinent distributional** features should be identified, and that slam Key Card Asks must be **economical** to be useful. Only then can we endeavor to achieve a "more perfect union" between partners ».

The author

---

1 NT opening   12/14 HL pts   4 3 3 3   4 4 3 2   5 3 3 2   5 4 ♦/♣ 2 2

Denies : a 5-card Major   **both** 4-card Majors   a 6-card suit

REBIDS, RESPONSES AND DEVELOPMENTS

We previously established why opening a strong NT, 15/17 H, is a serious error, pre-empting *the partner* instead of *the opponents*.
Beyond this, the *traditional* 1 NT opening is seriously handicapped by several flaws of its responses and rebids.
We are now going to illustrate the numerous advantages of opening a weak NT of **12/14** HL pts in **Optimal** Precision Relay.

First, this opening is in H<u>L</u> points, **not** H pts only; this enables opening 1 NT hands such as the ones below :

♠ Q 10 x	or	♠ K x	or	♠ Q 10 x
♥ K Q x x		♥ A x x		♥ A x
♦ x x		♦ x x x		♦ K Q x x x
♣ A x x x		♣ Q J 10 x x		♣ x x x
12 H		12 ½ HL		13 HL

Hands counted 10 or 11 H pts in *traditional* count – either *passed* or opened 1 ♣ or 1 ♦, open invitations to no-risk overcalls of 1 ♥ or 1 ♠.
Thus, it represents a very effective *"competitive initiative"* opening.
And its frequency is considerably greater than that of a strong 1 NT.

Second, its hand distribution is *precisely defined* : it **denies** a 5-card Major, **both** 4-card Majors as well as a semi-regular distribution with two doubletons (6 3 2 2 or 5 4 2 2) with the sole exception of 5 4 ♦/♣ 2 2.
Furthermore, we will see later that, on a Stayman-*relay* 2 ♣ bid from responder, the opener will have *unique* rebids to precisely describe his *minor-suit* holding when he does not have a 4-card Major.

Third, it enables the full and exact description of its distribution, all 13 cards if needed, on successive *relays* from responder.

And fourth, some direct responses, *unique and specific* to the method, are used to precisely describe some **5 4 3 1** hands.

I. THE METHOD'S "SYSTEMIC" PRECISION OF REBIDS ON RELAYS.

In **Optimal** Precision Relay, a 2 ♣ response is obviously a *relay* – and this relay is also *Stayman,* looking for a 4-card Major in opener's hand. But when the opener does **not** have a 4-card Major, he will describe his minor-suit holding as follows :

The opener can chose between four rebids on a 2 ♣ Stayman-*relay* :

2 ♥ : 4 hearts, **denies** 4 spades

2 ♠ : 4 spades, **denies** 4 hearts

2 ♦ : **Denies** a 4-card Major **and** *guarantees* 4 (or 5) **diamonds** !

2 NT : **Denies** a 4-card Major **and** 4 diamonds and *guarantees* 4 (or 5) **clubs** !

Furthermore, after a first rebid of 2 ♦, indicating 4 + diamonds, on a *second relay*, 2 ♥, the opener will then bid 2 ♠, to describe, *conventionally*, 4 clubs and, therefore, **both** 4-card minor suits, or 3 ♣ with 5 - 4 in ♦ / ♣.

These very precise 2 ♦ and 2 NT rebids, unique and specific to the method, have two key implications : A) they often allow the quick discovery of a Fit in a *minor* suit, allowing the count of Fit pts, and B) they eliminate the need for a *minor-suit Stayman* inquiry. Furthermore, they eliminate the rather problematic handling, in *traditional* bidding, of a 5 - 4 minor two-suiter in responder's hand, as an 8-card Fit in one of the minor suits can be identified, economically, through *relays*.

Illustration :

♠	x x x	♠	A x
♥	x x	♥	x x x x
♦	A Q x x	♦	K J x
♣	A Q x x	♣	K 10 x x

The bidding will be :

1 NT (12/14 HL)	2 ♣ ?
2 ♦ (4 + ♦)	2 ♥ ? (relay)
2 ♠ (4 ♣)	3 NT

Knowing about West's 4 clubs enables East to add 2 Fit pts to his initial 11 H pts (no Queen) : 13 H + 12 HL minimum = 25 HLF pts = 3 NT.

Another example :

♠	K x	♠	A x x x
♥	x x x	♥	A x
♦	A J x x x	♦	K 10 x x x
♣	A x x	♣	K x

The bidding being :

1 NT (12/14 HL)	2 ♣ ?
2 ♦ (4 + ♦)	2 ♥ ? (relay)
3 ♦ (5 ♦)	3 ♥ ? (relay)
3 ♠ (♠ doubleton)	4 ♣ ? (trump is ♦)
4 ♠ (2 Keys w/o ♦ Q)	4 NT ? (K & Q ♠ Ask)
5 ♥ (♠ King)	6 ♦

East, with his 16 ½ HLD pts (no Queen), knows his side is in slam zone right upon West's 2 ♦ rebid! (3 Fit pts minimum). Once the 5 diamonds and the ♠ doubleton are known, the side has 33 ½ HLDF pts = 4 ♣ Ask. East can safely bid 4 NT as he knows that a response that exceeds 5 ♦ guarantees a 6 ♦ slam.

This treatment now enables a 1 NT opener to describe a 5 - 4 minor two-suiter by rebidding 3 ♣ after a 2 ♦ response to a 2 ♣ *relay*-Stayman.

The **Optimal P**recision **R**elay method does so with 5 4 2 ♠ 2 ♥ hands with each doubleton "guarded" – by an Ace or a King. This is the **only** hand-shape with *two* doubletons that the method will open 1 NT.

On a further relay, 3 ♥, the opener will complete his hand description by indicating *which minor* is the 5-card suit : 3 NT with 5 ♦, 3 ♠ with 5 ♣.

This opening is particularly well suited for hands having honors in their short suits and to *"pre-empt"* a 1 ♥ or 1 ♠ or 1 NT overcall by the opponents. Hands such as the following :

♠ A x	♠ K x	♠ A x
♥ K x	♥ A x	♥ A x
♦ Q 10 x x x	♦ Q x x x	♦ Q J x x x
♣ Q 10 x x	♣ Q J x x x	♣ J 10 x x
12 ½ H pts	13 HL pts	14 HL pts (no K)

Note that the first hand would often **not** be opened in *traditional* bidding (11 H pts) or would be opened 1 ♦, inviting a 1 ♥, 1 ♠ or 1 NT overcall. The following deal illustrates this vividly :

♠ A x	♠ x x x
♥ A x	♥ x x x
♦ Q 10 x x x	♦ A K x
♣ J 10 x x	♣ K Q x x

In the tournament this deal comes from, most West players *passed*, North opened 1 NT and played there as all players *passed*.

In **Optimal P**recision **R**elay these hands would be bid as follows :

1 NT (12/14 HL)	2 ♣ ? (relay-stayman)
2 ♦ (4 + diamonds)	2 ♥ ? (relay)
3 ♣ (5 – 4 in minors)	3 NT

East can now add 2 Fit pts to his 11 ½ H pts (4 3 3 3) and bid 3 NT.

We will now cover the opener's hand description on successive relays.

II. OPENER'S HAND DESCRIPTION ON SUCCESSIVE RELAYS

As previously mentioned, the first *relay*, 2 ♣, is Stayman, looking for a 4-card Major in opener's hand. Then, the next relays look for the rest of the hand's distribution.

1. Hands with a **4-card M**ajor.

Process : the 4-card Major, followed by NT, without a second 4-card suit, or by the second 4-card *minor* suit. Then, the tripleton.

➤ With 4 ♥ – After : 1 NT   2 ♣ ?
                       2 ♥   2 ♠ ?

4 ♥ 3 3 3	:	2 NT – Final
4 ♥ 4 ♣ 3 2	:	3 ♣ 3 ♦ ?
4 ♥ 4 ♣ <u>3 ♠</u> 2 ♦ :		3 ♠
4 ♥ 4 ♣ <u>3 ♦</u> 2 ♠ :		3 NT the tripleton is in the *relay* suit.
4 ♥ 4 ♦ 3 2 :		3 ♦ 3 ♥ ?
4 ♥ 4 ♦ <u>3 ♠</u> 2 ♣ :		3 ♠
4 ♥ 4 ♦ <u>3 ♣</u> 2 ♠ :		3 NT the tripleton is the 4th suit.

The above covers all possible distributions with 4 hearts since a hand opened 1 NT with 4 hearts *cannot have* 4 spades.

➤ With 4 ♠ – After : 1 NT   2 ♣ ?
                       2 ♠   <u>3 ♣</u> ?

Watch ! On 2 ♠, the *next relay* is **3 ♣**, **not** 2 NT! This, to allow the partnership to settle in 2 NT when a Fit was looked for in hearts, not in spades.

4 ♠ 3 3 3	:	3 NT
4 ♠ 4 ♦ 3 2	:	3 ♦ 3 ♥ ?
4 ♠ 4 ♦ <u>3 ♥</u> 2 ♣ :		3 NT the tripleton is in the *relay* suit.
4 ♠ 4 ♦ <u>3 ♣</u> 2 ♥ :		3 ♠ the tripleton is the 4th suit.

With 4 ♠ <u>4 ♣</u> 3 2, the relay being in opener's second 4-card suit, the residual will be *directly described* by the two bids left available :

4 ♠ 4 ♣ <u>3 ♥</u> 2 ♦ :	<u>3 ♥</u>	– Final
4 ♠ 4 ♣ <u>3 ♦</u> 2 ♥ :	<u>3 ♠</u>	– Final

The above covers all possible distributions with 4 spades.

EXCEPTION : treatment of **"light"** 1 NT openings in **3rd** or **4th** seat.

In **Optimal** Precision Relay, there is no need to open "light" 1 ♠ or 1 ♥, below the "norm", in 3rd or 4th seat, as they are already "light" with a point-count of **12** HLD pts. Thus, the *"Drury"* convention is not needed.

However, there is a need for "light" **1 NT** openings in **3rd** or **4th** seat, *below the "norm"*, as two balanced hands of 11 HL pts each could turn into 25 HLF pts, for 3 NT, or 27 HLDF pts, for 4 ♠ or 4 ♥.
The **Optimal** Precision Relay method does enable opening "light" 1 NT in **3rd** or **4th** seat, *below "the norm"*, with **10/11** HL pts, and uses the following *"braking"* process to indicate to partner such "light" opening on a 2 ♣ Stayman-*relay* bid :

With 4 hearts, the 1 NT opener will rebid 2 ♥ and then 2 NT, a "brake" indicating **10/11** HL pts; with 4 spades, the 1 NT opener will rebid 2 ♦ first, a "brake", before bidding 2 ♠ next.

Any other direct rebid – 2 ♠, 2 NT, etc. – will, therefore, guarantee the "normal" **12/14** HL point-range.

To illustrate the above, here is an example deal used by *Bridge World*, in 1969, for a bidding contest :

♠ A Q x x	♠ K x x x
♥ A x x x	♥ x x x
♦ Q x	♦ K x
♣ J x x	♣ K Q x x

Two hands bid to 4 ♠ by the contestants but which only yield 9 tricks.

In **Optimal Precision Relay**, these hands would be bid as follows :

Pass (11 ½ H pts, no K)	1 NT **(10**/14 HL pts)
2 ♣ ?	2 ♦ **(10/11** HL pts)
2 ♥ ? (relay)	2 ♠ (4 spades)
3 ♣ ? (relay)	3 ♥ (4 ♠ 4 ♣ 3 ♥ 2 ♦)
3 ♠ – Final	

West, with only 11 ½ H pts, *passes*. East opens "light" in 3rd seat, after two passes. On East's 2 ♠ bid, the relay is 3 ♣, not 2 NT. The knowledge of East's 10/11 H pts and exact 3 ♥ 2 ♦ residual cards enables West to sign-off in 3 ♠ : 11 ½ H pts + 1 ♠ Fit point + 2 D pts for the ♦ doubleton with 4 trumps = 14 ½ HDF pts + 11 H pts minus 1 point for two "mirror" suits = 24 ½ pts = no game.

 Note that with a 3 ♦ 2 ♥ residual, West would then bid 4 ♠ : + 2 D pts for the ♥ doubleton with 4 trumps in East's hand = 27 ½ pts = 4 ♠.

The next example illustrates the method's 1 NT opening in another way:

♠ Q 10 x
♥ K 10 x
♦ x x x x
♣ A Q x

♠ A J x x	♠ K x x x
♥ Q x x	♥ x x x x
♦ K Q 10 x	♦ x x
♣ x x	♣ J 10 x

♠ x x
♥ A J x
♦ A J x
♣ K x x x x

In the tournament this deal comes from, the bidding was most often :

West	North	East	South
1 ♦	Pass	Pass	1 NT

On which all players passed and 3 NT was missed.

In **Optimal** Precision **Relay** the bidding would be :

1 ♦	Pass	Pass	1 NT
Pass	2 ♣ ?	Pass	3 ♣
Pass	3 NT		

The 3 ♣ bid indicates a "normal" NT of 12/14 HL and 5 clubs. With 1 pt for the 8-card Fit in clubs, North can now bid 3 NT.

Note that in **Optimal** Precision **Relay**, the West hand would be opened 1 NT, not 1 ♦, and would be played there as *all* would *pass*…

2. We will now cover the description of hands **without** a 4-card Major.

Process : with 4 + diamonds, bid 2 ♦ first. **Without** 4 diamonds, bid 2 NT : 4 + clubs without 4 diamonds. With 4 ♦ **and** 4 ♣, after bidding 2 ♦ first, rebid 2 ♠, *conventional*.

➤ With 4 ♦ – After : 1 NT   2 ♣ ?
                     2 ♦   **No** 4-card Major, 4 + diamonds
                                2 ♥ ? relay

4 ♦ 3 3 3 :	2 NT – Final.
4 ♦ 4 ♣ 3 2 :	2 ♠ *conventional* The next *relay* is **3 ♥** ?

Here, the next relay is **3 ♥** to allow the Stayman inquirer to stop in 2 NT or in 3 ♣ or 3 ♦.

This does not in any way impede the completion of the opener's hand description which has two bids left for two possible residuals :

                                  3 ♥ ?

4 ♦ 4 ♣ <u>3 ♠</u> 2 ♥ :	3 ♠ – the tripleton is spades.
4 ♦ 4 ♣ <u>3 ♥</u> 2 ♠ :	3 NT – the tripleton is in the *relay* suit.

➤ With 5 ♦ 3 3 2 :   1 NT   2 ♣ ?
                               2 ♦   **No** 4-card Major, 4 + diamonds
                                   2 ♥ ? relay

5 ♦ 3 3 <u>2 ♠</u> :	3 ♠
5 ♦ 3 3 <u>2 ♥</u> :	3 ♥
5 ♦ 3 3 <u>2 ♣</u> :	<u>3 ♦</u>

With a 5 ♦ 3 3 2 hand, it is the doubleton that is described – with the ♣ doubleton, the bid is, *exceptionally*, 3 ♦ (2 NT being for 4 ♦ 3 3 3).

➢ With 4 ♣ but **not** 4 ♦ –   1 NT   2 ♣ ?
                                 2 NT *conventional* 3 ♦ ?

Here, after 2 NT, the *relay* is 3 ♦, **not** 3 ♣, to enable the Stayman inquirer to stop in 3 ♣.

4 ♣ 3 3 3 :	3 NT
5 ♣ 3 3 2 ♠ :	3 ♠
5 ♣ 3 3 2 ♥ :	3 ♥
5 ♣ 3 3 2 ♦ :	3 NT

This is the only case where only one bid, 3 NT, is available to describe **either** a 4 ♣ 3 3 3 hand **or** a 5 ♣ 3 3 2 ♦ hand. In both cases, however, 3 cards in each Major are guaranted.

This concludes the description of opener's hand on successive relays after a 1 NT opening. In all cases, the level of 3 NT was never exceeded. A summary of these descriptions appears below.

SUMMARY OF HAND DESCRIPTION ON SUCCESSIVE RELAYS

DISTRIBUTION	ON 2 ♣ ?	2nd Relay	DESCRIPTION	FINAL BID
w/ a 4-card Mjr				
4 ♥ 3 3 3	2 ♥	2 ♠ ?	2 NT – Final	2 NT
4 ♥ 4 ♣ 3 2	"	"	3 ♣	tripleton
4 ♥ 4 ♦ 3 2	"	"	3 ♦	
4 ♠ 3 3 3	2 ♠	3 ♣ ?	3 NT – Final	3 NT
4 ♠ 4 ♦ 3 2	"	"	3 ♦	tripleton
4 ♠ 4 ♣ 3 2	"	"	tripleton	3 ♥ / 3 ♠
w/o a 4-card Mjr				
4 ♦ 3 3 3	2 ♦	2 ♥ ?	2 NT	3 NT
4 ♦ 4 ♣ 3 2	"	"	2 ♠	tripleton
5 - 4 ♦ / ♣ 2 2	"	"	3 ♣	5-card suit
4 ♣ 3 3 3	2 NT	3 ♦ ?	3 NT	3 NT
w/ a 5-card min				
5 ♦ 3 3 2	2 ♦	2 ♥ ?	2 NT	Doubleton
5 ♣ 3 3 2	2 NT	3 ♦ ?	doubleton	doubleton

III. DIRECT RESPONSES TO A 1 NT OPENING OTHER THAN RELAYS

GUIDING PRINCIPLES

We will see here that some of the direct responses to 1 NT in **Optimal Precision Relay** are quite different from those in *traditional* bidding. Before studying them in detail, let's first outline the key principles which guide these novel responses, as follows :

– The *"balanced hand principle"* dictates that, opposite a 1 NT opening, a hand which has a *singleton* should describe it to enable the opener to determine its positive or negative value (*"wasted honor pts"*). Yet, that is **not** what *traditional* responses do.

– Using *transfer* responses, at the two-level, is an absolute necessity. Therefore, *any other* use of two-level bids is inappropriate, such as a 2 ♦ game-forcing bid (not needed in a *relay* method), or the *puppet-Stayman* or any other form of *two-way Stayman*.

– Using a direct 2 NT response as *natural, game-invitational* is totally non-sensical. Not only is it based on a strict honor point count, with no consideration of Fit points in minor suits, but it is also very infrequent (specifically 11 or 12 H pts and no 4-card Major). And the same applies to the *"quantitative"* 4 NT double-jump raise !

– Using the direct response of 3 ♦ to identify, as some proponents do, a 5 - 5 Major two-suiter, *without* identifying which suit is *singleton*, is a total absurdity! Furthermore, its frequency, in a given 3 point zone, is less than… 1 %! And the same applies to *"smolen transfers"*.

And using the direct responses of 3 ♣ and 3 ♦ as natural, *invitational*, to identify a 6-card minor single-suiter is not of much value, and has a very low frequency. How often have you seen this lead to a minor-suit game contract ? It most often generates a bid of 3 NT.

– Using the direct responses of 3 ♥ and 3 ♠ as game-forcing, for strong Major single-suiters, but *without describing* the hand's short suit(s) (two doubletons or a singleton) is another absurdity, particularly in a *relay* method! The same applies to a direct jump to the *four-level* as it neglects to identify a singleton in that hand.

The **Optimal** Precision Relay method replaces the above non-sensical bids with novel solutions, base on the principles below :

– When the responder has a *singleton* in a *minor* suit, he should identify it, whenever possible, to enable the opener to assess *"wasted honor pts"*. However, a singleton in a *Major* suit should **not** be identified as it would indicate to opponents that they have an 8-card Fit in that Major suit.

Therefore, after a *transfer* bid for a Major, the responder's next bid, in a 10/12 HLD point zone, **must identify his singleton**, if he has one. Illustration : the following hands will be bid as follows :

♠ A x x	♠ K Q x x x
♥ K Q x x	♥ A x x x
♦ A x x	♦ x x x
♣ x x x	♣ x

1 NT (12/14 HL)	2 ♥ (*Transfer* for spades)
2 ♠ (*transfer*)	3 ♣ (♣ singleton, 10/12 HLD)
3 ♦ ? (relay)	3 ♥ (4 ♥ : 5 ♠ 4 ♥ 3 ♦ 1 ♣)
4 ♥ or 4 ♠	

While, with the opening hand below (♥ Q moved to clubs), the bidding would stop in 3 ♥ or 3 ♠ because of the "wasted honor pts" in clubs :

♠ A x x
♥ K x x x
♦ A x x
♣ Q x x

– Furthermore, the method uses the direct responses of 3 ♣ and 3 ♦ in a totally unique way : they are used to describe 5 4 3 1 hands with a 4-card Major, *specifically* **hearts**, a 5-card minor – the minor bid – and a singleton in the *other minor* suit, and 10/12 HLD pts.
Therefore, 3 ♣ describes a **5 ♣ 4 ♥ 3 ♠ 1 ♦** hand, while 3 ♦ describes a **5 ♦ 4 ♥ 3 ♠ 1 ♣** hand. Thus, both these direct responses are considerably "optimized" – *precise and pertinent invitational* bids !

An easy illustration is to reproduce the previous deal but with the spade and diamond suits, in East, reversed. The hands would now be :

♠ A x x	♠ x x x
♥ K Q x x	♥ A x x x
♦ A x x	♦ K Q x x x
♣ x x x	♣ x

1 NT (12/14 HL)	3 ♦ (5 ♦ 4 ♥ 3 ♠ 1 ♣, 10/12 HLD)
4 ♥	

The *corollary* of this is that a responder having gone through a 2 ♣ Stayman *before* bidding 3 ♣ or 3 ♦ **cannot be** of that type. Illustration :

1 NT		2 ♣ ?		
2 ♥	4 ♥	3 ♣	5 ♣	no ♥ Fit invitational to 3 NT
		3 ♦	5 ♦	no ♥ Fit invitational to 3 NT

– And to *replicate* the same benefits of these direct responses of 3 ♣ and 3 ♦, with **spades** as the 4-card Major, the method goes through the direct response of 2 ♠, first, followed by 3 ♣ or 3 ♦, with the very same meaning i.e. 3 ♣ describes a 5 ♣ 4 ♠ 3 ♥ 1 ♦ hand, while 3 ♦ describes a 5 ♦ 4 ♠ 3 ♥ 1 ♣ hand, and 10/12 HLD pts. And this direct response of 2 ♠ tells the opener that the responder has 5 ♣ 1 ♦ or 5 ♦ 1 ♣.
One can readily imagine the significant benefits these bids provide !

To learn about the responder's distribution in clubs and diamonds, the opener will relay, by 2 NT, on which the responder will rebid 3 ♣ or 3 ♦. Furthermore, the 2 ♠ response, being *natural*, is *non-forcing* and allows the opener to *pass* on 2 ♠ and play at the two-level. Illustration:

♠ A J x	♠ K Q x x
♥ K Q x x	♥ x x x
♦ K x	♦ A x x x x
♣ x x x x	♣ x
1 NT (12/14 HL)	2 ♠ (planning a 3 ♦ rebid)
Pass	

Without an 8-card Fit in either Major suit and knowing about a singleton in either minor, West cannot contemplate a NT game and settles in 2 ♠.

The same *corollary* applies here, as it did with hearts, i.e. a responder having gone through a 2 ♣ Stayman *before* bidding 3 ♣ or 3 ♦ **cannot have** 5 ♣ or 5 ♦ 4 ♠ 3 1 with the singleton in the *other* minor.

– The consequence of using the 2 ♠ response to a 1 NT opening for the above meaning is that 2 NT is used as a *transfer* bid response for *either* clubs *or* diamonds. On the opener's *transfer* to 3 ♣, the responder will correct to 3 ♦ when his long minor suit is diamonds, instead of clubs. Illustration : with a responder of fewer than **10** HLD pts :

♠ A x x	♠ x
♥ K Q x x	♥ J x x
♦ x x x x	♦ x x x
♣ K x	♣ A J 10 x x x
1 NT (12/14 HL)	2 NT (*transfer* for ♣ or ♦)
3 ♣	Pass

An excellent defense against a likely 4 ♠ contract by the opponents !

– Finally, the direct responses of 3 ♥ and 3 ♠ are natural and precisely describe a 6-card single-suit Major of 10/12 HLD pts **without** a singleton, as a singleton would have to be identified. Those responses are *invitational*, **not** game-forcing (*relay* with a strong hand).

204

Illustration : ♠ A x x   ♠ x x
                  ♥ K Q x   ♥ A J x x x x
                  ♦ K Q x x   ♦ A x x
                  ♣ x x x   ♣ x x

                1 NT (12/14 HL)   3 ♥ (6 ♥ 3 2 2, 10/12 HLD)
                4 ♥   Pass

These fundamental principles having been outlined, we can now go over the detailed responses to the 1 NT opening.

RESPONSES OTHER THAN SUCCESSIVE RELAYS

DETERMINING PARAMETERS

The same three key parameters applying to responses over a 2 ♣ or 1 ♥ or 1 ♠ opening apply to the responses over a 1 NT opening : the hand's **strength**, the search for a **Fit** in a **Major** suit, and without such Fit, the search for a potential 3 NT contract. A 4th parameter applies here : that is the presence, or not, of a singleton, which is of critical importance opposite a 1 NT opening.

1. The hand's **strength**, therefore its number of points.

We previously demonstrated that the *conventional wisdom* that 11 H pts are needed for a 2 ♣ Stayman on a weak NT is totally misguided. Opposite a maximum of 14 HL pts, the responder to a 1 NT opener needs to have **10** HLD pts – 3 more points than the 7 HL pts needed to bid opposite an opening limited to 17 HLD pts.
Here, these 10 pts must be counted as HL**D** pts – as **one** of the two hands of a partnership must count its distribution pts and since a hand opened 1 NT does **not** have D pts, the partner must count **his**.

So, with **less** than **10** HLD pts, partner can *pass* – unless his hand has a singleton and a long suit and he can easily foresee that his side would almost certainly be better off playing a suit contract, even at a higher level. He will then bid his long suit through a *transfer* bid : either 2 ♦ (for ♥) or 2 ♥ (for ♠) or 2 NT (for either ♣ or ♦), and then *Pass*.

With **10/12** HLD pts, he will need to make an invitational bid, or *relay*. He will do the same with a hand of **13/15** HLD pts **with a singleton** as the singleton could be opposite *"wasted honor pts"*, which would rule out a game contract.
With **16 +** HLD pts, a game is guaranteed (16 + 12 minimum = 28 pts, 25 HL pts without counting D pts) and he will *relay*.
Therefore, we only have two point zones to consider : 10/12 and 13/15 HLD pts.

2. The second parameter is to identify a potential **Fit** in a Major suit.

2.1 With **5 +** cards in a Major.

The responder will bid his long Major suit via a *transfer* bid : 2 ♦ with hearts, 2 ♥ with spades. With *less* than 10 HLD pts, he will then *pass*.
On a *transfer* bid, the opener **must** transfer – *unless* he has a 4-card support in the suit **and** a strong hand of **16** HLDF pts (14 HL + 2 Fit pts, or 13 HL + 3 Fit pts, or 12 HL + 2 Fit pts + 2 D pts for a doubleton).
In that case, and only then, he can *refuse to transfer* and *"super-accept"* by bidding the *next suit up* : 2 ♠ on 2 ♦, 2 NT on 2 ♥.

– With a balanced **5 3 3 2** distribution, the responder will then rebid 2 NT with 10/12 HL pts, 3 NT with 13 to 15 HL pts, giving the opener a choice between a contract in NT or in the Major suit.

– With an **unbalanced** hand i.e. with a **singleton** (5 4 3 1, 6 3 3 1), and this is critically important and novel, the responder's second bid will be his **singleton**, if in a *minor* suit : 3 ♣ or 3 ♦, with 10/15 HLD pts.

And a 5 - 4 Major two-suiter is described in a unique way :

With 5 ♥ 4 ♠ : the 5-card Major will be bid *first*, via a 2 ♦ *transfer* bid, followed by a bid of 2 ♠, on partner's *transfer* (2 ♥). This will now enable the responder to bid his **singleton** on opener's 2 NT *relay* : 3 ♣ or 3 ♦.
A 3rd bid of 3 ♥, instead of 3 ♣ or 3 ♦, will describe a 5 4 2 2 hand (a 6 ♥ 4 ♠ hand would necessarily have a singleton in a minor suit).

With 5 ♠ 4 ♥ : the 5-card Major will be *bid first*, via a 2 ♥ *transfer* bid, followed by bidding his **singleton** : 3 ♣, with a ♣ singleton, and then 3 ♥, to describe his four hearts, on opener's 3♦ *relay*. While with a ♦ singleton, his second bid will be 3 ♥ directly.
With 5 4 **2 2**, the responder will go through a *stayman-relay* bid of 2 ♣.

A 5 ♠ 5 ♥ two-suiter (low frequency), *necessarily* has a singleton in clubs or diamonds and will be treated the same as the 5 ♠ 4 ♥ two-suiter.

2.2 With **5 +** cards in a **minor** and a **singleton** in the **other** minor.

This was previously outlined : with 4 **hearts** : with **5 +** cards in a **minor**, and a singleton in the **other** minor, the responder will bid his **5 +** card minor suit *directly* at the 3-level : 3 ♣ or 3 ♦.
While, when with 4 **spades**, the responder will bid 2 ♠ first, *natural*, describing 4 spades, followed, on opener's 2 NT relay, by 3 ♣ or 3 ♦, in his 5 + card minor suit, also indicating a *singleton* in the *other minor*.

The treatment outlined above gives the 5 4 3 1 distributions – the most critical opposite a 1 NT opening and rather frequent – special attention in a unique way.

3. The third parameter is the search for a **4 – 4** Fit in a Major.

When the responder does **not** have a **5**-card Major but, instead, has a **4**-card Major, or *both* 4-card Majors, he will use a *relay-Stayman* bid of 2 ♣ to uncover a potential 4-card Major in opener's hand.
The opener will describe his hand's holding.

After his initial 2 ♣ *relay-Stayman*, the responder can either continue to *relay* or revert to *natural* bids, *invitational*, such as :

	1 NT	2 ♣ ?
	2 ♦	2 ♠ : 5 ♠ 4 ♣ 2 2 strong spades (invites ♠ vs NT)
		2 NT : 11/12 HL pts *Invitational* to 3 NT
		3 ♣ : 5 + ♣ one 4-card Major no ♦ singleton
Or :	1 NT	2 ♣ ?
	2 ♥	2 NT : 11/12 HL pts *Invitational* to 3 NT
		3 ♣ : 5 + ♣ 4-card ♠ suit no ♦ singleton

4. The fourth parameter is to facilitate the search for a **NT** game.

Without a 4-card or 5-card Major, the priority is to look for a possible 3 NT Game. To do so, the responder will *relay*. "guard" Asks can be made at the three-level, 3 ♦, 3 ♥ or 3 ♠. Over which, a 3 NT response is *positive* and indicates at least Q J x or K x x or A x x in the suit.

SUMMARY OF RESPONSES TO A 1NT OPENING

HLD POINTS	*With* 5-card Major	*W*/4-card Major	w/o 4 or 5-card Major
< than 10	*Transfer* to Major	Pass	Pass
10 / 12	2 ♦ : *transfer* / ♥ 2 ♥ : *transfer* / ♠ or : *Relay*	2 ♣ Stayman or 2 ♠ : 4 ♠ 5 3 1 or *Relay*	*Transfer* to minor suit or *Relay*
13 +	*Relay*	*Relay*	*Relay*

UNUSUAL CONVENTIONAL BIDS TO "FLAG"

OPENING	UNUSUAL CONVENTIONAL RESPONSE	POINTS
1 NT	2 ♠ : 4 ♠ 5 *min* 3 ♥ 1 *min*	10/12 HLD

Balanced hand   **18 +** H<u>L</u>D pts   **Open** 1 ♣

REBIDS, RESPONSES AND DEVELOPMENTS

OPENER'S 1 NT REBID ON A 1 ♦ RESPONSE

On a 1♦ response to a 1 ♣ opening, the opener's first rebid will be 1 NT with **18 +** HLD pts. But further bidding *developments* beyond this rebid will **not** be the same as **two** point zones must now be differentiated : **18/20** or **21/23 +** HL pts. The process to do this is described hereafter.

– For a hand with 4 **hearts**, the *"brake"* will be applied **after** bidding 2 ♥ first, i.e. :

1 ♣	1 ♦
1 NT	2 ♣ ?
2 ♥	2 ♠ ?
2 NT *"brake"*	**18/20** HL pts

Any rebid **other** than 2 NT indicates a hand of **21/23 +** HL pts.

Note : A *very* weak responder with 1, 2 or 3 HL pts may, *exceptionally,* ***pass*** on a 1 NT rebid by the opener. In those exceptional cases, the lack of communications with dummy will, most often, prevent a 3 NT contract, even opposite an opener of 23 + HL pts.

– For any other hand ***without*** 4 hearts, the *"brake"* will be applied *immediately* via a 2 ♦ bid, when in the *minimum* point zone. i.e. :

1 ♣	1 ♦
1 NT	2 ♣ ?
2 ♦ *"brake"*	**18/20** HL pts

Therefore, a direct response or rebid of 2 ♠, 2 NT, 3 ♣ or 3 ♦ describes a strong hand in the *maximum* point zone, **10/12** or **21/23 +** HL pts.

Caution : This means that, after a 1 ♣ opening, 1) a rebid of 2 ♦ no longer describes 4 + diamonds, and 2) a balanced hand cannot include a 5 - 4 minor two-suiter, which could not be described.

RESPONSE OF 1 NT (1 ♠) ON A 1 ♣ OPENING

A direct response of a balanced hand to a 1 ♣ opening is done via a ***transfer*** bid of 1 ♠ for NT. In response to a strong opening, having the weaker hand bid NT is simply inconceivable! To protect against a damaging defensive lead, No Trump **must** be bid by the stronger hand which dictates using a 1 ♠ response as a *transfer* bid for NT.

On responder's 1 ♠ bid, the opener's *transfer* to 1 NT is a *relay* on which the responder will describe his hand, in two point zones : **7/9** and **10/12** HL pts.

Reminder : On opener's transfer to 1 NT, the responder benefits from having the additional bid of 2 ♣ available. This 2 ♣ bid is used to identify holding **both Major** suits, either 4 ♠ 4 ♥, 5 ♠ 4 ♥ or 5 ♥ 4 ♠.
Their full description was outlined in the chapter on the 1 ♠ opening.

Let's conclude this chapter with deals taken from tournaments :

1965 World Championship (Buenos Aires)

♠ x x x	♠ A K J x x
♥ A J x x	♥ Q 10 x x
♦ A x x	♦ x x
♣ A x x	♣ x x

A. Truscott's comment on the above deal : *"Most pairs missed the 4 ♥ game after this bidding start :* 1 ♣ - 1 ♠ - 1 NT *as only a serious overbid of 3 ♥ would get you to 4 ♥"*.

A serious overbid of 3 ♥ ?! Only if you count East's hand for 10 H pts ! But East's hand has 14 HLD pts (1 point for 3 honors in a 5-card suit, 1 pt for 2 doubletons over a NT bid). Opposite 13 HL pts, it certainly would not be an overbid !

In **Optimal** Precision Relay, getting to 4 ♥ would be bid as follows :

1 NT (12/14 HL pts)	2 ♣ ?
2 ♥ (4 hearts)	4 ♥

East's hand is much too strong for a *transfer* bid and must relay.
On West's 2 ♥ bid, East can then add 2 pts for the 8-card ♥ Fit = 4 ♥.

Regional tournament, 1998.

♠ A J x x	♠ Q 10 x x x
♥ A J x	♥ K x x
♦ K x x	♦ Q J 10 x
♣ x x x	♣ x

In **Optimal** Precision Relay, these two hands would be bid as follows :

1 NT (12/14 HL)	2 ♥ (*transfer* for spades)
2 ♠ (*transfer*)	3 ♣ (♣ singleton, 10/12 HLD)
4 ♠	

On East's 3 ♣ bid, identifying a ♣ singleton, West can now add to his initial 12 H pts + 2 pts for the 9-card ♠ Fit + 2 pts for *"no wasted honor pts"* in clubs = 16 pts = 4 ♠ opposite 10 + HLD pts.

International tournament, 2003.

♠ x x x	♠ x
♥ A x x	♥ K x
♦ K Q x x	♦ A J x x x
♣ A x x	♣ K Q 10 x x

1 NT (12 / 14 HL)	2 ♣ ?
2 ♦ (4 + ♦)	2 ♥ ?
2 NT (4 ♦ 3 3 3)	4 ♣ ? (trump is ♦)
4 ♥ (3 Keys w/ ♦ Q)	4 ♠ ? (K & Q ♠ Ask)
4 NT (no ♠ K or Q)	6 ♦

East knows his side to be in slam zone right upon West's 2 ♦ bid (+ 2 pts for the ♦ 9-card Fit). His 4 ♠ Ask is to clarify West's number of Key Cards which could be 1, rather than 3. With nothing in spades, West has 3 Key Cards. 6 ♦ becomes easy to bid.

Example from *"The No Trump Zone"* (Danny Kleinman).

♠ x x	♠ A x
♥ K x x	♥ A x x
♦ A Q x	♦ K J x x
♣ A K x x x	♣ Q x x x

Comment from the book's author : *"If you open West's hand 1 NT, 15/17 H pts, your partner cannot be expected to consider a 6 NT contract with 14 H pts, as we all know that 34 pts are needed for that contract".*

And, indeed, West's hand has 18 HL pts, not 17, and should **not** be opened 1 NT. But there is more to this than just the point count…
In **Optimal Precision Relay**, these hands would be bid as follows :

1 ♣ (18 + HLD pts)	1 ♦
1 NT	2 ♣ ?
2 ♦ (18/20 HLD pts)	2 ♥ ?
3 ♣ (5 ♣ 3 3 2)	3 ♦ ?
3 ♠ (2 ♠ : 5 ♣ 3 3 2 ♠)	4 ♣ ? (trump is ♣)
4 ♦ (3 Keys w/o ♣ Q)	4 ♥ ? (K & Q ♥ Ask)
5 ♣ (♥ King)	5 ♦ ? (K & Q ♦ Ask)
5 ♠ (♦ Queen)	6 NT

East knows his side to be in slam zone right upon West's 3 ♣ bid (+ 3 pts for the ♣ 9-card Fit with the Q).

No confusion is possible on West's number of Key Cards with his 18/20 HL pts. After his ♥ and ♦ Asking bids, East knows that there is no grand slam (West does not have the ♥ Q, nor can he have the ♠ K, which would give him 22 HL pts).

And that last point is "the rest of the story" as should East have his spades and hearts reversed, he would play 7 ♣ knowing that West has 3 hearts, for one ruff. Knowing **all** of West's 13 cards is critical here !

European Championship, 2004.

♠ x x x	♠ A x
♥ A x	♥ K Q x
♦ A K x x x	♦ Q x x x
♣ A Q x	♣ K J x x

On a 15/17 H pts 1 NT opening, East players, with 15 H pts, rule out a No Trump slam and most teams play 3 NT. A few teams play 6 ♦.

But West has 19 ½ HL pts! And the *right* bidding should be :

1 ♣ (18 + HLD pts)	1 ♦
1 NT	2 ♣ ?
2 ♦ (18/20 HL pts)	2 ♥ ?
3 ♦ (5 ♦ 3 3 2)	3 ♥ ?
3 NT (5 ♦ 3 3 2 ♥)	4 ♣ ? (trump is ♦)
4 ♠ (4 Keys w/o ♦ Q)	4 NT ? (K & Q ♠ Ask)
5 ♣ (no ♠ Q or K)	5 NT ? (K & Q ♣ Ask)
6 ♦ (♣ Queen)	7 NT

East knows his side to be in slam zone right upon West's opening! and in grand slam zone upon West's 3 ♦ bid (+ 3 pts for the ♦ 9-card Fit). His 4 NT Ask is to clarify West's Key Cards which could be 2, rather than 4. With nothing in spades, West cannot have 2 Key Cards only.

A 5 ♠ Ask – a *repeat* Ask in spades – would be to clarify West's number of Key Cards, so a ♣ Ask must be made at 5 NT, a safe Ask as, if West responds 6 ♣, without the ♣ Queen, East can play 6 ♦ on a ♠ ruff (or a ♣ finesse) as he knows about West's three spades.

A rather satisfying 7 NT with the rest of the field in 3 NT or 6 ♦ !
Precise, pertinent description !

BIDDING AFTER INTERVENTIONS OVER A 1 NT OPENING

The table below summarizes **suggested** bids by the opener's **partner** following an intervention by the opposite team over a 1 NT opening. The suggested bids are guided by two key **principles** or **objectives** :

1. Over **double**, the priority is to ***escape*** in a suit at the *most economical level* possible, the two-level : thus, *redouble* replaces 2 ♣ as *relay*, to allow 2 ♣ to be a *transfer* bid for diamonds.

Any other overcall, *other* than *double*, gets the opener's side off the hook and therefore his partner *should only bid with a strong hand* of **11** + HL pts or **13** + HLD pts.

2. Retain, the direct responses of 2 ♠ and up whenever possible.

INTERVENTIONS over a 1 NT opening	SUGGESTED BIDS BY OPENER'S PARTNER Key principles : On *double*, Redouble to *relay* Retain 2 ♠ through to 3 ♠ responses
Double (*Take-out or penalty*)	**Redouble** : Relay replaces 2 ♣. 2 ♣ (for ♦), 2 ♦, 2 ♥ and 2 NT are all *transfer* bids 2 ♠, 3 ♣, 3 ♦, 3 ♥, 3 ♠ : *retain their same meaning*
2 ♣ (*Landy* : both Majors)	**Double** : Relay 2 ♦ : natural 2 ♥ / ♠ : ♥ / ♠ *guarded* to play 3 NT 2 NT, 3 ♣, 3 ♦ : retain their same meaning
2 ♦ (5/6 ♦ or ♥ if *transfer*)	**Double** : Relay 2 ♥, 2 ♠, 2 NT, 3 ♣, 3 ♦ : keep their meaning 3 ♥, 3 ♠ : Keep their meaning
2 ♥ / 2 ♠ (5 /6 ♥ / ♠)	**Double** : Relay 2 NT, 3 ♣, 3 ♦, 3 ♥, 3 ♠ : keep their meaning
2 NT (5 – 5 ♦ / ♣)	**Double** : Relay *"Sputnik"* type **with ♥ / ♠** 3 ♥, 3 ♠ : Keep their meaning
3 ♣ / 3 ♦ (*single-suiters*)	**Double** : Relay *"Sputnik"* type **with ♥ / ♠** 3 ♥, 3 ♠ : Keep their meaning

---

1 ♦ OPENING   **Balanced** distribution   **15/17** HL pts

Or **Two**-suiter with ♦ : 5 ♦ 4 ♠ or 4 ♥ or ♦/♣   **14/19** HLD pts

Denies : a 5-card Major **both 4**-card Majors a 6-card ♦ single-suit

REBIDS, RESPONSES AND DEVELOPMENTS

We previously established why opening a strong NT, 15/17 H, is a serious error, *pre-empting* the partner *instead of the opponents*.

We are now going to illustrate the numerous advantages of opening 1 ♦ balanced hands of 15/17 HL pts. Hands such as :

♠ A J 10 x	♠ A x x	♠ A x x
♥ K x x	♥ A x	♥ K Q x
♦ x x	♦ K Q 10 x x	♦ Q J x
♣ A J 10 x	♣ x x x	♣ A J x x
15 H pts	**16** HL pts	**17** H pts
(no Queen)		(4 3 3)

I. THE "SYSTEMIC" PRECISION OF REBIDS ON A 1 ♥ RELAY RESPONSE

In **Optimal P**recision Relay, priority is given to naming, first, a 4-card ♠ suit on partner's 1 ♥ *relay*. This not only identifies the 4-card Major at a very economical level, it also means that a 1 NT rebid **denies** four spades – a very useful precision, at a very early, economical stage !

It also means that any *other* rebid by the opener – 2 ♣ or 2 ♦ or 2 ♥ – **denies** 4 spades while describing a 5 – 4 two-suiter hand, and this, in a very precise, specific 3 HLD point zone ! (14/16 HLD for 2 ♣ and 2 ♦, 17/19 HLD for 2 ♥ and higher bids).

Furthermore, after a 1 NT rebid, the opener's responses to a 2 ♣ *relay*-Stayman by his partner are the very same as after a 1 NT opening i.e. 2 ♦ is "natural" and guarantees 4 + diamonds, and 2 NT guarantees 4 + clubs while denying 4 diamonds and denying a 4-card Major.

Last, but certainly not least, as the 1 ♦ opening **denies** a ♦ single-suiter hand, a 2 ♦ rebid can now be used to describe, *conventionally*, 4 ♥ in the *minimum* point zone of 14/16 HLD pts. And this applies, as well, on a response of 1 ♠ !

This definitely addresses a major problem of *traditional* bidding which **cannot rebid** hearts with **less** than 18 HD pts, on a 1 ♠ response.

Illustration :　　♠ x　　　　　　　　♠ A x x x x
　　　　　　　　♥ A Q x x　　　　　♥ K x x x
　　　　　　　　♦ K Q J x x　　　　♦ x x x
　　　　　　　　♣ x x x　　　　　　♣ x

While *traditional* bidding will be :

　　　　　　1 ♦　　　　　　　　　1 ♠
　　　　　　2 ♦　　　　　　　　　Pass

In **Optimal** Precision Relay, the bidding will be :

　　　　　　1 ♦　　　　　　　　　1 ♠　(5 ♠, 7/9 HL)
　　　　　　2 ♦ (♠ *Misfit*, 5 ♦ 4 ♥)　4 ♥

On West's 2 ♦ rebid, East can now add to his 7 ½ HL pts (no Queen), 2 pts for the 8-card ♥ Fit with the King + 1 point for the 8-card ♦ Fit + 3 D pts for the ♣ singleton with 4 trumps = 13 ½ HLDF pts = game.

II. THE "SYSTEMIC" PRECISION OF RESPONSES TO A 1 ♦ OPENING

In **Optimal** Precision Relay, a responder with a hand of **10 +** HL pts automatically *relays* (1 ♥) on his partner's 1 ♦ opening. That is because the 1 ♦ opening guarantees 14 + HLD pts and therefore 24 + pts to the side – enough points to play at the level of three and therefore to *relay*.

This means, and this is a major implication, that *any direct response* to 1 ♦, other than a 1 ♥ *relay*, is limited to **7/9** HL pts. One point zone only! Simplicity and precision !
Furthermore, in **Optimal** Precision Relay, any response from 1 NT up is a *transfer* bid, for the next suit up.
A *traditional* 1 NT response – balanced hand without a 4-card Major – would be counter-productive, bidding NT from the weak hand when a 1 ♥ *relay* will allow NT to be bid by the opener, the *stronger* hand.
Therefore, the 1 NT response can now be used, instead, to bid clubs, thus allowing all other bids, up the line, to be *transfer* bids, as well.

This now means that the responder can immediately identify a 6-card Major suit of 7/9 HL pts by a *transfer* bid response of 2 ♦ (for ♥) or 2 ♥ (for ♠), and *have it bid* by the opener, the *stronger* hand, while respecting the *bidding level safety* as he is assured of a minimum of 21 + HLD pts on his side. A most useful response to *pre-empt* a potential intervention.

This, in turn, allows using a direct 2 ♠ response as a *conventional* bid.
The **Optimal** Precision Relay method uses it to *specifically* describe a minor two-suiter **without** a singleton i.e. 5 ♦ 4 ♣ 2 2 or 5 ♣ 4 ♦ 2 2, of 7/9 HL pts. Another *"competitive initiative"* bid intended to raise the level of bidding to *pre-empt* opponents holding the Major suits.
At the same time, it is an invitation for 3 NT to an opener of 16 + HL pts

214

On such a 2 ♠ response, the opener can either *transfer* to 2 NT, or 3 ♣ or 3 ♦, or conclude in 3 NT, or *relay* in 3 ♥ to know partner's exact distribution (response : 3 NT with 5 ♦ 4 ♣, 3 ♠ with 5 ♣ 4 ♦).
Illustration :

♠ J x x x	♠ x x
♥ A x	♥ x x
♦ K Q x x	♦ A x x x
♣ A Q x	♣ K x x x x

While *traditional* bidding would most often be :

1 NT (15/17 H)	Pass (< than 8 H)

In **Optimal Precision Relay**, the bidding will be :

1 ♦	2 ♠ (♦ / ♣ *two-suiter*, 7/9 HL)
3 NT	

East's **2 ♠** bid enables the opener to add 2 Fit pts in ♦ / ♣ to his 16 ½ H pts for a total of 25 ½ HLF pts minimum for the side = 3 NT.
Furthermore, a ♣ or ♦ single-suit or minor two-suiter, in a weak hand *unfavorable* to a NT contract, can now be identified by the responder at the economical level of 1 NT (for ♣), and be bid by the *stronger* hand !

Last, but certainly not least, a direct response of 1 ♠ describes *specifically* **5** spades and 7/9 HL pts – **not 4** spades, as a 1 ♥ *relay* would be used to uncover a potential 4 – 4 spade Fit, and **not 6** spades, either, which would be described by a 2 ♥ *transfer* bid.
This fixes the *traditional* bidding's typical problem of not defining the length of spades when responding 1 ♠ on a 1 ♦ opening, and enables the opener to use several very useful rebids on a 1 ♠ response such as:
– He can *relay*, by 1 NT, to know more about the responder's hand residual distribution.
– Or, **without** a spade Fit, and minimum, he can *pass* or rebid 2 ♣ (♣ / ♦ two-suiter) or 2 ♦ (♦ / ♥ two-suiter).
– Or, **with** a spade Fit, he can raise spades, 2 ♠ or 3 ♠, or make a *trial* bid of 2 ♥ or 3 ♣, with a ♥ or ♣ singleton and **17** + HLDF. Illustration :

♠ K Q x	♠ A x x x x
♥ x	♥ x x x
♦ A x x x x	♦ K x x
♣ A x x x	♣ x x

While *traditional* bidding will most often be :

1 ♦	1 ♠
2 ♣	2 ♦
Pass	

West can only *pass* on East's 2♦ *preference* bid, not knowing about East's 5 spades. But, in **Optimal P**recision Relay, the bidding will be :

1 ♦	1 ♠ (5 ♠, 7/9 HL)
2 ♥ (♠ Fit, ♥ singleton)	4 ♠

On West's 2 ♥ *trial* bid, East can now add to his 7 ½ HL pts, 2 pts for no *"wasted honor pts"* in hearts and conclude in 4 ♠, assured of 26 ½ + pts. West's 2 ♥ rebid cannot mean to describe a strong 5 ♦ 4 ♥ two-suiter, as, with such a hand, he would relay (1 NT) on East's 1 ♠ to have his partner describe the rest of his hand. A jump *"mini-splinter"* to 3 ♥ would require 20 + HLDF pts (with 2 + Fit pts).

One can readily see the significant, multiple benefits of the **rebids** and **responses** after an **Optimal** Precision Relay 1 ♦ opening – which make this opening and its rebids another cornerstone of the bidding method.

Let's now cover the description of opener's hand on successive *relays*.

OPENER'S HAND DESCRIPTION ON SUCCESSIVE RELAYS

I. BALANCED HANDS : 4 3 3 3, 4 4 3 2, 5 minor 3 3 2, 5 4 minors 2 2.

A) WITHOUT 4 spades.

On a 1 ♥ *relay*, the 1 ♦ opener will rebid 1 NT, describing a balanced distribution of 15/17 HL pts, *without 4 ♠*.
On partner's next *relays*, starting with 2 ♣, the opener's rebids are exactly the same as they were after a 1 NT opening (2 ♦ = 4 diamonds, no 4-card Major, 2 ♥ : 4 hearts, 2 NT : 4 clubs, denies 4 hearts and 4 diamonds) .

B) WITH 4 spades.

On a 1 ♥ *relay*, the 1 ♦ opener will rebid 1 ♠, an *absolute priority*, to describe his 4 spades. On the next *relay*, 1 NT, the opener will bid 2 ♥, *conventional*, describing specifically a *balanced* distribution of 15/17 HL pts – as 2 ♥ cannot be a *natural* bid : 4 ♠ 4 ♥ hands are opened 1 ♥ or 1 ♠, *never* 1 ♦.
On the next *relay*, 2 NT, the opener will describe the rest of his hand as follows : 3 NT if 4 ♠ 3 3 3, 3 ♣ or 3 ♦ with 4 ♣ or 4 ♦, then his tripleton.

II. UNBALANCED HANDS.

A) WITH 4 spades.

On a 1 ♥ *relay*, the opener will rebid 1 ♠. Then, on the next *relay*, 1 NT :

– With a **strong** hand of **17/19** HLD pts, the opener will bid 2 ♠, describing a ♦/♠ two-suiter. On the next relay, 2 NT :
With 5 ♦ 4 ♠ 2 2 : 3 NT – Final.

5 ♦ 4 ♠ 3 ♥ 1 ♣ : 3 ♥ followed by : 3 NT, nothing else to describe.

5 ♦ 4 ♠ 3 ♣ 1 ♥ : 3 ♣ followed by : 3 NT, nothing else to describe.

5 ♦ 4 ♠ 4 ♣ 0 ♥ : 3 ♣ followed by : <u>3 ♥</u>   4 th suit = void.

5 ♦ 4 ♠ 4 ♥ 0 ♣ : *Not applicable* – a 4 ♠ 4 ♥ hand is **not** opened 1 ♦

4 ♦ 4 ♠ 4 ♣ 1 ♥ : 3 ♣ followed by : <u>3 ♠</u>   as *cannot* describe 5 spades

4 ♦ 4 ♠ <u>5</u> ♣ 0 ♥ : 3 ♣ followed by : 4 ♣

6 ♦ 4 ♠ 2 ♥ 1 ♣ : 3 ♦ followed by : 3 NT

6 ♦ 4 ♠ 3 ♥ 0 ♣ : 3 ♥ followed by : <u>4 ♣</u>   4 th suit = void, thus 6 ♦

6 ♦ 4 ♠ 2 ♣ 1 ♥ : 3 ♦ followed by : <u>3 ♠</u> as *cannot* describe 5 spades

6 ♦ 4 ♠ 3 ♣ 0 ♥ : 3 ♣ followed by : 4 ♦

– With a hand of **14/16** HLD pts, on a 1 NT *relay* the opener will bid :

5 ♦ 4 ♠ 2 2   : 2 ♦ followed by : 2 NT and then 3 NT.

5 ♦ 4 ♠ 3 ♥ 1 ♣ : 2 ♦ followed by : 3 ♥   – Final.

5 ♦ 4 ♠ 3 ♣ 1 ♥ : 2 ♣ followed by : 2 NT – Final.

5 ♦ 4 ♠ 4 ♣ 0 ♥ : 2 ♣ followed by : 3 ♣ then <u>3 ♥</u> 4th suit = void

4 ♦ 4 ♠ 4 ♣ 1 ♥ : 2 ♣ followed by : <u>2 ♠</u> – Final.

4 ♦ 4 ♠ <u>5</u> ♣ 0 ♥ : 2 ♣ followed by : 3 ♣ and then <u>3 ♠</u>

6 ♦ 4 ♠ 2 ♥ 1 ♣ : 2 ♦ followed by : 2 NT and then 3 ♦

6 ♦ 4 ♠ 3 ♥ 0 ♣ : 2 ♦ followed by : 2 NT and then 3 ♥ – Final.

6 ♦ 4 ♠ 2 ♣ 1 ♥ : 2 ♦ followed by : 3 ♦ – Final.

6 ♦ 4 ♠ 3 ♣ 0 ♥ : 2 ♣ followed by : 3 ♦ – Final.

Note that the rebids of 2 ♣ and 2 ♦ indicate *immediately* the *minimum* 14/16 HLD point zone, and that the 2 ♣ rebid guarantees **3 +** clubs **and denies 2** hearts, while the 2 ♦ rebid guarantees **5 +** diamonds **and denies 3** clubs. Note, as well, that the 2 ♣ rebid reveals, very *economically*, 12 cards of the hand and a ♥ singleton in a 5 ♦ 4 ♠ 3 ♣ hand structure.

B) WITHOUT 4 spades.

On a 1 ♥ *relay*, the 1 ♦ opener will rebid as follows :

– **Without 4 ♥**, thus a ♣/♦ two-suiter : 2 ♣ with **14/16** HLD pts.
                                              <u>2 ♠</u> with **17/19** HLD pts.

– **With** 4 ♥ and 4 + ♦ :   <u>2 ♦</u> with **14/16** HLD pts.
                              2 ♥ with **17/19** HLD pts.

This applies to 5 + ♦ 4 ♥ hands as well as to 5 ♣ 4 ♥ 4 ♦ 0 ♠ hands and to 4 ♦ 4 ♥ 4 ♣ 1 ♠ .

The use of the economical 2 ♦ rebid to describe a ♦ / ♥ two-suiter is unique and specific to the **Optimal** Precision Relay method as its 1 ♦ opening **denies** a ♦ single-suiter hand and can therefore use the rebid of 2 ♦ to describe, *conventionally*, 4 ♥ in the *minimum* point zone of 14/16 HLD pts. And this applies, as well, on a response of 1 ♠ !

This definitely addresses the problem that *traditional* bidding has as it *cannot rebid hearts* with *less* than 18 HD pts, on a 1 ♠ response. Illustration:

♠ x	♠ A x x x x
♥ A Q x x	♥ K x x x
♦ K Q J x x	♦ x x x
♣ x x x	♣ x

While *traditional* bidding will be :

1 ♦	1 ♠
2 ♦	Pass

In **Optimal** Precision Relay, the bidding will be :

1 ♦	1 ♠ (5 ♠, 7/9 HL)
2 ♦ (♠ *Misfit*, 5 + ♦ 4 ♥)	4 ♥

On West's 2 ♦ rebid, East can now add to his 7 ½ HL pts (no Queen), 2 pts for the 8-card ♥ Fit with the King + 1 point for the 8-card ♦ Fit + 3 D pts for the ♣ singleton with 4 trumps = 13 ½ HLDF pts = game.

The description of **unbalanced** hands **without** 4 spades will thus be as follows :

A) WITH 4 hearts.

On a 1 ♥ *relay*, the opener will rebid <u>2 ♦</u> with **14/16** HLD pts, 2 ♥ with **17/19** HLD pts. On the next *relay*, in both cases 2 ♠, the description of the residual cards will be the same for both point zones, as follows :

5 ♦ 4 ♥ 2 2   : 2 NT, and then, if necessary 3 NT.
5 ♦ 4 ♥ 3 ♠ 1 ♣ : 3 ♠   – Final.
5 ♦ 4 ♥ 3 ♣ 1 ♠ : 3 ♣ followed by : 3 NT, nothing else to describe.
5 ♦ 4 ♥ 4 ♠ 0 ♠ : 3 ♣ followed by : <u>3 ♠</u>   4 th suit = void.
5 ♦ 4 ♥ 4 ♠ 0 ♣ : *Not applicable* – a 4 ♠ 4 ♥ hand is **not** opened 1 ♦
4 ♦ 4 ♥ 4 ♠ 1 ♣ : *Not applicable* – a 4 ♠ 4 ♥ hand is **not** opened 1 ♦
4 ♦ 4 ♥ 4 ♣ 1 ♠ : 3 ♣ followed by : <u>3 ♥</u>   *cannot* describe 5 hearts
4 ♦ 4 ♥ <u>5 ♣</u> 0 ♠ : 3 ♣ followed by : 4 ♣

6 ♦ 4 ♥ 2 ♠ 1 ♣ : 2 NT followed by : 3 ♦ and then 3 NT
6 ♦ 4 ♥ 3 ♠ 0 ♣ : 2 NT followed by : 3 ♦ and then 3 ♠
6 ♦ 4 ♥ 2 ♣ 1 ♠ : 3 ♦ followed by : 3 NT
6 ♦ 4 ♥ 3 ♣ 0 ♠ : 3 ♣ followed by : 4 ♦

B) WITHOUT 4 hearts. Therefore a ♦ / ♣ two-suiter.

On a 1 ♥ *relay*, the opener will rebid 2 ♣ with **14/16** HLD pts, 2 ♠ with **17/19** HLD pts. After a 2 ♣ rebid, the next *relay* will be 2 ♥ and the description will be as follows :

5 ♦ 4 ♣ 2 2   : 2 NT followed on 3 ♥ ? by : 3 NT.
5 ♦ 4 ♣ 3 ♥ 1 ♠ : 3 ♥ − Final.
5 ♦ 4 ♣ 3 ♠ 1 ♥ : 2 ♠ followed by : 3 ♠ − Final.
5 ♦ 5 ♣ 2 ♥ 1 ♠ : 2 NT followed on 3 ♥ ? by : 4 ♣
5 ♦ 5 ♣ 3 ♥ 0 ♠ : 2 NT followed on 3 ♥ ? by : 3 ♠ 4th suit = void
5 ♦ 5 ♣ 2 ♠ 1 ♥ : 2 ♠ followed by : 3 ♣ and then 3 NT
5 ♦ 5 ♣ 3 ♠ 0 ♥ : 2 ♠ followed by : 3 ♣ and then 3 ♠
6 ♦ 4 ♣ 2 ♠ 1 ♥ : 2 ♠ followed by : 3 ♦ and then 3 NT
6 ♦ 4 ♣ 3 ♠ 0 ♥ : 2 ♠ followed by : 3 ♦ and then 3 ♠
6 ♦ 4 ♣ 2 ♥ 1 ♠ : 3 ♦ followed by : 3 NT
6 ♦ 4 ♣ 3 ♥ 0 ♠ : 3 ♦ followed by : 4 ♣ more economical than 4 ♥
4 ♦ 5 ♣ 2 2   : 3 ♣ followed on 3 ♥ ? by : 3 NT
4 ♦ 5 ♣ 3 ♥ 1 ♠ : 3 ♣ followed on 3 ♥ ? by : 3 ♠ impossible bid
4 ♦ 5 ♣ 3 ♠ 1 ♥ : 2 ♠ followed by : 3 ♣ and then 3 ♠
4 ♦ 6 ♣ 2 ♠ 1 ♥ : 2 ♠ followed by : 3 ♣ and then 3 NT
4 ♦ 6 ♣ 3 ♠ 0 ♥ : 2 ♠ followed by : 3 ♣ then 4 ♣ 6 ♣ and a void
4 ♦ 6 ♣ 2 ♥ 1 ♠ : 3 ♣ followed by : 4 ♣
4 ♦ 6 ♣ 3 ♥ 0 ♠ : 3 ♣ followed by : 4 ♥

With the same hands as above but **17/19** HLD pts, the opener will *conventionally* rebid, on a 1 ♥ *relay* : 2 ♠ directly, or 2 NT, with 5 ♦ 5 ♣ or 3 ♣ with 4 ♦ 6 ♣.
After the first rebid of 2 ♠, on the next *relay*, 2 NT, these hands will be described as follows :

5 ♦ 4 ♣ 2 2   : 3 NT − Final.
5 ♦ 4 ♣ 3 ♥ 1 ♠ : 3 ♥ − Final.
5 ♦ 4 ♣ 3 ♠ 1 ♥ : 3 ♠ − Final.
4 ♦ 5 ♣ 2 2   : 3 ♣ followed on 3 ♦ ? by : 3 NT
4 ♦ 5 ♣ 3 ♥ 1 ♠ : 3 ♣ followed on 3 ♦ ? by : 3 ♥
4 ♦ 5 ♣ 3 ♠ 1 ♥ : 3 ♣ followed on 3 ♦ ? by : 3 ♠
6 ♦ 4 ♣ 2 ♠ 1 ♥ : 3 ♦ followed on 3 ♥ ? by : 3 ♠
6 ♦ 4 ♣ 3 ♠ 0 ♥ : 3 ♦ followed on 3 ♥ ? by : 4 ♦
6 ♦ 4 ♣ 2 ♥ 1 ♠ : 3 ♦ followed on 3 ♥ ? by : 3 NT
6 ♦ 4 ♣ 3 ♥ 0 ♠ : 3 ♦ followed on 3 ♥ ? by : 4 ♣

The 5 ♦ 5 ♣ hands are described by a *direct jump* to 2 NT on the 1 ♥ *relay*, followed, on the next *relay*, 3 ♥, by :

5 ♦ 5 ♣ 2 ♠ 1 ♥ : 3 ♠
5 ♦ 5 ♣ 2 ♥ 1 ♠ : 3 NT
5 ♦ 5 ♣ 3 ♥ 0 ♠ : <u>4 ♣</u>
5 ♦ 5 ♣ 3 ♠ 0 ♥ : <u>4 ♠</u>

The hands with **6 clubs and 4 diamonds** are described by a *direct jump* to 3 ♣ on the 1 ♥ *relay*, followed on the next *relay*, 3 ♥, by :

6 ♣ 4 ♦ 2 ♠ 1 ♥ : 3 ♠
6 ♣ 4 ♦ 2 ♥ 1 ♠ : 3 NT
6 ♣ 4 ♦ 3 ♥ 0 ♠ : 4 ♣
6 ♣ 4 ♦ 3 ♠ 0 ♥ : <u>4 ♠</u>

This concludes the complete description of hands opened 1 ♦ on successive relays. A table on the next page summarizes this.

SUMMARY OF HAND DESCRIPTION ON SUCCESSIVE RELAYS

DISTRIBUTION	ON 1 ♥ ?	2nd Relay	DESCRIPTION	FINAL BID
<u>With</u> 4 spades				
15/17 HL	1 ♠	1 NT ?	<u>2 ♥</u>	
4 ♠ 3 3 3				3 NT
4 ♠ 4 ♣ or 4 ♦				3 ♦/3 ♥
14/16 HLD	1 ♠	1 NT ?		
4 ♦ 4 ♠ 4 ♣ 1 ♥			2 ♣	3 ♣
5 ♦ 4 ♠ 2 2			2 ♦	2 NT
5 ♦ 4 ♠ 3 ♥ 1 ♣			2 ♦	3 ♥
6 ♦ 4 ♠ 2 ♣ 1 ♥			2 ♦	3 ♦
17/19 HLD	1 ♠	1 NT ?	2 ♠	residual
<u>w/o</u> 4 spades				
15/17 HL	1 NT	2 ♣ ?		
with 4 ♥			2 ♥	the
without 4 ♥			2 ♦/2 NT	residual
♦ / ♣ two-suiter				
14/16 HLD	2 ♣	2 ♥ ?		
5 ♦ 4 ♣ 2 2			2 NT	3 NT
5 ♦ 4 ♣ 3 1			2 ♠ or 3 ♥	the
5 ♦ 5 ♣ 2 1			2 ♠ or 3 ♣	residual
6 ♦ 4 ♣ 2 1			2 ♠ or 3 ♦	
4 ♦ 5 ♣ 3 1			3 ♣	
4 ♦ 6 ♣ 2 1			3 ♣	
17/19 HLD	2 ♠	2 NT ?		
5 ♦ 4 ♣ 2 2			3 NT	
5 ♦ 4 ♣ 3 1			3 ♠ or 3 ♥	the
6 ♦ 4 ♣ 2 1			3 ♦	residual
4 ♦ 5 ♣ 3 1			3 ♣	
5 ♦ 5 ♣ 2 1	<u>2 NT</u>	3 ♥ ?		
4 ♦ 6 ♣ 2 1	3 ♣	3 ♥ ?	doubleton	

III. DIRECT RESPONSES TO A 1 ♦ OPENING OTHER THAN RELAYS

GUIDING PRINCIPLES

The direct responses to a 1 ♦ opening in **Optimal** **P**recision **R**elay are quite different from those in *traditional* bidding. Before studying them in detail, we will outline, first, the key principles which guide them. They are few and simple, as follows :

– The 1 ♦ opening being in a higher point-range, **14/19** HLD pts, than the 1 ♥ and 1 ♠ openings, enables a responder of **10** + HL pts to *relay*, assured of a *minimum* of **24** HLD pts on their side. This is significant as it means that any response *other* than a 1 ♥ *relay* can now be precisely limited to *one single* point-zone of **7/9** HL pts! This allows *"competitive initiative"* direct responses, with **7/9** HL pts, at the level of **two** that do not compromise the bidding level safety (14 + 8 = 22).

– Since a 1 ♥ *relay* response can be used to find out, *immediately*, whether the opener has a 4-card spade suit, a 1 ♠ response will describe a **5**-card spade suit, thus resolving a major problem of *traditional* bidding.

– And any *other* direct response, being a ***transfer*** bid, enables the opener, the *strong* hand, to bid the suit described, as well as giving the responder an opportunity to bid again.
And these *transfer* bids can start with 1NT, for clubs, as there is no reason to have the *weak* hand bid 1 NT to describe a balanced hand without spades, when an economical 1 ♥ *relay* can have NT bid by the opener. Therefore, the responses of 1 NT, 2 ♣, 2 ♦, etc. are all *transfers*.

So, responses to a 1 ♦ opening are : 1 ♥ is *relay*, 1 ♠ is natural, with **5** spades, 7/9 HL pts, and *all other* responses are *transfer* bids, 7/9 HL pts. As simple as can be !

We can now go over the detailed responses to the 1 ♦ opening.

RESPONSES OTHER THAN SUCCESSIVE RELAYS

DETERMINING PARAMETERS

The same three key parameters applying to responses over a 1 ♥ or 1 ♠ or 1 NT opening apply to the responses over a 1 ♦ opening : the hand's **strength**, the search for a **Fit** in a **Major** suit, and without such Fit, the search for a potential 3 NT contract.

1. The hand's **strength**, therefore its number of points.

As previously mentioned, there is only **one** point-zone to consider, **7/9** HL pts, since a responder with **10** + **HL** pts can simply and safely *relay*.

However, because the 1 ♦ opening is **2** pts *stronger* than a 1 ♥ or 1 ♠ opening, partner will have to respond with **5 +** HL pts, instead of **7**.
To keep things simple, his response will be assimilated to a **7/9** pt zone.

2. The second parameter is to identify a potential **Fit** in a Major suit.

2.1 With a **4**-card Major, **5 +** HL pts.

The responder will *relay*, by 1 ♥. Relaying is *mandatory*, to uncover a potential **4**-card Major in opener's hand.
With **4** spades, the opener will rebid 1 ♠, which **denies** 4 hearts.
If responder has 4 spades, a Fit has been found, while if he has 4 hearts, he knows that no heart Fit exists.
If the opener rebids 1 NT, he **denies** 4 spades.
If responder has 4 hearts, he can then *relay*-Stayman. Further bids by either partner are the very same as after a 1 NT opening (2 ♣ is Stayman, 2 ♦, 2 ♥ are *transfer* bids, etc.).
Any *other* rebid by opener will immediately either deny a 4-card Major (2 ♣ or 2 ♠ rebids on 1 ♥), or describe 4 hearts (2 ♦ or 2 ♥ on 1 ♥).

Note : 4 ♥ is the game contract that *eludes* expert pairs *most frequently*, often with 4 – 4 heart fits, as the heart suit is outranked by the spade suit or because a 4 heart-suit is with a 5-card minor in a point zone that does **not** allow a *reverse* bid. Therefore, it is critically important to identify the holding of 4 hearts, in a minimum point-zone, with hands such as : 5 ♦ 4 ♥, 5 ♣ 4 ♥ and 4 ♠ 4 ♥.
It is worth noting that the **Optimal** Precision Relay method addresses this issue in every case, i.e. with a 2 ♦ rebid with a 5 ♦ 4 ♥ hand of 14/16 HLD pts, or a 2 ♣ opening with a 2 ♥ rebid with a 5 ♣ 4 ♥ hand of 14/17 HLD pts or a 1 ♠ opening with a 2 ♥ rebid with 4 ♠ 4 ♥ hands of 12/14 HLD pts. And a 1 ♥ *relay* on a 1 ♦ opening will enable the responder to find out whether the opener has 4 hearts, or not.

2.2 With **5 spades** and **(5) 7/9 HL** pts.

The responder will bid 1 ♠ on which an opener with a ♠ **misfit** (singleton), will revert to 2 ♣ with a ♦/♣ two-suiter, or to 2 ♦ with a ♦/♥ two-suiter. Simple, economical and very descriptive !
While, **with** a ♠ **Fit**, the opener has several options :
With a **3**-card ♠ Fit : he can bid **2 ♥**, describing a 5 ♦ 4 ♥ 3 ♠ 1 ♣ hand of 14/16 HLD pts, or 2 ♠, describing a 5 ♦ 4 ♣ 3 ♠ 1 ♥ (or 5 ♣ 4 ♦) hand of 17/19 HLDF pts.
With a **4**-card ♠ Fit : he can bid 2 NT, with a 5 ♦ 4 ♠ 2 2 hand of 17/19 HL pts, or make a *trial* bid, with a singleton : 3 ♣ with a ♣ singleton (5 ♦ 4 ♠ 3 ♥ 1 ♣), 3 ♥ with a ♥ singleton (5 ♦ 4 ♠ 3 ♣ 1 ♥), or 3 ♦ with 4 ♦ 4 ♠ 4 ♣ 1 ♥, and 17/19 HDF pts.
Or he can *relay*, by 1 NT, to have the responder fully describe his hand.

2.3 With **5 hearts** and (5) **7 / 9 HL** pts.

The responder will ***conventionally*** bid 2 ♣, a *transfer bid, guaranteeing exactly* **5** hearts, while **denying** 4 spades. With this bid, the **Optimal Precision Relay** method resolves a *traditional* bidding age-old problem. Using a 2 ♣ *transfer* response to describe a long diamond suit would be of little value, particularly when it can be done with a much more effective, *pre-emptive*, and safe 3 ♦ response : either the opener has a balanced hand of 15/17 HL pts and a *minimum* of two diamonds : 16 HL + 7 HL = 23 pts + D and Fit pts, **or** he has a *minimum* of 4 diamonds : 15 HLD pts + 7 HL pts + 2 pts *minimum* for the ♦ Fit = 24 HLF pts + D pts.

Instead, using 2 ♣ as a *transfer* bid describing *specifically* 5 hearts – while **denying** 4 spades (with 4 spades, the responder will *relay*) – gives the opener several rebid options :
- With a ♥ ***misfit***, bid 2 ♦ (5 ♦ 4 ♠ 1 ♥ or 5 ♦ 4 ♣ 1 ♥ or 5 ♣ 4 ♦ 1 ♥).
- With a ♥ **Fit**, raise hearts to 2 ♥ (final), or 3 ♥, to invite a ♥ game, or conclude in 4 ♥.
- Invite a NT game by bidding 2 NT, or conclude in 3 NT.
- Or he can *relay*, by 2 ♠, to have the responder fully describe his hand (2 NT with a 5 3 3 2 hand, 3 ♣ or 3 ♦ with a 5 ♥ 4 ♣ or 5 ♥ 4 ♦ hand).
- With **17** + HLDF pts, a **3**-card ♥ Fit and a ♣ singleton, he can make a *trial* bid of 3 ♣ (3-card ♥ Fit, ♣ singleton, therefore 5 ♦ 3 ♥ 4 ♠ 1 ♣ or 6 ♦ 3 ♥ 4 ♠ 0 ♣). With a 4-card ♥ Fit, the opener will *relay*.

Hereunder is an illustration of the 3 ♣ *trial* bid :

♠ A x x x	♠ x x
♥ K x x	♥ A Q x x x
♦ A Q x x x	♦ J 10 x
♣ x	♣ x x x

Traditional bidding would likely bid these hands as follows :

1 ♦	1 ♥
1 ♠	2 ♦ (or 1 NT)
Pass	

East described 4 hearts, **not** 5. On his *preference* return to 2 ♦, West does not have the points to bid further. The 4 ♥ game will be missed.

In **Optimal P**recision Relay, these hands will be bid as follows :

1 ♦	2 ♣ (*transfer*, **5** ♥, 7/9 HL)
3 ♣ (*Trial* bid)	4 ♥

On West's 3 ♣ *trial* bid, East can now add to his own 8 ½ HL pts 2 pts for *no "wasted honor pts"* in clubs + 2 Fit pts in diamonds = 12 ½ pts + 17 pts minimum = 4 ♥.

2.4 With a **6**-card **M**ajor suit, **(5) 7/9** HL pts.

Such **6-**card Major single-suiter hands will be described by a direct *transfer* bid of 2 ♦, for 6 hearts, or 2 ♥, for 6 spades, and 7/9 HL pts.
The opener has several options on these responses :
– He can simply *transfer* to 2 ♥ or 2 ♠ with a *minimum* hand of 14/16 HLD pts. Or he can raise to 3 ♥ / ♠, *invitational*, or conclude to game.
– Or he can make a 3 ♣ *trial* bid (Fit in the Major suit bid and a ♣ singleton).
– Or he can *relay*, by the suit just *above*, 2 ♠, above the hearts suit, by 2 NT, above the spades suit, to have the responder fully describe his hand (his singleton or NT with a 6 3 2 2 hand).

Therefore, the **Optimal** Precision **R**elay method clearly identifies and differentiates a 4-card Major suit from a 5-card Major, from a 6-card **M**ajor! A significant precision and unique treatment !

2.5 With a **6**-card ♦ single-suiter, **(5) 7/9** HL pts.

Finally, the method uses a direct 3 ♦ natural bid to describe a 6-card ♦ single-suiter of **7/9** HL pts. Such a bid is "safe" as the side is guaranteed to have at least 24 total pts.

Furthermore, in keeping with the principle that *"the higher the bid, the more precise it must be"*, the method uses 2 other direct responses, 2 NT and 3 ♣, to distinguish 6 ♦ 3 2 2 hands from irregular 6 ♦ 3 3 1 hands.
So, a 2 NT direct response will describe semi-regular hands : 6 ♦ 3 2 2 or 7 ♦ 2 2 2 hands (on the next *relay*, 3 ♣, the responder will identify his tripleton, 3 ♥, or 3 ♠, or 3 NT for clubs, or will bid 3 ♦ with 7 ♦ 2 2 2, while a 3 ♣ direct response will describe a 6 + ♦ single-suiter with a ♣ singleton (on the next *relay* of 3 ♥, the responder will bid 3 NT with 6 ♦ 3 3 1 ♣ or 4 ♣ with 7 ♦ 3 3 0 ♣ or will identify his tripleton with a 7 ♦ 3 2 1 ♣ hand, 3 ♠ with a ♠ tripleton, 4 ♦ with a ♥ tripleton).

This means that a direct 3 ♦ response specifically describes a 6 + ♦ single-suiter with a heart or spade singleton, which will be identified on the next *relay*, 3 ♥.

3. Without a 4-card or 5-card or 6-card Major, the search for a NT contract becomes the next priority and is the third parameter.

Without a Major suit, this leaves single-suiter *minor* suits and *minor* two-suiters to deal with. Here again, the **Optimal** Precision Relay method brings a novel approach to treating both.
The 1 NT *transfer* bid will describe either a **6 +** card ♣ single-suiter or a **9 +** card ♣/♦ two-suiter (5 ♣ 4 ♦ or 4 ♣ 5 ♦ or 5 ♣ 5 ♦). On this bid, the opener has several options :

– He can *transfer* to 2 ♣, when *minimum*. Or invite a NT contract : bid 2 ♥, with "stoppers" in hearts, or 2 ♠ with "stoppers" in spades, or 2 NT, with "stoppers" in both Majors, or 3 ♣, without either Major guarded.
– Or he can conclude directly in 3 NT.
– Or he can *relay*, by 2 ♦, to have the responder fully describe *his* hand (2 NT with **6 ♣ 3 2 2**, 3 ♣ with **6 ♣ 3 3 1**, 2 ♥ with **5 ♦ 4 ♣** or **5 ♦ 5 ♣**, 2 ♠ with **5 ♣ 4 ♦**).

Furthermore, the method uses a direct 2 ♠ *transfer* bid to describe specifically a 5 ♦ 4 ♣ 2 2 *or* a 5 ♣ 4 ♦ 2 2 *minor* two-suiter of **9** cards and **7/9** HL pts. The 2 – 2 residual in the Majors is *mandatory* as the bid is an invitation for a 3 NT game (to be bid by the opener, the *strong* hand) and must **not** include a singleton, which would not be favorable to a NT contract and could find *"wasted honor pts"* opposite it.
On this 2 ♠ *transfer* bid, the opener can either transfer to 2 NT or to 3 ♣ or to 3 ♦, or he can *relay*, by 3 ♥, to discover the responder's exact distribution (3 ♠ with **5 ♣**, 3 NT with **5 ♦**).

This all means that : In any point zone, A) a responder with a **4-card** Major will always *relay* (1 ♥), and B) a responder with a **balanced** hand, including 5 ♣ or 5 ♦ 3 3 2 hands, will also always *relay* (1 ♥).

This concludes the responses to a 1 ♦ opening. You will find below a table **summarizing** these responses.

SUMMARY OF RESPONSES TO A 1 ♦ OPENING

HL POINTS	*W/4*-card Major	*W/5*-card Major	*W/6*-card Major	*Without* a Major
7 / 9	*Relay*	1 ♠ w/ 5 ♠ 2 ♣ w/ 5 ♥	2 ♦ w/ 6 ♥ 2 ♥ w/ 6 ♠	1 NT for ♣ 2 ♠ for ♦ / ♣ 3 ♦ for 6 ♦
10 +	*Relay*	*Relay*	*Relay*	*Relay*

UNUSUAL CONVENTIONAL BIDS TO "FLAG" (*INFREQUENT*)

OPENING	UNUSUAL CONVENTIONAL RESPONSE	PTS
1 ♦	2 ♣ : *Transfer* bid : **5 ♥** denies 4 ♠	7/9 HL
	2 ♠ : 5 ♦ 4 ♣ 2 2 *or* 5 ♣ 4 ♦ 2 2	7/9 HL

Balanced hands   **18 +** HL pts   **Open** 1 ♣

REBIDS, RESPONSES AND DEVELOPMENTS

OPENER'S 1 NT REBID ON A 1 ♦ RESPONSE

On a 1 ♦ response to a 1 ♣ opening, the opener's first rebid will be
1 NT with **18 +** HL pts, as if he had opened 1 NT. But further bidding
developments beyond this will **not** be the same as **two** point zones
must now be described : **18/20** and **21/23** + HL pts.
The **process** to differentiate **two** point zones, after 1 NT, was already
described in the previous chapter on the 1 NT opening.

RESPONSE OF 1 NT (1 ♠) ON A 1 ♣ OPENING

A direct response of a balanced hand to a 1 ♣ opening is done via a
transfer bid of 1 ♠ for NT. To protect against a damaging defensive
lead, No Trump **must** be bid by the stronger hand which dictates using
a 1 ♠ response as a *transfer* bid for NT.

On responder's 1 ♠ bid, the opener's *transfer* to 1 NT is a *relay* on
which the responder will describe his hand, in two point zones : **7/9**
and **10/12** HL pts. His hand description will then be the same as described in the previous chapter on the 1 NT opening.

Unbalanced hands   **20 +** HLD pts   **Open** 1 ♣

REBIDS, RESPONSES AND DEVELOPMENTS

RESPONSE OF 2 ♦ (2 ♣) ON A 1 ♣ OPENING

On a 1 ♣ opening, a responder with a diamond suit bids it through a
transfer bid of **2 ♣**, a jump which becomes necessary as a response of
1 ♦ is *relay*. On opener's transfer to 2 ♦, the responder describes his
hand as previously outlined in the chapter on the 2 ♦ opening.

As a reminder, the lack of bidding space dictates that these hands be
limited to **one** single point-zone, **9/12** HL pts, i.e. hands of 7/8 HL pts
are *assimilated* to hands with *less* than 7 HL pts and responded 1 ♦.

OPENER'S 2 ♦ REBID ON A 1 ♦ RESPONSE

On a 1 ♦ response to a 1 ♣ opening, the opener's first rebid will be 2 ♦
with **one** point-zone, **20 +** HLD.

Further bidding developments beyond this rebid must now describe two-suiters *without* the benefit of starting from a 1 ♦ opening.

Therefore, modifications must now be made to the description process. These modifications are as follows : On a 2 ♥ *relay*, the opener will now rebid 2 ♠ with 4 spades, 2 NT, *conventionally*, with 4 **hearts**, 3 ♣ with 4 clubs.

DESCRIPTION PROCESS :

– Single-suiter : **6 ♦ 3 2 2, 7 ♦ 2 2 2, 6 ♦ 3 3 1, 7 ♦ 3 3 0.**
  On the 2 ♥ *relay*, rebid 3 ♦ and then on the next *relay*, 3 ♥ ? :

  6 ♦ 3 2 2   : 3 NT The tripleton will *not* be identified.
  7 ♦ 2 2 2   : 4 ♦
  6 ♦ 3 3 1 ♠ : 3 ♠   the singleton
  6 ♦ 3 3 1 ♣ : 4 ♣   the singleton
  6 ♦ 3 3 1 ♥ : 4 ♥   the singleton

– Two-suiter with **4 spades** : 5 ♦ 4 ♠ 2 2, 5 ♦ 4 ♠ 3 1, 6 ♦ 4 ♠
  On the 2 ♥ *relay*, rebid 2 ♠ and then on the next *relay*, 2 NT ? :

  5 ♦ 4 ♠ 2 2   : 3 NT – Final.
  5 ♦ 4 ♠ 3 ♥ 1 ♣ : 3 ♥ and then 3 NT
  5 ♦ 4 ♠ 3 ♣ 1 ♥ : 3 ♣ and then 3 NT
  5 ♦ 4 ♠ 4 ♣ 0 ♥ : 3 ♣ and then 4 ♣
  6 ♦ 4 ♠ 2 ♥ 1 ♣ : 3 ♦ and then 3 NT
  6 ♦ 4 ♠ 3 ♥ 0 ♣ : 3 ♥ and then 4 ♣   4th suit = void = 6 ♦
  6 ♦ 4 ♠ 2 ♣ 1 ♥ : 3 ♦ and then 3 ♠
  6 ♦ 4 ♠ 3 ♣ 0 ♥ : 3 ♣ and then 3 ♠

– Two-suiter with **4 hearts** : 5 ♦ 4 ♥ 2 2, 5 ♦ 4 ♥ 3 1, 6 ♦ 4 ♥
  On the 2 ♥ *relay*, rebid **2 NT**, *conventional*, then on the next *relay*, 3 ♣ ?

  5 ♦ 4 ♥ 2 2   : 3 NT – Final
  5 ♦ 4 ♥ 3 ♠ 1 ♣ : 3 ♠   – Final
  5 ♦ 4 ♥ 3 ♣ 1 ♠ : 3 ♥   – Final   *Impossible* bid = 3 ♣, in the *relay*
  5 ♦ 4 ♥ 4 ♣ 0 ♠ : 4 ♣
  5 ♦ 4 ♥ 4 ♠ 0 ♣ : *Not applicable* – 4 ♥ 4 ♠ is never opened 1 ♦
  6 ♦ 4 ♥ 2 ♠ 1 ♣ : 3 ♦ and then 3 ♠
  6 ♦ 4 ♥ 3 ♠ 0 ♣ : 3 ♦ and then 4 ♠
  6 ♦ 4 ♥ 2 ♣ 1 ♠ : 3 ♦ and then 3 NT
  6 ♦ 4 ♥ 3 ♣ 0 ♠ : 3 ♦ and then 4 ♣

– Two-suiter with **diamonds** and **4 or 5 clubs**.
  On the 2 ♥ *relay*, rebid 3 ♣ and then on the next *relay*, 3 ♦ ? (A 3 ♥ *relay* would not leave sufficient bidding space for a full description).

5 ♦ 4 ♣ 2 2   : 3 NT
5 ♦ 4 ♣ 3 ♥ 1 ♠ : 3 ♥ and then 3 NT
5 ♦ 4 ♣ 3 ♠ 1 ♥ : 3 ♠ – Final
5 ♦ 5 ♣ 2 ♠ 1 ♥ : 4 ♣ – Final
5 ♦ 5 ♣ 3 ♠ 0 ♥ : 4 ♠
5 ♦ 5 ♣ 2 ♥ 1 ♠ : 3 ♥ and then 4 ♣
5 ♦ 5 ♣ 3 ♥ 0 ♠ : 3 ♥ and then 4 ♥
6 ♦ 4 ♣ 2 ♥ 1 ♠ : 3 ♥ and then 4 ♦
6 ♦ 4 ♣ 3 ♥ 0 ♠ : 3 ♥ and then 4 ♥
6 ♦ 4 ♣ 2 ♠ 1 ♥ : 4 ♦
6 ♦ 4 ♣ 3 ♠ 0 ♥ : 4 ♠

Let's conclude this chapter with deals taken from tournaments :

World Championship, Formose, 1971.

♠ A x	♠ K 10 x
♥ x	♥ x x x x
♦ K x x x	♦ A Q x x
♣ A Q 10 x x x	♣ x x

The American pair, Kaplan/Kay, bid as follows :

1 ♣	1 ♥ (!)
2 ♣	Pass

The pair from Taiwan, playing Precision Club, ended in 3 ♦, after a 2 ♣ opening. So did the French pair of Jais/Trezel, with this auction :

1 ♦	1 NT
3 ♣	3 ♦

In **Optimal** Precision **R**elay, these hands would be bid as follows :

1 ♦ (14/19 HLD)	1 ♥ ?
3 ♣ (6 ♣ 4 ♦, 17/19 HLD)	3 ♥ ?
3 ♠ (2 ♠ 1 ♥)	4 ♣ ? (trump is ♣)
4 NT (2 Keys w/ ♣ Q)	5 ♣

West, with 14 ½ HLD pts, opens and East knows that his side has the points to play at least 5 ♣ or 5 ♦ upon West's 3 ♠ bid. But 6 ♦ could be on if West has 3 Keys Cards, two Aces and the ♣ K, so he bids 4 ♣.
On West's 4 NT bid, East settles for 5 ♣ (he would prefer to play 5 ♦ but a 5 ♦ bid would be a K & Q ♦ Ask).

"How good is your Bridge hand ?" - 2000

> ♠ Q 10 x x
> ♥ K x
> ♦ A J 10 x x
> ♣ A x

In the above-mentioned book, the authors show the hand above and Comment on it as follows : *"After the following auction :*

1 ♦	pass	1 ♠	2 ♥

West is justified to "stretch" to 3 ♠ as the ♥ K is likely to produce a trick".

Stretch to 3 ♠ ?! But West has 18 ½ HLD pts + 2 Fit pts in spades + 1 D point for a doubleton with 4 trumps = 21 ½ pts. Opposite 6 + H pts that's 27 ½ pts = 4 ♠.

Regional tournament, 2010.

♠ A K x	♠ Q 10 x
♥ x x x	♥ A x x
♦ A Q x x x	♦ K x x
♣ x x	♣ x x x x

In the tournament, not a single pair bid the 3 NT contract! As none counted their points properly, or described West's 5 diamonds.

In **Optimal** Precision **Relay**, these hands would be bid as follows :

1 ♦ (14/19 HLD)	1 ♥ ?
1 NT (15/17 HL, w/o 4 ♠)	2 ♣ ?
2 ♦ (4 + ♦, w/o 4 ♥)	2 ♥ ?
3 ♦ (5 ♦)	3 NT

West's description of his **5** diamonds enables East to add 2 Fit pts in diamonds to his 9 H pts (4 3 3 3) for a minimum total of 26 HLF pts.

National Division 1, pairs, 2011.

♠ K x	♠ A Q x x
♥ J 10 x x	♥ x
♦ A Q 10 x x	♦ K x x x x
♣ x x	♣ A x x

In the tournament, not a single pair found the 6 ♦ slam. Half the field did *not* open West's hand and the contracts played were, most often, 3 NT or 5 ♦, or 4 ♦ or 3 ♦...

In **Optimal** Precision **Relay**, these hands would be bid as follows :

1 ♦ (14/19 HLD)	1 ♥ ?
2 ♦ (5 ♦ 4 ♥, 14/16 HLD)	2 ♠ ?
2 NT (2 spades)	3 ♣ ?
3 NT (5 ♦ 4 ♥ 2 2)	4 ♣ ? (trump is ♦)
4 ♥ (1 Key Card & ♦ Q)	4 ♠ ? (K & Q ♠ Ask)
5 ♦ (♠ King)	6 ♦

West, with 14 ½ HLD pts, opens and East knows that his side is in slam zone right upon West's bid of 2 ♦! (15 HL pts + 4 Fit pts + 2 D pts). The rest is "kid's play"...

National division 1, open, teams of four, 2011.

♠ A K x	♠ x
♥ A x x x	♥ K x x
♦ Q x	♦ K J x x
♣ K x x x	♣ J 10 9 x x

One of the two teams bid these hands as follows :

1 NT	2 NT
Pass	

In **Optimal** Precision Relay, these hands would be bid as follows :

1 ♦ (14/19 HLD)	1 NT (*transfer* for clubs)
2 NT (♥ & ♠ stoppers)	3 ♦ (5 ♣ 4 ♦, 7/9 HL)
3 NT	Pass

On East's *transfer* bid for ♣, West can add to his 16 H pts 2 pts for the 8-card ♣ Fit (East could have a 5 ♦ 4 ♣ two-suiter, with a singleton) = 18 HF. Therefore, instead of *transferring* to clubs, he invites a NT game while indicating stoppers in both hearts and spades.

International tournament, 2010.

♠ x	♠ x x x
♥ A J x x	♥ K 10 x x x x
♦ K Q 10 x x	♦ A x x
♣ A x x	♣ x

In the tournament, the bidding was, most often :

1 ♦	1 ♥
3 ♥	4 ♥

In **Optimal** Precision Relay, these hands would be bid as follows :

1 ♦	2 ♦ (*transfer* for ♥, 6 ♥, 7/9 HL)
2 ♠ ? (*forcing*, strong)	3 ♣ (♣ singleton)
3 ♦ ?	3 NT (6 ♥ 3 3 1 ♣)
4 ♣ ? (trump is ♥)	4 ♠ (2 Key Cards **w/o** the ♥ Q)
6 ♥	

West can count, in his hand : 23 HLDF pts (+ 3 for 10 hearts + 1 for his singleton with 4 trumps) + at least 10 HLDF pts in East (+ 1 for the 8-card ♦ Fit + 2 for the ♣ singeton) = slam zone.

International tournament, final, 2011.

♠ K J x x	♠ A Q x x x
♥ x x	♥ A x x
♦ A Q x x	♦ K J x
♣ A J x	♣ x x

The French team bid as follows :

1 NT	2 ♥ (*transfer* for ♠)
3 ♥ (♠ Fit, ♥ doubleton)	4 ♥ (repeat *transfer*)
4 ♠	

And the world champions Fantoni/Nunes did no better…
In **Optimal** **P**recision **R**elay, these hands will be bid as follows :

1 ♦	1 ♥ ?
1 ♠ (4 ♠)	1 NT ?
2 ♥ (balanced, 15/17 HL)	2 NT ?
3 ♦ (4 ♦)	3 ♥ ?
3 ♠ (3 ♣ 2 ♥)	4 ♣ ? (trump is ♠)
4 ♦ (3 Keys **w/o** the ♠ Q)	4 ♥ ? (K & Q ♥ Ask)
4 ♠ (no ♠ Q or K)	4 NT ? (K & Q ♦ Ask)
5 ♦ (♦ Q)	6 ♠

Knowing that West has 4 diamonds and 2 hearts, East can bid 6 ♠.

Regional tournament, 2012.

♠ x x	♠ A x
♥ K x x	♥ A Q J x
♦ A Q x x x	♦ K x x x
♣ A x x	♣ K Q x

No team in the tournament found a grand slam, whether 7 ♦ or 7 NT. West players having described 12/14 pts (1 ♦/rebid 1 NT), East players did not "see" a slam opposite 14 pts maximum and settled in 3 NT. But West's hand had **15** HL pts, not 13 or 14, and should have been opened 1 NT.

232

In **Optimal P**recision **R**elay, the bidding would be :

1 ♦	1 ♥ ? (relay)
1 NT (balanced, 15/17 HL)	2 ♣ ? (*relay*-Stayman)
2 ♦ (4 + ♦, no 4-card Mjr)	2 ♥ ? (relay)
3 ♦ (5 diamonds)	4 ♣ ? (OKC Ask, trump ♦)
4 NT (2 KC with the ♦ Q)	5 ♥ ? (K & Q ♥ Ask)
6 ♣ (♥ King)	7 NT

Upon West's 3 ♦ bid, East can add 3 pts for the 9-card ♦ Fit with the King and can count his side to have 15 + HL pts + 20 H pts + 3 Fit pts = 38 pts = grand slam point zone. West's 4 NT response also denies a Queen or King in spades which almost guarantees that he has the ♥ K.

233

BIDDING AFTER INTERVENTIONS OVER A 1 ♦ OPENING

The table below summarizes **suggested** bids by the opener's partner following *an intervention* by the opposite team over a 1 ♦ opening.
The *suggested* bids are guided by two key **principles** or **objectives** :

1. Over a **double**, the responses remain unchanged, except for two :
redouble replaces the 1 ♥ *relay*, so now a 1 ♥ response can describe
5 hearts and 2 ♣ can become a *transfer* bid for diamonds.
Over any *other* overcall, the responder's **double** is *take-out*.

2. **Retain**, whenever possible, the direct *transfer* responses of 1 NT, 2 ♣,
2 ♦, 2 ♥ and 2 ♠.

INTERVENTIONS over a 1 ♦ opening	SUGGESTED BIDS BY OPENER'S PARTNER Key principles : On *double*, Redouble is *relay* On other**s** : **Retain** the *transfer* responses.
Double (*Take-out*)	**Redouble** : *Relay* replaces 1 ♥ as *relay*. 1 ♥ : natural, 5 hearts 2 ♣ becomes a *transfer* for ♠ (*instead* of ♥). All *other* bids retain the same meaning.
1 ♥ (5 + ♥)	**Double** : *Relay* 2 ♣ becomes a *transfer* for ♠ (*instead* of ♥). All *other* bids retain the same meaning.
1 ♠ (5 + ♠)	**Double** : *Relay* All *other* bids retain the same meaning.
1 NT (Balanced)	**Double** : *Take-out*, looking for a 4-card Major 2 ♣, 2 ♦ become *transfer* bids for **5 ♥, 5 ♠**. 2 ♥, 2 ♠ become *natural* bids for **6 ♥, 6 ♠**.
2 ♣ (6 + ♣)	**Double** : *Take-out*, looking for a 4-card Major 2♦,2♥,2♠:natural
2 ♦ (cue-bid 5 ♠ 5 ♥)	Double : *conventional* for 5 ♦ 5 ♣ 2 ♥, 2 ♠ : *conventional* for 5 ♦ 4 ♣, 5 ♣ 4 ♦ 3 ♣, 3 ♦ : 6 + ♣, 6 + ♦.
2 ♥ / 2 ♠ (6 ♥/♠)	2 ♠ on 2 ♥ : 6 + spades 2 NT : 5 ♦ 5 ♣ 3 ♣, 3 ♦ : 6 + ♣, ♦.

OPTIMAL 4 ♦ CONTROL ASKING BID

Unique and **specific** to the **Optimal P**recision **R**elay method

RESPONSES AND DEVELOPMENTS

We all know that a **Key Card A**sk should **not** be bid when the inter-rogator has one (or more) suit with **two** direct losers i.e. two or more cards in a suit without the Ace or the King, or with a **void**, as responses to the Asking bid *may not indicate where* the responder's Key Cards are.

To address this, *traditional* bidding precedes using a 4 NT Blackwood by *"cue-biding"* its controls (Ace, King or singleton).
But this process, which relies on *dialogue* bidding, is not *applicable* in a *Relay* bidding method which uses *monologue* bidding.

To address this issue, the **Optimal** Precision Relay method uses the **4 ♦** bid as a **C**ontrol **A**sk and we will outline below how this works.

PROCESS

The **4 ♦** Control Ask is looking, *first and foremost*, for controls – Ace or King – in the Majors, hearts and spades. Beyond this, providing Key Card information *applies* and is done in the same manner as it is in response to the **4 ♣** Key Card Ask.
The responses to a 4 ♦ Control Ask are simple, as follows :

- 4 ♥ : **hearts** controlled – Ace or King. **Not spades.**
- 4 ♠ : **spades** controlled – Ace or King. **Not hearts.**
    On a 4 ♥ or 4 ♠ response, the interrogator asks for responder's Key Cards by bidding 4 NT. The responses to 4 NT – 5 ♣, 5 ♦, 5 ♥, 5 ♠ – indicate the same number of Key Cards as 4 ♦, 4 ♥, 4 ♠, 4 NT do on a 4 ♣ **Optimal** Key Card Ask.

- 4 NT : Do **not** control hearts **nor** spades.
- 5 ♣, 5 ♦, 5 ♥, 5 ♠ : hearts **and** spades **controlled**. The four bids indi-cate the same number of Key Cards as they do on a 4 NT Ask.

Let's illustrate this by a few examples :

1. The responder has *one* Major controlled, but *not* the one looked for
    :

♠ K x x x	♠ A Q J x x
♥ x x	♥ x x
♦ K Q J x x	♦ A x x x
♣ A K	♣ x x

The **Optimal** **P**recision **R**elay bidding of these hands will be :

1 ♦ (14/19 HL)	1 ♥ ?
1 ♠ (4 ♠)	1 NT ?
2 NT (17/19HL)	3 ♣ ?
3 NT (5 ♦ 4 ♠ 2 2)	4 ♦ ? (2 suits **not** controlled)
4 ♠ (♠ control, **not** ♥)	Pass

"Readers' mail".

♠ J 10	♠ Q x x
♥ A Q x	♥ K J x
♦ A K x	♦ Q J x x
♣ A Q x x x	♣ K J x

"Our auction was :   2 NT   4 NT

                6 NT   *could we have avoided this ?..."*

Yes! With bidding like this :

1 ♣ (18 + HLD)	1 ♠ (*tranfer for NT, 7/12 HL*)
1 NT ?	2 NT (no 4-card Mjr, 10/12)
4 ♦ ? (♠ **not** controlled)	4 ♥ (♥ control, **not** ♠)
5 ♣ – Final.	

World Championship, Shanghai, 2007.

♠ A K x x x	♠ x
♥ J x x x x	♥ Q 10 x
♦ ---	♦ A Q x x
♣ Q J x	♣ A K x x x

3 out of 4 teams bid 6 ♣ or 6 ♥, with A K of ♥ missing...

Instead of :	1 ♠	1 NT ? (relay)
	3 ♣ (5 ♠ 4 ♥ 2 + ♣, 15/17)	3 ♦ ?
	3 ♥ (5 ♥)	3 ♠ ?
	4 ♣ (3 ♣ : 5 ♠ 4 ♥ 3 ♣)	4 ♦ ? (*forced*)
	4 ♠ (♠ control, **not** ♥)	5 ♥ – Final.

     This is a case where the 4 ♦ Ask – which would have been used, anyway, as ♥ are **not** controlled – is "forced" by West's hand description ending in 4 ♣. The responses to the 4 ♦ Ask remain unchanged.

2. The responder controls *one* of the Majors only, the *one* looked for :
World Championships, Juniors, Final, 2004.

♠ x x x	♠ ---
♥ A Q 10 x x	♥ K x x
♦ A x	♦ K x x x
♣ A x x	♣ K Q x x x x

One team plays 6 ♥, the other plays 6 ♣. The "right" contract is 7 ♣,
which would be bid as follows, in **Optimal** Precision Relay :

1 ♥	1 ♠ ?
2 NT (5 ♥ 3 3 2, 15/17 HL)	3 ♣ ?
3 ♦ (♦ doubleton)	4 ♦ ? (void)
4 ♥ (♥ control, *not* ♠)	4 NT ? (RKC Ask, trump is ♥)
5 ♦ (3 KCs with the ♥ Q)	7 ♣

The 3 Key Cards described by West's 5 ♦ bid are known to be the Aces
of hearts, diamonds and clubs as West previously denied a ♠ control.
Precise and simple description, effective bidding.

"Technique : *To use Blackwood or not ?*" – Le Bridgeur, 2011.

♠ A Q x x	♠ K x x x x
♥ A K x x x	♥ x
♦ A x	♦ x x
♣ K x	♣ A Q x x x

Comments from the expert presenting the deal : *"After the following*
auction :   1 ♥   1 ♠
                 4 ♠   ?

*West having 20 + pts, East should consider a **grand** slam but, in addition to*
finding out West's Key Cards, he will also need to know about West's ♣ K.
*Even though a Blackwood Ask should **not** be used with the diamond suit **not***
being controlled, it sure would make life easier if used here, such as :

	4 NT
5 ♦ (3 Key Cards)	5 ♥ (♠ Queen ?)
6 ♣ (yes ♠ Q + ♣ K)	7 ♠

As it is very likely that West has the ♦ Ace, I would ignore the "rule" and
would use Blackwood here".

Wow! What an "opportunistic" recommendation, seeing both hands !
Instead of recommending *ignoring the rule*, the expert should have
suggested that the *strong* hand, West, should inquire the *weaker* hand !

In **Optimal** Precision Relay, the bidding would be :

1 ♣	1 ♥ (*transfer* for spades)
1 ♠ ? (transfer - relay)	2 ♣
2 ♦ ?	2 NT (5 ♠ 4 ♣ 2 + ♦, 10/12 HL)
3 ♣ ?	4 ♣ (5 ♠ 5 ♣ 2 ♦ 1 ♥)
4 ♦ ? (*forced*)	4 ♠ (♠ control, **not** ♥)
4 NT ? (♠ is trump)	5 ♥ (2 Key Cards w/o the ♠ Q)
6 ♣ ? (K & Q ♣ Ask)	6 ♥ (♣ Queen)
7 ♠	

West knows everything about East's hand! No guessing, no *ignoring of any rule* : precise description, effective and satisfying bidding !

Regional tournament.

♠ A J x x x	♠ K Q x
♥ J 10 x x	♥ x
♦ ---	♦ x x x x
♣ A x x x	♣ K Q x x x

In *traditional* point count, these two hands add up to 20 H/29 HDS pts, not quite the points for a slam !...

In **Optimal** Precision Relay, these hands would be bid as follows :

1 ♠	1 NT ? (relay)
3 ♣ (5 ♠ 4 ♥ 2 + ♣, 15/17)	3 ♦ ?
4 ♣ (5 ♠ 4 ♥ 4 ♣)	4 ♦ ? (*forced*)
4 ♠ (♠ control, **not** ♥)	4 NT ? (♠ is trump)
5 ♥ (2 KCs w/o the ♠ Q)	6 ♣

Upon knowing West's 5 4 0 4 distribution, East can count his hand for 11 HL pts + 3 double-Fit pts + 2 for his singleton + 3 for "no wasted honor pts" in diamonds = 19 HLDF pts = slam zone opposite 15 + HLD.

3. The responder controls **both** Major suits :

Bidding contest.

♠ K Q J x x x	♠ A x
♥ K x x	♥ Q J x x
♦ x x	♦ A x
♣ A x	♣ K Q x x

The question was : *"What do you bid after the following auction ?"*:

1 ♠	2 ♣
2 ♠	3 ♥
?	

The responses from the experts consulted were : 3 ♠, 3 NT, 4 ♥ and 4 ♠. Not a single attempt at a slam from any of them !

In **Optimal** Precision Relay, these hands will be bid as follows :

1 ♣	1 ♦ ?
2 ♠ (6 + ♠, 18/20 HLD)	2 NT ?
3 ♠ (6 ♠ 3 ♥ 2 2)	4 ♦ ? (♥ **not** controlled)
6 ♣ (♥ and ♠ controls,	6 ♠
2 KCs w/ ♠ Q + ♥ K)	

East knows his side to be in slam zone right from West's opening bid !

Regional tournament.

♠ A x x	♠ K Q 10 x x x
♥ A Q x x x	♥ K x x
♦ ---	♦ A x
♣ Q x x x x	♣ x x

In **Optimal** Precision Relay, these hands will be bid as follows :

1 ♥	1 ♠ ? (relay)
2 ♣ (5 ♥ 4 ♣)	2 ♦ ?
2 ♠ (2 + ♠, 15/17 HLD)	2 NT ?
3 ♣ (5 ♣)	3 ♦ ?
3 ♠ (5 ♥ 5 ♣ 3 ♠)	4 ♦ ? (♣ **not** controlled)
5 ♠ (♠ and ♥ controls,	Pass
2 Keys with ♥ Q)	

With the ♠ and ♥ Aces and the ♥ Queen, West cannot have the ♣ King which would give him 20 HLD pts – he would have opened 1 ♣.

The next example is a deal which Augie Boehm reported as having bid playing with his father a number of years ago. Their two hands were :

♠ K J 10 x x	♠ A x x x x
♥ A J x x x	♥ K Q x
♦ ---	♦ x x x x
♣ x x x	♣ x

And their bidding was :

Pass	Pass

Ah well, so much for the Goren point count…

In **Optimal** Precision Relay, the bidding would be :

1 ♠	1 NT ?
3 ♣ (5 ♠ 4 ♥ 2 + ♣, 15/17 HLD)	3 ♦ ?
3 ♥ (5 hearts)	3 ♠ ?
4 ♣ (3 clubs : 5 5 0 ♦ 3)	4 ♦ ? (Control Ask, *forced*)
5 ♥ (♥ & ♠ controls,	6 ♠
2 KC w/o ♠ Q)	

East knows their side is in slam zone upon West's 4 ♣ bid (18 ½ HLDF pts with 3 pts for "*no ♦ wasted honor pts*" opposite 15 HLD pts minimum).

Regional tournament, 2009.

♠ A K x x x x	♠ J 10 x x
♥ K x	♥ A Q J x x
♦ J 10 x	♦ A x
♣ A x	♣ x x

Not a single pair found the optimal 7 NT contract. Nothing surprising in *traditional* point count which gives these two hands a total of 27 H/30 HL pts – when they actually have 38 HLFit pts !
In **Optimal** Precision Relay, the bidding would be :

1 ♣	1 ♦ ?
2 ♠ (6 ♠, 18/20 HLD)	2 NT ?
3 ♦	3 ♥ ?
3 NT (6 ♠ 3 ♦ 2 2)	4 ♦ (♠ and ♣ **not** controlled)
5 ♣ (♥ and ♠ controls,	7 NT
3 Key Cards w/o the ♠ Q)	

No need to inquire about hearts as West's ♥ King is already known.

World Championship, open pairs, New Orleans, 1978.

♠ A K x x x x	♠ J 10 x x
♥ A x x x	♥ K
♦ x x x	♦ A K Q x
♣ ---	♣ J x x x

Only four pairs found the grand slam – less than 4% out of more than 100 pairs! *With these two hands ??...* Surely, this should have led all players to reconsider their bidding system !

In **Optimal** Precision Relay, these hands would be bid as follows :

1 ♠	1 NT ?
3 ♦ (5 ♠ 4 ♥ 3 ♦)	3 ♥ ?
3 ♠ (6 ♠ 4 ♥ 3 ♦)	4 ♦ ? (♠ **not** controlled)
5 ♣ (♥ and ♠ controls,	7 ♠
3 Key Cards w/o the ♠ Q)	

Simple, isn't it ?...

One more example, reported in the Bridge World magazine, of a hand played by the USA and India in an International tournament :

♠ K x	♠ A Q x x
♥ A K x	♥ Q J 10 x x
♦ A Q x x x	♦ K 10 x x
♣ A x x	♣ ---

One team opened the West hand a strong 2 ♣ and ended up in 6 ♦, the other team opened 2 NT and ended up in... 4 NT! Impressive !...

In **Optimal** Precision Relay, these two hands would be bid as follows:

1 ♣	1 ♦ ?
1 NT	2 ♣ ?
3 ♦ (5 ♦ 3 3 2, 21 + HL)	4 ♦ ? (♥ **not** controlled)
5 ♦ (♥ and ♠ controls,	5 ♥ ? (K & Q ♥ Ask)
3 Key Cards w/ ♦ Q)	
6 ♣ (♥ King)	7 NT

Occasionally (rather rare), when the interrogator has **all 4** Aces, a 4 ♦ Control Ask may be used, rather than 4 ♣, to learn about Kings in hearts and/or spades. Illustration :

National division, 2015.

♠ A x	♠ K x x
♥ A x x	♥ K x
♦ A J 10 x	♦ x x
♣ A K x x	♣ Q J x x x x

Only three pairs found the small slam, 6 ♣ or 6 NT. The most common auction was :   2 NT   3 NT

A common point miscount as West has 22 H pts (no Queen), not 20, and East has 12 HLD pts. And the 2 NT opening makes it rather difficult to discover the 10-card ♣ Fit !...

In **Optimal** Precision Relay, these two hands would be bid as follows :

1 ♣	1 NT (*transfer* for ♣, 7/12 HL)
2 ♣ ?	2 NT (6 ♣ 3 2 2, 10/12 HL)
3 ♣ ?	3 ♠ (♠ tripleton)
4 ♦ ? (Control Ask)	5 ♠ (♥ and ♠ controls,
6 ♣ or 6 NT	0 KCs w/ the ♣ Q)

The 4 ♣ RKC Ask would only provide West with the knowledge of the ♣ Queen, which is not needed. While using the 4 ♦ Control Ask will provide him with East's King(s) holding in hearts and/or spades.

4. The responder controls the Major suit looked for **and** has a **singleton** in the other Major suit.

This opens the interesting option to bid **in the singleton**. In **Optimal Precision Relay**, this bid is used to describe the control of **the other three** suits with specifically **two** Aces – not one Ace nor three Aces. This enables the responder to : A) bid directly to the 5-level with **3** Aces (rather rare), and B) to indicate, when he bids the Major suit controlled, that he either does **not** control one of the minor suits or that he does **not** have **two** Aces, an information often quite valuable.
Let's look at some example hands :

♠ ---	♠ Q 10 x x
♥ A x x x	♥ x
♦ A Q x x x	♦ K J x
♣ K x x x	♣ A Q J x x

In **Optimal** Precision Relay, these two hands will be bid as follows :

1 ♦	1 ♥ ?
2 ♥ (5 ♦ 4 ♥, 17/19 HLD)	2 ♠ ?
3 ♣ (3 ♣)	3 ♦ ?
4 ♣ (4 ♣ 0 ♠)	4 ♦ ? (*forced*)
4 ♠ (♥, ♣, and ♦ controls,	
2 Aces)	4 NT ? (Key Cards Ask)
5 ♠ (2 Key Cards w/ ♦ Q)	7 ♣

Upon West's 4 ♠ bid, East knows that West's ♥ control is the Ace, not the King, and that he has the ♣ King. He just needs to inquire about the ♦ Queen but bidding 5 ♦, the *assumed* trump, would be a conclusion.

Had West's bid been 4 ♥, instead of 4 ♠, his next bid of 5 ♠ on East's 4 NT inquiry would still leave the ♣ King undescribed.

National selection, final.

♠ x	♠ A x x
♥ A J x x x	♥ ---
♦ A x x	♦ K J 10 x x
♣ K x x x	♣ A J x x x

At both tables, the contract played was 3 NT (1 ♥ - 2 ♦ - 2 ♥ - 3 NT).

In **Optimal** P**recision** R**elay**, these two hands will be bid as follows :

1 ♥	1 ♠ ?
2 ♣ (5 ♥ 4 ♣)	2 ♦ ?
3 ♦ (3 ♦, 15/17 HLD)	3 ♥ ?
3 NT (3 ♦ 1 ♠)	4 ♦ ? (*void*, Control Ask)
4 ♠ (♥, ♣, and ♦ controls, 2 Aces)	6 ♣

East knows all of West's controls. For a grand slam, West would need to have both ♣ and ♦ Queens, which he cannot have as this would give him 19 HLD pts and he would have opened 1 ♣. Without either Queen, the small slam is odds-on with one of two finesses succeeding. Therefore, no need to interrogate further.

International tournament.

♠ x	♠ x x x
♥ A x x	♥ K Q x x x
♦ A K x x	♦ x x
♣ K 10 x x x	♣ A Q x

Most teams played 4 ♥ (1 ♣ - 1 ♥ - 2 ♣ - 3 ♣ - 3 ♥ - 4 ♥).

In **Optimal** P**recision** R**elay**, these two hands will be bid as follows :

1 ♦	1 ♥ ?
2 ♠ (5 ♦ 4 ♣, 17/19 HLD)	2 NT ?
3 ♣ (4 ♦ 5 ♣)	3 ♦ ?
3 ♥ (3 ♥ 1 ♠)	4 ♦ ? (♦ **not** controlled)
4 ♠ (♥, ♣, and ♦ controls, 2 Aces)	5 ♦ ? (K & Q ♦ Ask)
5 NT (♦ King)	6 ♥

Regional tournament.

♠ A J x x x	♠ K x
♥ x	♥ A K J 10 x x
♦ A x	♦ K x
♣ K x x x x	♣ Q J x

In **Optimal** Precision Relay, these two hands will be bid as follows :

1 ♠	1 NT ?
2 ♣	2 ♦ ?
2 NT (5 ♠ 4 ♣ 2 + ♦, 15/17 HLD)	3 ♦ ?
4 ♣ (5 ♣)	4 ♦ ? (*forced*)
4 ♥ (♠, ♣, and ♦ controls,	6 ♣
2 Aces)	

5. On a response of 4 ♥ to a 4 ♦ Control Ask, the **Optimal** Precision Relay method uses 4 ♠ **not** as a sign-off bid but instead as a **Control** Ask in the **minor** suits. Used in this manner, this bid is much more useful and much more frequent.

The responses to such a 4 ♠ Control Ask are very similar to the ones used in response to the 4 ♦ Control Ask and are as follows :

4 NT : **No** ♣ or ♦ control.
5 ♣ : ♣ control, **not** ♦.
5 ♦ : ♦ control, **not** ♣.
5 ♥, 5 ♠, 5 NT, 6 ♣ : ♣ and ♦ controls, 5 ♥ : 1, 3 or 5 Key Cards **without** the trump Q, 5 ♠ : 1, 3 or 5 Key Cards **with** the trump Q, 5 NT : 0, 2 or 4 Key Cards **without** the trump Q, 6 ♣ : 0, 2 or 4 Key Cards **with** the trump Queen.

Let's look at some examples :

♠ x x	♠ A K J x x x
♥ K Q x x x	♥ A J x
♦ K x x	♦ A x
♣ A x x	♣ x x

In **Optimal** Precision Relay, these two hands will be bid as follows :

1 ♥	1 ♠ ?
1 NT (5 + ♥, 12/14 HLD)	2 ♣ ?
2 NT (5 ♥ 3 3 2)	3 ♣ ?
3 ♠ (♠ doubleton)	4 ♦ ? (♣ **not** controlled)
4 ♥ (♥ control, **not** ♠)	4 ♠ ? (Control Ask for ♣ / ♦)
6 ♣ (♣ and ♦ controls,	6 ♥
2 KCs w/the ♥ Q)	

Regional tournament.

♠ x	♠ A K Q x x x x
♥ A K J x	♥ x x
♦ K Q x x x	♦ A
♣ x x	♣ x x x

In **Optimal** Precision Relay, these two hands will be bid as follows :

1 ♦	1 ♥ ?
2 ♥ (5 + ♦ 4 ♥ 17/19 HLD)	2 ♠ ?
3 ♦ (6 ♦)	3 ♥ ?
3 NT (2 ♣ 1 ♠)	4 ♦ ? (♥ and ♣ **not** controlled)
4 ♥ (♥ control, **not** ♠)	4 ♠ ? (Control Ask for ♣/♦)
5 ♦ (♦ control, **not** ♣)	5 ♠ – Final

Regional tournament.

♠ A x x	♠ x
♥ K J x x x	♥ A 10 x x x
♦ A Q x x x	♦ K x x
♣ ---	♣ J 10 x x

The bidding was often : 1 ♥   4 ♥
                        Pass   And the slam was missed.

In **Optimal** Precision Relay, these two hands will be bid as follows :

1 ♣	1 ♥ (*transfer* for spades)
1 ♠ ?	2 ♣ (4 ♣)
2 ♦ ?	2 ♥ (5 ♥)
2 ♠ ?	2 NT (7/9 HL pts)
3 ♣ ?	2 ♦ (3 diamonds)
4 ♦ ? (Control Ask, *void*)	4 ♥ (♥ control, not ♠)
4 ♠ ? (Control Ask for ♣/♦)	5 ♦ (♦ control, **not** ♣)
7 ♥	

A 4 NT Ask would not be helpful here as the ♥ Queen is not needed while the ♦ King is of critical importance for a grand slam. Should East bid show no ♦ control, West will settle in 6 ♥. Note that these two hands add up to 36 ½ HLDF pts, not 22 H/31 HDS pts…

Rubber bridge.

♠ x x	♠ A x
♥ K Q	♥ x x x
♦ A J 10 x x x	♦ K x x x
♣ K x x	♣ A Q J x

In **Optimal** Precision Relay, these two hands will be bid as follows :

2 ♦ (6 + ♦, 15/17 HLD)	2 ♥ ?
2 NT (6 ♦ 3 2 2)	3 ♣ ?
3 NT (3 ♣)	4 ♦ ? (♥ **not** controlled)
4 ♥ (♥ control, **not** ♠)	4 ♠ ? (Control Ask for ♣/♦)
5 ♥ (♣ and ♦ controls, 1 KC)	6 ♦

A 4 NT Ask would not help here as the ♦ Queen is not needed while the ♣ King is of critical importance for a slam.
The 4 ♠ Control Ask solves that problem. Should West bid 5 ♦ (clubs **not** controlled), East will *pass* to play 5 ♦.

6. After a response of 4 ♠ on a 4 ♦ Control Ask, a bid of 5 ♣ or 5 ♦ by the interrogator is a K & Q Ask in that suit. The responses to them are the same as previously defined i. e. first step : No Q or K, second step : the Queen, third step : the King, fourth step : K and Q. Illustrations :

National Championship, pairs, 1964.

♠ K x	♠ A x x x x
♥ K Q J x x x	♥ x x
♦ ---	♦ x x x
♣ A K x x x	♣ Q J x

Only 5 pairs out of 34 (15 %!) bid the small slam. Understandably so, as, in *traditional* count, the two hands add up to no more than 30 HDS pts... When, in fact, they add up to 26 ½ (+ 1 for 3 Kings + 2 for 3 honors in a 6-card and 4 pts for a void) + 12 ½ HLDF pts (2 Fit pts in clubs, + 3 for "no wasted honor pts" in diamonds) = 39 pts !

In **Optimal** **P**recision Relay, these two hands will be bid as follows :

1 ♣	1 ♥ (*transfer* for spades)
1 ♠ ?	1 NT (5 Major 3 3 2)
2 ♣ ?	2 ♠ (5 ♠ 3 3 2, 7/9 HL)
2 NT ?	3 ♥ (♥ doubleton)
4 ♦ ? (void)	4 ♠ (♠ control, **not** ♥)
5 ♣ ? (K & Q ♣ Ask)	5 ♥ (♣ Queen)
6 ♥ (or 6 ♣)	

West knows his side has a minimum of 33 ½ pts right upon East's 1 ♥ response! Should East have bid 5 ♦ (no ♣ Queen) on West's 5 ♣ inquiry, West would have concluded in 5 ♥.

World Championship, teams of four, 1963.

♠ K x	♠ A Q x x
♥ A Q x x x	♥ K x x
♦ A Q x	♦ x x x x
♣ x x x	♣ A K

A "historic" deal in the 1963 Bermuda Bowl's final as the famous American pair of Schenken and Leventritt missed the slam and played 4 NT (1 NT - 4 NT *quantitative* - Pass).

This gave the great Italian Blue Team its 6th consecutive world championship as Garozzo and Forquet bid and made 6 ♥.

Jose Le Dentu, famous French player and champion, commented on the deal : *"The East hand is worth considerably more than 16 pts with its 4 "quick tricks" : 2 Aces and 2 Kings".*

Thinking rather typical of the times, in 1963. But wouldn't today's best world-class players bid the very same way, 55 years later ?…

What's wrong with that picture ? Just about everything…

First, the East hand is not at all undervalued – it is worth exactly 16 H pts. Instead, it is West's hand that is undervalued at 16 pts when it has 17 HL pts. But the biggest mistake is the 4 NT *"quantitative"* bid! As if one H point was going to make all the difference! It is the 8-card ♥ Fit with the ♥ King, missed by the Americans, that is the decisive factor. And opening 1 NT with a 5-card Major is not going to help find it !

In **Optimal** Precision Relay, these two hands will be bid as follows :

1 ♥	1 ♠ ?
2 NT (5 ♥ 3 3 2, 15/17 HL)	3 ♣ ?
3 ♠ (♠ doubleton)	4 ♦ ? (♦ **not** controlled)
5 ♠ (♥ and ♠ controls,	6 ♥
2 Key Cards w / ♥ Q)	

West cannot have the ♦ King which would give him 18 HL pts, he would have opened 1 ♣, not 1 ♥. And with the ruff of a club, the ♦ Queen is not needed for the small slam.

Note that these two hands add up to 36 HLDF pts and would add up to 34 pts without the ♦ Queen.

This concludes the chapter on the **Optimal** 4 ♦ Control Ask. We will now cover, next, the **4 NT** Control Ask.

OPTIMAL **4 NT CONTROL ASKING BID**

Unique and specific to the **Optimal P**recision **R**elay method

RESPONSES AND DEVELOPMENTS

When the responder ends his hand's description at the level of 4 ♦ or higher, the interrogator will have to use 4 NT as a slam inquiry bid.

In those cases, **Optimal** Precision Relay uses 4 NT as the equivalent of a 4 ♣ Ask, that is a RKC **6** Key Card Ask, with the same responses, i.e. 5 ♣ : 1 or 3 Key Cards without the trump Queen, 5 ♦ : 1 or 3 Key Cards with the trump Queen, etc. Illustrations :

Here is an example from a deal reported in Bridge Winners, 2018 :

♠ A Q x x x	♠ K J 10 x
♥ K	♥ J 10 x x x
♦ A K x x	♦ Q J x x
♣ x x x	♣ ---

In **Optimal** Precision Relay, these two hands will be bid as follows :

1 ♣	1 ♠ (*transfer* for NT, 7/12 HL)
1 NT ?	2 ♣ (Major two-suiter)
2 ♦ ?	2 ♥ (5 hearts 4 spades)
2 ♠ ?	4 ♦ (4 diamonds, 10/12 HL)
4 NT ? (RKC Ask)	5 ♥ (**no** KCs w/o ♥ Q)
6 ♠	

Precise description of East's hand, in both shape and strength.
East having no Key Card nor the ♥ Queen, must have K J of spades, J 10 of hearts and Q J of diamonds + one 10 in either diamonds or spades for his 10 + HL pts. Thus the 6 ♠ conclusion.

International tournament.

♠ A Q x	♠ K J 10 x x x
♥ Q J x	♥ A x x x
♦ A K Q x	♦ x x x
♣ x x x	♣ ---

An excellent ♠ slam, over 70 % odds-on (either with the ♥ King in the south hand or the missing diamonds divided 3 – 3 or a ♥ / ♦ squeeze).

In **Optimal** Precision Relay, these two hands will be bid as follows :

1 ♣	1 ♠ (*transfer* for NT, 7/12 HL)
1 NT ?	2 ♣ (Major two-suiter)
2 ♦ ?	2 ♠ (5 spades 4 hearts)
2 NT ?	3 ♦ (3 diamonds, 10/12 HL)
3 ♥ ?	4 ♠ (6 ♠ 4 ♥ 3 ♦ 0 ♣)
4 NT ?	5 ♥ (2 KCs w/o the ♠ Q)
5 NT ? (K & Q ♥ Ask)	6 ♣ (no ♥ Q or K)
6 ♠	

East's 5 ♥ bid ensures a play for 6 ♠. So, there is no risk for West to inquire about a possible ♥ King and a grand slam which would be bid should East's response be 6 ♥ (♥ King).

International tournament, final.

♠ K x x x	♠ A x
♥ K J x x x	♥ A x
♦ A 10 x x	♦ K J x x x x
♣ ---	♣ x x x

An excellent grand slam, missed by both teams.

In **Optimal** **P**recision **R**elay, these two hands will be bid as follows :

1 ♥	1 ♠ ?
4 ♦ (5 ♥ 4 ♠ 4 ♦, 15/17 HLD)	4 NT ? (RKC Ask)
5 ♥ (2 KCs w/o the ♥ Q)	5 ♠ ? (K & Q ♠ Ask)
6 ♦ (♠ King)	7 ♦

West's 5 ♥ bid ensures a play for 6 ♦. So, there is no risk for East to inquire about a possible ♠ King, for a grand slam.

"Bidding contest".

"What do you bid, after this auction, with the following hand :

			♠ x
1 ♥	2 ♠	3 ♦	pass ♥ Q J x
3 NT	pass	?	♦ A J 10 x x x
			♣ A J x

All experts consulted unanimously responded : 4 ♥, and commented as follows : "3 NT *is rather discouraging; 5 ♥ could go down. The 2 ♠ overcall suggests an unfavorable distribution of the missing hearts"*. But the opener's hand was :

♠ A x x
♥ A K 10 x x
♦ x
♣ K Q x x

And the slam was missed – and a grand slam at that...

For those concerned that overcalls hamper strong 1 ♣ openings, in **Optimal** Precision Relay, these two hands would be bid as follows :

1 ♣	2 ♠	double (strong, relay)
3 ♥ (5 + ♥)	pass	3 ♠ (*cue-bid*, relay)
4 ♣ (4 ♣)	pass	4 ♦ ? (relay)
4 ♠ (3 ♠)		4 NT ? (RKC Ask)
5 ♣ (3 KCs w/o ♥ Q)		5 NT ? (K & Q ♣ Ask)
6 ♠ (♣ K & Q)		7 ♥

West's 5 ♣ bid ensures a play for 6 ♥. So, there is no risk for East to inquire about West's ♣ holding, for a possible grand slam.

– Furthermore, the opportunity exists to use 4 NT, instead of 4 ♣ or 4 ♦, as a slam Ask. The **Optimal** Precision Relay method uses 4 NT as a **Control** Ask for the *minor* suits whenever it *bypasses* the 4 ♣ or 4 ♦ Asks. It is used when the interrogator does **not** need to know about the ♥ or ♠ controls, but absolutely needs to know about the ♣ or ♦ controls.

The responses to this 4 NT Control Ask are the same as on a 4 ♦ Control Ask i.e. 5 ♣ : ♣ control, **not** ♦, 5 ♦ : ♦ control, **not** ♣, 5 ♥ : neither ♣ nor ♦ controls, 5 ♠ : ♣ **and** ♦ controls, 3 Key Cards **without** the trump Queen, 5 NT : ♣ **and** ♦ controls, 3 Key Cards **with** the trump Q, etc.

Let's illustrate this through a few examples :

Readers' mail.

♠ A x	♠ x
♥ A J x	♥ K Q x x x
♦ A K J 10 x x	♦ x x x x
♣ x x	♣ A J x

Comment from the player submitting the deal : *"We played 6 ♦, but this only gave us an average score as many other pairs played 6 NT and some played 7 ♦, 7 ♥ or 7 NT".*

In **Optimal** Precision Relay, these two hands will be bid as follows :

1 ♣	2 ♠ (5 ♥ 4 ♦, 9/12 HL pts)
2 NT ?	3 ♣ (3 clubs)
3 ♦ ?	3 NT (5 ♥ 4 ♦ 3 ♣ 1 ♠)
4 NT ? (Control Ask for ♣/♦)	5 ♣ (♣ control, **not** ♦)
5 ♦ ? (RKC Ask, ♥ is trump)	6 ♣ (2 Key Cards w/ ♥ Q)
7 NT	

East's 5 ♣ bid ensures a play for 6 ♦. So, there is no risk for West to inquire about East's Key Cards as the ♥ Queen will yield a grand slam.

Rubber bridge.

♠ K Q J x x	♠ A x x
♥ A J x x x	♥ K 10 x x
♦ A x x	♦ K J x
♣ ---	♣ x x x

In **Optimal** **P**recision **R**elay, these two hands will be bid as follows :

1 ♣	1 ♠ (*transfer* for NT)
1 NT ?	2 ♥ (4 ♥)
2 ♠ ?	3 NT (4 3 3 3, 10/12 HL)
4 NT ? (Control Ask for ♣/♦)	5 ♦ (♦ Control, **not** ♣)
5 NT ? (RKC Ask)	6 ♥ (2 KCs w/o the ♥ Q)
Pass	

East's 5 ♦ bid ensures a play for 6 ♥. So, there is no risk for East to inquire about a possible ♥ Queen, for a grand slam. 5 ♥ would be a conclusion in ♥, 5 ♠ would be a K & Q ♠ Ask, so 5 NT is the RKC Ask.

Rubber bridge.

♠ x x	♠ A K Q x x x
♥ Q x x	♥ x
♦ A K x x	♦ x x
♣ A x x x	♣ K Q x x

In **Optimal** **P**recision **R**elay, these two hands will be bid as follows :

1 NT	2 ♣ ?
2 ♦ (4 ♦)	2 ♥ ?
2 ♠ (4 ♣)	2 NT ?
3 ♥ (4 ♦ 4 ♣ 3 ♥ 2 ♠)	4 NT ? (Control Ask for ♣/♦)
5 ♠ (3 KCs w/o ♦ Q)	6 ♠

West's 5 ♠ bid indicates clubs **and** diamonds controls and 3 Key Cards.

---

2 NT (♦) OPENING   –   **RESPONSES AND DEVELOPMENTS**

6 + ♦ single-suit   **12/14** HLD pts   **9 +** H pts

The purpose of the 2 NT (♦) and 3 ♣ openings is two-fold :
A) To be *precisely descriptive* of a **6 +** card single-suit *minor*, in a clearly defined 12/14 HLD point-zone, while preserving the option of playing a NT or Major suit contract – a *"semi-constructive"* opening,
B) To be a *"competitive initiative"* opening with *"pre-emptive"* intentions to make it more difficult for the opposing team to find their potential *optimal* contract in a Major suit.

While the first objective of these openings is **not** to be fully described *economically*, that option still exists, so we will start, first, with the description of the opener's hand on successive *relays*.

DESCRIPTION OF OPENER'S HAND ON SUCCESSIVE RELAYS

1. **Semi-regular** hands (**no** singleton) : 6 ♦ 3 2 2 and 7 ♦ 2 2 2

   Process : On a first *relay*, 3 ♣ : with 6 ♦ 3 2 2 : Rebid 3 NT.
   with 7 ♦ 2 2 2 : Rebid 3 ♦, then 3 NT.

If responder favors a 3 NT contract, over identifying opener's 3-card suit (or *singleton*), he can bid 3 NT directly. While, with a 5 + card Major suit, he can bid 3 ♥ or 3 ♠, instead of relaying.

2. **Unbalanced** hands (**with** a singleton) : 6 ♦ 3 3 1, 7 ♦ 3 2 1, 7 ♦ 3 3 0

   Process : On a first *relay*, 3 ♣ : Opener's rebid will be in his *short* suit.
   With a 6 3 3 1 hand : 3 ♥ or 3 ♠ or 4 ♣ with a ♥ or ♠ or ♣ singleton.
   With a 7 3 3 0 hand : 4 ♦ (♣) or 4 ♥ or 4 ♠.
   With a 7 3 2 1 hand : the singleton first, followed by the 3-card suit.

RESPONSES OTHER THAN SUCCESSIVE RELAYS

DETERMINING PARAMETERS

Two key parameters apply here : the hand's **strength** and the search for a **Fit** in a **Major** suit.

1. The hand's **strength**, therefore its number of points.

Opposite a maximum of 14 HLD pts, the responder to a 2 NT (♦) opener does **not** need to bid with **less** than 10 pts (HL or HLF pts). With less than 10 pts, he will simply transfer to 3 ♦, which will be final. While, with **13 +** pts, he can *relay*, by 3 ♣. Any other response will be **10/12** pts

253

2. The second parameter is to identify a potential **Fit** in a **M**ajor suit.

With **5 +** cards in a Major, and **10 / 12** HL or HLF pts, the responder will bid his **5 +** card Major suit : 3 ♥ or 3 ♠.
With a Fit in the major suit bid, the opener will either *pass*, if minimum, or bid game when his Fit pts bring his hand's total to **16** HLDF pts.
With a doubleton in the Major bid and no singleton, he can bid 3 NT.
While with a misfit (singleton) in the Major bid, he can revert to 4 ♦.

---

6 + ♦ single-suit   **18/20** HLD pts   OPEN 1 ♣

REBIDS, RESPONSES AND DEVELOPMENTS

OPENER'S 2 NT REBID ON A 1 ♦ RESPONSE

On a 1♦ response to a 1 ♣ opening, with a **6 +** ♦ single-suit, the opener's first rebid will be 2 NT with **18 / 20** HLD pts. Further description and developments beyond this rebid will be the same as described above.

RESPONSE OF 2 NT ON A 1 ♣ OPENING

The same applies to a direct response of 2 NT to a 1 ♣ opening : it will be made with a **6 +** ♦ single-suit and **7/9** HL pts. On responder's 2 NT bid, the opener will *relay* and the responder will describe *his* hand, in the same manner as previously described above.

Some example deals, now :

Bidding contest, 2010 – Le Bridgeur.

"What do you bid, in West, with the hand below after the following auction ?:

♠ x x				
♥ x x x	1 ♦	4 ♠	*double* *	pass
♦ A K x x x x	?			
♣ A x				

* "optional"double, not a penalty double.
"Pass was the overwhelming majority answer with the comment : "hard to conceive making 5 ♦ with this semi-regular hand".
"But, in the tournament this deal comes from, pass was disastrous as 5 ♦ made while the opponents made 4 ♠ doubled. Partner had the hand below" :

> ♠ ---
> ♥ A K x x x
> ♦ J 10 x
> ♣ Q x x x x

Typical problem of a 1 ♦ opening made with a 6-card ♦ single-suiter...

In **Optimal** **P**recision **R**elay, these hands would be bid as follows :

2 NT (6 ♦, 12/14 HLD)   4 ♠   5 ♦

On West's 2 NT opening, East knows immediately about the 9-card ♦ fit and with his 18 HLDF pts, he will have no difficulty bidding 5 ♦.

International tournament, final.

♠ Q x	♠ K J x x
♥ A x x	♥ x x x
♦ K J x x x x	♦ Q x x
♣ x x	♣ A x x

In the closed room, no team found itself fit to open in West and all *passed*. In the open room, some Wests opened 1♦ but North/South intervened and most ended up playing, and making, 3 ♣.

In **Optimal** **P**recision **R**elay, these hands would be bid as follows :

2 NT (6 ♦, 12/14 HLD)   3 ♦

West's 2 NT opening will not likely enable the opponents to intervene – but should they, East will over-bid them with 3 ♦.

Regional tournament, 2012.

♠ J 10 x	♠ Q x x
♥ A x	♥ x x x
♦ A K x x x x	♦ J 10 x x
♣ A x	♣ K x x

At two tables, West opened 1 NT, on which both Easts *passed*.
At the other two tables, both Wests opened 1 ♦ followed by a 2 NT rebid (18/19 H), on which both Easts *passed*, as well.
In both cases, the 6-card ♦ single suit remained a well-kept secret !...

In **Optimal** **P**recision **R**elay, these hands would be bid as follows :

1 ♣ (18 + HLD)   1 ♦ (< than 7 HL pts)
2 NT (6 ♦, 18/20)   3 ♣ ?
3 ♦ (6 ♦ 3 2 2)   3 NT

East *relays* to uncover a possible singleton in West's hand. Without one, he can play 3 NT, with 9 ½ HF pts opposite at least 17 HL pts.

255

International tournament, 2010.

♠ x x	♠ A x x
♥ A K x	♥ Q J x x
♦ K J 10 x x x	♦ A x x x
♣ A x	♣ K x

Not a single pair found a slam contract, whether 6 ♦, 6 NT or 7 NT.
The bidding was most often:

1 NT (15/17)	2 ♣ (Stayman)
2 ♦ (no 4-card Major)	3 NT

Counting his hand for 14 H pts, East, without a ♥ fit, doesn't "see" a
slam opposite a partner limited to 17 H pts.
But West has 19 HL/20 HLD pts, not 17 pts! In **Optimal** Precision **Relay**,
these hands would be bid as follows :

1 ♣ (18 + HLD)	1 ♦
2 NT (6 + ♦, 18/20)	3 ♣ ?
3 NT (6 ♦ 3 2 2)	4 ♦ ? (♥ **not** controlled)
4 ♥ (♥ control, **not** ♠)	4 NT ? (trump is ♦)
5 ♣ (3 Keys w/o ♦ Q)	5 ♥ ? (K & Q ♥ Ask)
6 ♣ (♥ King)	7 NT

Simple, precise description and a rather satisfying result !

International tournament, pairs, 1978.

♠ A x	♠ x x x
♥ K Q x	♥ A x x
♦ A x x x	♦ K J x x x x
♣ A x x x	♣ x

Most pairs opened the West hand 1 NT – and all pairs missed the slam.

Indeed, it is hard to imagine a slam after a 15/17 H 1NT opening !
But West's hand has 18 ½ H pts, not 17, and the two hands have a
10-card ♦ Fit! In **Optimal** Precision **Relay**, these hands would be bid as
follows :

1 ♣	2 NT (6 + ♦, 7/9 HL)
3 ♣ ?	4 ♣ (6 ♦ 3 3 1 ♣)
4 ♦ ? (Control Ask)	4 ♥ (♥ control, **not** ♠)
4 NT ? (trump is ♦)	5 ♥ (2 KCs w/o ♦ Q)
6 ♦	

On East's 4 ♣ bid, West can add 3 ♦ Fit pts + 2 D pts for the ♠ doubleton
with 4 trumps + 2 D pts for East's singleton = 32 ½ pts = slam zone.

International tournament, 1972.

♠ J x	♠ A x x
♥ K x x	♥ A x x
♦ K Q J x x x	♦ A x x x
♣ x x	♣ A x x

In the tournament this deal comes from, not a single pair found the only makeable contract, 3 NT, as most looked for a ♦ slam and ended up playing 5 ♦ – or 6 ♦ for some. But, with no ruff from the short hand in sight, these hands only yield 10 tricks.

In **Optimal P**recision **R**elay, these hands would be bid as follows :

2 NT (6 + ♦, 12/14 HLD)	3 ♣ ?
3 NT (6 ♦ 3 2 2)	Pass

Even a maximum of 13 HL pts in West (minus 1 D point for the two doubletons) will only give the side a total of 32 HLF pts. Not the points for 6 NT, thus the conclusion in 3 NT.

Note that West's 2 NT opening will likely hamper an intervention from the opponents.

---

3 ♣ OPENING – **RESPONSES AND DEVELOPMENTS**

6 + ♣ single-suit   **12/14** HLD pts   9 + H pts

The purpose of the 3 ♣ opening is *the same* as that of the 2 NT opening :
A) To be *precisely descriptive* of a **6 +** card single-suit *minor*, in a clearly defined 12/14 HLD point-zone, while preserving the option of playing a NT or Major suit contract – a *"semi-constructive"* opening ;
B) To be a *"competitive initiative"* opening with *"pre-emptive"* intentions to make it more difficult for the opposing team to find their potential *optimal* contract in a Major suit.

However, the option to describe the hand, *economically*, exists, so we will start, first, with the description of the opener's hand on successive *relays*. Its description, however, will *not* be the same as what it is on a 2 NT opening as the *relay*, here, is 3 ♦, not 3 ♣.

DESCRIPTION OF OPENER'S HAND ON SUCCESSIVE RELAYS

1. **Semi-regular** hands (**no** singleton) : 6 ♣ 3 2 2 and 7 ♣ 2 2 2
   Process : On a first *relay*, 3 ♦ : Rebid 3 NT (*no further description*).

2. **Unbalanced** hands (**with** a singleton) : 6 ♣ 3 3 1, 7 ♣ 3 2 1, 7 ♣ 3 3 0

   Process : On a first *relay*, 3 ♦ : Opener's **rebid** will be in his *short* suit:
   With a **6 3 3 1** hand : 3 ♥ or 3 ♠ or 4 ♣ (♦).
   With a **7 3 3 0** hand : 4 ♦ or 4 ♥ or 4 ♠.
   With a **7 3 2 1** hand : first, the singleton, then the 3-card suit.
     With spades as the *short* suit, 3 ♠ is final – *no further description*.
     With diamonds as the *short* suit, 4 ♣ is final – *no further description*.

RESPONSES OTHER THAN SUCCESSIVE RELAYS

DETERMINING PARAMETERS

The same two key parameters applying to the 2 NT opening apply here as well : the hand's ***strength*** and the search for a **Fit** in a **Major** suit.

1. The hand's ***strength***, therefore its number of points.

Opposite a maximum of 14 HLD pts, the responder to a 3 ♣ opener does **not** need to bid with **less** than **10** pts. With *less* than 10 pts (HL or HLF pts), partner will simply *pass*. While with **13 +** pts, he can *relay*, by 3 ♦.

Therefore, we only have to consider responses in the **10/12** point-zone.

2. The second parameter is to identify a potential **Fit** in a **M**ajor suit.

With **5 +** cards in a Major, and **10/12** HL or HLF pts, the responder will bid his **5 +** card Major suit : 3 ♥ or 3 ♠.
With a Fit in the major suit bid, the opener will either *pass*, if minimum, or bid game when his Fit pts bring his hand's total to **16** HLDF pts.
With a doubleton in the Major bid and no singleton, he can bid 3 NT.
While with a misfit (singleton) in the Major bid, he can revert to 4 ♣.

---

6 + ♣ single-suit   **18/20** HLD pts   OPEN 1 ♣

REBIDS, RESPONSES AND DEVELOPMENTS

OPENER'S 3 ♣ REBID ON A 1 ♦ RESPONSE

On a 1 ♦ response to a 1 ♣ opening, with a **6 +** ♣ single-suit, the opener's first rebid will be 3 ♣ with **18/20** HLD pts. Further description and developments beyond this rebid will be the same as described above.

RESPONSE OF 3 ♣ ON A 1 ♣ OPENING

The *same* applies to a direct response of **3 ♣** to a 1 ♣ opening.
The opener's partner will respond **3 ♣** directly with a **6 +** ♣ single-suit and **7/9** HL pts. On responder's 3 ♣ bid, the opener will *relay* and the responder will *describe his* hand as previously described above.

Let's look at some example deals now :

Bidding contest, 1972.

♠ x x	♠ A
♥ Q x	♥ A K x x x x
♦ A x x	♦ K Q x x
♣ A Q x x x x	♣ K x

South overcalls 1 or 2 ♠. Some pairs played 7 ♥, down one as the suit broke 4 – 1. None of the contestants found the 7 NT slam.
Without the ♣ or ♥ Jacks, rather than picking hearts or clubs as trump, the solution is to play No Trump which only requires that one of the two suits break 3 – 2.

In **Optimal P**recision Relay, these hands would be bid as follows :

3 ♣ (6 ♣, 12/14 HLD)	3 ♦ ?
3 NT (6 ♣ 3 2 2)	4 ♣ ? (RKC Ask)
4 NT (2 Keys with ♣ Q)	5 ♥ ? (K & Q ♥ Ask)
5 NT (♥ Queen)	7 NT

Rubber game.

♠ x	♠ A x x x x
♥ A x x	♥ x
♦ A x x	♦ K Q J x x
♣ A Q x x x x	♣ K J

In **Optimal Precision Relay**, these hands will be bid as follows :

1 ♣	1 ♦ ?
3 ♣ (6 ♣, 18/20 HLD pts)	3 ♦ ?
3 ♠ (6 ♣ 3 3 1 ♠)	4 ♣ ? (OKC Ask)
4 ♥ (3 Keys with ♣ Q)	7 NT

National tournament, 2010.

♠ x	♠ A K Q x
♥ A x x	♥ K x x
♦ x x x	♦ A x x
♣ A K Q x x x	♣ x x x

At one table, 6 ♣ is played, at the other 7 NT. The right contract is 6 NT.

In **Optimal Precision Relay**, these hands would be bid as follows :

1 ♣ (18 +HLD)	1 ♦ ?
3 ♣ (6 ♣, 18/20 HLD)	3 ♦ ?
3 ♠ (6 ♣ 3 3 1 ♠)	4 ♣ ? (RKC Ask)
4 ♥ (3 Keys w/ ♣ Q)	6 NT

West has shown all 20 of his HLD points. Therefore, he cannot have the ♥ Queen for a grand slam = 6 NT.

Auction pairs, London, 2012.

♠ x x	♠ K Q J 10 x
♥ A x	♥ Q x
♦ x x x	♦ A K Q 10 x
♣ A Q x x x x	♣ K

Most Wests did not open and very few pairs found the 6 ♠ slam.

In **Optimal Precision Relay**, these hands would be bid as follows :

3 ♣ (6 ♣, 12/14 HLD)	3 ♦ ?
3 NT (6 ♣ 3 2 2)	4 ♦ ? (♥ **not** controlled)
4 ♥ (♥ control, **not** ♠)	4 NT ? (trump is ♣)
5 ♠ (2 Keys with ♣ Q)	6 ♠

Who said, again, that 10s are mostly valuable at NT contracts ?!...

CHAPTER 4

---

1 ♣ OPENING – RESPONSES AND DEVELOPMENTS

18 + HLD PTS – ANY DISTRIBUTION

PREAMBLE

The 1 ♣ opening is the cornerstone of the **Optimal** Precision Relay method – but it is a far cry from the Precision Club strong club opening which is based on H pts, and 16 + H pts at that! A huge flaw that dooms it from the word "go"!

In **Optimal** Precision Relay, a hand can be opened 1 ♣ with as little as 11 H or even 10 H pts, as some of these hands can have enormous *distributional* power and should therefore be opened with a *forcing* opening bid. Illustration :

This hand :　　♠ Q J x　　♥ A K J x x x x　　♦ ---　　♣ x x x

has 21 ½ HLD pts, **not** 11 ½ H pts ! (4 pts for the void, 4 L pts for 7 clubs + 2 pts for 3 honors in a 6 + card suit). If opened a *non-forcing* 1 ♥, as it would in most bidding systems, including the Precision Club, such an opening bid would elicit a *pass* from a partner with the following hand:

♠ K x x　　♥ x x x　　♦ x x x x x　　♣ x x

when a 4 ♥ game should be bid. And responder has, in fact, 6 HDF pts (minus 1 for no Queen but 3 Fit pts for the 10-card ♥ suit and 1 D point for the ♣ doubleton). Opposite 21 ½ HLD pts, that's 27 ½ pts !

In **Optimal** Precision Relay, these hands would be bid as follows :

1 ♣ (18 + HLD)	1 ♦ (< 7 HL or 13 + HL pts)
1 ♥ (5 + hearts, *forcing*)	2 ♦ (*transfer* / ♥ Fit, < 7 HL pts)
3 ♦ (*short* in ♦, 21 + pts)	4 ♥ (no *wasted H pts* in ♦)

Before delving further into some more specificities of the **Optimal** Precision Relay 1 ♣ opening, let's just analyse a few more example deals to illustrate how flawed and crippling some of the Precision Club opening bids are.

The most glaring one is, undoubtedly, its continued use of a strong, 20/21 H pt 2 NT opening :

261

"Bidding contest", 1977.

"What is your bid, with the following hand in East, after this auction ?" :

		♠ x
		♥ x x x x
2 NT	3 ♣	♦ A x x
3 ♠	?	♣ A J x x x

Comment from the contest organizer : *"A very challenging hand. Going over the level of 3 NT is risky as it likely commits you to play 5 ♣ which could go down, while the ♠ singleton may make a slam impossible. The opener would be in a much better position to make the "right" decision if only **he knew** about East's ♠ singleton. But the 2 NT opening makes that description impossible."*

Well, the organiser's comment says it all! And the opener's hand was :

> ♠ A Q x x
> ♥ A x
> ♦ K Q x
> ♣ K Q x x

6 ♣ should be bid.

In **Optimal P**recision Relay, these hands would be bid as follows :

1 ♣ (18 +HLD pts)	1 NT (*transfer* for clubs)
2 ♣ ?	2 ♥ (4 ♥, 9/12 HL pts)
2 ♠ ?	3 ♦ (3 ♦)
3 ♥ ?	3 NT (5 ♣ 4 ♥ 3 ♦ 1 ♠)
4 ♣ ? (RKC Ask)	4 ♠ (2 KCards w/o ♣ Q)
6 ♣	

The 1 ♣ opening enables East to describe his hand and his ♠ singleton. A 5 ♣ contract is not at risk, thus the 4 ♣ RKC Ask.

And requiring 16 **H** pts to open 1 strong Club can be disastrous, as well :

Open tournament, mixed pairs, 2007.

♠ A x x	♠ K Q J x
♥ A K Q x x x x	♥ x x
♦ x x	♦ A x x
♣ x	♣ A x x x

Not a single pair found the 7 NT slam. In 2007?! Hard to imagine…

Well, the opening hand does not have the prescribed 16 H pts to be opened 1 strong club… So, all bidding systems are in the same boat !

In **Optimal** Precision **Relay**, these hands would be bid as follows :

1 ♣ (18 +HLD pts)	1 ♦ ?
1 ♥ (5 + ♥)	1 ♠ ?
2 ♥ (6 + ♥, 21 + HLD)	2 ♠ ?
3 ♣ (♣ singleton)	3 ♦ ?
3 ♠ (3 ♠ : 7 ♥ 3 ♠ 2 ♦ 1 ♣)	4 ♣ ? (RKC Ask)
4 ♥ (3 Key cards w/ ♥ Q)	7 NT

West's hand has 22 HLD pts, not 13 H pts! It must be opened 1 strong ♣! And these two hands add up to 37 HLF pts, not 27 H/30 HL pts !

Here is another example of the same "systemic" flaw :

World Championship, 1971.

♠ x	♠ x x x
♥ A x x x x x	♥ x x
♦ K x x	♦ A Q x x x x
♣ A K x	♣ x x

Not a single pair (out of 6) bid a game (4 ♥ or 5 ♦) with the above hands. The bidding was, either :

	1 ♥ (Precision Club)	Pass (less than 8 H pts)
or :	1 ♥	1 NT
	2 ♥	pass

Two of the six pairs played Precision Club and one played the Roman Club. After such bidding, shouldn't *any* system have been questioned ?

In **Optimal** Precision **Relay**, these hands would be bid as follows :

1 ♣ (18 +HLD pts)	2 NT (6 + ♦, 7/9 HL)
3 ♣ ?	3 NT (6 ♦ 3 2 2)
4 ♥	

West's hand has 18 HLD pts, not 14 H pts! It must be opened 1 *strong* ♣ ! Upon East's 2 NT response, West can count 28 + HLDF pts on his side (18 + 7 HL minimum + 3 Fit pts for the 9-card ♦ Fit with the ♦ King). He now just needs to know whether East has a ♥ singleton, or not.

Let's conclude this brief "review" of the 1 ♣ opening with the following two example hands, taken from a 2010 column in Le Bridgeur.

Entitled "exercises", the question asked was : *"What do you rebid with each of these hands after the following auction :*

1 ♣	1 ♥
?	

Hand A   ♠ x   ♥ J 10 x x   ♦ A K x   ♣ A K 10 x x

Prescription : "3 ♥. *A 15 H point hand with unbalanced distribution*".

With no mention of where the singleton is, spades or diamonds? And an *invitational* bid only with a hand that has **22 ½** HLDF pts !

Had this hand been opened 1 strong Club of 18 + HLD pts instead, its rebid would be 1 ♠, *relay* – the most economical way to know more about the responder's hand !

Hand B   ♠ Q x   ♥ K Q x x   ♦ x   ♣ A K J 10 x x

Prescription : "4 ♣. *Describes a* ♥ *Fit with a 6* ♣ *4* ♥ *distribution*".

So, now we make a *double-jump* rebid, "burning" 12 bidding steps, with no mention of the singleton or its location, in spades or diamonds ?! But this hand has **23 ½** HLDF pts, enough points for a 4 ♦ "*splinter*" bid!

Again, had this hand been opened 1 strong Club of 18 + HLD pts, its rebid would be 1 ♠, *relay* – to have the responder's hand described. The above examples clearly illustrate again and again the absurdity of *traditional* bidding systems' opening bids or needing **16 H** pts to open 1 strong Club !

RESPONSES TO 1 ♣ AND MODIFICATIONS TO REBIDS AFTER 1 ♣

While most rebids after a 1 ♣ opening and responses to a 1 ♣ opening are the same as an opening bid would be, we previously identified the few cases which require modifications : the 1 NT rebid and response, which need to describe **two** point zones – and how to do this was previously covered – the 2 ♣ rebid, which also needs to describe two point zones, as well as rebids with hands that would be opened 1 ♦, a bid not available to describe such hands after a 1 ♣ opening. These last two cases will now be addressed next.

RESPONSES TO A 1 ♣ OPENING

Minor two-suiter hands opposite a 1 ♣ opening were previously addressed through *transfer* bids of 1 NT (for clubs) and 2 ♣ (for diamonds) in one point-zone of 9 / 12 HL pts.

MODIFICATIONS TO REBIDS AFTER A 1 ♣ OPENING

1. MODIFICATIONS APPLYING TO HANDS WITH 5 + ♣

These hands are the following two-suiters : 5 + ♣ with 4 ♥ or 4 ♠, but, as well, 5 + ♣ with 4 ♦, which cannot be described with a 1 ♦ opening, and, as well, 4 4 4 1 hands with a *Major*-suit *singleton* : 4̲ ♠ 1̲ ♥ 4 ♦ 4 ♣ and 4̲ ♥ 1̲ ♠ 4 ♦ 4 ♣ (with a *minor*-suit *singleton*, the hand has 4 ♠ 4 ♥ and would be rebid 1 ♠ or 1 ♥, depending upon their number of points).

A. 5 + ♣ WITH 4 ♥ OR 4 ♠

– After a 1 ♣ opening, these hands need to be described in two point zones. To do this, the **Optimal** Precision Relay method uses the 2 ♣ rebid to describe the **minimum** point zone : 18/20 HLD pts. Further developments after a 2 ♦ *relay* are the same as previously covered.

– For the strong point zone of **21/23** + HLD pts, the method uses an *unusual* process : bidding the 4-card Major first, followed by clubs *twice*. The description of the various distributions is, therefore, as follows :

```
4 ♥ 5 + ♣        :  1 ♣      1 ♦ ?
                    1 ♥      1 ♠ ?
                    2 ♣      2 ♦ ?
                    3 ♣ :  4 ♥  5 + ♣   21/23 + HLD
```
Then, on the next relay :   3 ♦ ?

4 ♥ 5 ♣ 2 2   : 3 NT
4 ♥ 5 ♣ 3 ♠ 1 ♦ : 3 ♠
4 ♥ 5 ♣ 3 ♦ 1 ♠ : 3 ♥ *impossible* bid = 2 + ♦ then, on 3 ♠ ? : 3 NT
4 ♥ 5 ♣ 4 ♦ 0 ♠ : 3 ♥ *impossible* bid = 2 + ♦ then, on 3 ♠ ? : 4 ♦
4 ♥ 5 ♣ 4 ♠ 0 ♦ : *Not applicable* – 4 ♠ 4 ♥ hands : 1 ♥ / rebid 2 ♠
4 ♥ 6 ♣ 2 ♦ 1 ♠ : 3 ♥ *impossible* bid = 2 + ♦ then, on 3 ♠ ? : 4 ♣
4 ♥ 6 ♣ 2 ♠ 1 ♦ : 4 ♣ directly
4 ♥ 6 ♣ 3 ♦ 0 ♠ : 4 ♦ directly
4 ♥ 6 ♣ 3 ♠ 0 ♦ : 4 ♠ directly

The same description process applies to 4 ♠ 5 + ♣ hands.

Example : "Bidding contest".

```
♠ x x x x               ♠ A x x x
♥ ---                   ♥ A K Q
♦ A x                   ♦ K 10 x
♣ A Q J x x x x         ♣ K x
```

There is no room here for mistakenly picking spades as trumps as the above deal has no play for 6 ♠, while 7 NT is 100 % odds-on.

In **Optimal** Precision Relay, these two hands will be bid as follows :

```
1 ♣                              1 ♦ ?
1 ♠                              1 NT ?
2 ♣                              2 ♦ ?
3 ♣ (4 ♠ 5 ♣, 21/23 + HL)       3 ♦ ?
4 ♣ (7 ♣ 4 ♠ 2 ♦ 0 ♥)           4 NT ? (RKC Ask)
5 ♠ (2 Keys w/ ♣ Q)             7 NT
```

B. 5 + ♣ WITH 4 ♦ — WITHOUT A 4-CARD MAJOR

These hands must be described starting with the longest suit first, clubs, and only need to be described in one point zone, **20 +** HLD pts. The bidding method does so through a *conventional* **2 NT** rebid, following its initial 2 ♣ rebid.

5 + ♣ 4 ♦ hands will therefore be described as follows :

```
5 + ♣  4 ♦        : 1 ♣     1 ♦ ?
                    2 ♣     2 ♦ ?
                    2 NT   conventional  5 + ♣  4 ♦   20 + HLD
On the next relay :          3 ♣ ?
  5 ♣ 4 ♦ 2 2     : 3 NT
  5 ♣ 4 ♦ 3 ♥ 1 ♠ : 3 ♥   followed, on 3 ♠, relay, by : 3 NT
  5 ♣ 4 ♦ 3 ♠ 1 ♥ : 3 ♠   Final
  6 ♣ 4 ♦ 2 ♥ 1 ♠ : 3 ♥   followed, on 3 ♠, relay, by : 4 ♣
  6 ♣ 4 ♦ 2 ♠ 1 ♥ : 4 ♣   directly
  6 ♣ 4 ♦ 3 ♥ 0 ♠ : 3 ♥   followed, on 3 ♠, relay, by : 4 ♥
  6 ♣ 4 ♦ 3 ♠ 0 ♥ : 4 ♠   directly
```

Furthemore, the *conventional* rebid of 2 NT to describe 5 ♣ 4 ♦ hands allows the use of a **direct** 3 ♦ rebid, on a 2 ♦ relay, to describe 5 ♣ 5 ♦ hands – an *unusual* treatment, which is needed, as bidding these hands starting with diamonds first, and rebidding clubs next, would not allow the description of 5 ♣ 5 ♦ hands economically.

These **5 – 5** minor two-suiters will therefore be described as follows :

```
5 ♣ 5 ♦           : 1 ♣     1 ♦ ?
                    2 ♣     2 ♦ ?
                    3 ♦    conventional  5 ♣ 5 ♦   20 + HLD pts
On the next relay :          3 ♥ ?
  5 ♣ 5 ♦ 2 ♠ 1 ♥ : 3 ♠
  5 ♣ 5 ♦ 2 ♥ 1 ♠ : 3 NT
  5 ♣ 5 ♦ 3 ♥ 0 ♠ : 4 ♥
  5 ♣ 5 ♦ 3 ♠ 0 ♥ : 4 ♠
```

– The 2 NT rebid now being used to describe 5 + ♣ 4 ♦ hands, a direct jump-rebid of 3 NT , after a 2 ♣ rebid, will be used to describe the semi-regular 6 ♣ 3 2 2 and 7 ♣ 2 2 2 single-suiter hands, without differentiating between the two shapes.

C. 4 ♣ 4 ♦ 4 1 HANDS WITH A MAJOR SUIT SINGLETON

These hands will also be described in **one** point zone only, the **9/12** H point zone, in response to a 1 ♣ opening, **20 +** H point zone as a rebid. The ones in the 7/8 H point zone will be treated as "weak" (1 ♦ response to a 1 ♣ opening).

These 4 4 4 1 hands are described by *one single bid*, 3 ♦ or 3 ♥, as these **direct** responses, or rebids – *pre-emptive* openings which *do not apply* after a 1 ♣ opening – can be given *conventional* meanings. These bids are in the suit just *below* the *singleton*, as follows :

4 ♦ 4 ♣ 4 ♠ 1 ♥	: 1 ♣	3 ♦ directly	(1 ♣ - 1 ♦ - 3 ♦ rebid)
4 ♦ 4 ♣ 4 ♥ 1 ♠	: 1 ♣	3 ♥ directly	(1 ♣ - 1 ♦ - 3 ♥ rebid)

Note : An opener's bid in the singleton suit can be used as a RKC Ask, *instead of* 4 ♣, since that bid could not possibly have any other meaning. Here are a couple of example deals illustrating the use of these bids :

"Bidding contest", 2009.

♠ K x x x	♠ A x x x
♥ A K Q	♥ x
♦ A K J x	♦ Q 10 x x
♣ A x	♣ K x x x

Comment fron the contest organizer : *"Very difficult to find the 7 ♦ grand slam when there is an easy 6 ♠. None of the contestants found it".*
in **Optimal** Precision Relay, the bidding would be as follows :

1 ♣ (18 + HLD)	3 ♦ (4 ♠ 1 ♥ 4 ♦ 4 ♣, 9/12 HL)
3 ♥ ? (RKC Ask)	3 NT (1 Key Card w/o ♠ Q)
4 ♣ ? (K & Q ♣ Ask)	4 ♠ (♣ King)
4 NT ? (K & Q ♦ Ask)	5 ♦ (♦ Queen)
7 ♦ *Simple and effective…*	

National Division 1, pairs, 2011.

♠ x x	♠ A
♥ A K 10 x x x x	♥ x x x x
♦ K x	♦ A x x x
♣ K x	♣ A x x x

Not a single pair found the 7 ♥ grand slam! *Hard to imagine…*
In **Optimal** Precision Relay, these hands will be bid as follows :

1 ♣ (18 + HLD)	3 ♥ (4 ♥ 1 ♠ 4 ♦ 4 ♣, 9/12 HL)
3 ♠ ? (RKC Ask)	3 NT (3 Key Cards w/o ♥ Q)
4 ♠ ? (Key Cards check)	5 ♦ (3 Aces)
7 ♥ *Again, simple and effective…*	

2. MODIFICATIONS APPLYING TO HANDS WITH 5 + ♦

These hands are the following two-suiters : 5 + ♦ with 4 ♥ or 4 ♠ or 4 ♣, which cannot be described with a 1 ♦ opening, and, as well, 4 4 4 1 hands with a *Major*-suit singleton : 4 ♠ 1 ♥ 4 ♦ 4 ♣ and 1 ♠ 4 ♥ 4 ♦ 4 ♣.
(4 4 4 1 hands with a *minor*-suit singleton necessarily have both 4-card Majors and are bid or rebid 1 ♠ or 1 ♥, based on their number of points).

270   267

– While hands opened 2 ♦ describe single-suiter ♦ hands in just one point zone of 15/17 HLD pts, now a 2 ♦ response or rebid must also describe two-suiter hands and this can only be done in a *one-point* zone. To do this, the method considers hands of 7/8 pts in response as "weak" (1 ♦ response on 1 ♣) and describes hands in only one point zone of 9/12 HL pts (20 + HLD pts as a rebid after a 1 ♣ opening), as follows :

With a 5 + ♦ 4 ♠ : 2 ♦, then rebid 2 ♠ on the 2 ♥ *relay*.
With a 5 + ♦ 4 ♣ : 2 ♦, then rebid 3 ♣ on the 2 ♥ *relay*.
With a 5 + ♦ 4 ♥ : 2 ♦, then rebid <u>2 NT</u> on the 2 ♥ *relay*.
The latter is an *unusual, conventional* treatment.
These hands will, therefore, be described as follows :

A. 5 + ♦ WITH 4 ♠ HANDS

5 + ♦ 4 ♠	: 1 ♣	2 ♦ (1 ♣ - 1 ♦ ? - 2 ♦ rebid)
	2 ♥ ?	2 ♠ 5 + ♦ 4 ♠ **9/12** HL
	2 NT ?	

5 ♦ 4 ♠ 2 2 :		3 NT
5 ♦ 4 ♠ 3 ♣ 1 ♥ :		3 ♣
5 ♦ 4 ♠ 3 ♥ 1 ♣ :		3 ♥
5 ♦ 4 ♠ 4 ♣ 0 ♥ :		3 ♣ followed, on a 3 ♦ *relay*, by : 4 ♣
5 ♦ 4 ♠ 4 ♥ 0 ♣ :		*Not applicable* – 4 ♠ 4 ♥ *are described via* 1 ♥ *or* 1♠
6 ♦ 4 ♠ 2 ♣ 1 ♥ :		3 ♦ (6 ♦) then, on 3 ♥ ? : <u>3 ♠</u>
6 ♦ 4 ♠ 2 ♥ 1 ♣ :		3 ♦ (6 ♦) then, on 3 ♥ ? : 3 NT
6 ♦ 4 ♠ 3 ♣ 0 ♥ :		3 ♣ (3 ♣) then, on 3 ♦ ? : <u>3 ♠</u>
6 ♦ 4 ♠ 3 ♥ 0 ♣ :		3 ♥ (3 ♥) then, on 3 ♠ ? : 4 ♦

B. 5 + ♦ WITH 4 ♥ HANDS

5 + ♦ 4 ♥	: 1 ♣	2 ♦ (1 ♣ - 1 ♦ ? - 2 ♦ rebid)
	2 ♥ ?	<u>2 NT</u> 5 + ♦ 4 ♥ **9/12** HL
	3 ♣ ?	

5 ♦ 4 ♥ 2 2 :		3 NT
5 ♦ 4 ♥ 3 ♠ 1 ♣ :		3 ♠
5 ♦ 4 ♥ 3 ♣ 1 ♠ :		<u>3 ♥</u>
5 ♦ 4 ♥ 4 ♣ 0 ♠ :		4 ♣
6 ♦ 4 ♥ 2 ♠ 1 ♣ :		3 ♦ (6 ♦), then, on 3 ♥ ? : <u>3 ♠</u>
6 ♦ 4 ♥ 2 ♣ 1 ♠ :		3 ♦ (6 ♦), then, on 3 ♥ ? : 3 NT
6 ♦ 4 ♥ 3 ♠ 0 ♣ :		3 ♦ (6 ♦), then, on 3 ♥ ? : <u>4 ♣</u>
6 ♦ 4 ♥ 3 ♣ 0 ♠ :		3 ♦ (6 ♦), then, on 3 ♥ ? : <u>4 ♥</u>

C. 5 + ♦ WITH 4 + ♣ HANDS

These hands are described as follows :

5 + ♦ 4 ♣	: 1 ♣	2 ♦ (1 ♣ - 1 ♦ ? - 2 ♦ rebid)
	2 ♥ ?	3 ♣ 5 + ♦ 4 ♣ **9/12** HL

3 ♦ ?

5 ♦ 4 ♣ 2 2	:	3 NT
5 ♦ 4 ♣ 3 ♠ 1 ♥ :		3 ♠
5 ♦ 4 ♣ 3 ♥ 1 ♥ :		3 ♥
5 ♦ 4 ♣ 4 ♥ or 4 ♠ : N/A		rebid describes the 4-card *Major* first.
6 ♦ 4 ♣ 2 ♥ 1 ♠ :		3 ♥ followed by : 4 ♦
6 ♦ 4 ♣ 2 ♠ 1 ♥ :		4 ♦ 6 ♦ 2 ♠
6 ♦ 4 ♣ 3 ♠ 0 ♥ :		4 ♠ directly
6 ♦ 4 ♣ 3 ♥ 0 ♠ :		4 ♥ directly

This concludes the modifications needed on a 1 ♣ opening.
Let's now look at some example hands that reflect these modifications.

European Championships, pairs, final - 2004.

♠ A x	♠ J 10 x
♥ A x x	♥ x
♦ A Q J x	♦ K 10 x x
♣ A K x x	♣ Q J x x x

One team played 3 NT while the other played 4 NT! The minor suits are not described, neither is the ♥ singleton… 7 ♦ was missed.
In **Optimal** Precision Relay, these two hands will be bid as follows :

1 ♣ (18 + HLD)	1 NT (5 + ♣, 9/12 HL pts)
2 ♣ ?	2 ♦ (5 ♣ 4 ♦)
2 ♥ ?	3 ♠ (5 ♣ 4 ♦ 3 ♠ 1 ♥)
4 ♣ ? (RKC Ask, ♣ trump)	4 NT (no KC w/ ♣ Q)
5 ♦ ? (K & Q ♦ Ask)	5 NT (♦ King)
7 ♦	

European Championships, 2008.

♠ A K x x	♠ Q J
♥ K x x	♥ A Q J x x
♦ A K x x x	♦ x x x
♣ x	♣ A x x

Comment from the expert reporting on the deal : "*A 7 ♥ grand slam very difficult to bid. Bidding 6 ♥ would be difficult enough…*".
In **Optimal** Precision Relay, these hands would be bid as follows :

1 ♣	1 ♦ ?
2 ♦ (5 + ♦, 20 + HLD)	2 ♥ ?
2 ♠ (4 ♠)	2 NT ?
3 ♥ (3 ♥)	3 ♠ ?
3 NT (5 ♦ 4 ♠ 3 ♥ 1 ♣)	4 ♦ ? (Control Ask)
5 ♣ (♥ and ♠ controls,	5 ♠ ? (K & Q ♠ Ask)
3 Key Cards w/o ♦ Q)	
6 ♦ (♠ King)	7 ♥

East knows his side is in grand slam zone right from West's opening bid!

International tournament.

♠ A Q J x x	♠ K x
♥ A x x	♥ x x
♦ A x x	♦ K Q 10 x x x
♣ A x	♣ x x x

In **Optimal Precision Relay**, these two hands will be bid as follows :

1 ♣ (18 + HLD)	2 ♣ (5 + ♦, 7/12 HL)
2 ♦ ?	3 ♦ (6 + ♦, 10/12 HL)
3 ♥ ?	3 NT (6 ♦ 3 ♥ or 3 ♣ 2 2)
4 ♣ ? (RKC Ask)	4 ♥ (1 KCard w/ ♦ Q)
4 ♠ ? (K & Q ♠ Ask)	5 ♦ (♠ King)
7 NT	

West knows his side is in slam zone right upon East's 2 ♣ bid ! (+ 1 point for an 8-card ♦ Fit + 1 D point for the ♣ doubleton). And the two hands actually add up to 36 HLF pts with + 1 point for the doubleton King in West's long suit = the points for a 7 NT grand slam !

European Championship, teams of four, 2009.

♠ A x	♠ x
♥ A x x	♥ x x
♦ A J 10 x x	♦ K x x x x
♣ A J x	♣ K Q x x x

Only 3 pairs out of 22 bid a small slam. None found the 7 ♦ grand slam. In **Optimal Precision Relay**, these two hands will be bid as follows :

1 ♣ (18 + HLD)	1 NT (5 + ♣, 7/12 HL)
2 ♣ ?	2 ♦ (5 ♣ 4 ♦, 9/12 HL)
2 ♥ ?	3 ♦ (5 ♦)
3 ♥ ?	3 NT (2 ♥ 1 ♠)
4 ♣ ? (RKC Ask)	4 ♦ (1 Key w/o ♦ Q)
4 NT ? (K & Q ♣ Ask)	5 ♠ (♣ K Q)
7 ♦	

International tournament (French Cup), final, 2014.

♠ A K x x x	♠ x
♥ A x	♥ K Q x
♦ A K Q x	♦ x x x x x
♣ K x	♣ A Q x x

Neither team could do better than 6 NT – after a strong 2 ♣ opening. In **Optimal Precision Relay**, these two hands will be bid as follows :

1 ♣ (18 + HLD)	2 ♦ (5 + ♦, 7/12 HL)
2 ♦ ?	3 ♣ (4 ♣, 9/12 HL)
3 ♦ ?	3 ♥ (2 + ♥)
3 ♠ ?	3 NT (5 ♦ 4 ♣ 3 ♥ 1 ♠)
4 ♣ ? (RKC Ask)	4 ♦ (1 Key w/o ♦ Q)
4 ♥ ? (K & Q ♥ Ask)	5 ♦ (♥ K Q)
5 NT ? (K & Q ♣ Ask)	6 ♦ (♣ Queen)
7 NT	

Spingold tournament, final, 1978.

♠ A J x	♠ K Q x x
♥ A K x x x x	♥ x
♦ A K x	♦ Q J x x x
♣ x	♣ x x x

The US pair of N. Kay/E. Kaplan could only bid these hands to 4 ♠ while the French *Relay* pioneer, P. Ghestem, stopped in 5 ♥.
In **Optimal** Precision **Relay**, these two hands will be bid as follows :

1 ♣ (18 + HLD)	2 ♣ (5 + ♦, 7/12 HL)
2 ♦ ?	2 ♠ (4 ♠, 9/12 HL)
2 NT ?	3 ♣ (2 + ♣)
3 ♦ ?	3 NT (5 ♦ 4 ♠ 3 ♣ 1 ♥)
4 ♣ ? (RKC Ask)	5 ♥ (0 Key w/ ♦ Q
6 ♦	and ♠ K Q)

Regional tournament, 1998.

♣ ---	♠ x x x
♥ A Q x x x x	♥ K x
♦ A x x	♦ x x x
♣ A K x x	♣ Q J x x x

Most pairs played 4 ♥ or 5 ♣. None found the 7 ♣ slam.

In **Optimal** Precision **Relay**, these two hands will be bid as follows :

1 ♣ (18 + HLD)	1 ♠ (*transfer* for NT, 7/12 HL)
1 NT ?	2 ♦ (7/9 HL)
2 ♥ ?	3 ♣ (5 ♣)
3 ♦ ?	3 ♥ (5 ♣ 3 3 2 ♥)
4 ♦ ? (Control Ask)	4 ♥ (♥ control, *not* ♠)
4 NT ? (RKC Ask)	5 ♠ (0 Keys w/ ♣ Queen)
7 ♣ !	

BIDDING AFTER INTERVENTIONS OVER A 1 ♣ OPENING

The table below summarizes **suggested** bids by the opener's partner following *an intervention* by the opposite team over a 1 ♣ opening. The *suggested* bids are guided by **two** key **principles** or **objectives** :

1. Over a **double**, the responses remain *unchanged*, except for one : *Redouble* replaces the 1 ♦ *relay*, to enable a 1 ♦ response to describe the *very same hands* opened 1♦ (with 7/12 HL pts) – a huge benefit! Over any *other* overcall, the responder's *double* is *relay* or *take-out*.

2. All other responses to **retain** their meaning, whenever possible.

INTERVENTIONS over a 1 ♣ opening	SUGGESTED BIDS BY OPENER'S PARTNER Key principles : On *double*, Redouble is *relay* On others : *double* is *relay*, others *remain same*
Double (*Take-out*)	**Redouble** : *Relay* replaces 1 ♦ as *relay*. 1 ♦ : same as 1 ♦ opening, w/ 7/12 HL pts All **other** bids retain their same meaning.
1 ♦ (5 + ♦)	**Double** : *Relay* replaces the 1 ♦ *relay*. 2 ♦ becomes a *cue-bid* describing 5 ♠ – 5 ♥ 2 NT becomes a *cue-bid* for 5 ♣ – 5 ♥ or 5 ♠ All **other** bids retain their same meaning.
1 ♥ (5 + ♥)	**Double** : *Relay* 2 ♥ becomes *cue-bid* for 5 ♠ - 5 ♣ or 5 ♦ **Other** bids retain their same meaning.
1 ♠ (5 + ♠)	**Double** : *sputnik* indicating 4 ♥ 2 ♠ becomes a *cue-bid* for 5 ♥ - 5 ♣ or 5 ♦ **Other** bids retain their same meaning.
1 NT (Balanced)	**Double** : *Take-out* signaling a 4-card Major All **other** bids retain their same meaning.
2 ♣ (??)	**Double** : *Take-out*, looking for a 4-card Major 3♣:*cue-bid* 5♠ 5
2 ♦/2 ♥/2 ♠ (6 ♦/♥/♠)	**Double** : *penalty* double

OPTIMAL PRECISION RELAY : **OVERCALLS** OVER A **1** ♣ **OPENING**

Contrary to what is often claimed by many, *direct overcalls* over a strong 1 ♣ opening are **not** necessarily "highly disruptive" – and the above table of suggested responses by opener's partner dispel such a claim. Against any 1 club opening, overcalls of 1 ♦ and 1 ♥ have no impact, and against the **Optimal** Precision Relay 1 ♣ opening, the overcall of *double* enables the opener's partner to use a 1 ♦ bid as equivalent to a 1 ♦ opening bid – with all its positive implications !

Any *other* overcall over a 1 ♣ opening offers no *additional* benefit than it would over *other* opening bids, while it is considerably more vulnerable as the opener's partner knows about the opener's strength and is in a better position to select the most appropriate response.

Here are three examples of overcalls over a 1 ♣ opening that illustrate their lack of negative impact :

International tournament.

♠ x x	♠ x
♥ A K x x x	♥ Q x x x
♦ x	♦ A x x x
♣ A Q x x x	♣ K x x x

At most tables the auction was :

1 ♥	1 ♠	4 ♥

In **Optimal** Precision Relay, these two hands would be bid as follows:

1 ♣	1 ♠	3 ♥ (4 ♥ 1 ♠ 4 4, 9/12 HL)
4 ♣ ? (RKC Ask)		4 ♥ (1 Key w/ ♥ Q)
5 ♣ ? (K & Q ♣ Ask)		5 ♠ (♣ King)
6 ♥		

The 1 ♠ overcall has no impact whatsoever.

Deal reported in Bridge World magazine.

♠ K 10 x x	♠ A Q x x x
♥ A x x x x x x	♥ x
♦ A	♦ J x x x
♣ A	♣ x x x

The expert from Bridge World presenting this deal comments : *"We can easily imagine much of the field playing this grand slam in… 2 ♥, after :*

1 ♥	1 NT	pass	pass
2 ♥	pass	pass	pass

In **Optimal** Precision Relay, these two hands would be bid as follows :

1 ♣	1 NT	2 ♠ (5 + ♠, 7/12 HL)
2 NT ?		3 ♦ (4 ♦)
3 ♥ ?		4 ♣ (3 ♣)
4 ♦ ? (Control Ask)		4 ♠ (♠ control, not ♥)
4 NT ? (RKC Ask)		5 ♦ (1 Key w/♠ Q)
7 ♠		

The key is that there is no risk for East to bid 2 ♠ because he knows that the opener has 18 + HLD pts for a total of 25 pts on their side.

Bidding contest – Bridge World, 1969.

♠ A x x	♠ x
♥ A	♥ J 10 x x
♦ K 10 x	♦ A Q J x x
♣ Q J x x x x	♣ A K x

After a 1 ♣ opening by West and a 1 ♠ overcall by North, both pairs of American experts ended up in 3 NT for one, the other in 5 ♣. Instead of:

1 ♣	1 ♠	double
3 ♣ (18/20, 6 + clubs)		3 ♦ ?
3 ♥ (♥ singleton)		4 ♣ ? (RKC Ask)
4 NT (2 KC w/♣ Q)		5 ♦ ? (K & Q ♦ Ask)
5 NT (♦ King)		7 ♣

Here again, the 1 ♠ overcall has no negative impact on the 1 ♣ opening.

In closing, the benefits of the **Optimal Precision Relay 1 ♣ opening** far outweigh the occasional negative impact that overcalls may have on it while its *considerably greater* frequency than that of the *traditional* strong club opening makes it operational much more often – immediately enabling the responder to know his side's *minimum* point zone.

Furthermore, the **Optimal Precision Relay** bidding method has bids of its own that hamper opponents' bidding, such as the *competitive initiative* openings represented by : the 12/14 HLD pre-emptive 2 NT opening, openings of 2 ♠, 2 ♥, 2 ♦ and 2 ♣ in the 15/17 HLD point zone, the 12/14 HL weak 1 NT opening, much more frequent than the strong NT opening, the light openings of 1 ♥ and 1 ♠, and the low frequency of the 1 ♦ opening – all being serious impediments to the opponents' bidding!

Considering *only* the *occasional* competitive disadvantages of a 1 ♣ opening *without* considering its substantial benefits as well as the bidding method's *other* openings would be seriously misguided !

RESPONSES TO A 4 ♣ ASK – WITH HANDS < THAN 7 HL PTS

AFTER A 1 ♦ RESPONSE TO A 1 ♣ OPENING

With hands having fewer than **7** HL pts – after a 1 ♦ response to a 1 ♣ opening – the Roman Key Card replies to a 4 ♣ KC Ask do **not apply**, as : A) the cases for 2 or 3 or 4 Key cards do not exist with fewer than 7 HL pts, and B) the responder's hand description may only have been partial and an *"assumed"* trump suit may **not** have been identified.

The honors held by the responder can only be : **no Ace and no King**, with or without Queens, or **1 King**, with or without one or two Queens, or **2 Kings** (no Queen), or **1 Ace**, with or without one or two Queens. With such hands, The **Optimal Precision Relay** method uses specific replies to a 4 ♣ Ask, with the following guidelines :

– The "negative" reply, **no** Ace, **no** King, is 4 ♠, allowing the 4 ♣ interrogator to *pass* or to play 5 ♣ or 5 ♦ or 5 ♥ on a *"puppet' transfer* bid of 4 NT. Any *other* bid (5 ♣, 5 ♦, 5 ♥, 5 ♠) is a *suit-specific* Queen Ask.

– Any other reply, 4 ♦, 4 ♥, 4 NT, 5 ♣ and 5 ♦ is considered "positive" and allows the *next bid up* to be an inquiry for *further* description of the honors held by the responder (5 ♦ is final).

The specific replies and further developments are as follows :

REPLY	ACE	KING	FURTHER DEVELOPMENTS
4 ♦	0	1	On 4 ♥ ? *relay* : The King in ***double***-transfer to describe K Q *in the **same** suit*, when needed
4 ♥	1	0	On 4 ♠ ? *relay* : Identify Queen(s), if any (5 ♣, 5 ♦, etc.). *Without* any Queen, bid 4 NT.
4 ♠	0	0	4 NT is a *"**puppet**" transfer* for 5 ♣. Any *other* bid (5 ♣, 5 ♦) is a *suit-specific* **Q** Ask
4 NT	0	2	*Transfer* for ♣ **K** DESCRIBE OTHER **K** ON 5 ♣
5 ♣	0	2	*Transfer* for ♦ **K** DESCRIBE OTHER **K** ON 5 ♦
5 ♦	0	2	*Transfer* for ♥ **K** AND ♠ **K** – FINAL

Let's now cover specific developments, beyond the direct responses, as applied to some example hands, as they will illustrate how they work.

Rubber game.

♠ A Q	♠ J x x
♥ A K x x x	♥ J 10 x x x
♦ A K x x x	♦ x x
♣ x	♣ A x x

In **Optimal** Precision Relay, these two hands will be bid as follows :

1 ♣ (18 + HLD)	1 ♦
1 ♥ (5 + ♥)	2 ♦ (*transfer* for ♥, < 7 HL)
2 ♠ ? (relay)	2 NT (balanced)
3 ♣ ? (relay)	3 ♥ (5 ♥)
4 ♣ ? (KC Ask)	4 ♥ (1 Ace)
5 ♦ ? (♦ Queen ?)	5 ♥ (no ♦ Queen)
6 ♥	

Rather than looking for *which suit* the Ace is in, an information rarely needed, Asking bids beyond the 4 ♠ *relay* look for a Queen in a specific suit. The hand **cannot** have a King, along with the Ace, as such a combination will be treated as in the 7/9 HL point zone, with 7 ½ pts.

Column *"technique"*.

♠ K x	♠ x x x
♥ A K x x x	♥ Q x x x
♦ A x x	♦ x
♣ A Q x	♣ K x x x x

"Does your bidding system enable you to bid these hands to 6 ♥ ?".

In **Optimal** Precision Relay, these two hands will be bid as follows :

1 ♣ (18 + HLD)	1 ♦
1 ♥ (5 + ♥)	2 NT (*transfer* for ♣, 10 / 12 HLDF)
3 ♣ ? (relay)	3 ♦ (♦ *singleton*, ♥ Fit)
4 ♣ ? (KC Ask)	4 ♦ (1 King)
4 ♥ ? (describe)	4 ♠ (*double-transfer* for ♣ King)
4 NT ? (continue)	5 ♥ (♥ Queen)
6 ♥	

The *double-transfer* (*two* suits below the one where the King is) is used after a 4 ♦ response to enable the description of K Q in the *same* suit i.e. on 4 NT, 5 ♣ would describe **K**ing **and Q**ueen of clubs.

Note the 2 NT *transfer* for clubs, instead of 1 NT which would describe the **7/9** HLDF point-zone (versus 10/12 HLDF).

276

Spingold tournament, final, 2008.

♠	A K	♠	Q x x
♥	K x	♥	x x x
♦	A K Q	♦	x x x x
♣	A K x x x x	♣	Q x x

Ron Smith and Bill Cohen land in 3 NT, after a stong 2 ♣ opening.

In **Optimal** Precision **Relay**, these two hands will be bid as follows :

1 ♣ (18 + HLD)	1 ♦
2 ♣ (5 + ♣)	3 ♣ (< 7 HLDF, 3 + clubs)
3 ♦ ? (relay)	3 NT (balanced, 3 clubs)
4 ♣ ? (KC Ask)	4 ♠ (**no** Ace, **no** King)
5 ♣ ? (♣ Queen ?)	5 ♠ (yes, ♣ Q **and** ♠ Q)
6 ♣	

6 ♣ is played, by West, to protect against a lead through the ♥ King, rather than 6 NT which would have to be played by East.

International tournament, pairs, 2007.

♠	A Q x x x	♠	K x x x
♥	x	♥	x x x x
♦	A Q x x	♦	K x x x
♣	A x x	♣	x

Most pairs bid : 1 ♠		2 ♠
	3 ♦ or 3 ♥ (*trial bid*)	4 ♠

In **Optimal** Precision **Relay**, these two hands will be bid as follows :

1 ♣ (18 + HLD)	1 ♦
1 ♠ (5 + ♠)	2 ♣ (*transfer* for ♦, < 7 HL)
2 ♥ ? (forcing)	3 ♣ (♣ *singleton*, ♠ Fit, 7 + HLDF)
3 ♦ ?	3 NT (4 4 4 1 ♣)
4 ♣ ? (KC Ask)	5 ♣ (*transfer* for the ♦ King)
5 ♦ ? (other King ?)	5 ♠ (♠ King)
6 ♠	

The 2 ♥ *forcing relay* is used, instead of just transferring to diamonds, as West now has **21 ½** HLDF pts (+ 1 for the ♦ Fit + 1 for the ♥ *singleton*). The first King is described by a *transfer* bid to enable the description of the *second* King on the transfer.

PRE-EMPTIVE OPENINGS 3 ♦ AND UP < THAN 9 H PTS

RESPONSES AND DEVELOPMENTS

Pre-emptive openings in **Optimal** Precision Relay are the same as in *traditional* bidding – except for the *transfer* opening itself and for the 3 ♠ opening which describes a 5 – 5 minor two-suiter of **10 / 12 H** pts. That is : *less* than 9 H pts, no more than **one** Ace, and **7** + cards for a 3 ♦ (♥) or 3 ♥ (♠) opening, **8** + cards for an opening of 3 NT (♣) and up.

On these openings, which are obviously *forcing* by their *transfer* nature, the response will most often be to *transfer* into the intended suit, that is 3 ♥ over 3 ♦, 3 ♠ over 3 ♥. With the right number of tricks for game (6 + 4 tricks, non-vulnerable, 7 + 3, vulnerable), or to further extend the *pre-emptive* effect, the responder can transfer directly to 4 ♥ or 4 ♠.

In rare cases, a responder with a *void* in the intended Major and with 7 + spades or 8 + hearts may elect to bid 3 ♠ over a 3 ♦ (♥) opening or 4 ♥ over a 3 ♥ (♠) opening, with the appropriate number of tricks.

This leaves the response of 3 NT, over a 3 ♦ or 3 ♥ opening, to be explored, as using this response as *natural*, to play 3 NT, would be very rare and generally misguided. As illustration, consider this deal:

♠ K Q 10 x x x x	♠ J x
♥ x x x	♥ A x x
♦ K x	♦ Q J x x
♣ x	♣ K Q J x

In response to a 3 ♥ opening (♠), a responder with the above hand must **not** consider playing a 3 NT contract, which has no chance as West does not have a re-entry to his hand to run his long suit.
But with the hearts and clubs reversed in West's hand, 4 ♠ is on as there are no "*wasted honor pts*" in clubs. The location of the singleton in West's hand is the key and it would be best for East to locate it.
To do so, using 3 NT as a *relay* would be considerably more useful.
On the *relay* bid of 3 NT, West will bid his singleton, 3 ♣ or 3 ♥.
In both cases, East will end up in 4 ♠, a winning contract with a ♥ singleton, while he will only be down two with the hand above.

Similarly, a specific meaning needs to be assigned to the responses of 4 ♣ and 4 ♦. Here too, using these responses as natural, to play, in preference to 3 ♥ or 3 ♠ would be very rare (void in the Major and an 8 + card minor suit) and misguided. Instead, the 4 ♣ and 4 ♦ bids should be used as direct Key Card Asks – the very same Asks as used otherwise.

In the tournament this deal comes from, bidding these two hands was problematic for most pairs and very few reached 7 ♥ :

♠ Q x	♠ A x x
♥ A Q 10 x x x x	♥ K x x
♦ x x	♦ ---
♣ x x	♣ A K x x x x x

The bidding invariably started with a 3 ♥ pre-emptive opening by West, overcalled by 3 ♠ in North. All that is needed to bid 7 ♥ is to know whether West has the ♥ Ace but very few pairs tried to find out.
In **Optimal** Precision Relay, a direct 4 ♦ Control Ask would enable East to determine whether West has, or not, the ♥ Ace.

– The 3 ♠ opening being an invitation to 3 NT must specify a precise number of **H** pts, **10/12 H** pts. A responder of **14 + HLF** pts with *complementing* honors in the minors *and stoppers* in *each* Major can bid 3 NT, to play, or he can *transfer* into his best minor suit : 4 or 5 ♣ or ♦.

Hereunder is an illustration of this opening "at work".

Bidding contest, 2015.

"What do you bid, in third and even vulnerability, with the hand below ? :

♠ x
♥ x
♦ K J 10 x x
♣ A Q 10 x x x

The experts consulted proposed 4 different bids with their comments :
"1 ♣ : *as a pre-emptive 3 ♣ would "hide" the diamonds".*
"3 ♣ : *Pass or 1 ♣ just won't do! No free ride for my opponents…".*
"4 ♣ : *5 ♣ would be excessive while 1 ♣ or 3 ♣ won't hinder opponents".*
"5 ♣ : *I won't have an opportunity to bid again – this way, I won't have to".*

Frankly, none of these bids are satisfactory. The **Optimal** Precision Relay 3 ♠ opening is a much better alternative : it describes, in one bid, both 5 - 5 *minors* and does so at a pre-emptive level much higher than 3 ♣! And still enables the side to play 3 NT – and from the right hand !

The power and effectiveness of the **O**ptimal **P**recision **R**elay bidding method are multi-faceted and lie in the following features :

– First and foremost, it is based on the **O**ptimal **H**and **E**valuation, the only point count which captures the full **distributional** value of an opening hand as well as the **combined** value of **two** hands.

– Its 1 ♣ opening of all hands of 18 + HLD pts is **unique** among any other bidding system as it is **the only one** that enables limiting any other opening to a maximum of 17 HLD pts and therefore to no more than **two** HLD point zones within the "bidding safety" level.
As well, the responses to the 1 ♣ opening (other than the 1 ♦ response) are **limited** to a 12 HL point "ceiling" and describe precisely just **two** point zones, unlike any other bidding system.
Furthermore, on a 1 ♦ response, the 1 ♣ opening **rebids** "mirror" other openings, also describing just **two** point zones.

– Its 1 ♦ opening, an opening highly vulnerable to interventions, is designed to be of **limited frequency** and the responses to it (other than the 1 ♥ relay) are uniquely limited to **one** single point zone, 7/9 HL pts, and precisely describe a 5-card or 6-card suit, and do so via *transfer* bids.
Furthermore, the **rebids** following a 1 ♦ opening (on a 1 ♥ relay) are of **unmatched precision** as they describe at once **both** the **shape** and the **point zone** of the opening hand, including the economical description of a 5 ♦ - 4 ♥ two-suiter in the minimum point zone !

– Its 1 ♥ and 1 ♠ openings enable "light" openings of 12 HLD pts and **rebids** that precisely describe one of only two point zones, as well as describing **economically** the minimum point zone through the use of "braking" bids, instead of space-consuming "jumps".
Furthermore, *transfer* responses to a 1 ♥ or 1 ♠ opening are of unmatched effectiveness in enabling the responder to describe either a **misfitted** hand **or** one with a **4-card fit** and a specific feature.

– Its 1 NT opening is unique in two ways : it is the only one to **describe its minor suit**(s) without a 4-card Major, and **responses** to the 1 NT opening describe a specific minor **singleton** after a transfer bid or directly, with 4 ♥ or 4 ♠ and a 5-card minor. And the same precision applies after a 1 ♦ opening / 1 NT rebid !

– Its 2 ♠, 2 ♥ and 2 ♦ openings precisely describe a 6 + card single-suit within a 3 HLD point zone of 15/17 HLD pts, while its 2 ♣ opening denies **both** 4-card Majors as well as 4 diamonds as a second suit, in one single point zone limited to 4 HLD pts – unmatched precision !

– It does away with the "horrible 3" openings : the strong 2 NT opening with a balanced hand, the game-forcing 2 ♣ opening and the strong 1 NT

– In all cases, the **O**ptimal **P**recision **R**elay method describes the **residual** distribution of a hand at the level of three, all 13 cards when needed, without exceeding the level of 3 NT (for most hand distributions).
This, in turn, enables the method to use 4 ♣ as the RKC Ask, instead of the uneconomical 4 NT.

– Its economical 4 ♣ 6 key RKC Ask, combined with subsequent K & Q Asks in specific suits, is uniquely effective in identifying the presence or absence of key control cards needed for a slam.

– Furthermore, the method benefits greatly from the *economical **precision*** of its rebids, from its ***pertinent description*** of singletons, whenever possible, and from the ***competitive initiative*** nature of most of its openings.

The above features of the **O**ptimal **P**recision **R**elay bidding method can be expected to provide a significant competitive advantage.
Naturally, this now remains to be verified by world-class partnerships adopting and playing the method in international tournaments…

This concludes the description of the **Optimal** Precision Relay method. I welcome any comments or questions you may have which you can e-mail to this address : patrick.darricades@gmail.com

The next pages show a summary table of *unusual **conventional*** bids as well as a sample **Convention** card, for reference and potential use.

UNUSUAL CONVENTIONAL BIDS TO "FLAG"

OPENING	UNUSUAL CONVENTIONAL MEANING	POINTS
1 ♣	**Forcing** opening bid – **any** distribution	18 + HLD
2 NT	Opening bid for 6 + **diamonds** single-suit	12/14 HLD
3 ♦ up	Pre-emptive *Transfer* openings – 7 + cards	< 9 H
3 ♠	Pre-emptive *Transfer* bid for 5 + ♦ 5 + ♣ *without* 3 cards in a Major	10/12 H

OPENING	UNUSUAL CONVENTIONAL RESPONSE	POINTS
1 ♣	1 ♥ and up : *Transfer* bids for **next** suit up	7/12 HL
	2 ♠ : 5 ♥ 4 ♦ (rest of the hand to follow)	9/12 HL
	3 ♦ : 4 ♠ <u>1 ♥</u> 4 ♦ 4 ♣ ♥ singleton	9/12 HL
	3 ♥ : <u>1 ♠</u> 4 ♥ 4 ♦ 4 ♣ ♠ singleton	9/12 HL
1 ♦	1 NT up : *Transfer* bids for **next** suit up	7/9 HL
	2 ♣ : *Specifically* <u>5 ♥</u> denies 4 ♠	7/9 HL
	2 ♠ : 5 ♦ 4 ♣ 2 2 *or* 5 ♣ 4 ♦ 2 2	7/9 HL
1 ♥ / 1 ♠	2 ♣ and up : *Transfer* bids for **next** suit up	7 + HL
	2 ♠ : *Splinter* bid w/a **void** and <u>5</u> trumps	16/18 HLDF
1 NT	3 ♣/♦ : 5 - 1 in minors with **4 hearts**	10/12 HLD
	2 ♠ : 5 - 1 in minors with **4 spades**	10/12 HLD
2 ♣	2 NT : Exactly 5 ♠ 4 ♥	7/12 HL
2 ♥	2 NT : Exactly **5 spades**	7/12 HL

283

OPTIMAL PRECISION RELAY

Openings, Responses and Overcalls

SYSTEM SUMMARY	RESPONSES	OVERCALL

GENERAL APPROACH / OPENING BIDS :
 	
1 ♣ **18+** HLD (forcing), 1 ♦ 14/19 HLD
Weak 1 **NT** : 12/14 HL
1♠/1♥: **5**-card Mjr - can be 4 ♠ 4 ♥
  12/17 HLD pts *light opening* : **9** + H
2 ♣ to 2 ♠ openings : **6** + cards
    15/17 HLD
2 NT : 6 + ♦, 3 ♣ : 6 + ♣ single-suiter
    12/14 HLD
3♦ & up : *pre-emptive* **transfer** bids
	On ***any*** opening, the *next suit up* is a **relay**, forcing.
	
	On 1NT : 2♦ / ♥ : *transfers*
	On 1♦, 1♥ : 1 NT to 2 NT
	are *transfer* bids.
	On 1♥/♠ : 2♠/3♣/♦/♥
	are *mini-splinter* bids.
		Y
		O
		U
		R

OPENING BIDS
 	
1 NT : **12/14** HL pts   Balanced
  On 2 ♣ Stayman, rebids of :
  2 ♦ = 4 + ♦, 2 NT = 4 + ♣, < 4 ♦
 	
1 ♠/1♥ : **12/17** HLD pts **5** + cards
        or **4** ♠ **4** ♥
Over *relay*, jump-rebids of 3 ♣ / ♦ =
5 – 4 in Majors **15/17** HLD
 	
1 ♦ : **14/19** HLD two-suiter ♦ / ♣
        or **5** + ♦ **4** ♥ or **4** ♠
  or **15/17** HL pts   Balanced
 	
2 ♦ *rebid* : 5 ♦ <u>4 ♥</u> **14/16** HLD
2 ♠ *rebid* : minor 5 - 4 **17/19** HLD
 	
1 ♣ : **18** + HLD Any distribution
  on 1♦, *relay* : Rebids are the *same*
  as openings
	2 ♠ : <u>4 ♠</u> with **5** + ♣ or ♦
	3 ♣ / ♦ : **5** + ♣ or ♦ *w/* 4 <u>♥</u>
	    10/12 HLD
	2 NT : *transfer* for ♣ *or* ♦
	
	1 NT to **2 NT** are *transfers*
	2 ♠ : *splinter* with a *void*
	    and **5**-card *trump* Fit
	
	1 ♠ : **5** ♠ *exactly* 7/9 HL
	1 NT to 2 ♥ : *transfer* bids
	2 ♠ : *minor* 5 4 2 ♥ 2 ♠
	
	1 ♦ : *Relay*, < 7 or 13 + HL
	1 ♥ and up : *transfer* bids
	      7/12 HL pts
		O
		V
		E
		R
		C
		A
		L
		L
		S

CONVENTION CARD

OPTIMAL PRECISION RELAY

OPENINGS, RESPONSES AND OVERCALLS

SYSTEM SUMMARY	RESPONSES	OVERCALL
OPENING BIDS 2 ♠/♥/♦ : 6 + card single-suiter 15/17 HLD Rebid in the *singleton*, 3 ♣/♦/♥ *without* a singleton, rebid NT 2 ♣ : 6 + ♣ or 5 + ♣ 4 ♠ or 4 ♥ 14/17 HLD On 2 ♦ *relay*, rebid of 2 ♥ = 4 ♥, 2 ♠ = 4 ♠, 2 NT or 3 ♣ = 6 + ♣	3 ♣/♦/♥ : *singleton* with 3-card Fit On 2 ♥ opening : 2 NT = 5 ♠ 7/9 HL 2 ♥, 2 ♠ : 5 + ♥/♠ 7/9 HL 2 NT : 5 ♠ 4 ♥	Y O U R O V E R
2 NT (♦), 3 ♣ : 6 + ♦/♣ single- suiter **12/14** HLD 3 ♦ **and up** : *pre-emptive* **transfer** bids	3 ♥/♠ : 5 + ♥/♠ 10/12 HL	C A L L S

OPTIMAL PRECISION RELAY

SLAM ASKINGS BIDS AND RESPONSES

SLAM ASKING BIDS, RESPONSES AND RE-ASKS

4 ♣ ? 6 Key Card Ask

    4 ♦ : **1** or **3** Key cards *without* the trump **Q**

    4 ♥ : **1** or **3** Key cards *with* the trump **Q**

    4 ♠ : **0** or **2** or **4** Keys *without* the trump **Q**

    4 NT : **0** or **2** or **4** Keys *with* the trump **Q**

RE-ASK : Suit-specific King and Queen Ask

5 ♣ ? ♣ Ask   **5 ♦** : no K or Q   **5 ♥** : ♣ Q   **5 ♠** : ♣ K   **5 NT** : ♣ KQ

5 ♦ ? ♦ Ask   **5 ♥** : no K or Q   **5 ♠** : ♦ Q   *etc, same as above.*

5 ♥ ? ♥ Ask   **5 ♠** : no K or Q   **5 NT** : ♥ Q   *etc, same as above.*

4 NT ? Suit Ask for *highest ranking* suit *other than trump. Responses as above.*

4 ♦ ? Control Ask   Responses identify Ace or K control of *either* Major

    Responses : **4 ♥** : Control (**A** or **K**) ♥, *not* ♠. **4 ♠** : Control ♠, *not* ♥.

               4 NT : Control *neither* ♥, *nor* ♠. **5 ♣/5 ♦/5 ♥/5 ♠** :

               Same as Key Card responses to **4 ♣**, *with* ♥ *and* ♠ Controls.

Responses to **4 ♣ ?** Ask with hands having < than **7 HL** pts (**1 ♦** reply to **1 ♣**)

    4 ♦ : **1 K**   **4 ♥** : **1** Ace   **4 ♠** : No **A** or **K** (only **Q**s)   **4 NT, 5 ♣, 5 ♦** :

    transfer bids for **2 K**s : **4 NT** for ♣ **K**   **5 ♣** for ♦ **K**   **5 ♦** for ♥ **K** & ♠ **K**

DEFENSIVE LEADS

	Vs **a suit** contract	Vs **No Trump**
With : **A** K x x or **K Q** x x	Top H : Ace, King	same
Q J 10 x or **Q J** x	Top H : **Q**	same
x x	Hi-lo	*only in* partner's suit
K x x x or **Q** x x x	Do not lead	4th best

DEFENSIVE SIGNALING – ON PARTNER'S LEAD

Low card to encourage **continuing** the suit (Honor in suit or doubleton)

High card to **discourage** pursuing the suit

Discard : *Suit preference* : **Low** for *lowest* ranking suit, **High** for *highest* ranking

---